# Successful Direct Marketing Methods

# Successful Direct Marketing Methods
## *Second Edition*

**Bob Stone**
Chairman, Stone & Adler, Inc.
Board Member, Young & Rubicam Affiliates

Crain Books
A Division of Crain Communications Inc.
740 Rush Street
Chicago, Illinois 60611

To Dorothy, my "one and only" for more than thirty years, who did extra duty in raising five wonderful kids while her husband was almost constantly "in flight." This book is but another manifestation of a wonderful partnership.

Published by Crain Books Division of Crain Communications Inc. All rights reserved. This book may not be reproduced in whole or in part in any form or by any means without written permission from the publisher.

International Standard Book Number: 0-87251-040-9
Library of Congress Classification: LC 78-74973

Printed in the United States of America.

Design and typesetting: North Coast Associates.

# Contents

Definition. Direct marketing sales volume. Factors affecting growth. Criteria for entering direct marketing. The impact of credit cards. Cost of direct mail. Direct response expenditures. Six big keys to direct marketing success. Checklist for applying the six big keys to direct marketing success. The uniqueness of direct mail. Opportunities for retailers. Eight major responsibilities of direct marketing executives. Self-quiz. Pilot project.

Example of dramatic differences. Checklist of basic offers. Yes-no. Free gift. Load-ups. Get-a-friend. Short- and long-term effects on offers. Offers relate to objectives. Ways to hypo response. Danger of overkill. Effect on bad debts. Make it easy to order. Self-quiz. Pilot project.

What business are you really in? What are your capabilities? What is your image with your prospect? Examine the characteristics of your customer list. What is the life style of your customers? What new products are people buying? Look at the new life styles. How do you evaluate products? Price/value relationships. Other areas to consider. Products may determine media. The use of research. Reliable sources. Summary. Self-quiz. Pilot project.

Mailing lists as market segments. Eight usually reliable truths. When to use mailing lists. Every list has a profile. Working with list brokers and compilers. List rental arrangements. Lists as a profit center. 32 questions to ask a prospective list manager. Duplication elimination. Lists age rapidly. Analyzing response by timing and locale. Determining proper test quantities. Problem: high testing costs. Market segmentation. Environmental influences. ZIP code areas as market segments. Penetration of the market. Segmentation of the market. Retrieval of market segments. Alternative marketing units. AID analysis. Self-quiz. Pilot project.

# Foreword

When writing the foreword to the first edition of this book, the admired and revered Edward N. Mayer, Jr. said: "This is a great book."

As usual, Ed was an excellent judge and prophet. But, he had only the advantage of reading the galleys of copy before the book was enclosed in hard covers.

It is a much easier task three years later to heap praise upon *Successful Direct Marketing Methods* and its ingenious author, Bob Stone. This book is unique in business circles, a best seller in its own right, a textbook in many college classrooms, and a reference guide for marketers and agencies.

Yes, the book did have time on its side. The explosion that has occurred and continues in the use of direct marketing methods was just in its beginnings. How lucky that this excellent guide to direct marketing was made available to amplify the few voices in marketing and advertising circles who were espousing this "new way of selling."

The second edition adds the use, testing results, and sophistication of literally hundreds of practitioners who have found direct marketing an exciting complement to their normal marketing methods, or, in many cases, a whole new way of life. Direct marketing as a vehicle has become a recognized convenience to the consumer. It has transformed many ordinary products into a service. The 35,000 copies of the previous edition of this book have probably saved millions of dollars for marketers, for it has given them straightforward guidance in a new medium. For those who read the book and referred to it often, the old method of trial and error was reduced substantially and measurability became a watchword.

What more could one ask of a book?

Just one thing. All of the royalties have been donated by the author to the Direct Mail/Marketing Educational Foundation to assist college and university students and professors in finding out more about this exciting method of selling!

Robert F. DeLay
*President*
*Direct Mail/Marketing Association*

# About the Author

**Positions**  Chairman of the Board, Stone & Adler, Inc.
Board Member, Young & Rubicam Affiliates

**Articles**  Author of more than 160 articles since 1967 for the feature column "Stone on Direct Marketing" appearing in *Advertising Age* magazine published by Crain Communications Inc.

**Awards**  Six-time winner of the Direct Mail/Marketing Association's Best of Industry Award. His firm, Stone & Adler, has received Direct Mail/Marketing Association's highest honor including the Silver and Gold Mail Box Awards as well as the International Direct Marketing & Mail Order Symposium's Bronze Carrier Pigeon Award.

**Affiliations**  Former director of the Direct Mail/Marketing Association
Former president of the Chicago Association of Direct Marketing
Former membership chairman of the Direct Mail/Marketing Association
Former president of the Associated Third Class Mail Users
Member of the Professional Division of Alpha Delta Sigma fraternity
Board member of the Direct Mail/Marketing Educational Foundation

"$50 billion plus. That's a lot." So started the first chapter of the first edition of *Successful Direct Marketing Methods*. The time was January 1975. Six printings and about 35,000 books later, December 31, 1977, the Direct Mail/Marketing Association was reporting annual sales of $70 billion—a spectacular 40 percent growth. And a conservative prediction for this explosive marketing phenomonon by 1981 is sales of $120 billion per year.

Concurrent with this galloping growth have come new breakthroughs. Laser beam printing. Scintillating graphics. New computer technology. Segmented marketing techniques. New ways to cut sales costs. A tremendous growth in catalog selling. An awakening of direct marketing opportunities among retailers.

And research. The sophisticated, those who are tallying the big breakthroughs, have "discovered" research. Focus testing. Pretesting. Quantitative research. Qualitative research. Post research. All the tools.

Moreover, leaders in direct marketing have faced up to a gnawing problem—a dearth of talent. In the year 1978 alone DMMA sponsored more than 75 direct marketing seminars and institutes. Many major universities are now regularly sponsoring direct marketing adult education courses.

Meanwhile the Direct Mail/Marketing Educational Foundation continues to invite the brightest of the bright college students to its collegiate institutes twice yearly. As a long-time lecturer I come away from each institute secure in the feeling that our future is in good hands. "I learned more in your five-day intensive course than I did in four years of college"—an expression from an exuberant student—is a somewhat typical statement from marketing students exposed to the disciplines of direct marketing for the first time.

What has become clear to the traditional marketer is that direct marketing is an additional alternative, an opportunity to add a separate profit center. And, more often than not, advertising geared towards direct marketing becomes *plus advertising* for retail outlets.

But the appeal of direct marketing is in no way limited to the traditional marketer. It's there for the entrepreneur, the individualist with the courage and the foresight to start from "scratch" and build a direct response business where one never existed before.

Like the growth of direct marketing, this second edition of *Successful Direct Marketing Methods* has also expanded—in scope, in size and especially in what I hope will be knowledge gained by you, the reader. For those of you who are statistics oriented (an important element in the world of direct marketing), I have revised about 60 percent of the book and attempted to retain the best of the first edition.

So, in this new edition, you will find not only new case histories of entrepreneurs who entered the direct marketing stream for the first time and succeeded, but major corporations as well.

There's a new look at mailing lists with an update on life-style market segmentation. The chapter on broadcast is all new, providing the latest techniques for producing and airing television commercials. Telephone marketing is completely updated. The chapter on catalogs is greatly expanded to reflect the latest techniques of catalog preparation and distribution.

Two important chapters have been added to this new edition: Selecting and Selling Merchandise, and Techniques of Producing Leads for Salespeople. Detailed instructions are given on how to select the right merchandise for mail order, how to evaluate merchandise, and how to establish price/value relationships. Recognizing the high cost of sales calls, the chapter on lead production lays out a complete program for smooth lead flow in the right quantity, the right quality and at the right cost.

Chapter 15, Research and Testing Techniques, details the many research techniques being applied to direct marketing, including background research, pretesting research and post-testing research. Case histories include all new examples of telescopic testing.

In addition, you will find for the first time a glossary of direct marketing terms which has been prepared and endorsed by the Direct Mail/Marketing Association.

Two popular features from the first edition of *Successful Direct Marketing Methods* have been retained: a self-quiz and a pilot project at the end of each chapter. Quizzes enable the reader to review thoroughly the chapter content, thus creating a permanent reference to all the basic materials in the book. Pilot projects are structured in such a way that the reader can, if he wishes, promptly put into practice the information provided in the chapter.

But let's get on with it. This book is for you, be you seasoned professional or student seeking a career in direct marketing. The best of success to you in all your efforts.

Bob Stone

# Acknowledgments

As with the first edition, the materials in this second edition are in no way the thinking solely of the author. Instead this book is a reflection of all that is happening in direct marketing, with generous contributions from a host of people and organizations.

Thanks go to the Direct Mail/Marketing Association for the statistics it has provided. To Pete Hoke, publisher of *Direct Marketing* for his contributions. To Sy Levy and his staff at March Advertising for their input on broadcast. To Stan Rapp and Tom Collins of Rapp & Collins for their input on magazines and the techniques of creating print advertising.

Thanks too to Martin Baier of Old American Insurance Company for his expertise on life-style market segmentation. Thanks also to Murray Roman of CCI for his contribution on telephone marketing.

Numerous staff members of Stone & Adler contributed to this book. Special thanks go to Mark Duchene for his contributions on mailing lists. To Marilyn Gottlieb and Marsh Edinger for their media expertise. To Don Kanter and Bill Gregory for their insights on writing direct mail copy. To Bob Ingalls for his contributions on creating catalogs. To Aaron Adler for contributing his life-long experience on mail order merchandise selling.

Thanks too to John Mecchella who provided the basics for successful lead-producing programs. And thanks to Frank Daniels for his contributions on the techniques for producing creative breakthroughs.

My thanks and appreciation to Mel Brisk, publisher of Crain Books, who urged me to write this revised and enlarged edition and contributed his expertise for the benefit of all who read this book.

# Section I

# Getting Started in Direct Marketing

# 1

## The Scope of Direct Marketing

The incomparable David Ogilvy, founder of Ogilvy, Benson & Mather, in an address at the first Direct Marketing Day in London, England in October 1977, stated, "Ladies and gentlemen, how I envy you. Your timing is perfect. You have come into the direct response business at the right time. It has exploded, and it is going to go on exploding. You are on to a good thing."

At about the same time Mr. Edward Ney, chairman of Young & Rubicam, stated, "Direct marketing and direct response will be the biggest growth area in the next 25 years."

Yes, direct marketing is indeed exploding. Opportunities abound. Direct marketing has come into its own.

**Definition**  But before we jump aboard the glittering bandwagon, let us review an accepted definition of direct marketing created by the Direct Mail/Marketing Association (DMMA).

> Direct (response) marketing is the total of activities by which products and services are offered to market segments in one or more media for informational purposes, or to solicit a direct response from a present or prospective customer or contributor by mail, telephone or other access.

Let's analyze this definition. Direct marketing is a marketing system not an industry. Our "reach" includes both present and potential customers. Our choice of media—direct mail, newspapers, magazines, radio, television—is ours to use singly or in combination. Our objective can be to get inquiries, to sell merchandise or services direct, to get contributions, to get people to visit stores. But underlying all direct marketing success is the ability to trigger a direct action, a *measurable action* at the right cost. And we don't care if that action is by mail, or telephone, or personal visit. Our franchise is broad.

**Direct marketing sales volume**  Bob DeLay, president of the DMMA, reported in an October 1976 speech that direct marketing accounted for 12 percent of all consumer goods purchased in 1976. And in an address in New York City on September 14, 1977, before the Direct Marketing Idea Exchange, an elite group of direct marketers, I stated, "I predict that by the end of 1981, direct marketing—incremental sales not included—will reach a recorded sales volume of 120 billion dollars—double the direct marketing volume recorded in 1976." Sales volume for the year 1977 was estimated to be in excess of 70 billion dollars. So my estimate by year end 1981 may indeed prove to be conservative.

**Factors affecting growth**

There are many positive factors that have affected the phenomenal growth of direct marketing:

1. *Changing consumer life styles resulting in part from:*
   a. greater emphasis placed on leisure time activities
   b. the dual roles of working homemakers
   c. the demand for more services and conveniences in shopping

2. *Availability of consumer credit*

3. *Problems consumers encounter when shopping at retail:*
   a. congested parking lots and streets
   b. inadequate parking facilities and long walking distances to shopping centers
   c. uninformed sales clerks
   d. difficulties encountered in locating retail sales personnel
   e. long waiting lines at check-out stations
   f. in-store congestion during peak shopping hours

4. *Increased consumer demand for more "wants" due in part to increasingly higher levels of discretionary income*

5. *Innovations in computer technology which have resulted in:*
   a. personalization of messages at greater production speeds than previously possible
   b. mathematical models that predict the effect of various levels of multimedia expenditures
   c. reliable prospect lists

*Better Homes & Gardens* surveyed readers of their publication to determine their attitudes towards shopping by mail. The two major reasons for shopping by mail were: "can't find items elsewhere" (33 percent) and "convenience" (27 percent). Other reasons given were "fun," "price" and "better quality."

The entry of scores of Fortune 500 firms has provided tremendous impetus to direct marketing growth. These giants of industry have found direct marketing to be a viable profit center. Members of the exclusive Fortune 500 club who have entered into direct marketing include Avon Products, Bell & Howell, Boise Cascade, CBS, R. R. Donnelley, Dart Industries, General Foods, General Mills, General Motors, W. R. Grace, Hewlett-Packard, Honeywell, International Business Machines, Kraftco, Macmillan, Mobil Oil, McGraw-Hill, NCR, New York Times, Pitney-Bowes, Shell Oil, Sperry Rand, Polaroid, Standard Oil (Cal.), Standard Oil (Ind.), Sun Oil, Minnesota Mining & Manufacturing, and Time Inc.

**Criteria for entering direct marketing**

While more and more major corporations which built their businesses through traditional distribution methods are testing and entering direct marketing, there are still thousands who question whether they should explore this new wave of the marketing future. Robert Kestnbaum of R. Kestnbaum & Company of Chicago has served as counsel to scores of mass marketers who have explored direct marketing. To help mass marketers establish direct marketing criteria, I conducted an in-depth interview with Bob Kestnbaum on behalf of *Advertising Age.* The questions I put forth and Mr. Kestnbaum's answers follow.

Q. What criteria do you follow to determine whether it is advisable to use direct marketing?

A. Basically, I like to see a compelling reason for a company to consider this form of marketing. Examples of such reasons would be (1) a unique product or service for which other distribution channels are unsatisfactory, too expensive, or unavailable; (2) a market where the best prospects have some highly recognizable or definable characteristic, and where lists of other media can be found to match this characteristic; and (3) a product which needs to be fully and carefully explained.

Q. What types of merchandise lend themselves to direct marketing?

A. The range of merchandise and services that can be sold by direct marketing appears almost unlimited. I hesitate to assign any restrictions. Direct marketing thrives on products (1) that have poor retail distribution, (2) for which the purchase decision is difficult because of a multiplicity of brands and models to choose from, or because of the need to have a full explanation of the product or service, or (3) for which impulse and ease of purchase are dominant factors.

Q. How important is selling price?

A. On the upper side, there hardly seems to be a limit. Products costing several hundred dollars have been sold directly by mail. Where businesses or institutions are the buyers, there are innumerable examples of elaborate direct marketing programs to generate qualified leads which are subsequently converted with ease into orders by a salesperson calling on a prospect who has been largely pre-sold.

On the other hand, there is a growing limitation on the minimum price of a product that can be sold by mail. If a product sells for $10, even with a very high gross margin and minimal handing costs yielding a contribution as high as $7 or $8, twenty or more orders per thousand are required at a $175 per thousand promotion cost just to break even. A substantial number over that are needed to produce a good profit. Contrast this example with another product bearing the same promotion cost, but contributing $50 per order instead of $7 or $8 and we find we need only 3.5 sales per thousand pieces mailed to break even, with additional orders multiplying profits rapidly.

Q. How important is credit?

A. With the shift to sale of higher cost items, availability of credit becomes increasingly important. Credit availablity through commercial credit cards is one answer. But commercial credit cards are not a complete answer. Travel-and-entertainment cards require high discounts. Bank charge cards, while they offer lower discounts, have floor limits and other restrictions that are very cumbersome for many marketers. Finally, many consumers simply are unwilling or unaccustomed to charging mail order purchases to their credit card.

In the industrial market, credit problems are much easier to solve. Charge cards are less significant here. Even a small direct marketer can utilize procedures that permit him to offer net 30-day billing to companies and organizations with minimal risk of bad debts.

Q. How should a mass marketing company be structured for a direct marketing program?

A. The program must start with the attention and active support of top management. Direct marketing is very different from other forms of marketing. It operates with different strategies, employs a specialized kind of sales presentation, utilizes arithmetic and budgeting that vary significantly from typical corporate methods. And it often requires specially tailored approaches to product design, packaging, and instruction material.

Launching a direct marketing program, even in its test stages, is a very complex activity. It requires attention from an experienced and effective executive. If the test program is substantial, this executive may have to devote full time and may require a supporting staff. And he should be permitted to manage with *autonomy*, guided by general policies and budgets laid down at the start of the program.

The other necessary ingredient is that the company should have access to and should freely utilize comprehensive direct marketing expertise. To some extent, this can be provided by an advertising agency specializing in direct marketing. Most of these organizations, however, are not geared to provide comprehensive management, analytical, organizational, and other inputs that can make the difference between failure or mediocrity on the one hand and success on the other. There is something to say for the objective, dispassionate consultant, without any ax to grind, operating entirely on management's side of the desk and applying direct marketing know-how to management decisions.

Q. Should a mass marketer test direct marketing with existing products or different products?

A. The answer to this depends very much on the criteria described in my reply to your second question. There is not much reason to use direct marketing for a highly recognizable product in mass distribution. There is reason to use it for products that otherwise do not receive enough selling attention.

Another consideration is related to the question of contribution which was discussed in your third question. Maximizing the dollar contribution to selling cost and profit is of major importance. Many direct marketers find they can improve their gross margin, and, therefore, their contribution, by using a somewhat different model or product line in their direct marketing program. Frequently, extra features or product quality will command a greater price differential in direct marketing where the advantages of these extras can be fully explained and merchandised.

Q. Which offers a better opportunity—syndication or direct sales to the consumer?

A. The deciding factor as to whether to use syndication (allowing other marketers to sell your products to their customer list) or to sell direct to the consumer hinges primarily upon *profitability*. In other words, the question is: Is it more profitable to go direct to lists or markets to which a company has access, or are more sales volume and profit likely to be achieved through a syndicated sales activity? (With syndication, other marketers handle all the complexities of the selling transaction and usually pay for the mailings to their customers, assuming credit to their customers as well.)

    Another consideration is whether multiple opportunities exist to sell to the same customer. If a company makes one product and has nothing else to offer to the buyer of that product, there is much less reason to attempt to sell direct to that buyer. In contrast, if the buyer of the first product automatically becomes a prime prospect to purchase accessories or additional items, it then becomes much more worthwhile for the company to undertake the entire marketing job.

Q. Don't dealers complain when a mass marketer goes the direct marketing route?

A. Dealers do complain, but usually from lack of understanding or knowledge of the program. While a direct marketing program should not be viewed as an advertising effort, a large-scale direct marketing program does circulate great amounts of very dramatic and effective advertising. This effort heightens product awareness and demand. While only a small percentage of the audience may actually order direct, another substantial portion will go to a conventional sales outlet to request the same product. Bell & Howell increased its retail share of the market at the same time that it created a whole new market by mail. Manufacturers of all types have repeated the experience of seeing retail sales and share of market increase immediately following a large direct marketing effort.

    With good communications, retailers can be appraised in advance of the benefits of a direct marketing program and can be offered the opportunity to participate by making mailings or sponsoring ads to their own customers. This sort of thoughtful attention reduces dealer objections.

Q. Should direct sales to the consumer be promoted under a different name?

A. There are two parts to this answer. First, brand names are important. Offering a product to a consumer under a brand name that he recognizes and trusts will always be more successful than offering an unknown brand. This applies to direct marketing as well as to any other form of marketing. Second, people prefer to do business with a company with which they have had a happy and successful relationship in the past. This is especially important in direct marketing.

I have seen several cases where well-established direct marketing companies tested identical offers to their customers, changing only the company name under which the offer was made. Mailings made under a name unfamiliar to prospects invariably produced one-third to one-half the response.

Q. How do sales costs for a successful direct marketing program compare with sales costs for a traditional marketing program?

A. There are a handful of cases I know of where direct marketing expenses are as low as 8 to 10 percent of sales. These are not typical. Ordinarily, direct marketing selling costs are as high as 30 to 35 percent. The important thing is to compare the selling costs of direct marketing with those for other forms of distribution.

Q. What is the value of customer lists?

A. Bob, I'm glad you asked that question, because it is so often misunderstood by mass marketers. The thing that makes a list valuable is its responsiveness. The more orders that can be generated by contacting people on a list, the more profit will be earned and the more each name on the list will be worth.

Responsiveness is generally a reflection of two factors. The first is a history of direct marketing purchases. Individuals who purchased by mail or telephone as a result of a direct marketing contact are much more responsive than people who did not purchase in this manner. The more merchandise people have purchased, the more frequently they purchase; and the more recently they purchased, the more responsive they will be.

The next best thing to a list of people who purchase as a result of a direct marketing contact is a list of people who have responded in some other way, for example, by returning a survey or a warranty card. Such nonpurchaser lists are typically low in value, however, and unfortunately, the lists that most mass marketers possess fall into this category.

The second factor affecting responsiveness is the ability to isolate people who have a compelling interest in a product or service. I referred a moment ago to owner lists which usually are not very responsive. But the fact that an owner of one product is a prime prospect to purchase needed accessories or other related items can outweigh the fact that the list was not generated from responses to direct marketing appeals.

Unfortunately, both you and I have seen innumerable instances where major companies have been in possession of large lists of people who are good prospects for additional purchases, but where these lists have gone unused. A variation of this sort of neglect occurs when one division of a company generates a responsive list and possibly even uses that list itself, but other divisions of the same company fail to capitalize on its existence.

Q. Name some situations that you believe will call for the expanded use of direct marketing over the next five to ten years.

A. Over the next few years more and more companies will realize they are in situations where they should be using direct marketing. Some examples are these:

I see direct marketing expanding for firms that derive a major portion of their business from a relatively small, highly identifiable audience. A classic example is airline travel where a small number of high-frequency travelers provide 70 to 80 percent of total revenues.

Another example relates to financial institutions such as banks and brokerage houses. Generally, the only regular contact such institutions have with their customers is a monthly statement which is impersonal and often minimally informative. How often do these organizations solicit other kinds of business or inform their customers about other kinds of business or inform their customers about other kinds of available services?

A major opportunity exists for companies having accessories and follow-up products to sell to purchasers of primary products. Why doesn't IBM offer me additional elements for my Selectric typewriters? Why doesn't the store that sold me a winter suit a few months ago tell me about the summer suits they have in the same style?

I see great opportunities for companies that do not wish to create additional sales forces or open additional stores in given areas. This is particularly significant when a new product does not fit the existing sales force or type of outlet, and there is not a base sufficient to warrant building a new sales force or group of outlets. Direct marketing often can establish a product and create a sales base that permits subsequent expansion by other sales channels.

Q. How long does it usually take to determine if direct marketing is viable for a mass marketer?

A. If good testing procedures are employed, it can frequently be determined if a program is very successful within three to six months. Often, it is necessary to go through several testing cycles before a program can be "engineered" to produce the desired profitability and before the total market potential can be estimated. It is safest to allow from nine months to one year to develop a program and acquire a clear picture of its potential.

**The impact of credit cards**  When the first edition of *Successful Direct Marketing Methods* was published, credit cards—particularly bank cards—were just starting to have a strong impact on direct marketing. During the past five years, offering charge privileges through travel-and-entertainment cards (American Express, Diners Club, and Carte Blanche) as well as through bank cards (Visa and Master Charge) has become commonplace. Cases where credit cards account for 35 to 50 percent of all orders received from a promotion are not unusual. Charge card arrangements offer two advantages to the marketer: (1) the opportunity to sell bigger ticket items, and (2) freedom from credit problems.

In addition to the travel-and-entertainment cards and bank cards, consider the fact that scores of retail stores offer their own credit cards. In the DMMA *Fact Book of Direct Response Marketing*, it is estimated that consumers hold more than 150 million retail charge cards. As of 1977, DMMA estimated that there were 133 million oil company credit cards in circulation. Breakout for the travel-and-entertainment cards and bank cards is shown in Table 1.1.

### Table 1.1. Number of credit cards in use in the United States, 1977.

| Credit Card | Number in Use |
| --- | --- |
| American Express | 6,560,000 |
| Carte Blanche | 725,000 |
| Diners Club | 915,000 |
| Master Charge (InterBank) | 44,000,000 |
| Visa (BankAmericard) | 39,000,000 |

**Cost of direct mail**

While direct marketers today use a host of media, direct mail is still the major one. But rising postage costs have raised the question, "Is direct mail pricing itself out of existence?" In 1960, third-class regular bulk mail was $20.00 per thousand pieces. By 1976, the bulk rate had risen to $77.00 per thousand pieces. And by 1978, the rate had reached $85.00 per thousand pieces.

In spite of these spiraling postage costs, some research indicates that the total cost per thousand mailing packages rose less than the Consumer Price Index for the 1960-1976 period. Table 1.2 indicates that the increase in costs for the private business sector during the 16-year period amounted to 54 percent, the increase in postage charges by the federal government was 285 percent. The relatively small increase in costs by the private business sector has held the total increase for the 16-year period to 108 percent. During the same 16-year period, the Consumer Price Index rose 114 percent.

### Table 1.2. Comparative advertising mail costs, based on a one-million piece mailing, 1960 versus 1976.

| Items | 1960 Cost per M | 1976 Cost per M | Percent Increase |
| --- | --- | --- | --- |
| 1. Brochure, four colors | $19.14 | $ 26.13 | 36 |
| 2. Premium insert, four colors | 8.60 | 10.30 | 19 |
| 3. Order card, four colors | 3.81 | 7.36 | 93 |
| 4. Letter, two colors | 4.17 | 6.64 | 59 |
| 5. Reply envelope, one color | 2.22 | 4.11 | 85 |
| 6. Outer envelope, two colors | 4.83 | 6.69 | 38 |
| 7. Mailing list | 15.00 | 30.00 | 100 |
| 8. Lettershop charge | 6.50 | 7.75 | 19 |
| Total, items 1–8 | $64.27 | $ 98.98 | 54 |
| 9. Third-class postage | 20.00 | 77.00 | 285 |
| Total cost per thousand | $84.27 | $175.98 | 108 |

**Direct response expenditures**

Total expenditures for direct response include not only direct mail, but also television, radio, newspapers, and magazines. The DMMA *Fact Book on Direct Response Advertising* shows the figures in Table 1.3 for major direct response media.

# Table 1.3. Summary of annual direct marketing expenditures.

**Direct mail expenditures, including postage and production costs, but excluding creative services.**

| Year | Amount |
|------|--------|
| 1936 | $266,010,365 |
| 1937 | 277,851,087 |
| 1938 | 269,869,569 |
| 1939 | 277,292,494 |
| 1940 | 278,221,589 |
| 1941 | 293,981,595 |
| 1942 | 274,369,636 |
| 1943 | 268,036,086 |
| 1944 | 271,991,230 |
| 1945 | 241,960,283 |
| 1946 | 278,797,152 |
| 1947 | 482,737,477 |
| 1948 | 574,527,477 |
| 1949 | 863,989,380 |
| 1950 | 918,660,480 |
| 1951 | 1,056,296,826 |
| 1952 | 1,171,088,984 |
| 1953 | 1,256,393,834 |
| 1954 | 1,374,882,915 |
| 1955 | 1,485,261,000 |
| 1956 | 1,554,068,971 |
| 1957 | 1,615,826,302 |
| 1958 | 1,777,039,094 |
| 1959 | 1,930,588,964 |
| 1960 | 2,027,016,075 |
| 1961 | 2,111,523,778 |
| 1962 | 2,029,308,000 |
| 1963 | 2,215,172,000 |
| 1964 | 2,354,015,000 |
| 1965 | 2,408,275,000 |
| 1966 | 2,551,148,000 |
| 1967 | 2,581,634,000 |
| 1968 | 2,796,013,000 |
| 1969 | 2,725,618,000 |
| 1970 | 2,827,026,000 |
| 1971 | 3,432,191,000 |
| 1972 | 3,406,483,000 |
| 1973 | 3,990,063,000 |
| 1974 | 4,749,689,000 |
| 1975 | 5,063,525,000 |
| 1976 | 6,025,639,000 |
| 1977 | 6,966,680,000 |

**Newspaper preprints of all types, including card, multi-page, and roll-fed.**

| Year | Number of Preprints (In Billions) |
|------|-----------------------------------|
| 1970 | 8.0 |
| 1971 | 10.0 |
| 1972 | 11.8 |
| 1973 | 12.8 |
| 1974 | 16.0 |
| 1975 | 16.0 |
| 1976 | 18.0 |
| 1977 | 20.0 |

**Insert expenditures, including printing and inserting.**

| Year | Amount |
|------|--------|
| 1977 | $1,086,000,000 |

Source: Newspaper Advertising Bureau, New York.

**Magazine expenditures for retail and mail order ads.**

| Year | Amount (In Millions) |
|------|----------------------|
| 1971 | $58.8 |
| 1972 | 65.8 |
| 1973 | 68.6 |
| 1974 | 69.9 |
| 1975 | 71.1 |
| 1976 | 86.3 |
| 1977 | 86.2 |

Source: Magazine Publishers Association, New York.

**Television**

| Year | Amount (In Millions) |
|------|----------------------|
| 1969 | $ 22 |
| 1973 | 106 |
| 1974 | 200 |
| 1975 | 280* |
| 1976 | 300* |
| 1980 | 500* |

*Estimated

**Radio**

| Year | Amount |
|------|--------|
| 1975 | $1,892,300,000 |
| 1976 | 2,270,000,000* |

Information as to what portion of radio advertising expenditures is attributable to direct response advertisers is not available. Judging by case histories, however, those companies using radio in conjunction with other direct response activities find it to be highly successful.

Source: Radio Advertising Bureau, New York; FCC Radio Report.

**Six big keys to direct marketing success**

Regardless of media used, the big question to be answered is, "What makes direct marketing successful?" An oversimplified answer might be: *Offering the right products or services via the right media, with the most enticing propositions, presented with the most effective formats, proved successful as a result of the right tests.*

Sounds pretty simple. But, of course, it isn't! Let's explore the six big keys to direct marketing success and some basic questions relating to them.

1. *Right product or services.* Success in any endeavor starts with the product. No matter what the selling medium, no business can long survive unless the product is *right.* Time was when direct sale of products via mail, space, or broadcast advertising was looked upon as a means of "dumping" merchandise that did not sell well through retail channels. Time was when off-brand merchandise, which couldn't get shelf space in retail stores, was offered direct to the consumer. That's all changed today. Successful direct marketers offer quality merchandise of good value.

2. *Right media.* Some authorities give half or more of the credit for the success of a mailing to the lists that are used. You can't prove the figure. But you can bet on this: one of the most important keys to success is lists! Likewise, selection of the publications used for print ads and the stations used for broadcast are vital keys to success. (Chapters 4 through 9 cover each major medium in depth.)

3. *Right offer.* There is no key to success more important than the offer. You can have the right product, the right mailing lists, the right print and broadcast media. But you still won't make it big if you don't have the right offer. You've got to overcome human inertia, whatever the medium. (Chapter 2 covers 25 different offers designed to overcome human inertia.)

4. *Right formats.* The number of formats for presenting offers is almost endless. This is particularly true of direct mail, where there are few restrictions on format. The marketer can use anything from a simple post card to a $9 \times 12$ mailing package which could include a giant four-color brochure, letter, giant order card, tokens, stamps, pop-ups, and so on.

   Restrictions on print and broadcast advertising are, of couse, more stringent, because of controls by the publishers and the stations. But the important point is that there is a *right* format for a given mailing package, a given ad, and a given commercial. Depending on format selected, the results can be anywhere from disastrous to sensational.

5. *Right tests.* With literally thousands of chances to do the wrong thing, the way to achieve direct marketing success is to test to determine the *right* thing. Indeed, direct marketing is the most *measurable* type of marketing there is.

   Mailing packages can be tested scientifically to determine such vital factors as best offer, best format, best lists, best copy, best postage, and so on.

The print medium, with the advent of regional editions, has also made an endless variety of tests possible. Direct marketers now test by regions. They test for size and color. They test for position. They test bind-in cards, bingo cards. They test special against general interest magazines. Newspapers can be tested to learn all you have to know.

It is also possible to test the efficiency of broadcast on a control basis. Testing is likewise possible when the telephone is used as a selling medium. (Chapter 15 clearly spells out the techniques that enable you to get the right answers.)

6. *Right analyses.* The final element essential to a successful direct marketing program is right analyses. Direct marketers live by figures, but misinterpretation of figures often leads to erroneous conclusions. Fortunes have been lost by counting *trial orders* instead of counting *paid-ups*. Fortunes have been lost by *averaging* response, by not really knowing break-even points, by never determining the value of a customer, by never preparing cash-flow charts.

Section IV of this book, "Managing Your Direct Marketing Business," is devoted to applying the mathematics of direct marketing properly.

**Checklist for applying the six big keys to direct marketing success**

1. The product or service you offer
   - ☐ Is it a real value for the price asked?
   - ☐ How does it stack up against competition?
   - ☐ Do you have exclusive features?
   - ☐ Does you packaging create a good first impression?
   - ☐ Is the market broad enough to support a going organization?
   - ☐ Is your product cost low enough to warrant a mail order markup?
   - ☐ Does your product or service lend itself to repeat business?

2. The media you use

   *Customer lists*
   - ☐ Is your customer list cleaned on a regular basis?
   - ☐ Do you keep a second copy of your list in a secure place to avoid loss?
   - ☐ Have you developed a profile of your customer list, giving you all the important demographic characteristics?
   - ☐ Have you coded your customer list by recency of purchase?
   - ☐ Have you worked your customer list by the classic mail order formula: recency-frequency-monetary?
   - ☐ Have you thought of what other products or services may appeal to your customer list?
   - ☐ Do you mail your customer list often enough to capitalize on the investment?

*Prospect lists*

☐ Do you freely provide facts and figures to one or more competent mailing list brokers, enabling them to unearth productive lists for you?

☐ Have you worked with competent list compilers in selecting names of prospects who match the profile of those on your customer list?

☐ Do you test meaningful, measurable, projectable quantities?

☐ Have you measured the true results of prospect lists, computing for each list the number of inquiries, the quantity of returned goods, net cash receipts per thousand mailed, and repeat business?

☐ Have you determined how often you can successfully mail to the same prosepct list?

*Print*

☐ Have you matched your offers with your markets and used print publications with good direct response track records?

☐ Have you measured the true results of print media, computing for each newspaper or magazine the number of inquiries, the amount of returned goods, net cash receipts per insertion, and repeat business?

☐ Have you determined how often you can successfully use the same print media?

*Broadcast*

☐ Have you selected broadcast media that best fit your objective: (a) to get inquiries or orders; (b) to support other advertising media?

☐ Have you measured the true results of broadcast media, computing for each station the number of inquiries, the amount of returned goods, net cash receipts per broadcast schedule, and repeat business?

☐ Have you determined the proper times and frequency for broadcast schedules?

3. The offers you make

☐ Are you making the most enticing offers you can within the realm of good business?

☐ Does your offer lend itself to the use of any or all of these incentives for response: free gift, contest, free trial offer, installment terms, price savings, money back guarantee?

☐ Does your offer lend itself to the development of an "automatic" repeat business cycle?

☐ Does your offer lend itself to a "get-a-friend" program?

☐ Have you determined the ideal introductory period or quantity for your offer?

☐ Have you determined the ideal introductory price for your offer?

☐ Have you determined the possibility of multiple sales for your offer?

4. The formats you use

*Direct mail*

☐ Are your mailing packages in character with your product or services and the markets you are reaching?

☐ Have you developed the ideal format for your mailing packages, with particular emphasis on mailing envelope, letter, circular, response form, and reply envelope?

☐ Do you work with one or more creative envelope manufacturers?

☐ Are your sales letters in character with your offers?

☐ Are your circulars graphic, descriptive, and in tune with the complete mailing package?

☐ Does your response form contain the complete offer? Is it attractive enough to grab attention and impel action?

*Print*

☐ Are your ads in character with your product and services and the markets you are reaching?

☐ Have you explored newspaper inserts, magazine inserts, bind-in cards, tip-on cards, Dutch door newspaper inserts, plastic records?

*Broadcast*

☐ Are your commercials in character with your products and services and the markets you are reaching?

☐ Have you determined the efficiency of stand-up announcer commercials vs. staged commercials?

☐ Have you explored the efficiency of noted personality endorsements?

5. The tests you make

☐ Do you consistently test the big things: product, media, offers, and formats?

☐ Have you tested to determine the best timing for your offers, the best frequency?

☐ Have you determined the most responsive geographical areas?

☐ Do you consistently test new direct mail packages against control packages, new ads against control ads, new commercials against control commercials?

☐ Do you use adequate test quantities?

☐ Do you follow your test figures through to conclusion, using net revenue per thousand as the key criterion?

☐ Do you interpret your test figures in the light of the effect on the image and future profits of your company?

6. The right analyses

☐ Do you track results by source, computing front-end response, returned goods factors, and bad debt factor for each source?

□ Do you analyze results by ZIP codes, by demographics?

□ Do you compute the level of repeat business by original source?

**The uniqueness of direct mail**

While direct marketing embraces all media today, the one medium that is truly unique is direct mail. You can select a mailing list that zeroes in on a certain type of person or a specific geographic area. You can pick only people with known interest or a specific buying history, with little or no waste circulation. And you can make your message a personal one by using a computer letter that addresses each individual by name. Or you can use a printed letter that includes copy directed to the specific lists selected.

Your mailing package can be as simple or as elaborate as you wish. You can include a four-color circular that opens up as big as a tablecloth, or you can include a sample of your product in the mailing. You can control the distribution so the quantity of a mailing can be as small as you like or as large as the available universe. And you can mail whenever you prefer.

While other media permit some types of testing, none offer the wide spread of test capability that direct mail does. Thanks to the computer's ability to select a perfect "nth" name sample (such as every tenth name), your mailings can include as many split tests as necessary to provide a wide variety of answers from a single mailing.

The classic formula for direct marketing success is to build a list of satisfied customers and then go back to them for repeat sales. Direct mail is the only medium that allows you to concentrate your promotion efforts on just your present customers. Absolutely no waste circulation.

Compared with other media, direct mail will usually produce the highest percentage of response. So if mail pays out for you, you build your sales, profit, and customer list more rapidly. Direct mail has a one-on-one advantage which cannot be matched by any other media. Its very uniqueness leads to unique applications.

No more unique application of direct mail could be found than the famous Admiral Byrd saga. In 1968, Hank Burnett, a famous direct response writer, and his associates, Christopher Stagg and Dick Benson, accepted the challenge of selling a $10,000 around-the-world trip. The total marketing budget was a mere $5,000. This ruled out any chance of producing a deluxe four-color booklet picturing the points of call on this fabulous journey. Faced with the challenge of reaching the objective with words alone, Hank Burnett wrote one of the classic letters of all time—seven pages of copy, no enclosures. This famous letter convinced 60 men that the Admiral Byrd trip would be the adventure of a lifetime. They paid a total of $600,000 for the experience! It was my good fortune to secure one of the few copies of this classic letter, and it is reproduced as Exhibit 1.1.

EDWARD C. BURSK
SOLDIERS FIELD
BOSTON, MASSACHUSETTS 02163

EDITOR
HARVARD BUSINESS REVIEW

Please reply to me in care of:
Transpolar Expedition
Admiral Richard E. Byrd Polar Center
18 Tremont Street
Boston, Massachusetts   02108

September 3, 1968

Mr. Richard N. Archer
121 Corlies Ave.
Pelham, N.Y.   10803

Dear Mr. Archer:

As Chairman of the Admiral Richard E. Byrd Polar Center, it is my privilege to invite you to become a member of an expedition which is destined to make both news and history.

It will cost you $10,000 and about 26 days of your time.  Frankly, you will endure some discomfort, and may even face some danger.

On the other hand, you will have the rare privilege of taking part in a mission of great significance for the United States and the entire world. A mission, incidentally, which has never before been attempted by man.

You will personally have the chance to help enrich mankind's fund of knowledge about two of the last earthly frontiers, the polar regions.

I am inviting you to join a distinguished group of 50 people who will fly around the world longitudinally, over both poles, on an expedition which will commemorate Admiral Richard E. Byrd's first Antarctic flight in 1929.

Among the highlights of this transpolar flight - the first commercial flight ever to cross both poles and touch down on all continents - will be stopovers at the American military/scientific bases at Thule, Greenland, and McMurdo Sound, Antarctica.

Because this expedition has the interest and support of much of the Free World, you and your fellow members will be honored guests (in many cases, even celebrities) at state and diplomatic receptions throughout the itinerary. You will have the opportunity to meet and talk with some of the world's important national leaders and public figures, such as Pope Paul VI, the Emperor of Japan, General Carlos Romulo, and many others who are already a part of history.

By agreeing to join this expedition, you will, in a sense, establish yourself in history too.  For you will become a Founding Trustee of the new Admiral Richard E. Byrd Polar Center, sponsor of the expedition.

Your biography will be recorded in the Center's archives, available to future historians.  The log, photographs and memorabilia of the expedition will be permanently  displayed in the Center.  And your name will be inscribed, with those of the other expedition members, on a bronze memorial tablet.

Before I continue with the details of the expedition, let me tell you more about the Byrd Polar Center and the reasoning which led to its establishment this summer.

Located in Boston, home of the late Admiral and point of origin for each of his seven expeditions, this nonprofit institution will house, catalog and preserve the papers and records of both Admiral Byrd and other Arctic and Antarctic explorers.

But the Center will have a more dynamic function than merely to enshrine the past. It will be a vital, viable organization devoted to furthering peaceful development of the polar regions, particularly Antarctica.

It will become, in effect, this country's headquarters for investigation and research into the scientific and commercial development of the poles. The Center will sponsor, support, initiate and conduct studies and expeditions. It will furnish comprehensive data or technical assistance to the United States, or to any university, institution, foundation, business organization or private individual legitimately interested in polar development.

In other words, the Center has set for itself a course which the Admiral before his death endorsed wholeheartedly. He foresaw that mankind would one day benefit enormously from development of Antarctica's vast potential. And he perceived that Antarctica's unique and diverse advantages and resources might best be developed by private capital in a free enterprise context.

The Byrd Polar Center is dedicated to these objectives. And the essential purpose of this commemorative expedition is to dramatize the role that private enterprise - and private citizens - can play in the opening of these last frontiers.

At the same time, the expedition should help prove a few other important points. It should demonstrate the feasibility of shrinking the world through longitudinal navigation. It should also help blaze a trail for commercial air travel over the South Pole. Presently, to fly from Chile to Australia, you must go by way of Los Angeles, even though a straight line trans-Antarctic route would be far shorter.

There is another factor I should mention, one which I think lends a certain urgency to the work of the Center. Development of the polar regions enjoys a high official priority in the Soviet Union - higher, some believe, than in the United States.

The Center's activities can provide a tangible, effective complement to those of our own government, and over the long term, contribute meaningfully to preservation of the Arctic and Antarctic regions for peaceful purposes.

These objectives, I think you will agree, are entirely valid. And important, for the future of humanity. It is for this reason that the inaugural activity of the Byrd Polar Center will be an expedition of such scope and magnitude.

The expedition will be led by Commander Fred G. Dustin, veteran of six polar expeditions, advisor to Admiral Byrd and one of the intrepid group which spent the winter of 1934 in Little America on Byrd's Antarctic Expedition II. Commander Dustin is a member of the U.S. Antarctica Committee and President of the Byrd Polar Center.

Considered the ranking American authority on the polar regions, Fred Dustin is probably better qualified to lead this expedition - and brief members on virtually every aspect of the polar regions - than any man on earth. The Center and the expedition are fortunate to have Commander Dustin, as you will discover should you decide to participate.

The flight will be made in a specially outfitted, four-engine commercial jet with lounge-chair-and-table cabin configuration. A full flight crew of six will be headed by Captain Hal Neff, former pilot of Air Force One, the Presidential plane. Special clothing and equipment, such as Arctic survival gear, will be provided by the expedition and carried aboard the plane.

The expedition members will meet in Boston on the evening of November 7, 1968, for briefing and a reception and send-off party with the Governor of Massachusetts, Mayor of Boston, local officials and directors of the Byrd Polar Center. Next day, we will take off, head due north from Boston's Logan International Airport and follow this itinerary (as I have not yet visited all these places myself, I have drawn on the descriptions submitted to me by Commander Dustin and the other experienced people who have planned the expedition):

Thule, Greenland

Far above the Arctic Circle, past the chill reaches of Baffin Bay, lies desolate Thule, the northernmost U.S. air base. Almost 400 miles further north than the northern tip of Alaska, Thule was originally surveyed as a possible military site by Admiral Byrd and Commander Dustin. Here, in the deepening Arctic winter, you will get your first taste of the rigors of polar existence. You will have the chance to inspect the installation and meet the men for whom Arctic survival is a way of life.

North Pole

According to those who have crossed the North Pole, you will completely lose your day-night orientation. Sunrise and sunset can occur within minutes of each other, a strange and unforgettable phenomenon. After Thule, you will cross the geographic North Pole, just as Admiral Byrd did in his pioneering trans-Arctic flight with Floyd Bennett in 1926. A memorial flag will be dropped.

Anchorage, Alaska

After crossing the pole, the plane will bank into a 90° left turn and head south, over the Arctic Ocean and Beaufort Sea, past Mt. McKinley, North America's highest peak, and on to Anchorage. There, you will meet the Governor and key officials.

Tokyo, Japan

The highlight of your stopover in Japan will be an opportunity to meet the Emperor and Premier. (Fishing; excursion to Hakone and Atami by bullet train; tea ceremony at private homes.)

Manila, Philippines

General Carlos Romulo, the legendary patriot and statesman, an old friend of Admiral Byrd, will give the expedition a warm welcome in Manila. (Folklore performance; hunting for duck, deer, wild boar and a special species of water buffalo; fishing for tuna and marlin.)

You will note that here and elsewhere we have prearranged a considerable amount of hunting, fishing, and so on. These activities are optional. (Members of the expedition will be asked to indicate their preferences 30 days before the flight.) For those who do not want to participate in any of these events, there will be sight-seeing, golf and many other things to do.

Darwin, Australia

Hard by the Timor Sea, tropical Darwin offers some of the world's most superb beaches. You will have time not only to sample the sand and water sports, but to see Australia's great outback. With its spectacular chasms, canyons and gorges, the rarely visited outback is a scenic match for our own West.

Sydney, Australia

You can look forward to an enthusiastic reception in Sydney by the Prime Minister and government officials. For one thing, Australia is on particularly good terms with the United States. For another, Australia has traditionally been in the vanguard of nations involved in Antarctic exploration and development. (Hunting for kangaroo, crocodile, buffalo, wild boar, duck, and geese; or off-shore fishing for rifle fish, salmon, and giant grouper.)

Christchurch, New Zealand

This is our staging point for the flight to Antarctica, and it couldn't be more appropriate. Most of the early expeditions departed from New Zealand, and Admiral Byrd is still considered a national hero there. New Zealand is Antarctic-conscious and its people take almost a proprietary interest in the frozen continent. You will be something of a celebrity in New Zealand, and can expect a thoroughly enjoyable visit while the expedition awaits favorable weather reports from McMurdo Sound. (Deer hunting - where deer are so plentiful that they pay a bounty; fishing for all of the great species of marlin - in an area known for the greatest marlin fishing in the world - also Mako shark.)

McMurdo Sound, Antarctica

I am told that only a total eclipse of the sun is comparable, in emotional impact, to the first sight of Antarctica. Once experienced, neither can be forgotten. If you prove to be like most who have seen Antarctica, you will need somehow, someday, to return. And when you do, the emotional impact will be just as profound. That is what the Antarctic veterans say.

For Antarctica exists well beyond the boundaries of the world you know. You will see there a sun you have never before seen, breathe air you have never before breathed. You will see menacing white mountains towering for thousands of feet over a black ocean in which, with luck, you might survive for 45 seconds. You will see the awesome Ross Ice Shelf, as large as France, with its 50 to 200 foot ice cliffs cleaving the sea for 400 miles. You will see the active volcano, Mt. Erebus, 13,000 feet of fire and ice.

And you will see the huts, so well preserved they seem to have been inhabited only yesterday, which Shackleton used in 1908 and the ill-fated Scott in 1911. Antarctica, apparently, is not subject to the passage of time as we know it.

At McMurdo Base, you will meet the military men and scientists who inhabit this strange, alien territory. And you will inhabit it for a while too - long enough to feel its bone-chilling cold, to hear its timeless silence, to perceive, at the very edge of your composure, the terror of its mindless hostility to human beings.

While you are there, you will learn, as few men have ever had the opportunity to learn, about Antarctica. You will learn about survival, but more important, about what men must accomplish to truly open this formidable frontier.

South Pole

Admiral Byrd was the first man to fly over the South Pole. In all of history, probably fewer than 200 men have crossed the pole, by air or otherwise. As a member of this expedition, you will join that select group.

Punta Arenas, Chile

From the South Pole, you will fly to Punta Arenas, on the tortuous Strait of Magellan which separates continental South America from bleak Tierra del Fuego. The visit here will be brief, but you should get some idea of the flavor of this nearly forgotten outpost.

Rio de Janeiro, Brazil

This memorable stopover will include a diplomatic reception. You will also have a chance to relax and sample the sights and sounds of fabulous Rio. (Special plane to Belo Horizonte for hunting boar, duck, jaguar, panther, water buffalo, crocodile and deer.)

Dakar, Senegal

You may never have expected to see Dakar, but you will on this expedition. (Tribal dancing; safari.)

Rome, Italy

No trip would be complete without a stop in Rome, where we will be received enthusiastically. During our stay there we will have a private audience with the Pope.

London, England

From London, the expedition will fly back across the Atlantic and terminate with a debriefing, critique and farewell dinner in Boston, on December 3.

As mementos of the expedition, you will receive a leather-bound, personalized copy of the log book and a piece of the fabric from Admiral Byrd's original plane, mounted in crystal.

You will also be presented with a framed certificate from the Admiral Richard E. Byrd Polar Center, affirming your appointment as a Founding Trustee and expressing appreciation for your interest in, contributions to and efforts on behalf of the Center and its objectives. In the future, you will be kept fully advised of the plans and activities of the Center, and be invited to participate to whatever extent you wish. And of course, you will have life-long access to the Center's archives and services.

Most important, you will take back with you a once-in-a-lifetime experience. The day may come when journeys to and over the poles are commonplace. But today, the privilege is available to very few.

It is true, I think, that this privilege does carry responsibility with it. By the time you return, you will have received a comprehensive indoctrination course in the polar regions by the world's leading authorities. Your responsibility will be to make the most of the knowledge you will gain, to become an active advocate - perhaps even a disciple - of polar research and development.

It is a responsibility which, I trust, will weigh easily upon you. For once the polar air has been absorbed into your bloodstream, there is no cure. Like others who have been stricken, you will probably find yourself reading every word you can find on the North and South Poles. And, most likely, thinking about your next trip.

But first of all, you must decide about this trip. If you have a sense of adventure, a certain pioneering spirit, and if the prospect of taking part in a mission of worldwide significance and historical importance appeals to you, perhaps you should consider joining the expedition. It is doubtful that you will ever have another chance like this.

Obviously, you can't make a decision of this magnitude instantly. But a word of caution: reservations will be accepted in the order received - a total of only 60, including ten standbys. The departure date, remember, is November 8, 1968, so there is little time to waste.

The price of $10,000 includes food and beverages, all accommodations (the best available under all circumstances) transportation, special clothing, insurance, side excursions - virtually everything except your travel to and from Boston.

Money received will go into escrow at the United States Trust Company in Boston until the time of the flight. To the extent that revenues from the trip will exceed costs, the activities of the Polar Center will be accelerated.

To reserve your place in the expedition, just drop me a note on your letterhead or personal stationery, with your deposit check for $2,500, made out to the United States Trust Company. Incidentally, if anything prevents your leaving as planned, you can send another in your place; otherwise, cancellations cannot be accepted later than 30 days before departure.

If you have further questions, please write to me in care of the Transpolar Expedition, Admiral Richard E. Byrd Polar Center, 18 Tremont Street, Boston, Massachusetts 02108.

I hope we may hear from you soon - and that we will welcome you to the expedition.

Sincerely yours,

*Edward C. Bursk*

Edward C. Bursk

P.S.: We have just made arrangements for a professional camera crew to accompany the flight, and as a result we will be able to provide you with a short film clip and sound tape of your experiences.

## THE KIPLINGER WASHINGTON EDITORS, INC.

1729 H STREET, NORTHWEST, WASHINGTON, D. C. 20006   TELEPHONE: 298-6400

THE KIPLINGER WASHINGTON LETTER  THE KIPLINGER TAX LETTER
THE KIPLINGER AGRICULTURAL LETTER  THE KIPLINGER FLORIDA LETTER
THE KIPLINGER CALIFORNIA LETTER  THE KIPLINGER EUROPEAN LETTER
CHANGING TIMES MAGAZINE

Will There Be BOOM and More INFLATION Ahead?

The next few years will see business climb to the highest
level this country has ever known.  And with it...inflation.  Not
a boom, but steady growth accompanied by rising prices.

Those who prepare NOW for the growth and inflation that
lies ahead will reap big dividends for their foresight...and avoid
the blunders others will make.

You'll get the information you need for this type
of planning in the Kiplinger Washington Letter...
and the enclosed form will bring you the next 26
issues of this helpful service on a "Try-out" basis.
The fee:  Only $21 for the six months just ahead.

During the depression, in 1935, Kiplinger warned of inflation and told what to do about it.  Those who heeded his advice were
ready when prices began to rise.

Again, in January of 1946, Kiplinger renounced the widely-
held view that a severe post-war depression was inevitable.  Instead
he predicted shortages, rising wages and prices, a high level of
business.  And again, those who heeded his advice were able to avoid
losses, to cash in on the surging economy of the late 40's, early
50's and mid-60's.

Now Kiplinger not only foresees expansion ahead, but also
continuing inflation, and in his weekly Letter to clients he points
out profit opportunities in the future...and also dangers.

The Kiplinger Letter not only keeps you informed of present
trends and developments, but gives you advance notice of new government
policies...political moves and their real meaning...money policy...
foreign affairs...taxes...prices...union plans and tactics...
employment...wages...anything that will have an effect on you, your
job, your personal finances, your family.

To take advantage of this opportunity to try the Letter and
benefit from its keen judgments and helpful advice during the fast-

(Over, please)

---

changing months ahead...fill in and return the enclosed form along
with your $21 payment.  And do it with this guarantee:  That you may
cancel the service and get a prompt refund of the unused part of
your payment, any time you feel it is not worth far more to you than
it costs.

I'll start your service as soon as I hear from you, and
you'll have each weekly issue on your desk every Monday morning
thereafter.

Sincerely,

*Stanley Mayes*

Stanley Mayes
Assistant to the President

SM:kbi

P.S.  More than half of all new subscribers sign up for a full year.
In appreciation, we'll send you FREE an important Kiplinger
Special Report if you decide to take a full year's service,
too.  Details are spelled out on the enclosed slip.

---

**Exhibit 1.2. The Kiplinger Letter. Kiplinger has mailed almost three-quarters of a billion letters using the boom-or-bust theme over a sixteen-year period.**

**Opportunities for retailers**

Among the last to get on the direct marketing bandwagon have been retailers. But this is changing rapidly. The most visible evidence of retail entries into direct marketing has been retail catalogs. (See chapter 10.)

Retailers have three big advantages that cannot be matched by those who do not have retail stores.

1. *The advantage of local identity.* This is a big plus in the local trading area. The reluctance to order by mail from an unknown firm in a distant city is overcome when a mailing comes from a local retailer.

2. *The advantage of additional traffic.* A firm that sells solely through mail order either gets an order direct by mail or phone, or it's dead. The retailer, on the other hand, can have his cake and eat it too. Orders are generated direct by mail or by phone. And he can expect additional store traffic as well.

3. *Buying power.* Giant retailers and buying groups have buying power going for them. They have the sources of supply and the possibility of volume discounts.

There are three disadvantages which retailers must overcome.

1. *Lists.* Most retail customer lists consist of charge customers, those who have charged purchases at the retail store. They are *not,* for the most part, mail order buyers. Few retail charge lists are arranged by recency, frequency, or amount of purchase. Most retail direct mail promotions are across-the-board: metro and suburban areas alike. And you just don't sell many power mowers to apartment dwellers! The merchandise retailers stock in suburban stores is different from that in downtown stores to cater to different preferences. But retailers seem to ignore this necessity when it comes to direct mail.

2. *Installment credit.* Without installment credit, the sale of big ticket merchandise by mail is a virtual impossibility. There is a real hang-up for retailers who want to retain their identity with their own charge card—offering 30-day terms—to the exclusion of other charge cards which allow for installment payments. The answer lies in choosing one of two alternatives: instituting a revolving credit plan for the existing store credit card, or working through one of the bank credit card systems.

3. *Merchandise selection.* Selecting merchandise for mail order sales and selecting merchandise for sale over the counter can be as different as day and night. Few mail order practitioners could sit in the chair of the retail store buyer and vice versa! The types of merchandise to be selected, the manner of promotion, the economics involved, differ greatly.

Since the retailer enjoys the great advantages of store traffic resulting from his direct marketing effort, there are many objectives that can be explored.

1. *Activating existing charge customers.* The area with the most sales potential in any business is existing customers. And the charge card list is

the prime list. There's no more effective way to activate a charge list than to give special recognition to charge customers and to show this recognition with special offers.

2. *Getting new customers.* Close behind the objective of activating existing customers is the goal of getting new customers. And here's where direct marketing methods can prove a bonanza. Pinpoint marketing makes it possible to seek new customers in most trading areas with the most potential around existing stores. Merchandise offers can be tied to efforts to acquire new customers, with the objective of making such efforts break even or do better.

3. *Increasing store traffic.* Store traffic is still the name of the game. Direct marketing efforts will automatically create store traffic spillover. But beyond this, the retailer can direct mail a special offer not generally advertised, designed to increase store traffic. A well-organized store traffic program can pay off big.

4. *Leveling out sales volume.* The retail sales cycle has been a fact of life ever since the early days of Wanamaker, the Penneys, and the Fields. It still is today. Direct marketing efforts can be a big factor in filling in the valleys of the cycle.

5. *Pretesting merchandise and price.* Direct marketing methods offer perhaps the most accurate means of pretesting the appeal of merchandise and the most appealing price level. I have yet to see retailers use direct marketing for this purpose, but it could prove to be imaginative and profitable.

6. *Selling a wider range of merchandise.* This can be the most desirable and most profitable objective of all. Mail order thrives on the sale of merchandise and merchandise combinations not generally available in the retail store. But who is to say that a retailer should not sell merchandise *not generally available in his retail store?* It's being done right now—successfully. Cameras, radios, dinnerware, tool sets, delicacies, paint guns, magazine subscriptions, insurance—an endless variety of merchandise and services, and all extra business.

And if the retailer works with a syndicator, there are two distinct advantages: (1) properly prepared mailing packages at minimal cost, and (2) no inventory or handling by the retail store.

So the time is ripe for retailing to get on the direct marketing bandwagon. The elements are all here for those who will grasp the opportunities and run with them. Three basic ingredients are vital to success: (1) a separate department headed by a direct marketing manager or direct marketing consultant reporting directly to a store official; (2) an installment credit program in conjuction with the store's own charge card or with one or more charge card systems; and (3) a planned, continuing program.

**Eight major responsibilities of direct marketing executives**

The world of direct marketing is a big world, an exciting world, an awesome world for those who have never operated within it. As more and more major corporations enter direct marketing (and they are doing so at a rapidly accelerating speed), it is becoming clear that those who are succeeding are doing so by setting up direct marketing separate and apart from other marketing functions. It is safe to predict that in the next decade all major corporations having products or services that can be sold direct will have staffs of direct marketing experts. Exhibit 1.3 lists in detail the major responsibilities of the direct marketing executive—a total of 66 individual functions. A review of the eight major responsibility categories with their attendant functions is very much in order.

---

**Exhibit 1.3. Direct marketing evaluations and functions checklist.**

1. **Product selection and development**
   Market potential
   Competition
   Reliability of sources
   Value comparison
   Packaging
   Shipping costs
   Unit of sale
   Profit margin
   Ease of use
   Instructions
   Refurbishing costs
   Repeat potential
   Evaluation of syndication

2. **Markets and media selection**
   Mailing lists
   Magazines
   Newspapers and supplements
   Radio and television
   Co-ops
   Telephone
   Car cards, match books, etc.

3. **Creative development and scheduling**
   Strategy and concept
   Offers
   Copy
   Layouts
   Formats
   FTC regulations
   Scheduling of ads and mailing packages

4. **Testing procedures**
   Compiled vs. direct response lists
   Regional testing
   Testing by ZIP codes
   Testing by socioeconomic factors
   Seasonal testing
   Price testing
   Offer testing

Establishing control ads and control mailing packages
Determining media duplication
Using probability scales
Preevaluation of ads and mailing packages
Measuring readership

5. **Fulfillment**
   Shipping facilities
   Replacement procedures
   Returned goods procedures
   Distribution centers
   Shipping method (carriers)

6. **Budgeting and accounting**
   Cash flow charts
   Bad debt reserves
   Financing costs
   Attrition scales
   Forms and systems
   Commercial credit card affiliations
   Credit and collection procedures
   Recency, frequency, and monetary criteria

7. **Customer service**
   Sales correspondence
   Complaints and adjustments
   Activation and reactivation

8. **Personnel and supplier relations**
   Advertising department
   Fulfillment sources
   Accounting department
   Customer service
   Advertising agency
   List brokers
   Space reps
   Suppliers of merchandise and services
   Printers, engravers, and typesetters
   Artists and art studios
   Envelope houses

## Product selection and development

Direct marketing fails right here for many companies. Selecting or developing the right product or products requires special know-how and special considerations peculiar to direct marketing.

What is the market potential? Is it too small to pursue? Is it too competitive? Can supply sources meet requirements fast? Can they offer good value? Is packaging attractive enough to sell the product or service on its arrival? Is packaging sturdy enough to prevent damage or breakage? Are shipping costs killers to the consumer if he must pay, or killers to the marketer if *he* must pay?

What about unit of sale and profit margin? It's hard to chew up selling costs with a small unit of sale, no matter what the profit margin. And if the unit of sale will be sold using installment credit, is there an extra margin to carry the costs of a credit operation?

Then there's the matter of ease of use. Some of the most appealing items are mechanical, but give the most astute adult something mechanical and he frequently shows the intelligence of a high school dropout. Getting the consumer to read even the most lucid instructions is a difficult task.

And how about refurbishing costs, the amount the marketer must pay to have returned merchandise checked and refurbished? These can run sky-high, killing off front-end profits.

What about repeat potential? Do profits have to come from a one-time sale? Who is to make all these evaluations? If not a company direct marketing executive, a professional direct marketing agency is needed. Such an organization should be able to match product selection with a company profile and marketing objectives.

## Markets and media selection

When the product or products have been developed or selected, the marketing executive must consider the most profitable route or routes to reach potential buyers. The route can involve the existing customer list, especially where syndicated offers are used.

Marketing beyond one's existing customer list may involve a wide variety of media. Direct marketing relies heavily upon lists of mail order buyers, and print media should have a direct response atmosphere.

## Creative development and scheduling

The creative arm of a direct marketing department is a key factor in the success or failure of a direct marketing operation. It can be said that the creative people who are great in the world of direct marketing are a rare breed. They're creative, but they are accustomed to receiving positive feedback on their creativity from periodic results.

Creative development starts with selling strategies and concepts, and these are translated into propositions. The propositions are presented through copy and illustrations. To get the recipient to read the copy and look at the illustrations, you need a unique combination of layouts and formats. Copywriters should have at least a working knowledge of increasingly stringent FTC regulations. More and more copy must go through legal channels before release.

Creative people should also have a hand in scheduling and in making certain all their ads and mailing packages appear as conceived and are keyed properly to allow results to be traced.

**Testing procedures**  Because direct marketing lives by measured results, testing procedures are vital. And it is in this area that many a direct marketing program falls apart. Erroneous testing procedures lead to faulty conclusions. Factors to test include media, regions, ZIP code areas, socioeconomic factors. The season of the year can be a key factor. Then there's testing for best price and best proposition. Control ads and control mailing packages must be established.

In the case of print media, circulation duplication must be considered. In the case of mailing lists, duplication between direct response lists must be eliminated. Publication studies and readership measurements may well be considered under testing procedures.

**Fulfillment**  One of the real stumbling blocks to many companies that enter direct marketing is fulfillment, the process of making delivery of the product or service ordered. I've seen giant corporations flunk out on this. Filling orders promptly, within 48 hours if possible, is critical. Mail order respondents cool off mighty fast.

Of no less importance are prompt replacement of damaged or improperly sized items and prompt credit for returned merchandise. Lack of efficient systems can lead to nightmares. Distribution centers can alleviate or complicate problems. Having the right carriers is essential for efficient distribution.

**Budgeting and accounting**  No direct marketing executive can hit the big time without a watchdog treasurer backed by an efficient force steeped in mail order procedures.

This treasurer will develop cash-flow charts that will show management how quickly it will get its money back at various levels of success. He'll be smart enough to set up bad debt reserves that will cover unusually high uncollectables. He'll take the cost of money into account as a direct cost of direct marketing.

And in this very same department, facts and figures will be developed, probably through the computer, that will enable the direct marketing executive to build the business rapidly and profitably. He'll be able to determine acquisition cost and the value of a customer.

**Customer service**  Probably right down the hall from budgeting and accounting will be "the boys in the white hats," customer service. Direct marketing departments get lots of letters with questions, questions, questions. "How do I put part A into B?" "Where's my free gift?" "How do I stop my membership?" The answers had better be prompt, courteous, and accurate. A good customer service department is a key link in the direct marketing chain.

**Personnel and supplier relations**  The ideal direct marketing executive not only must know and evaluate all the functions involved in direct marketing, but he must also be able to work well with all the internal and external forces involved in his world of direct marketing. And it's quite a world!

His advertising agency should be as steeped in direct marketing as he is. He should have a close relationship with leading list brokers and space reps of direct response publications. A knowledge of suppliers is essential. He should be able to pick the right art studio, engraver, typesetter, envelope house, and printer for each given job.

Direct marketing is indeed a wide, wide world. It requires specialized knowledge and specialized skills, but for those who have them or develop them, it's a beautiful world.

**Self-quiz**

1. Define direct marketing.

   _____

   _____

   _____

   _____

   _____

   _____

   _____

2. Why have changing lifestyles had a favorable effect on direct marketing?

   _____

   _____

   _____

   _____

   _____

   _____

   _____

3. Give three examples of compelling reasons for a firm to consider direct marketing?

   a. _____

      _____

   b. _____

      _____

   c. _____

      _____

4. Name the three major commercial credit cards.

   a. _____

   b. _____

   c. _____

5. Name the two major bank cards.

   a. _____

   b. _____

6. What are the six big keys to direct marketing success?

   a. _____

   b. _____

   c. _____

   d. _____

   e. _____

   f. _____

7. What are the three advantages unique to retailers using direct marketing methods?

   a. _____

      _____

   b. _____

      _____

   c. _____

      _____

8. What are the eight major responsibilities of direct marketing executives?

   a. _____

   b. _____

   c. _____

   d. _____

   e. _____

   f. _____

   g. _____

   h. _____

## Pilot project

Educators agree that one of the best ways to learn is by doing. For the industrious, pilot projects will be suggested so that you can apply the material contained in each chapter.

Assume you are the advertising manager of a department store organization with one central city store and three suburban stores. You have 50,000 charge accounts, but only 40 percent of these customers have made charge purchases in the past 12 months.

You have a budget that will enable you to mail to each inactive account four times over the next four months. Develop an outline that spells out precisely what your proposition will be in each of these four mailings.

# 2

# Importance of the Offer

The propositions you make to customers—more often referred to as *offers*—can mean the difference between success or failure. Depending on the offer, differences in response of 25, 50, 100 percent, and more are commonplace.

Not only is the offer you make the key to success or failure, but the manner in which an offer is presented can have an equally dramatic effect. For example, here are three ways to state the same offer:

1. Half price!
2. Buy one—get one *free!*
3. 50% off!

Each statement conveys the same offer, but statement number 2 pulled 40 percent better than statement number 1 or number 3. Consumers perceived statement number 2 to be the most attractive offer.

**Example of dramatic differences**
The following case history illustrates the dramatically different results that can be obtained from two propositions offering the same product to the same audience.

The "product" was a series of 12 sales bulletins produced by Harry Simmons, a nationally known sales consultant. The market was sales managers. The objective was to sell the series of bulletins in quantity for distribution to sales forces. Two different offers were devised and tested.

Offer A asked the sales manager to send for one complete set of 12 sales bulletins for personal review. He was told that on receipt he would have the following options: (1) 15 days' free review, (2) the right to return the bulletins at the end of the trial period at which time the memo invoice in the amount of $3.75 would be cancelled, (3) the right to keep the set and honor the memo invoice, or (4) the right to keep the set and order additional sets for the sales force.

Offer B involved sending the sales manager one sample bulletin with a solicitation letter. The offer was, "Tell us how many salesmen you employ.

We'll send you a free copy of the enclosed bulletin for every member of your sales force. Then, every two weeks thereafter, we'll send you an equal quantity until all 12 bulletins are received. If there are any bulletins you don't like, you can return them for full credit."

Here are the comparative results. Offer A produced an average order of $5.25 for a single set and multiple-set order combined. Offer B pulled a third more responses than Offer A. The average order was $27.50 compared to an average order of $5.25 for Offer A. The same "product" was offered to the same market, and it must be said that the quality of copy was the same. But Offer B pulled a third more responses and an average order which was almost five times larger! Why the difference?

Under Offer A, the sales manager had to read all 12 bulletins to decide whether he wished to distribute them. Human inertia got in the way. Obviously, a very large percentage of sales managers never got around to the chore. Under Offer B, the decision to become involved depended on reading just one bulletin. No wonder B did so much better than A.

Whatever medium may be employed to make the offer, the objective is to overcome *human inertia*—the natural resistance to becoming involved with an offer. And since hundreds of offers are proffered through every available medium daily, there is a strong, strong resistance out there! Theoretically, the more attractive you can make your offer, the easier you make it for the prospect to respond; the less resistance there is likely to be and, therefore, the more response.

**Checklist of basic offers**
The following checklist briefly describes 25 basic offers that may be used singly or in various combinations, depending on the marketer's objectives. Variations on some of these basic offers are illustrated in Exhibits 2.1–2.4.

1. *Free information.* This is often the most effective offer, particularly when leads for salespeople are the prime objective or nonprospects must be screened out at low cost before expensive literature is sent to prime prospects.

2. *Samples.* A sample of a product or service is often a very effective sales tool. If a sample can be enclosed in a mailing package, results often more than warrant the extra cost. Consideration should be given to charging a nominal price for a sample. The recipient's investment in a sample promotes trying it and this usually results in a substantial increase in sales.

3. *Free trial.* Bellwether of mail order. Melts away human inertia. Consider fitting the length of the trial period to the nature of the product or service, rather than the standard 15 days.

4. *Conditional sale.* Prearranges the possibility of long-term acceptance based on a sample. Example: "Yes, please send me the current issue of *Psychology Today* and enter my name as a trial subscriber at the special introductory rate of $6 for 12 issues (half the regular price). However, if not delighted with the first issue, I will simply write 'cancel' on the bill and return it without paying or owing anything, keeping the first issue as a complimentary copy."

**USE THE POSTCARD BELOW TO TAKE ADVANTAGE OF**

# Two FREE United Hawaii Vacation Offers

1. Fly/Drive  2. As You Like It  3. Life Style  4. Unwinders  5. One-O  6. Privacy In Paradise

## I. A FREE PINEAPPLE

can be yours. Just mark an X in this pineapple and you may be one of 5,000 lucky people to receive a luscious, juicy, fresh pineapple. Enter now, whether you order any vacation guides or not — there's no obligation. Void where prohibited by law.

## 2. FREE VACATION GUIDES

They're yours, easy as marking in the numbers of your choices in the outlined boxes. Then detach this postcard, and mail it today. We'll be glad to send your brochures to you at no cost whatever.

**Yes,** please enter my name in your Hawaii Vacations Drawing for a free pineapple. Void where prohibited by law.

```
CHI                      118
ROBERT STONE
150 N WACKER DR 8TH FL
CHICAGO         IL 60606
```

**Yes,** please send me the free Hawaii vacation guides that I have numbered.

**Exhibit 2.1.**
**Dual free offer...with limitations. United Airlines gives the consumer an opportunity to get a free pineapple, if among the first 5,000 to reply. And an opportunity to select 2 of 6 free tour folders being offered.**

5. *Till forbid.* Prearranges for continuing shipments on a specified basis. The customer has the option to forbid future shipments at any specified time. Works well for business services offers and continuity book programs.

6. *Yes-no.* An involvement offer. The prospect is asked to respond, usually through a token or stamp, indicating whether he accepts or rejects the offer. Historically, more favorable responses are received with this offer than when no rejection option is provided.

7. *Time limit.* Setting a time limit on a given offer *forces* action, either positive or negative. Usually it is more effective to name a specific date rather than a time period. It is important to test for the most effective time limit because a short period may not allow sufficient time for deliberation. Too long a period, on the other hand, may promote inertia.

8. *Get-a-friend.* Based on the axiom that the best source for new customers is one's present list of satisfied customers. Many get-a-friend offers get

**Exhibit 2.2.**
**Tentative commitment offer. Involvement card with token offers the first issue of *Money* free with a commitment to buy 11 issues unless bill is returned marked "cancel." (Front-end pull on this type of offer normally exceeds other subscription offers. Cancellations, however, usually exceed those for more stringent offers.)**

new customers in a large volume at low acquisition cost. The best response for a get-a-friend offer usually results from limiting the number of friends' names requested and offering a reward for providing names or securing new customers.

9. *Contests.* These create attention and excitement. Stringent FTC rules apply. Highly effective in conjunction with magazine subscription offers and popular merchandise offers.

10. *Discounts.* A discount is a never-ending lure to consumers as well as businessmen. Discounts are particularly effective where the value of a product or service is well established. Three types of discounts are widely offered: (a) for cash, (b) for an introductory order, and (c) for volume purchase.

11. *Negative options.* This offer prearranges for shipment if the customer doesn't abort the shipment by mailing the rejection form prior to deadline date. In popular use by book and record clubs. FTC guidelines must be followed carefully.

12. *Positive option.* Every shipment is based on a *direct action* by the club member, rather than a *nonaction* as exemplified by the negative option feature of most book and record clubs. Front-end response to a positive option is likely to be lower, but long-pull sales are likely to be greater.

**Exhibit 2.3. Employing the laser-beam typesetting process (with various type styles and sizes), *Time* magazine offers a special price for as many issues as desired (from 25 to 100) and a free *Hammond World Atlas* with a paid subscription.**

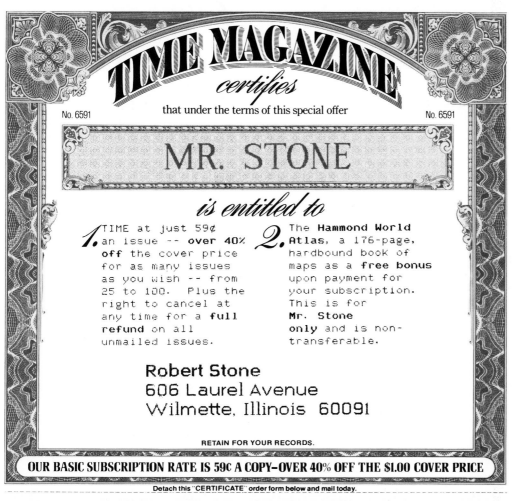

# TIME MAGAZINE
## *certifies*

that under the terms of this special offer

No. 6591                                                                 No. 6591

## MR. STONE

### *is entitled to*

**1.** TIME at just 59¢ an issue -- **over 40% off** the cover price for as many issues as you wish -- from 25 to 100. Plus the right to cancel at any time for a **full refund** on all unmailed issues.

**2.** The Hammond World Atlas, a 176-page, hardbound book of maps as a **free bonus** upon payment for your subscription. This is for **Mr. Stone only** and is non-transferable.

**Robert Stone
606 Laurel Avenue
Wilmette, Illinois 60091**

RETAIN FOR YOUR RECORDS.

**OUR BASIC SUBSCRIPTION RATE IS 59¢ A COPY—OVER 40% OFF THE $1.00 COVER PRICE**

- - - - - - - - - - Detach this "CERTIFICATE" order form below and mail today. - - - - - - - - - -

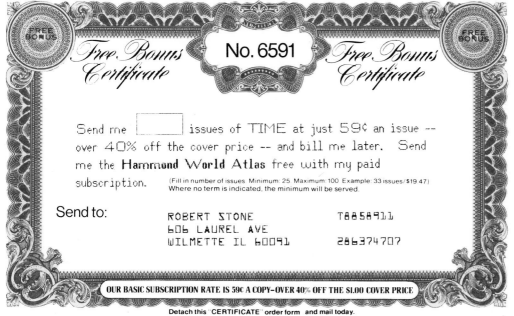

*Free Bonus Certificate*   **No. 6591**   *Free Bonus Certificate*

Send me [        ] issues of TIME at just 59¢ an issue -- over 40% off the cover price -- and bill me later. Send me the Hammond World Atlas free with my paid subscription.

(Fill in number of issues. Minimum: 25. Maximum: 100. Example: 33 issues/$19.47) Where no term is indicated, the minimum will be served.

Send to:

ROBERT STONE                    T8858911
606 LAUREL AVE
WILMETTE IL 60091               286374707

**OUR BASIC SUBSCRIPTION RATE IS 59¢ A COPY—OVER 40% OFF THE $1.00 COVER PRICE**

Detach this "CERTIFICATE" order form and mail today.

## Certificate of Application

*Advertising Age Professional Development Program in Advertising*

☐ YES...Please enter _____ charter enrollment(s) in the new Professional
         (quantity)

Development Program in Advertising. The complete program comes to me hand-somely packaged in a deluxe vinyl carrying case, containing 16 lessons in profes-sional development, including self-quizzes and involvement assignments, a mar-keting case study, three supplementary advertising books, six interviews with leading advertising professionals on cassettes, and one deluxe binder with 16 color-coded section dividers.

### *Guarantee of Satisfaction.*

The Professional Development Program In Advertising is uncon-ditionally guaranteed by *Advertising Age.* The Program(s) may be returned for credit or full refund within 15 days after receipt.

### *Check the Terms of Your Choice:*

☐ **Cash Payment In Full.** Enclosed is payment in full—$250 for each enrollment. *Advertising Age* is to pay all shipping and handling costs. (Full refund(s) for Program(s) returned within 15 days after receipt.)

☐ **Installment Cash Payment.** Enclosed is $62.50 as the first of four equal monthly install-ments for each enrollment. (Ship Deluxe carrying case, introduction lessons 1 thru 4, one of three books, Deluxe binder and color-coded dividers, and two of six cassettes.) If not completely satis-fied, Program(s) will be returned within 15 days after receipt for full refund. Otherwise *Advertis-ing Age* is to invoice 30 days in advance of each of the three remaining shipments at the rate of $62.50 each, plus shipping and handling charges. Installment shipment will follow within 5 days of payment.

☐ **Charge to Credit Card.** Ship complete Prog-ram(s) at $250 each and charge to:
☐ AMERICAN EXPRESS
☐ BANK AMERICARD ☐ MASTER CHARGE
My COMPLETE CARD NO.
IS _____
EXPIRATION DATE:_____
If using Master Charge, please include 4-digit bank number appearing on card just above your name ☐☐☐☐

☐ **Bill In Full to Company.** Ship complete Prog-ram(s) and bill to my firm at $250 each, plus ship-ping and handling charges. Terms: 30 days net (available to rated firms only). Full return privileges within 15 days after receipt.

☐ **Bill In Installments to Company.** Ship com-plete Program(s) and bill in four equal monthly installments of $62.50 for each program, plus shipping and handling charges. Terms: 30 days net (available to rated firms only). Full return privileges within 15 days after receipt.

**Optional Equipment**

☐ YES...please send_____cassette player/recorder(s) for just $29.95 each. (Payment must accompany order.)

Name _____
Firm _____
Home or Business Address_____
City _____ State_____ Zip_____
Phone _____
Signature_____
(If billed to credit card. must be signed by cardholder.)

Crain Books Division • Advertising Age • 740 N. Rush Street • Chicago, Illinois 60611

6975F                                                                                    IMC

---

**Exhibit 2.4.**
**Multiple terms order form. Crain Books Division of Crain Communications Inc. offers several purchase options for its *Professional Development Program in Advertising*: cash payment in full, installment cash payments, full amount billed to company, installment billing to company, and charge to credit card.**

13. *Lifetime membership.* Under this plan, the member pays one fee, $5.00, for instance, at the time of becoming a member. In return the member is guaranteed substantial reduction from established retail prices. There is no requirement that the respondent make a specified number of pur-chases. But the safeguard to the marketer is that the member is more likely to make purchases because of his front-end investment.

14. *Load-ups.* This proposition is a favorite of publishers of continuity series. Example: The publisher offers a set of 12 books, one to be re-leased each month. After the purchaser has received and paid for the first three books, the publisher invites him to receive the remaining nine, all in one shipment, with the understanding that payments can continue

to be made monthly. This load-up offer invariably results in more *complete sets* of books being sold.

15. *Free gift.* Most direct response advertisers have increased response through free gift offers. For best results, you should test several gifts to determine the most appealing. There's no set criterion for the cost of a gift as related to selling cost. The most important criteria are: (a) appropriateness of the gift; (b) its effect on repeat business; and (c) net profit per thousand circulation or distribution including cost of the gift.

16. *Deluxe alternative.* Related to the famous Sears tradition of *good, better, best* are offers for deluxe alternatives. A classic example would be a dictionary offered in a regular edition or in a thumb-indexed edition for $2.00 more. By giving the prospect the choice, the advertiser often increases total response and total dollars.

17. *Charters.* A charter offer by its very nature denotes something special. The offer plays on the human trait that many people want to be among the first to see, try, and use something new. The most successful charter offers include special rewards or concessions for early support.

18. *Guaranteed buy-back.* "Satisfaction guaranteed" is the heart of mail order selling. But the guaranteed buy-back offer goes much further. This guarantee pledges to buy back the product (if the customer so requests) at the original price for a period of time after original purchase.

19. *Multiproduct.* Multiproduct offers may take the form of a series of postcards or a collection of individual sheets, each with a separate order form. Each product presentation is structured to stand on its own feet.

20. *Piggybacks.* These are "add on" offers which ride along with major offers at no additional postage cost. The unit of sale is usually much smaller than the major offer. Testing is advocated to determine whether piggybacks add to or steal from sales of the major offer.

21. *Bounce-backs.* Bounce-back offers succeed on the premise, "the best time to sell a person is right after you have sold him." Bounce-back order forms are usually included in shipments or with invoices or statements. Bounce-backs may offer (a) more of the same, (b) related items, or (c) items totally different from those originally purchased.

22. *Good-better-best.* The essence of the offer is to give the prospect a choice between something and something. Example: For their State of the Union series, the Franklin Mint gave the prospect three choices: 24k gold on sterling at $72.50 monthly, solid sterling silver at $43.75 monthly, and solid bronze at $17.50 monthly.

23. *Optional terms.* The technique here is to give the prospect the option of choosing terms at varying rates. The bigger the commitment, the better the buy.

24. *Flexible terms.* A derivative of optional terms is flexible terms. The potential subscriber to a magazine is offered a bargain weekly rate of, say, 25 cents a week for a minimum period of 16 weeks. But, if he

wishes, the subscriber may choose to enter his subscription for any number of weeks beyond the minimum at the same bargain rate.

25. *Exclusive rights.* This is an offer made by publishers of syndicated newsletters. Under the terms of such an offer, the first to order—an insurance broker, for example—has exclusive rights for his trading area so long as he remains a subscriber.

Some of these 25 basic offers warrant additional explanation.

**Yes-no**
Yes-no offers add an extra dimension to other offers, for instance, the free-trial offer. The yes-no alternative *involves* the reader; it encourages him to make a conscious decision and express that decision with a yes or no response. With the basic free-trial offer, it's easier to say "no" by simply taking no action. But the yes-no device, with its added dimension, plays on a basic human trait. It's probably true that most people dislike saying "no." Therefore, they are more likely to say "yes" if confronted with making a yes-no decision.

Businessmen's Record Club conducted many tests using the yes-no offer in conjunction with the free-trial offer. It was generally found that lists which would pull 1 percent without the yes-no involvement would pull close to 1½ percent in free-trial orders with the yes-no involvement.

Also, some interesting results emerged as related to the percentages of yeses and noes on given lists. Generally, there was little difference in total response between lists. A well-performing list that produced 1½ percent in free-trial orders would produce about 2½ percent noes. A poorly performing list which brought 1 percent in trial orders would produce 3 percent noes. In both cases, the total response was about 4 percent.

When it comes to sweepstakes contests, of course, the yes-no feature is a legal necessity. The standard language is, "Yes, I am ordering at this time. Let me know if I have won (or what I've won)"; or "No, I am not ordering at this time. But let me know if I've won (or what I've won)." In sweepstakes, too, there are wide variances between yes-no response percentages. It isn't unusual at all to get 10 to 15 no responses for every yes response when mailing to prospect lists. On the other hand, a sweepstakes offer to an active customer list often produces one or more yes responses for each no response.

**Free gift**
Giving free gifts for inquiring, for trying, and for buying has got to be as old an incentive as trading stamps. It is not unusual at all for the right gift to increase response by 25 percent and more. On the other hand, a free-gift offer can actually reduce response or have no favorable effect on the basic offer. Joan Manley, publisher of Time-Life Books, states that the company has been consistently unsuccessful with free gifts in conjunction with their Time-Life continuity book offers.

What's more, there is a tremendous variance in the appeal of free gifts. For example, the Airline Passengers Association tested two free gifts along with a membership offer: an airline guide and a carry-on suit bag. The suit bag did 50 percent better than the guide.

A fund-raising organization selling to schools tested three different gifts:

a set of children's books, a camera, and a 30-cup coffee maker. The coffee maker won by a wide margin; the children's books came in a poor third.

Testing for the most appealing gifts is essential because of the great differences in pull. In selecting gifts for testing purposes, follow this good rule of thumb: Gifts that are suited to personal use tend to have considerably more appeal than those that aren't.

There is yet another consideration about free gifts: Is it more effective to offer a selection of free gifts of comparable value than to offer only one gift? The answer is that offering a selection of gifts of comparable value usually reduces response. This is perhaps explained by the inability of many people to make a choice.

Adopting the one-gift method (after testing for the one with the most appeal) should not be confused with offering gifts of varying value for orders of varying amounts. This is quite a different situation. A multiple-gift proposition might be a free travel clock for orders up to $15, a free transistor radio for orders from $15 to $30, and a free Polaroid camera for orders over $30.

Offering gifts of varying value for orders of varying amounts is logical to the consumer. The advertiser can afford a more expensive gift in conjunction with a larger order. His prime objective is accomplished by increasing his average order over and above what it would be if there were no extra incentive.

The multiple-gift plan works for many but it can also boomerang. This usually happens when the top gift calls for a purchase over and above what most people can use or afford. The effect can also be negative if the gift offered for the price most people can afford is of little value or consequence. The multiple-gift plan tied to order value has good potential advantages, but careful tests must be conducted. An adaptation of the multiple-gift plan is a gift, often called a "keeper," for trying (free trial), plus a gift for keeping (paying for the purchase). Under this plan the prospect is told he can keep the gift offered for trying even if he returns the product being offered for sale. However, if the product being offered is retained, the prospect also keeps a second gift of greater value than the first. Columbia House, to name one big mass marketer, has successfully applied the gift for trying and the gift for buying technique many times.

Still another possibility with gift offers is giving more than one gift for either trying or buying. If the budget for the incentive is $1.00, for example, the advertiser can offer one gift costing $1.00, two gifts costing $1.00 combined, or even three gifts totaling $1.00. From a sales strategy standpoint, some advertisers spell out what one or two of the gifts are and offer an additional "mystery gift" for prompt response. Fingerhut Corporation of Minneapolis is a strong proponent of multiple gifts and "mystery" gifts.

Free gifts are a tricky business, to be sure. Gift selection and gift tie-ins to offers require careful testing for best results. The $64 question always is, "How much can I afford to spend for a gift?" Aaron Adler, president of Stone & Adler, maintains that most marketers make an erroneous arbitrary decision in advance, such as "I can afford to spend 5 percent of selling price." He maintains that a far more logical approach is to select the most appealing gift possible, without being restricted by an arbitrary cost figure, than to be guided by the net profit figures resulting from tests. For example, Table 2.1 shows a comparison of net profits for two promotions, one with a gift costing $1.00 and the other with a gift costing $2.00 on a $29.95 offer, given a 50 percent better pull with the $2 premium.

**Table 2.1. Comparison of profits from promotions with free gifts of different costs.**

| Item | $1 Gift | $2 Gift |
|---|---|---|
| Net pull of promotion ....... | 1% | 1.5% |
| Sales per thousand pieces .. | $299.50 | $449.25 |
| Less: | | |
| Mailing cost ........... | $120.00 | $120.00 |
| Merchandise cost (45%) .. | 134.98 | 202.16 |
| Administrative cost (10%) . | 30.00 | 44.93 |
| Premium cost ......... | 10.00 | 30.00 |
| Total costs ............. | 294.98 | 397.09 |
| Profit per thousand pieces ... | $ 4.52 | $ 52.16 |

It is interesting to note that, in this example, when the $1.00 gift was offered, the mailing just about broke even. But when the cost of the gift was doubled, the profit jumped from $4.52 to $52.16 per thousand mailed.

Another advantage of offering more attractive gifts (which naturally cost more) is to offer gifts of substantial value tied to cumulative purchases. This plan can prove particularly effective when the products or services being offered produce consistent repeat orders. A typical offer under a cumulative purchase plan might be: "When your total purchases of our custom-made cigars reach $150, you receive a power saw absolutely free."

**Load-ups**  Load-up offers are peculiar to continuity bookselling programs. The technique, however, should interest all direct marketers in that it shows how to attract customers with one offer and change the arithmetic favorably through a subsequent offer. The load-up technique came into vogue early in the 1960s and is still enjoying great success. The director of administration of Britannica Home Library Service describes load-ups as follows.

The subscriber sends in an order card requesting the first volume in a set of books. Usually, the first volume is offered free, but it could also require a token payment, the most common being a 10 or 25¢ offer. If the subscriber does not cancel after receiving the first book, volumes 2 and 3 will be shipped separately at monthly intervals. Then all remaining volumes are sent in one shipment. It is important to note that a subscriber can cancel at any time, and the return of any book constitutes automatic cancellation.

The success of the mailing depends not only on front-end response but also on the shipment retention factor, or "load factor," as it is commonly called. No mailer, to my knowledge, will release 12 volumes in a set without receiving at least one payment. In some cases three (or more) payments are required before the final volumes are released.

It is the end result of the load-up technique that makes the method attractive to book publishers. Under the one-book-a-month plan with no load-up, attrition is more likely to occur after four or five books are received in a 12-book series, for example.

But under the load-up technique, the subscriber receives the balance of 12 books after he has received and paid for the first two or three in a series. Even though the subscriber need pay for only one book a month and even though he may return the load-up shipment if he wishes, statistics prove that a higher percentage of complete sets are sold with this method.

**Get-a-friend**  Perhaps one of the most overlooked and yet most profitable of all offers is the get-a-friend offer. If you have a list of satisfied customers, it is quite natural for them to want to let their friends in on a good thing.

The basic technique for get-a-friend offers is to offer an incentive in appreciation for a favor. Nominal gifts are often given to a customer for the simple act of providing friends' names, with more substantial gifts awarded to the customer for friends who become customers.

Based on experience, here is what you can expect in using the get-a-friend approach: You will get a larger number of friends' names if the customer is guaranteed that his name will not be used in soliciting his friends. Response from friends, however, will be consistently better if you are allowed to refer to the party who supplied their names.

To get the best of two worlds, therefore, you should allow the customer to indicate whether his name may be used in soliciting his friends. For example: "You may use my name when writing my friends," or "Do not use my name when writing my friends."

Response from friends becomes progressively less in relation to the number of names provided by a customer. One can expect the response from three names provided by one person to be greater than the total response from six names provided by another person. The reason is that is it natural to list the names in order of likelihood of interest.

Two safeguards may be applied to getting the maximum response from friends' names: (1) limit the number of names to be provided, for example, to three or four, and (2) promote names provided in order of listing, such as all names provided first as one group, all names provided second as another group, and so forth. Those who have mastered the technique of getting friends' names from satisfied customers have found that, with very few exceptions, such lists are more responsive than most lists they can rent or buy.

**Short- and long-term effects on offers**  A major consideration in structuring offers is the effect a given offer will have on your objectives.

- Is your objective to get a *maximum* number of new customers for a given product or service as quickly as possible?
- Is it your objective to determine the *repeat business factor* as quickly as possible?
- Is it your objective to break even or make a profit in the shortest possible period?

So, the key question to ask when designing an offer is, "How will this offer help to accomplish my objective?"

**Offers relate to objectives**  Say you are introducing a new hobby magazine. You have the choice of making a short-term offer (three months, for instance) or a long-term offer (say 12 months). Since you want to determine acceptances as quickly as possible (your objective), you would rightly decide on a short-term offer. Under the short-term offer, after three months you will be getting a picture of renewal percentages. If you made an initial offer of 12-month subscriptions, you would have to wait a year to determine the publication renewal rate. In the interim, you would be missing vital information important to your magazine's success.

If the three-month trial subscriptions are renewed at a satisfactory rate, you could then safely proceed to develop offers designed to get initial long-term subscriptions. It is axiomatic in the publishing field that the longer the initial term of subscription, the higher the renewal rate is likely to be. Professional circulation men know from experience that if they are getting, say, a 35 percent conversion on a three-month trial, they can expect a conversion of 50 percent or more on 12-month initial subscriptions. This knowledge, therefore, can be extrapolated from the short-term objective to the long-term objective.

Sol Blumenfeld, a prominent direct marketing consultant, when addressing a Direct Mail/Marketing Association convention, made some pertinent remarks about the dangers of looking only at front-end response. Blumenfeld stated, "Many people still cling to the CPA (cost per application) or CPI (cost per inquiry) response syndromes. In their eagerness to sell now, they frequently foul up their chances to sell later."

He then asks, "Can the practice of those who concern themselves only with front-end response at least partially explain book club conversions of only 50 to 60 percent? Magazine renewal rates of only 30 percent? Correspondence school attrition factors of as much as 40 percent?"

Blumenfeld gives us a case in point. A control for the Britannica Home Study Library Service (a division of Encyclopaedia Britannica) was run against several test ads developed by the agency. Control ads offered free the first volume of *Compton's Encyclopedia*. Major emphasis was placed on sending for the free volume; small emphasis was placed on the idea of ultimately purchasing the balance of the 24-volume set. Front-end response was excellent; the rate of conversion to full 24-volume sets was poor. Profitability was unacceptable.

Against the control ad, the agency tested several new ads which offered Volume I free but also revealed the cost of the complete set—right in the headline. Here's what happened: The cost per coupon for the new ads was 20 percent higher than the control ad, but conversions to full sets improved a full 350 percent!

**Ways to hypo response**     Once you have decided on your most appealing offer, either arbitrarily or by testing, you should ask a very specific question: How can I hypo my offer to make it even more appealing? There are several ways.

Terms of payment     Where a direct sale is involved, the terms of payment you require can hypo or depress response. A given product or service can have tremendous appeal, but if payment terms are too stringent—beyond the means of a potential buyer—the offer will surely be a failure. Five general categories of payment terms may be offered: (1) cash with order, (2) C.O.D., (3) open account, (4) installment terms, and (5) revolving credit.

If a five-way split test were made among these categories, it is almost certain that response would be in inverse ratio to the listing of the five categories. Revolving credit would be the most attractive and cash with order the least-attractive terms. With each loosening of terms, the appeal of the offer is hypoed. In a four-way split test on a merchandise offer, here's how four terms actually ranked (The least-appealing terms have a 100 percent ranking.): cash with order, 100 percent; cash with order—free gift for trying, 144 percent; bill me offer (open account), 177 percent; and, bill me offer (open account) and free gift, 233 percent.

As the figures disclose, the most attractive terms (bill-me offer and free gift) were almost two-and-one-half times more appealing than the least attractive terms (cash with order).

While C.O.D. terms are generally more attractive than cash-with-order requirements, the hazard of C.O.D. terms is refusal on delivery. It is not unusual to sustain an 8 percent refusal rate when C.O.D. terms are offered. (Many C.O.D. orders are placed emotionally, and emotion cools off when the delivery man or letter carrier calls and requests payment.)

When merchandise or services are offered on open account, payment is customarily requested in 15 or 30 days. Such terms are naturally more appealing than cash with order or C.O.D. Open account terms are customary when selling to business firms. When used in selling to the consumer, however, such terms, while appealing, can result in a high percentage of bad debts, unless carefully selected credit-checked lists are used.

The best appeals lie in installment terms and revolving credit terms. Both mechanisms require substantial financing facilities and a sophisticated credit collection system. Installment selling in the consumer field is virtually essential for the successful sale of "big ticket" merchandise—items selling for $69.95 and up.

One can have the best of two worlds—most-appealing terms and no credit risk. This can be accomplished by making credit arrangements through a sales finance firm or commercial credit card operations, such as American Express, Diners Club, Carte Blanche, or one of the bank cards—BankAmericard (Visa), or Master Charge.

Bank cards and travel-and-entertainment cards have proved a boon to mail order operations, especially catalog operations. It is not unusual to hypo the average order from a catalog by 20 percent when bank card privileges or travel-and-entertainment card privileges are offered. Not only do these privileges tend to increase the amount of the average order, they also tend to increase the total response.

When arrangements are made through commercial credit card operations, any member may charge purchases to his card. The credit of all members in good standing is ensured by the respective credit card operations. The advertiser is paid by the agency for the total sales charged less a discount charge, usually about 3 percent for bank cards and 7 percent for travel-and-entertainment cards.

**Sweepstakes**

Perhaps the most dramatic hypo available to direct marketers is sweepstakes. A sweeps overlayed on an offer adds excitement and interest. Three major direct marketers who have used sweepstakes all through the '60s and '70s are *Reader's Digest*, Publishers Clearing House, and Sunset House. The techniques they use are the ultimate in sophistication.

**TV support**

Both *Reader's Digest* and Publishers Clearing House are using TV support as an integral part of their sweepstakes promotions. Success depends upon (1) heavy market penetration of the printed materials, (2) time-controlled delivery of the printed offer to coincide with TV support, and (3) sufficient TV impact to excite interest in the printed promotion. Careful testing is required to determine the most cost-efficient amount of TV laid over the print offer.

**What should the commercial say?**

"Keep it simple," cautions Publishers Clearing House. Current PCH commercials prove they practice what they preach: They feature the sweepstakes, using past winners to carry the message, leaving the magazine savings story to the mailing package.

**Early entries**

Astute direct marketers like RD, PCH, and Sunset House know incentives for prompt response tend to increase total response. Each has built incentives for prompt response into its sweepstakes contests.

**Reader's Digest**

This publication, for example, provides the following bonus award information: "$1,000 a day for every day your entry beats the deadline of January 31." This means that, if the grand prize is $50,000 and your entry is postmarked before January 21, you, as the grand prize winner, will win an extra $10,000.

**Involvement devices**

The direct marketing sweepstakes sophisticates invite involvement on the reader's part. "Seven Chances to Be a Winner," states PCH in announcing its current $400,000 sweepstakes. Then it provides the entrant not one prize number, but seven.

**Sunset House**

This company, a master at developing involvement devices, provides five lucky stamps, each to be matched against a list of eleven lucky numbers on the entry form. In a "Red Nose Reindeer" contest, the entrant opens a secret panel to learn the name of his reindeer, then rubs the nose of his reindeer to learn what he might win. Fun. Anticipation. Involvement. It works!

**Umbrella sweepstakes**

A big sweepstakes requires a bushel of money for prizes and administration. Direct marketers, bottom-line people that they are, have found ways to overlay a major sweeps on more than one proposition. *Reader's Digest*, for example, can overlay the same sweeps on a magazine subscription offer, a book club offer, and a record offer—each falling under the umbrella of one prize budget.

These are some of the things the big boys in direct marketing are doing to make sweepstakes highly effective under today's conditions.

Thomas J. Conlon, president of D. L. Blair, the largest sweepstakes judging agency in the country, points out that there are many questions to be answered for anyone contemplating a sweepstakes. Here are the questions we put to Mr. Conlon and his replies during the course of an interview for *Advertising Age.*

Q. Currently, what are the most popular prize structures?

A. Cash, automobiles, and trips—in that order—continue to be the most appealing and popular prize structures. According to our most recent research, almost no appeal attaches to apparel (fur coats, designer dresses). As for other merchandise, we generally prefer to echew the use of merchandise prizes except when we have conclusive research indicating greater consumer preference for the prize item than for its equivalent cash value.

Q. When a sweeps is tested against a non-sweeps, what range of increase might be expected for a magazine subscription offer or catalog offer?

A. Using a sweepstakes overlay, we have never seen less than a 15 percent increase in orders for either a catalog or a magazine subscription. The greatest increase we have ever seen is 350 percent. Generally, the increment falls between 30 and 100 percent.

Q. Can a low-budget sweeps be successful?

A. To avoid violating any client confidences, I cannot answer this question. I might comment, however, that we tend to see a clear correlation (at the lower levels) between the value of the prize structure and the level of consumer response.

Q. From a legal standpoint, must all prizes be awarded in a sweepstakes contest?

A. Regardless of the legal questions, we believe that an overwhelming moral imperative exists for awarding all prizes. More to the point, D. L. Blair would refuse to handle any sweepstakes in which all prizes were not awarded.

Q. Is the average order from a catalog, for example, likely to be smaller with a sweeps entry?

A. It depends on whether the order is from a former buyer or a new customer. The average order from former buyers tends to be larger. I've seen a sweepstakes increase the value of each catalog order by more than 40 percent. New customer orders, on the other hand, tend to be lower than average, probably because these are fringe buyers coming in as a result of the sweepstakes overlay.

Q. Having acquired a new customer with a sweepstakes contest, would you say that repeat business is likely to depend on additional sweepstakes contests?

**Exhibit 2.5. Sweepstakes offer.** *Playboy* Dreamstakes offers a $50,000 grand prize on the front cover of a four-page folder and on personalized entry certificate.

**Exhibit 2.6. Devices to hypo response.** Included in the *Playboy* Dreamstakes mailing package are two devices designed to hypo response: an "Early Bird" bonus notice and a "publisher's letter."

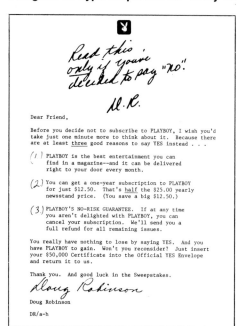

A. Yes, to some degree it is true that continuing sweepstakes promotions might be necessary to maintain a normal level of repeat business. I would say this is true to the same extent that a customer first acquired with incentives such as price-off coupons, free gifts, discount offers, and the like would be conditioned to such offers in the future.

Q. What is the profile of sweepstakes entrants these days?

A. It's becoming broader with more geographic, economic, and educational homogeneity. This "flattening" process extends to the sex of respondents: men account for almost 47 percent of sweepstakes entrants.

**Telephone**   Sweepstakes add dramatic impact to any given offer and historically tend to hypo response. The telephone serves quite another purpose. The telephone makes is *easier* to respond. This is another way to overcome inertia. Consider the hypo effect of telephone ordering privileges as related to the following mini-case histories.

1. A major upscale catalog operation found, to its surprise, that when toll-free ordering privileges nationally with use of an 800 number were offered, 50 percent of the total orders were placed by phone. The real payoff was that the average telephone order was 20 percent larger than the average mail order.

2. An office equipment manufacturer seeking leads for his national sales force added an 800 number to the response card, giving the prospect the privilege of either phoning and requesting that a salesman call or simply mailing in the card. The addition of phone privileges increased response by 10 percent.

3. A publisher selling a home study program for $250 answered all inquiries by mail. Prospects who did not respond were followed up by telephone, and 25 percent of those who had not responded by mail were closed by phone.

4. A fund-raising organization added toll-free ordering privileges to its catalog and found that the average telephone order was 21 percent larger than the average mail order. Today more than one-half of all of that group's orders are placed by telephone.

Many direct marketers have been hesitant to offer the privilege of calling via 800 numbers, fearing that the cost would not warrant it. One way to test the appeal of telephone ordering privileges is to offer the opportunity to reverse the charges. But, in testing the appeal of telephone with collect-call privileges, the direct marketer should realize that, in carefully controlled tests, it has been found that toll-free privileges via an 800 number have about twice the appeal of collect phone-call privileges. In an attempt to explain this difference, theorists have claimed that there is a natural hesitancy about phoning collect, whereas the 800 number implies that it is not costly to the marketer.

**Publisher's letter**    An innovative device that has been developed for hypoing responses during the past decade is an extra mailing enclosure known as the "publisher's letter." It gets its name from its first usage—a short letter from a magazine publisher enclosed in the basic mailing package.

The publisher's letter usually carries a headline: "If you have decided not to respond, read this letter." The letter copy typically reinforces the offer made in the basic mailing package, assures the reader it is valid, and guarantees the terms. This extra enclosure often increases response by 10 percent and more. While the publisher's letter was originated for subscription letters, this device was soon adopted by other direct marketers selling goods and services. Results have been equally productive.

**The guarantee**    No matter what the terms or basic offer may be, a strong guarantee is essential when selling products or services direct. For more than 90 years, Sears, Roebuck and Company has guaranteed satisfaction for every article offered. Over the years, no one else has ever succeeded in mail order operations without duplicating the Sears guarantee or offering a similar assurance.

> **SEARS GUARANTEE**
>
> *Your safisfaction is guaranteed or your money back.*
>
> We guarantee that every article in this catalog is accurately described and illustrated.
>
> If, for any reason whatever, you are not satisfied with any article purchased from us, we want you to return it to us at our expense.
>
> We will exchange it for exactly what you want, or will return your money, including any transportation charges you have paid.
>
> SEARS, ROEBUCK AND CO.

The importance of the guarantee is perhaps best understood by recognizing a negative fact of life. It is this. Ninety years after Sears first established its ironclad guarantee, it is still a fact of human nature that one is hesitant to send for merchandise unless he knows that, should the product not come up to expectation, it may be returned for full credit. Guaranteed satisfaction should be a part of any offer soliciting a direct sale.

Many marketers have developed unique guarantees that go beyond the trial period. Madison House, for instance, advertised a new fishing lure in a March issue of *Family Weekly*. The company knew, of course, that in northern areas, lakes were frozen over and that there would be no opportunity to test and use this lure before spring. Madison House overcame the problem beautifully by urging the fishing buff to send for the lure *now*, with the proviso that the lure could be returned any time within six months for a full cash refund. This guarantee had two advantages: It assured the fishing buff that, even though he was ordering the lure out of season, he could return it after he tried it in season; and it enabled Madison House to advertise and get business out of season.

One of the most successful manuals ever produced at National Research Bureau was the 428-page *Retail Advertising and Sales Promotion Manual*. It was offered on a ten-day free trial basis with the guarantee: "If this manual isn't all we say it is, you may return it any time within twelve months for full refund." National Research Bureau sold over 20,000 manuals at $19.95. It is significant that, after several years, no one has ever asked for a refund!

Many marketers reinforce their own guarantees with a "third party" guarantee. "Approved by Underwriters Laboratory" can make the difference where electrical appliances are concerned. The *Good Housekeeping Seal of Approval* has long been accepted as a guarantee of validity of claim.

Publishers Clearing House makes this statement: "In addition to the publisher's own warranties, Publishers Clearing House makes you this unconditional guarantee: You may have a full cash refund at any time, or for any reason, on the unused part of any subscription ordered through the clearing house. This guarantee has no time limit. It is your assurance that you can order from Publishers Clearing House with complete confidence."

In direct sales, the right proposition and the right terms of payment are only two-thirds of the impetus. A clear, strong guarantee completes the equation.

**Danger of overkill**    The power of an offer cannot be over-estimated. But there's such a thing as too much of a good thing—offers that sound too good to be true or that produce a great front-end response but make for poor pay-ups or poor repeat customers. Here are two thought-provoking examples.

A comprehensive test was structured for a fund-raising organization to determine whether response would best be maximized by (a) offering a free gift as an incentive for an offer; (b) offering a combination of free gift plus a cash bonus for completing a sale, or (c) offering a cash bonus only. The combination of free-gift-plus-cash-bonus pulled the lowest response by far; the free-gift proposition far outpulled the cash-bonus proposition.

The second example: A $200 piece of electronic equipment was offered for 15 days' free trial. This was the basic proposition. But half the people on the list also were invited to enter a sweepstakes contest. The portion of the list who were not invited to enter a sweepstakes responded 25 percent better than the portion who were invited to enter.

In both these examples, the more generous offer proved to be "too much." One must be most careful not to make the offer so overwhelming that it overshadows the product or services being offered. Another important consideration in structuring offers is the axiom, "As you make your bed, so shall you lie in it." Here's what we mean. If you obtain thousands of new customers by offering free gifts as incentives, don't expect a maximum degree of repeat business unless you continue to offer free gifts. Similarly, if you build a big list of installment credit buyers, don't expect these buyers to respond well to cash-basis offers, and vice versa.

Given offers attract given types of customers. Make sure these are the types you really want. Here is an illustration of our axiom. A firm selling to businesses built a large customer list based on a series of soft-sell offers. The firm then went into another product line, offering products to their customers and to cold prospect lists. Three offers were tested: (1) a free gift for ordering, (2) a discount for ordering, and (3) no incentive. The results of the three offers against cold lists and against the customer list are provided in Table. 2.2.

**Table. 2.2. Results of testing three types of offers with both cold and customer lists.**

| | Results (In Percent) | |
| --- | --- | --- |
| | Cold Lists | Customer List |
| Free gift . . . . . . . . . . . . . | 2.2 | 3.2 |
| Discount . . . . . . . . . . . | 5.2 | 3.1 |
| No incentive . . . . . . . . . | 2.5 | 3.9 |

Note the dramatic differences in response between cold lists and the customer list. The discount offer was more than twice as attractive to cold lists. But, to the customer list, not nurtured in this manner, the discount offer was the least attractive. Note also that the offer with no extra incentive was the most attractive to the customer list.

**Effect on bad debts**

It is rarely mentioned that a misleading offer can have a devasting effect on bad debts. A misleading offer causes the consumer, without consciously thinking about it, to feel that he has been rooked and often leads him to conclude, "They can whistle for their money." The justice, if it may be called that, is that those who would mislead usually end up paying dearly for their misdeeds.

The fact that it is poor business to make misleading offers is underscored by the following true story. For many years two large publishers exchanged mailing lists—each making noncompeting offers to the list of the other. The two publishers exchanged bad-debt lists. Time after time, the publisher known for its misleading offers would send the other publisher a list of customers with whom it had bad-debt experience. When the names were compared, it was found that, in over 80 percent of the cases where both publishers had the same customers, the publisher who practiced forthrightness had no bad-debt experience with the identical customers. Honesty does pay.

**Make it easy to order**

The structure of an offer should not be taken lightly. The impact an offer can have on immediate and long-term results can be tremendous. Sad, but true, some of the most brilliant of offers fail, not because the offers aren't appealing, but because they are poorly presented, verbally or graphically or both. The greatest sins of execution are to be found in coupon space ads.

Tony Antin, director of creative services of *Reader's Digest*, lays down this mandate for coupon order forms. "A coupon (order form) should be—*must be*—an artistic cliche. Rectangular. Surrounded by dash lines. Not even dotted lines. Because one connects dots. One cuts along dashes. Moreover, the coupon should be where it belongs, at the lower outside. The coupon should stand out from the rest of the ad."

So, construction of offers boils down to this: Your primary job is to overcome human inertia. Your offers should relate to objectives. Consider the short- and long-term effects. And, by all means, make it easy to order!

## Self-quiz

1. The primary objective of any offer is to over-come_____

2. One particular offer has long been the bell-wether of mail order. What is that offer called?

    _____

3. What is a "bounce-back" order?

    _____

    _____

4. What is the basic rule to follow in testing a variety of free gifts to determine which is most appealing?

    _____

    _____

    _____

    _____

5. The effect of offers should be tracked from front-end response to_____

6. Give the five general categories of payment terms:

    a. _____

    b. _____

    c. _____

    d. _____

    e. _____

7. What is an "umbrella" sweepstakes?

    _____

    _____

    _____

8. Name the three most popular sweepstakes prize structures in order of popularity.

    a. _____

    b. _____

    c. _____

9. Generally, what range of increased response can be expected when a sweeps promotion is tested against a nonsweeps promotion? Between 30 percent and ____percent

10. Does a sweeps promotion tend to decrease the average catalog offer?

    To prospects?          ☐ yes          ☐ no

    To customers?          ☐ yes          ☐ no

11. What is the advantage of offering toll-free ordering privileges with an "800" number as opposed to offering collect-call ordering privi-eges?

    _____

    _____

    _____

    _____

12. What is the purpose of a publisher's letter?

    _____

    _____

    _____

    _____

13. What is a "third-party" guarantee?

    _____

    _____

    _____

    _____

14. Check the requirement for an effective coupon (order form):

    Coupons should be ☐ rectangular          ☐ oval

    Coupons should be surrounded by
    ☐ dotted lines          ☐ dash lines

## Pilot project

Assume that David Ogilvy—one of the world's most famous copywriters—has just completed a home study course entitled "How to Be a Professional Copywriter." The course is to consist of 14 lessons and is to sell for $300.

Develop three specific offers designed to produce maximum response. In developing your plan for each offer, cover the following:

1. Specifications for terms of payment and methods of payment
2. Free gifts, if any
3. Telephone ordering privileges, if any
4. Guarantees.

# 3

## Selecting and Selling Merchandise

When someone asks Aaron Adler, president of Stone & Adler, how to determine what new product or service to offer, he asks, "What business are you in?" Nine times out of ten, the person will say, "Oh, I'm in the catalog business," or, "I sell collectibles," or, "I sell books," or something similar.

**What business are you really in?** That type of answer is true, of course, so far as it goes. But it probably doesn't go far enough if you really want to explore all the possibilities of your operation. The executive of a company who thinks of himself as being in the "catalog business" or in the "record business" limits his options severely. His thinking is confined so narrowly that it becomes difficult to come up with new offers for customers. On the other hand, if he gives serious thought to the total character of his business, new avenues of possibility are opened, perhaps leading to the development and promotion of a wider range of products and services.

To illustrate: Is a mail order insurance company merely in the business of selling insurance? Not at all. It is really in the business of helping to provide financial security to its policyholders and prospects. From that perspective, management of an insurance company can think of offering not only other kinds of insurance policies but also financial planning services, loans, and the sale of mutual funds, assuming, of course, there is no conflict with insurance or investment laws and regulations.

More and more successful mail order companies have adopted this kind of thinking. A classic example is the Franklin Mint, whose management recognized that the company was not simply in the business of selling limited edition medallions. Franklin Mint was actually in the business of producing fine art objects on a limited edition basis for those who enjoy the pleasure and status provided by owning handsome objects not available to the majority of the general public. In addition, the possibility existed that the value of these objects would increase as time went on. As a result, the company has successfully offered limited-edition art prints, books, glassware, and a myriad of other items.

Another example is Baldwin Cooke Company. This firm for many years had offered an executive planner (desk diary) that businesspeople found made an excellent Christmas gift for their clients and friends. Then came the realization that the company was not simply in the business of selling desk diaries, but rather was in the business of selling executive gifts. This led to the development of a broad line of successful new products. The company's gift catalog today runs 32 pages with a circulation of one million.

An outstanding example of this broad-based thinking is the Meredith Publishing Company, publishers of *Better Homes and Gardens,* among other publications. Recognizing that the company was not simply in the magazine publishing business but rather in the business of disseminating useful, helpful information to large segments of middle America, management moved into such product areas as geographic atlases, world globes, gardening books, cookbooks, and a whole range of similar materials.

So, if you are exploring new products or services you can offer your customers or those you can use to reach new prospects, think about what kind of business you are really in. When you make that determination you'll find that many new areas will open for you.

If you are not already using direct marketing to promote your products or services and would like to explore this technique for your company, the key question is totally different from the one we have been discussing. Such a plan requires an understanding of the arithmetic of direct marketing, an analysis of which direct marketing media are available, knowledge of the demographic and psychographic profiles of you prospective customers, and many other factors.

For the moment, let's pursue the idea that you are in direct marketing, that you have a list of customers built by offering products or services that they have found eminently satisfactory, and that you would like to expand your sales to those customers with new offerings. Let's also assume that you have answered the question of what business you are really in and have concluded that there are broader areas of endeavor available than you had previously realized. What then?

**What are your capabilities?**
First, review your capabilities and those of your organzation and, again, try to think in the broadest possible terms. To illustrate this general instruction, let's consider the experience of a major publisher in the development and marketing of a new product.

George Collins, the dynamic vice-president of Encyclopaedia Britannica, came to Stone & Adler with the challenge to assist Britannica in developing new products and services that this eminent, highly respected organization could market to its customers as well as to outside audiences. We approached the question not from the perspective of an "encyclopedia company," but from that of a company with broad, expert capabilities in the procurement and dissemination of knowledge and information. How EB reached its objective is a fascinating new-product development and marketing story. The story is told in the words of George Collins:

Recently, management of Britannica Home Library Service began work on a mail order new-product testing program. We were interested in developing new profit centers that related to mass marketing on a national scale. We wanted new, innovative products supported by highly creative marketing strategies and advertising. We wanted means of researching and test marketing that would provide rapid roll-out for successful product ideas. We wanted to test all selling media thoroughly, including direct mail, space, television, package inserts, and co-op mailings. We also hoped to find products that had potential for syndication and cooperative ventures with other companies.

Our first step was to establish a close working relationship with a direct marketing agency to assist us in the formulation and development of the products and programs. I'd like to give you a close-up and personal look at how we created, refined, and marketed a highly successful product that came out of a mere idea.

The product I'm referring to is EB's new Fix-It-Fast Reference File on Home Repairs. Its success has been so instantaneous that I think it makes an exciting educational story. Fix-It-Fast emerged a runaway success as a result of a tedious, structured new-product development.

Working with the agency, we set up a structured, new-product development/review organization for the systematic processing of ideas, suggested strategies, budgets, and research. An EB top management screening committee, chaired by myself, was balanced with a suitable creative and marketing team at the agency. We established a point rating system to evaluate the new product possibilities.

## Ten steps provide checks, balances

Additionally, we used a 10-step product development system that provided the checks and balances necessary throughout the development process. We felt that a precisely managed system was necessary to ensure that each new idea was subjected to the same checklist evaluation as all other ideas.

Step one involved a detailed review of our present EB product line, to determine what existing products might fit—or might suggest—new direct marketing opportunities.

Next we took an objective assessment of our present corporate image, consumer awareness, and our general reputation in the consumer marketplace. (And I might add the EB name is a great asset to have going for you.) From there we moved to a careful evaluation of in-house editorial strengths.

At the agency, six new-product brainstorming sessions were held, supplemented by Synetic sessions and lateral thinking techniques they've developed. Additionally, a number of new-product ideas were suggested by members of my own staff.

Result: we developed 58 new-product concepts that appeared to hold promise. Each was supported by a brief product concept description. Let me read just one of the 58 product concepts, so you can see how it was initiated.

## Fix-It-Fast reference file

Various do-it-yourself book sets have done well for the EB house list, which is natural considering that EB customers are primarily homeowners. We borrowed an idea from other publishers who have been successful with recipe card files. Do-it-yourself repairs and craft projects could be put together in a card file for quick and easy reference. Like the recipe cards, they could be printed on heavy stock that could be wiped off.

Step two was a careful review of each of the 58 new-product ideas by the management screening committee. Ideas were then ranked on a point system. Those of us with more experience in the direct marketing field held an overriding veto position if we felt it would be necessary. Result: we identified 16 new-product ideas that were judged suitable for immediate further exploration.

At this point, Fix-It-Fast was just one of a group of 16 with nothing to suggest an out-of-the-ordinary potential, except that some of us really liked it (which sometimes amounts to the kiss of death).

## Marketing profiles developed

Step three involved the further development of marketing profiles for each of the 16 products: How would the product be positioned? What were the primary and secondary market audiences? How accessible or reachable was the primary market through available lists and media? How big was it? What was competition in the marketplace at present? What was the estimated size of competitive sales?

What offers could be adopted to each of our new products? What price points should be tested? Which method of fulfillment should be considered? What were back-end projections based on experience with similar products and offers? What major problems would we face and what alternatives were available to deal with these potential problems?

Finally, what investments would be required to test and roll out a successful product. These were just a few of the many questions to be answered. A massive amount of thinking and planning time was required by our agency and my own staff.

Next, we submitted written analyses to our review committee. Each concept was again voted upon using our numerical rating system. Here, four products were dropped. Twelve were judged suitable for continued evaluation.

## Focus groups provide solid lead

Our next step involved a look at subjective consumer reaction to each of the products still in the running. For this we utilized focus group research. Each of our 12 products was submitted to two separate focus research panels. Many interested aspects surfaced from the analysis of these sessions.

For instance, although women's lib was a hot subject at the time, two test panels comprised solely of women showed virtually no interest and indeed were critical of a proposal for a women's book club.

It was at this phase in our procedure that we got our first solid hints that Fix-It-Fast was a product that might have the potential of a winner. Fix-It-Fast made a strong showing with the focus groups. We suspect Fix-It-Fast scored well with focus groups because do-it-yourself home repairs and improvements are hot subjects with consumers today. With escalating labor costs, the home handyman market is rapidly expanding.

The Fix-It-Fast Card Reference File was conceived as a new method of providing do-it-yourself information for home repairs and maintenance. It would consist of plasticized cards with step-by-step instructions and diagrams for a wide variety of home repairs. The cards would be enclosed in a convenient file storage box, and individual cards could be easily removed for on-site utilization.

The initial shipment would consist of the file box, divider cards, and the first project deck of 24 cards. The subsequent 19 project decks, to be shipped on a continuity basis, would be purchased at $1.98 each.

Here's a capsule summary of the key thoughts of our research audience:

- All groups liked the concept of an indexed box and washable cards—it was perceived as very practical.
- The name "Fix-It-Fast" left some question of whether the cards showed a simple way of doing complex repairs or rather how to make simple repairs yourself without paying an expert, but we decided it was still a strong name.
- Most group members who had attempted home repairs had found how-to manuals difficult to understand and were discouraged from trying do-it-yourself repairs again.
- Home repairs are most often attempted in order to save money.

Now we have moved ahead into step six. Using our point ranking system, we again voted on the marketing potential of the 12 products still with us. This time 5 of 12 were either "tabled" or returned to the agency for further development. Seven products were okayed for the next step.

## Enter cost evaluations

Now it was time to put each of these seven ideas into a realistic cost-evaluation mode. Detailed marketing budgets were developed by the agency for our review. Copy and art cost, media plan, and test cost. Most importantly, a five-year profit-and-loss potential was projected for each product.

As a result of this analysis, two products are presently being developed as joint ventures with other companies, since this was the most economically feasible approach. Two products were eliminated because they didn't meet our profit objective. Three products, Let's Travel, Discovery Library, and Fix-It-Fast, were okayed for full-scale market testing. Copy and layout were started for the advertising, simultaneously with product development.

In the case of Fix-It-Fast, we assigned editorial development to Len Hilts, one of the nation's outstanding authors of "do-it-yourself" books. Design and engineering for the file box was handled by Western Printing Company. Design of dividers and project cards was prepared by the agency.

Step 10 was that final, revealing trip to the marketplace to watch consumers vote with their dollars for the products that had passed through our development program. You already know Fix-It-Fast was successful. But, just how successful was it compared with the other two entries?

For Let's Travel, the future looks dim. Ads appeared in November. Response to both space ads and direct mail was clearly unsatisfactory. (That's a polite way of saying this one was a bomb.) In retrospect, we feel parents may be restricting book purchases for their children to products with stronger educational overtones. Here's an example of an important point that just did not surface in our focus research phase.

Discovery Library, happily, was another story. Initial repsonse was encouraging, but definitely not a landslide. The program is currently in the process of fulfillment. The final chapter can only be written after careful evaluation and tracking of payments, returns, subscriber longevity, and so forth.

With Fix-It-Fast, the painstaking planning and development paid off in spades. Sales have been very successful. The success of other card files is well known, and EB now had a winner in the same format.

**Exhibit 3.1. Shown is an ad for the Fix-It-Fast card reference file created at Encyclopaedia Britannica.**

## Importance of product specs

But there's much more to marketing a new product concept than the physical format to be used. The product editorial content has to be carefully selected to fill a contemporary need in society. The functional character of our EB kit offers the unique difference so essential to a successful direct marketing product.

The 20 full-color dividers attractively illustrate the "end result" that can be achieved. The color tabs on these dividers are cleverly arranged to give a chromatic "rainbow" color effect in the box, just to add eye appeal.

The heart of the product is carefully designed and contains professionally written instructions on precisely how to repair almost 500 different household problems. Washable, sturdy cards. Handy card size to carry to your problem. Easy to file and refile. A handy portable carrying case that looks neat and trim—and is so waterproof it will float.

Fix-It-Fast is a true success story, a story that grew out of long hours of planning, researching, and testing by both EB and the agency.

In sum, when you look at what we went through with our 10-step product development system, you might say it was a pretty elaborate exercise. But remember, only three products have been tested so far . . . and we've already got one big winner, plus another that might still make it. Whether you're talking about general advertising or direct marketing, coming up with one winning product out of three is a pretty darn good batting average.

Very few marketers explore their capabilities as thoroughly as did Encyclopaedia Britannica. But thinking in the broadest possible terms is the first logical step.

In a field entirely different from that of Encyclopaedia Britannica, the G.R.I. Corporation, which originally launched the World of Beauty Club, decided to utilize the ability it had developed in working with cosmetic manufacturers to set up a similar arrangement of sampling with a group of food manufacturers. In this case the market consisted of large numbers of people who want to sample new foods and save money on a regular basis.

Other companies which have looked at their own expertise and facilities to determine what new products and services they could develop range all the way from the Donnelley Company, which utilized their co-op mailings to include the sale of their own products to Time-Life, which used its editorial and photographic expertise to produce probably the most successful series of continuity books in the publishing industry.

So along with determining the business you're in, probably the second most important factor to investigate is your company's capabilities. As you can see, determining what business you are in and examining your capabilities go hand in hand in helping you pinpoint new merchandise or services. But there are significant differences between these areas and they must be considered individually. By doing so, you will be able to broaden your horizons even more.

**What is your image with your prospect?** A third area to consider in this entire process is one which, paradoxically, instead of expanding your horizons is more likely to limit them or at least put some boundaries on them. Unlike the first two considerations—determining the business you are really in and examining your capabilities—this third area requires you to carefully analyze the "image" customers have of your company.

Every customer has an image of the company he or she deals with. This image may differ from customer to customer (and probably does in degree if not in kind) based on the relationship each customer has had with that company. If one customer has had nothing but satisfactory dealings with a company, that cutomer's image would differ from that of one who may have had an unsatisfactory experience, regardless of the cause. But the company's basic image will vary only slightly from customer to customer and will be essentially the same for all customers.

For example, General Motors has a particular image with most Americans. That image exists even for those who have never owned a GM car. The buyer of a GM car who was not happy with his or her purchase may have a somewhat different image of that company based on how his or her complaints were treated. But, in general, the American public believes that General Motors is a responsible, reputable company selling various forms of transportation among which are cars they enjoy using and driving.

Another example in an entirely different field is International Business Machines. Here is a company with which, I dare say, the majority of Americans have never had direct contact. But the image of IBM with most people is probably that of a major American, multinational corporation with unsurpassed technical and scientific skill in the development of the most advanced computers. As in the case of Henry Ford of an earlier day, IBM is probably regarded by most Americans as the developer and the most advanced proponent of a particular technology. In the case of IBM, this technology is concerned with sophisticated computers and with office equipment such as typewriters.

This perceived image is a vitally important factor when you are considering what new products or services to offer your customers or your prospects, if your company is sufficiently well known. It has been proved over and over in direct marketing as well as in other distribution channels that a company has great difficulty selling merchandise or services that do not fit the public's preconceived image of that company. This can be illustrated in the case of one company that built its customer list on the sale of power tools and then failed dismally in an offer of books of general interest to the same audience.

Let's take the case of the Minnesota-based Fingerhut Company. This firm has built a fine reputation by offering good values in medium- to low-priced merchandise ranging from power tools to tableware. While the company was able successfully to sell medium- to low-priced men's and women's wear to the same audience, it is highly doubtful that they could just as successfully sell fine bound books or Yves St. Laurent clothing. This is true not only because the demographics of the Fingerhut list probably are not suited to the higher-priced category, but also because the Fingerhut image does not conform to that high-priced merchandise.

On the other hand, let's take a look at Joe Sugarman of the highly successful JS&A Company of Northbrook, Illinois, a company that specializes in high-technology electronic equipment. Sugarman probably could not successfully sell (and I might suggest would not offer) his customers a $29.95 set of cookware, no matter how good a value it might be. His customers would find it hard to understand and accept the idea that JS&A was a qualified source for cookware.

Unless your customers or prospects are willing to believe that you are a qualified source for the products you are offering, they are unlikely to buy. But if those prospects *expect* certain products from you, because they fit your company image, your chances of success are vastly enhanced.

Thus, it is extremely important that you fully recognize the image you present to your customers, and that you select offerings that are appropriate to that image. This recognition, as mentioned earlier, narrows your choices. But it narrows them to your ultimate advantage if it keeps you from going so far afield that what you offer will stand little chance of success.

At this point we might discuss the kinds of factors that tend to create a company's image. The combination of such factors consists of approximately equal parts of the following:

- The products or services offered in the past
- The style and quality of the new product itself
- The price level
- The presentation of the product, whether it is an ad, a commercial, or a mailing piece. The "sound" of the copy and the appearance of the graphics send a definite message to the prospect.
- The "look" of the merchandise package received by the customer.
- The "sound" and appearance of any other communication with your customer, e.g., the invoice, the way complaints are handled, and the way telephone communications are conducted
- The "tone" of any publicity your company receives

An excellent example of the difference a company's image can make can be given in a comparison of two companies featuring outdoor products: L. L. Bean of Maine and Norm Thompson of Seattle, Washington. Just as they are at opposite ends of the country, both companies successfully present different, yet equally acceptable, images. L. L. Bean's image is that of an old-

**Exhibit 3.2. Typical JS & A ad. Through hundreds of magazine ads, JS & A has created a strong image as a reliable supplier of electronic equipment.**

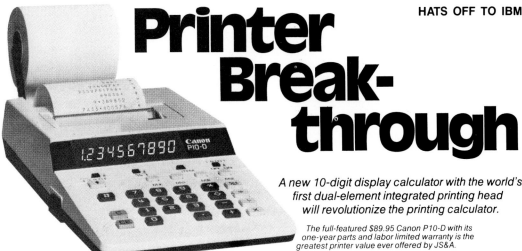
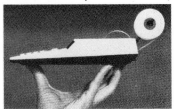

63

line, conservative company with the Yankee habit of underplaying its product, a company featuring timeless styles that appeal primarily to a mature male audience. Norm Thompson, on the other hand, shows an image of a company that appeals to men and women with a more youthful lifestyle. The company prides itself on its ability to come up with interesting, often exotic new products from abroad.

**Examine the characteristics of your customer list**

Another most important "mine" to explore for products or services is your own customer list. Study your list from a number of different perspectives, such as:

- How your list was developed
- How your customers have been "educated"
- What they are buying, if you give them choices
- The demographics and psychographics of your customers
- The "product experience" of your list

Let's start with the first point, how your list was developed. In other words, what type of merchandise have your customers been buying? At what prices? How have they paid: cash, charge, time payment? These may appear to be obvious questions, but it is surprising how often they are overlooked when new product planning is under consideration.

Your customers are constantly "telling" you what they like and are interested in every time they make a purchase. Catalog companies are following this rule every time they analyze each product in their catalog for profitability. By doing this, they automatically determine which products are most popular and, as a corollary, which new products they should add to their line and at what prices.

If you are successfully selling a vacuum cleaner through direct marketing, it is likely your customers would be logical prospects for such products as sets of dishes, tableware, glassware, and similar items. If you are selling clothing through the mail, as does the Haband Company and New Process, your customers might well be tempted by offerings of economical housewares, luggage, towel sets, and so forth.

Moreover, the price levels of your merchandise are standards by which to judge any new offering. There is one proviso: you should be constantly testing higher price levels to determine the upper pricing limits of your customer list. Just a 10 or 15 percent increase in the price level your customers will accept may open many more profitable products or services for you to offer.

This, of course, raises the question of methods of payment used by your customers. If they pay in cash or by credit card, they will probably prefer to continue to purchase on that basis. This will probably add to the difficulty of introducing a new item that requires a higher purchase price. On the other hand, if your customers are used to paying on the installment plan, they more likely will be willing to purchase higher-priced merchandise, especially if you can increase the number of installments. Customers who prefer to pay for their merchandise on a monthly basis are generally speaking more likely to be concerned with the amount of the individual payment rather than the total price of the product.

The second point is, "How have your customers been educated?" The way in which you first got your customers has an important influence on what they expect of you in future offers. An example of the power of this "educating" process is the Fingerhut Company, whose customers have been conditioned to expect a host of free gifts with every purchase. It is unlikely that Fingerhut would be successful with a new offering that did not include such free gifts.

The Grolier Corporation has built a large list of book customers by offering free the first volume of a set of books, whether or not the prospect decides to continue with the series. Again, an offering to these customers of a new series without the free volume would probably fail. At the same time, Time-Life Books has been extremely successful in a program of selling books with an offer that only permits the prospect to examine a new volume for a limited time, without getting it free.

From its beginning, JS&A has offered its products strictly for cash or on credit cards without a free trial. The company's customers are not educated to expect a "free gift" or anything other than a straight money-back offer.

Especially if you are just starting in business, give serious thought to your front-end offer. Be sure you are clear on how you want your customers "educated." The way you start out is probably the way you will have to continue. If you'd rather not adopt the pattern of free gifts, free volumes, and sweepstakes, you probably ought not to start with such an offer.

**What is the life style of your customers**
Now we get to your customers themselves. What kind of a life style do they have. If you haven't already, you should do a comprehensive analysis to develop a "profile" of your "typical customer."

More and more we are finding that the demographic profiles of customers combined with their psychographic (life style) profiles give many clues to successul new product development and sales.

With such a profile, you will find all kinds of "road signs" to new products or services. How your customers live, the kinds of vacations they take, the type of entertainment they enjoy, whether they prefer books to movies, as well as their income level, education, size of family, whether they live in a house or apartment, and other demographic characteristics—all are hints as to the new products or services they might be interested in.

Obviously, people who live in an apartment are less likely to be prospects for a set of power tools than people who live in a house. Similarly, people who prefer movies to books are not very good prospects for a best seller.

But what do you do if you don't have a list of customers? What if you are just starting out in direct marketing? How do you determine what to sell? Let's suppose you're a company that can produce anything (a farfetched supposition!). Or you have access to all kinds of merchandise and services. How do you decide which to select and promote?

One way in which knowledgeable direct marketing people decide whether an item or a service has a chance to be promoted successfully is to determine whether there are media that can reach the logical market for that offering. Let's take an example. Suppose you came up with an item you believe might appeal to mothers of preschool children. That's exactly the situation which existed for Science Research Associates, a Stone & Adler client. The company had an excellent program for helping preschool children develop interest in and appreciation for mathematics.

The first problem was how to reach these mothers economically. Of course, the key word is *economically*. Any group of people can be reached if you don't care about cost. But, to a direct marketer, the cost of getting to a prospect or customer is all important. You might expect that finding media to reach this rather restricted group would be difficult. As a matter of fact, it is not as easy as finding, say, a group of business executives. But media do exist—both periodicals and mailing lists—that enable one to reach mothers of preschool children, *Parent's Magazine* in the magazine field and the subscription list for *Cricket Magazine* in the mailing list category are excellent examples.

Only after we had established the fact that media were available did it make sense to consider developing a campaign for the SRA Math Skills program. Conversely, if we had not been able to locate such media, it would have been fruitless to go ahead. Thus, if you have no customer list and are trying to determine whether it would be feasible to sell a particular item or service through the direct response method, one of the first things to determine is whether media are available for reaching your best prospects.

Another technique used by direct marketers for developing merchandise ideas is to look at the specialized markets being served by various media. They study the new, successful publications. One of the most important trends in the magazine field in the last few years has been the proliferation of special-interest magazines. So marketers search for product offerings that might appeal to subscribers to particular publications.

Publications directed to the senior-citizen market may give you ideas for products and services that would appeal to this market, such ideas as supplementary hospital insurance or a mail order prescription service.

Looking at subscriber lists of beer can collectors might suggest that you consider selling a set of beer steins or a display cabinet for holding the beer cans. If you find that magazines are being successfully launched to tell people how to handle their finances think about products or services that would appeal to people concerned with conserving and increasing their capital. Magazines devoted to physical fitness (and their subscriber lists) might suggest products that would help people in their fitness programs.

**What new products are people buying?**

When you want to determine whether an offering will work in direct marketing, review the products that people are currently buying at retail. Examples are LED watches and paperback books.

Formerly, direct marketers tended to shy away from products available at retail. But that is no longer true. A wide variety of products ranging from Polaroid cameras to General Electric toasters have been and are being sold through the direct response method in increasing volume. Only a few years

Exhibit 3.3. Insert ad in *Parents* magazine. The demographics of the *Parents* magazine readership proved to be appropriate for the SRA Math Skills offer. (Reverse side of this insert appears on page 68.)

# Introduce your youngster to SRA's
# Skills Ladder for BASIC MATH
## Free for 15 Days.

**Reusable plastic overlay lets child check *own* answers.**

Child simply hooks overlay on card, lines up "smiling faces" before doing exercises, then turns card over to check answers. The Activities Cards can then be used again.

**From SRA, one of the most respected names in American education . . . a special invitation for parents who want to help their children excel in school and beyond . . .**

Here is an opportunity for your youngster to practice and learn important math skills . . . and have a good time in the process.

SRA's MATH SKILLS LADDER translates the basic concepts of mathematics into a *step-by-step* series of enjoyable exercises geared to the interests and abilities of children in the crucial early learning years from 5 to 7. Based on a program used in schools nationwide, the methods and vocabulary in SKILLS LADDER are consistent with instruction in schools.

**The SKILLS LADDER is a kit of 200 colorfully illustrated Activities Cards divided into 7 units. The first 2 units include counting, writing, adding and subtracting numbers up to 10. The other 5 units expand these activities for numbers up to 100. Also included are simple concepts of geometry, measuring, telling time, and counting money.**

A child's attention is maintained by cleverly drawn animals and objects and a variety of fun-to-do exercises.

SKILLS LADDER has been structured so that even youngsters just beginning to read can do the exercises and check the answers *themselves.* Only an occasional bit

of guidance and encouragement is required on your part to keep your child involved and motivated from beginning to end of the Program.

When you complete and return the postage-paid Free Examination Certificate below, SRA will send you the *Skills Ladder for Basic Math* Starter Kit to use in your own home, for a full 15 days, without cost or obligation.

**The Starter Kit includes . . .**
- **Parent's Guide** with helpful ideas for getting the most out of the program.
- **30 Activities Cards,** covering basic addition, subtraction, counting and writing numbers.
- **Storage Case,** with 7 section dividers, to organize all Cards.
- **Reusable Plastic Overlay** for recording and checking answers, plus 2 special Markers.

You can keep your Starter Kit for just $4.95. Or if you're not completely satisfied, simply return the Kit and pay nothing.

If you do decide to continue, then you will receive six more units of 25 to 35 Activities Cards each in the months ahead, as explained on the Free Examination Certificate. But there is no minimum purchase required, and you may cancel at any time after receiving your Starter Kit.

---

FIRST CLASS
Permit No. 1736
Hicksville,
New York
11801

## BUSINESS REPLY MAIL
No Postage Stamp Necessary if Mailed in the United States

POSTAGE WILL BE PAID BY

S R A

**Skills Ladder for Basic Math**
6 Commercial Street
Hicksville, New York 11801

---

ago the Quality Paperback Book Club was started, successfully, on a direct response basis, to take advantage of the tremendous popularity of paperbacks. When you consider that paperbacks are sold in virtually every drugstore, cigar shop, candy store, railroad station, and airport—as well as every bookstore—QPB's success can be seen as a tribute to the convenience and acceptance of direct marketing.

**Look at the new life styles**

American life styles seem to be changing more rapidly all the time. A few years ago the women's liberation movement initiated a continuing change in the life style of many women that influences the life style of a great many men as well. Over half of all women in America now work outside the home. Obviously, employed women have different needs from those who don't work. More convenient food preparation products, for instance. The number of unmarried women who head households also keeps growing. Their needs, too, are different. Their need for financial advice, for example, is certainly different from that of married women. For many years senior citizens have constituted a growing segment of U.S. society. Older people have many needs that differ from those of younger age groups. An example of how one group is addressing those needs is the American Association of Retired Persons. The assocation offers people over 55 a wide variety of services ranging from travel opportunities to insurance. Membership is over 6,000,000. All of these groups have particular needs that frequently can be met by the perceptive direct marketer.

**How do you evaluate products?**

Once you have selected a product or service, how do you evaluate its potential—its acceptance by and suitability for your market? This is an area that can be treacherous, especially for the amateur. Everyone has his own preconceived ideas as to what is a good product or service. The judgment is based on the person's own desires and experiences. And that is the pitfall. A mark of the professional is the ability to set aside personal prejudices and be able to analyze an offer objectively, from the point of view of his prospect.

You may think that fur-lined mufflers are just the niftiest idea going, but do your prospects? On the other hand, you may turn up your nose at Lawrence Welk's music. But there's a big market out there that thinks he's great. You may have no interest in a 74-piece socket-tool set. But through the years, hundreds of thousands of people have bought such kits by mail. This objectivity is one of the marks of a successful marketer: If you're called on to choose a product, remember that it's not what *you* like that counts. Consider the value of the product you will select from the point of view of the person to whom you're going to sell it.

To estimate the potential marketability of a product, ask yourself:

1. Does the product or service have a "reason for being?" Is there a perceived need? Or can one be created?
2. Does the product suit your prospect's tastes, life style, and the price he or she may be willing to pay?

3. Does the product have a perceived beauty, utility, or value for the individual prospect?
4. Will it appeal to the majority of your prospects?

Let's start with the first questions: Is there a perceived need for your product? Can one be created? Does the product have a reason for being?

Science Research Associates looked at the tremendous increase in the purchase of indoor plants and the highly successful Betty Crocker "recipe file technique." They combined the two into the "SRA Greenhouse" and developed a direct response program which quickly became highly successful. SRA was sufficiently alert to recognize that a perceived need existed in the marketplace for products like this.

Of course, a most dramatic example of taking advantage of a perceived need is the specialty mail order catalog which has increased greatly in variety and number. The publishers of these catalogs have recognized the need of appealing to a distinctive audience for two reasons: (1) To provide an easier way to shop than to drive miles to a shopping center, park blocks from the stores, and endure long waits for a salesperson only to discover the product you want is either out of stock or not available in the color, size, or style you wanted; and (2) to meet an increasing desire of Americans to own products that enhance their individuality because they are not advertised and available in every local store.

Question: Does the product fit your prospect's taste, life style, and attitude about price?

Prospects with similar demographic and psychographic profiles have important similarities with respect to the types of merchandise and services they purchase and the prices they are willing to pay. The more the offer you are considering matches the characteristics and desires of the group to whom you are appealing, the more likely it is to be successful. An excellent example of this is the New Process Company of Warren, Pennsylvania. The company has developed a line of attractive but not too highly styled clothes for women and extremely low prices and a similar line of men's slacks. New Process has established the fact that such clothes at the right price levels meet the desires of millions of Americans. As a consequence, the company has built a mult-million-dollar operation by appealing to a certain segment of the market.

Question: Does the product have beauty, utility, or value for your prospect?

Perhaps the best example of this ideal combination of perceived beauty and value was the Franklin Mint's offer of limited edition commemorative medallions in sterling silver or gold. Millions of Americans perceived these medallions as works of art in precious metal that were and could be even more valuable. Franklin Mint created one of the most successful direct response ventures in the past decade.

Perceived value has been a major reason for the outstanding success of Publishers Clearing House, a company that built a very successful business by offering prospects magazine subscriptions for far less than their regular price. The prospects they mail to can readily determine how much money they can save by subscribing through Publisher's Clearing House. And they have—by the millions.

An extremely successful offer by several mail order firms is a large selection of all the screws and bolts the average person will probably ever need. The items are in individual drawers and housed in a plastic case. The perceived utility benefit of this offer is apparently very high for millions of men and women who can never find the screw or bolt they need, when they need it.

So, look for one or all three of these benefits (beauty, utility, perceived value) in the product or service you are offering. The more benefits your product has and the greater degree to which it has them, the more likely you will be successful.

Question: Will the product appeal to the majority of your market segment?

When you choose an item, ask yourself, will it appeal to most of my prospects or only a chosen few? If your answer is "the chosen few" your chances of success have suddenly diminished. The reason, of course, is quite apparent. Selling by direct response, as with any other kind of selling, is difficult, at best. If, for any given market, you limit your approach to only a segment of that market, you adversely affect the results you might have achieved. So, opt for a stereo outfit that will fit in a small apartment as well as a home. Or a camera that won't seem too formidable to novices, rather than one which appeals only to the sophisticated user. Your chances of success will be brighter

Obviously, it is not always possible to select an item that will appeal to 100 percent of your market. But the closer you can come to that figure, the greater the chances of success.

Just because a product has failed in the past, don't write it off at some future date. Most products have a "life cycle." They are developed, they grow in popularlity and sales, they reach a peak, and they begin to dwindle. The product that may not have been successful five years ago may have been introduced too soon. Or, something may have been developed in the interim years that will enable you to add more appeal to it.

A recent example of a product's life cycle is the microwave oven. These devices have been around for many years, slowly building up acceptance and sales, until the fall of 1977, when they suddenly took off and proved to be one of the biggest sellers of the season.

In the direct response field, there was a time when multi-band radios and heavy-duty vacuum cleaners were hot. Today, sophisticated electronic items (calculators, burglar alarms, telephone answering devices) collectibles (books, medals, plates), and card file sets of recipes, gardening information, and home repairs are all on the upswing.

Conclusion: Keep a lookout for the products and services that seem to be on the way up. As in playing the stock market, just as you want to buy a stock that's on the way up and sell it at its peak, so in direct response. You want to promote a product that's rising in appeal and stop promoting that product when its life cycle is ended.

**Price/value relationships**  Once you have selected your product or service, you are faced with the problem of pricing it. How much can you get for it? Whatever price you select, it must appear to the prospect as the "right" price for that item. He or she must perceive your price as being a value. And that perception depends on the item and the person to whom you are appealing.

A person earning $175 per week has one set of price/value relationships. Another earning $750 per week has a different set. To the first person, a $7.00 tie may have just the right price/value relationship. To the second, the tie may seem "cheap."

A piece of merchandise in itself has a perceived price/value relationship with the consumer. One expects a set of cookware to cost less than a set of bone china dishes. A price of $49.00 for a set of cookware might sound just right. But $49.00 for bone china dinnerware set sounds suspiciously inexpensive.

As an example of how people establish a price/value relationship for a product, here's a test conducted by a direct marketer selling a set of four kitchen knives. Five offers were tested with the results indicated.

> Offer 1—four knives at $19.95 plus $1.00 shipping and handling. Pull: 1.3 percent.
>
> Offer 2—four knives at $19.95, plus hanging board at $1.50 (optional), plus $1.00 shipping and handling. Pull: 1.3 percent; 80 percent took the hanging board.
>
> Offer 3—four knives, plus hanging board, plus shipping and handling at $24.95. Pull: 0.9 percent.
>
> Offer 4—three knives at $19.95, plus $1.00 shipping and handling. Pull: 0.8 percent.
>
> Offer 5—five knives at $29.95, plus hanging board at $1.50, plus $1.00 shipping and handling. Pull: 0.7 percent.

As you can see, the prospects saw offer 2 as the best in terms of price and value, far better than offer 3, which was only $2.50 more.

We have been through this time after time, and we have found that the assumption that there is a right price for every item invariably holds true. Certain cookware sets can only be sold at $39.95. Certain clock radios can only be sold at $49.95. Certain sets of stainless tableware can only be sold at $24.95

Conversely, we have also found that the customer will, in some cases, accept a higher price than you would have chosen as the proper price/value relationship. For example, a paint gun was tested at both $49.95 and $59.95. And sales at the $59.95 price were better. So, while you may think you have a good idea what the right price for an item should be, you should test that price, but also test at a higher and lower price. You may be pleasantly surprised.

Price/value relationships change, too. Inflation has an affect on them. So does competition. And the relative popularity of the item is important. The same paint gun that sold successfully at $59.95 now sells for $89.95 in about the same quantities as it did at the lower price. Remember when Sharp came out with the first electronic calculator? It was only a four-function model, but American Express sold thousands at $300. Today you'd be lucky to get $39.95 for it.

**Other areas to consider**

Finally, let's consider several other marketing factors apart from the product or service itself. These are such factors as the offer, the advertising medium to be used, and how to use research in reaching your decisions.

So far as the offer is concerned, regard it as an opportunity to say to the prospect, "Here is a special reason for acting now rather than waiting to order at a future date." The best offers flow from the product or service being offered. A good example is the Franklin Mint five-year buy-back guarantee, an offer which corresponded perfectly with the firm's assumption that their products might increase in value. Book club and record club offers of X number of books or records for as little as 10 cents are other examples. Free gift offers, limited time or quantity offers, free trial periods, and a wide variety of others can be useful. Try to develop an offer that relates to the general character of your merchandise best. It can pay big dividends.

**Products may determine media**

When it comes to deciding which advertising medium to use, a number of basic factors must be considered. Generally speaking, if the product doesn't carry at least a $15.00 profit at a $29.95 retail price, you probably won't be successful in a solo mailing, unless the pull is really sensational.

A further consideration in your decision as to whether to use the direct mail system is the amount of copy and illustration you need. The more of both you require, the more likely your product belongs in the mail. If your item is suited to a visual demonstration, television becomes a likely medium, especially if the item's price is under $20.00.

There was a time when we thought that a high-priced, highly technical product would require too much space to be promoted successfully in magazines or newspapers. But Joe Sugarman of JS&A proved that "ain't necessarily so." Which, of course, is a reminder that there are exceptions to every rule. So, don't hesitate to experiment.

Newspaper inserts should not be overlooked as a viable medium today. Inserts lately have brought a new dimension which offers as much copy space as needed with a wide variety of interesting formats, plus a return envelope, quality reproduction, and often, market segmentation. Newspaper inserts have opened opportunities fo a wide range of offers—from insurance to limited-edition commemoratives and free credit cards.

**The use of research**

Over the past few years an activity that has been receiving more attention in determining product selection is market research. For many years, direct marketers believed that the only way to determine the appeal of a product or service was to put it in the mail or run an ad and see if it sold. Today, sophisticated direct marketers are more and more turning to research as a means of helping to determine whether an item stands a chance of success. You will recall that research was an integral part of the successful

Encyclopaedia Britannica new-product development program. Consider the various research techniques available to help in selecting your product or service so as to increase your prospects for success. Research such as Focus Group testing can give you valuable insights into the appeal (or lack thereof) of your offering. It can also help you determine which one of two or more items have the strongest appeal. Often this procedure can even help you add to the appeal of your product or service by suggesting additional benefits to be added.

For Science Research Associates, focus group interviews provided valuable insights for two different programs. In one case, focus group findings considerably improved the appeal of the program. In another, research results caused the client to completely re-think his approach to the project.

**Reliable sources**
Everything we've said so far presupposes that you have a dependable source for supplying your product, or that you will have a supplier once you determine what you are going to sell. Seasoned direct marketers always make certain they are ready to deliver when they put a promotion in the mail, or advertise in a magazine, or offer the item via broadcast. A cardinal point to remember is: the product must be on hand before you start your promotion. Once you have mailed or placed your ad, you have committed yourself fully. You can't recall the mailing or magazine. And in the direct response business, if you can't deliver in a reasonable length of time, you will lose a large percentage of your orders. You will create much expensive, time-consuming correspondence. You will engender a lot of ill-will and undoubtedly lose the bulk of your investment.

**Summary**
Everything covered in this chapter about selecting merchandise or services to sell via direct marketing may be summed up with the phrase, "Look at all your options." You have a great many!

Investigate the potentialities of your business, your company's capabilities, what your customers are telling you in their dealings with you, and what your prospects are telling you about their life styles and buying habits. Consider also the popularity (is it growing or decreasing?) of products in the marketplace and examine the available media and *their* relative popularity. Give thought, too, to pricing and perceived values and then investigate the potential help you can get in making your decisions from today's research techniques.

The options and techniques available today to help you choose an item for direct marketing are infinitely greater than they were even a few years ago. Take advantage of them and you will immeasurably increase your chances of success.

## Self-quiz

1. In attempting to expand your horizon with new products or services, what is the first question you should ask yourself?

   _____

   _____

   _____

   _____

2. What is the second question you should ask?

   _____

   _____

   _____

   _____

3. How does the image of your company influence your selection of various types of products?

   _____

   _____

   _____

   _____

   _____

   _____

4. In determining what other products you might offer your customers, you should look at your list from five different angles. They are:

   a. _____

   b. _____

   c. _____

   d. _____

   e. _____

5. In what way are media important in determining what products to promote?

   _____

   _____

   _____

   _____

6. What are the four questions you should ask in assessing the potential marketability of a product?

   a. _____

   b. _____

   c. _____

   d. _____

7. Define price/value relationships.

   _____

   _____

   _____

   _____

8. The more copy and illustration you need to adequately present your product, the more likely it is that

   ☐ space is your best medium.

   ☐ direct mail is your best medium.

9. When does television become a likely medium for presenting a product?

   _____

   _____

   _____

   _____

10. What is the cardinal point to remember before making a product offer?

   _____

   _____

   _____

   _____

   _____

## Pilot project

You are a film processor. You have a list of 250,000 customers who have ordered film processing by mail. Following are the demographic characteristics of your customer list.

- 85 percent are married
- Average age, 38
- Median family income, $17,000
- 51 percent own their own home
- 62 percent live in the suburbs
- 72 percent have one or more children
- 39 percent have more than one car
- 41 percent have graduated from college

Your management has asked that you structure a new product development program. Develop a list of fifteen products that you believe can be sold profitably to this list.

# Section II

# Choosing Media for Your Message

# 4

## Mailing Lists

Mailing lists are the heart of every direct marketing operation. This is true whether the prime medium for getting inquiries or orders is direct mail lists or print or broadcast. Ultimately every inquiry or order ends up on a mailing list.

It's been said that mailing lists may be compared to people. They come in various sizes and shapes. And grooming among them varies tremendously. Some are meticulous. Some are just plain sloppy.

**Mailing lists as market segments**

For those engaged in direct response marketing, various structures of mailing lists (or subscriber lists for newspapers and magazines and viewer/listener lists for broadcast media) evolve quite naturally as well as logically into market segments. Such structures may be categorized as *house lists, mail response lists,* and *compiled lists.* Let's look at each of these categories individually.

**House lists**

Within the direct marketer's own firm rests his most valuable asset—his list of customers. They may be active, recently active, or long-since active customers or merely inquirers. They may have made many purchases, just one, or maybe none at all as in the case of inquiries. Individual purchases may have been quite large or small in monetary terms. Customers may be differentiated by the types of products in which they express interest. Or perhaps they can be classified by the promotional strategy used to obtain them: direct mail, space advertisements, broadcast media, or personal salesmen. Furthermore, they may be considered in terms of a host of other variables: how long they have been customers, their credit vs. cash experience, and so on.

In addition to all these factors, customers have other characteristics as *individuals:* geographic, demographic, and psychographic. They are located in a certain geographic area of the country where climate influences purchase behavior. They are a certain age and subject to environmental influences. One thing they have in common, however, is their relationship with your firm. This intangible, sometimes called goodwill, is your most valuable asset, though it never appears as such on your balance sheet.

Mail response lists  Next in importance to those who have made a direct response to your own promotional efforts are those who have responded to another firm's direct response offer, preferably related to your marketing situation in terms of buyer qualification. Thousands of such so-called mail order lists are available from an endless array of firms. Such lists are most commonly rented (they are rarely sold) through mailing list brokers. In effect, they are the house lists of other direct reponse marketers. That is what makes them of value to you: the persons represented by the list have a history of responding to direct market appeals, especially if the offers are similarly qualified. Such lists can also be further qualified into market segments, just like your own lists, in terms of geography and demography. Frequently, the type and nature of their purchases may even allow them to be qualified psychographically according to life styles and values.

Compiled lists  Next in direct response expectations, but generally first in potential volume, come a great variety of lists which have been compiled for one purpose or another from one or more sources. Examples of such lists are automobile registrations and telephone directory, city directory, or crisscross directory listings. There are also major compilations by age, occupation, educational attainment, or even manufacturer warranty card returns. Marketers sometimes create variations by merging one or more such compiled lists—auto registrations by age of owner, for example—into a further qualified list. Sometimes large mail response lists are similarly merged to identify *multiple appearances* on such lists in the manner we have described earlier. The sophistication of computer routines makes such qualifications—or market segmentations, as we prefer to call them—increasingly possible.

**Eight usually reliable truths**  In the body of knowledge garnered from hundreds of thousands of list tests, certain findings have emerged. The following statements may be regarded as being reliable *most of the time:*

- A direct response list (with names of those who have shown a propensity to respond by mail) will outpull a compiled list.
- A customer list will outpull outside lists, whether the outside lists are direct response lists or compiled lists.
- People over 35 years old tend, as a group, to respond by mail at a greater rate than people under 35 years old.
- Rural areas tend to respond by mail at a higher rate than urban areas.
- "Hot line" names (those who have responded by mail within the past six months) are likely to be the most productive names available.
- Multiple buyers (those who have purchased two or more times within a season) outpull buyers who have purchased just once within a season.

- The pull from any given list will vary by seasons, January being the best pulling month except for offers tied to the Christmas season.
- The pull from any given list will vary by regions, states, sectional centers, ZIP codes, and census tracts.

So much for the body of knowledge which is reliable *most of the time*. Exceptions abound. For example, how valid is the rural-better-than-urban thesis when you apply it to a Neiman-Marcus or Horchow Collection catalog operation? Probably not very valid at all.

Why? Because Neiman-Marcus and Horchow offer upscale high-fashion merchandise. A lady in Winnetka, Illinois, attired in a cocktail dress from Neiman-Marcus, may be more likely to feel at ease in her surroundings than her counterpart in Ottumwa, Iowa, wearing the same dress.

Now let's test the statement, "A customer list will outpull an outside list." You'd expect this to be on solid ground, but I've seen scores of exceptions.

For example, let's say that a direct marketer has built a customer list of 250,000 people who have purchased pocket calculators. That's a nice customer list. The list owner decides to cash in on the list. So he makes a deal with a cheese processor to offer cheese packs to his calculator buyers at Christmas. Chances are 100 to one the mailing will be a dismal failure. He'd probably do better with outside lists of Christmas gift buyers.

Why? The value of a customer list notwithstanding, the reputation of the list owner lies with calculators, not with cheese. Customer loyalty does not usually carry over to unrelated products. Exceptions . . . exceptions.

**When to use mailing lists**

With the rising costs of mailing pieces and postage, it is increasingly important that our direct marketing efforts be directed toward the best qualified market segments that we can reach.

Imagine that you are a direct marketer attempting to sell do-it-yourself oriental flower arranging programs through the mail for $25 each. As a marketer of this product you couldn't very well consider everyone your prime prospect. Therefore certain forms of media may not be as useful to your campaign as others. Using a medium like television could result in a great amount of wasted exposure and expense. Mailing lists, however, allow us to aim our efforts at very defined market segments and thereby reach a greater proportion of preferred prospects.

For instance, we could use the LeeWards Mail Order Craft Buyers List, with appropriate selections, to reach highly qualified prospects for our do-it-yourself flower arranging program. A portion of the LeeWards list consists of 500,000 middle-class women catalog buyers who have purchased creative craft kits in the past 90 days. We could further select from this file only those women who have spent at least $15 on craft kits, thereby qualifying our prospects even further. The ability to reach these narrowly defined markets is what makes mailing lists one of the most valuable tools available to the direct marketer today.

**Every list has a profile**

A person isn't in direct marketing long before he learns that every list of respondents has common characteristics. Thus a profile soon emerges. Once this happens, selection of lists for future promotion is simplified.

Consider the profile of 7.2 million active subscribers to *Better Homes & Gardens*, for example. Meredith Direct Marketing of Des Moines provides the following data.

Median family size: 3.3
Median household income: $16,000
Median age: 43
Percentage owning home: 80
Percentage owning one or more cars: 89

The profile of active subscribers to *Better Homes & Gardens* serves two purposes: (1) it provides prospective list renters with statistics necessary for determining whether this list would match the profile of their customers, and (2) it gives *Better Homes & Gardens* a true picture of the typical subscriber and thus provides direction for selecting lists available from others for prospecting purposes.

A prospective renter of this list with products or services that appeal to home owners would consider the list attractive (80 percent own their own home). Conversely, this list would not be attractive to an organization whose products appeal primarily to consumers in the 18 to 25-year-old bracket (median age is 43).

If *Better Homes & Gardens* were seeking additional active subscribers, they would no doubt consider the Spring Hill Nursery Mail Order Buyers list as test-worthy. Table 4.1 shows several similarities as they relate to some of the key demographics.

Direct response lists—names of people who respond by mail—develop profiles from propositions. It is axiomatic, for instance, that an inquiry list of a home study school will predominantly comprise names of people who have not gone to college and in many cases have not completed high school. So the educational level of a home study inquiry list would be on the low side. Another example—the customer list of a

**Table 4.1. Similarities between *Better Homes & Gardens* and Spring Hill Nursery mail order buyers lists.**

| Demographic Characteristic | *Better Homes & Gardens* | Spring Hill Nursery |
|---|---|---|
| Median income | $16,000 | $15,000 |
| Median age | 43 | 46 |
| Median family size | 3.3 | 3.2 |
| Percentage owning home | 80 | 95 |

classics book club—would almost certainly contain in its profile a high educational level, with a major percentage having attended college.

While profiles of a direct response list result from the proposition, compiled lists can be created to have various profiles within the universe.

A good example of selectivity within a compiled list is the "Young Family Index" maintained by Market Development Corporation of Hazelwood, Missouri. The Young Family Index is a birth list. Market Development Corporation assembles about two million new names each year. Selectivity is possible by region, state, city, size of city, sales area, income, and so forth. Reviewing the data, we see clearly the wide variety of profiles which exist within a compiled list. If a proposition caters or appeals only to high-income groups, then maybe only groups 1, 2, and 3 will respond satisfactorily.

**Table 4.2. Selectivity criteria and number of names available per category for the "Young Family Index" list maintained by Market Development Corporation of Hazelwood, Mo.**

| By State | Monthly Average | Yearly Total |
|---|---|---|
| Alabama | 1,936 | 23,238 |
| Arizona | 1,525 | 18,303 |
| Arkansas | 1,316 | 15,789 |
| California | 18,130 | 217,561 |
| Colorado | 1,335 | 16,024 |
| Connecticut | 2,410 | 28,919 |
| Delaware | 469 | 5,633 |
| District of Columbia | 422 | 5,070 |
| Florida | 3,492 | 41,910 |
| Georgia | 3,568 | 42,820 |
| Idaho | 786 | 9,434 |
| Illinois | 9,442 | 113,396 |
| Indiana | 5,432 | 65,190 |
| Iowa | 2,552 | 30,620 |
| Kansas | 1,936 | 23,231 |
| Kentucky | 2,607 | 31,288 |
| Louisiana | 1,923 | 23,081 |
| Maine | 687 | 8,244 |
| Maryland | 3,135 | 37,620 |
| Massachusetts | 5,253 | 63,037 |
| Michigan | 9,902 | 118,820 |
| Minnesota | 3,360 | 40,316 |
| Mississippi | 428 | 5,131 |
| Missouri | 4,136 | 49,629 |
| Montana | 630 | 7,559 |
| Nebraska | 1,400 | 16,795 |
| Nevada | 254 | 3,050 |
| New Hampshire | 791 | 9,492 |
| New Jersey | 4,653 | 55,837 |
| New Mexico | 851 | 10,218 |
| New York | 13,800 | 165,598 |
| North Carolina | 4,046 | 48,556 |
| North Dakota | 635 | 7,615 |
| Ohio | 11,475 | 137,702 |
| Oklahoma | 1,977 | 23,729 |
| Oregon | 1,395 | 16,736 |
| Pennsylvania | 9,534 | 114,413 |
| Rhode Island | 740 | 8,879 |
| South Carolina | 855 | 10,259 |
| South Dakota | 489 | 5,872 |
| Tennessee | 2,861 | 34,331 |
| Texas | 12,509 | 150,106 |
| Utah | 1,576 | 18,907 |
| Vermont | 405 | 4,857 |
| Virginia | 2,164 | 25,967 |
| Washington | 2,936 | 35,231 |
| West Virginia | 1,635 | 19,619 |
| Wisconsin | 4,562 | 54,748 |
| Wyoming | 285 | 3,421 |
| Alaska | 117 | 1,405 |
| Hawaii | 781 | 9,253 |
| Totals | 169,538 | 2,034,459 |

**By Income Groups (Highest to Lowest)**

| Group Number | Monthly | Yearly |
|---|---|---|
| 1 | 41,004 | 492,044 |
| 2 | 10,460 | 125,522 |
| 3 | 13,728 | 164,738 |
| 4 | 14,735 | 176,827 |
| 5 | 19,572 | 234,863 |
| 6 | 14,322 | 171,868 |
| 7 | 13,549 | 162,595 |
| 8 | 12,352 | 148,219 |
| 9 | 8,561 | 102,726 |
| 10 | 21,255 | 255,057 |
| Totals | 169,538 | 2,034,459 |

**By Percentage of Nonwhite Population**

| Percentage | Monthly | Yearly |
|---|---|---|
| 0 | 49,800 | 597,601 |
| 1-5 | 76,829 | 921,958 |
| 6-9 | 12,285 | 147,416 |
| 10-13 | 6,331 | 75,969 |
| 14-17 | 4,328 | 51,926 |
| 18-21 | 3,583 | 42,993 |
| 22-25 | 2,739 | 32,871 |
| 26-29 | 1,772 | 21,268 |
| 30-35 | 3,069 | 36,826 |
| 36-39 | 1,363 | 16,361 |
| 40 and above | 7,439 | 89,270 |
| Totals | 169,538 | 2,034,459 |

**By Nielsen Market Area**

| | Monthly | Yearly |
|---|---|---|
| A | 66,039 | 792,472 |
| B | 49,406 | 592,866 |
| C | 33,229 | 398,750 |
| D | 20,864 | 250,371 |
| Totals | 169,538 | 2,034,459 |

**By Geographic Region**

| | Monthly | Yearly |
|---|---|---|
| New England | 10,286 | 123,428 |
| Mid Atlantic | 27,987 | 335,848 |
| East North Central | 40,828 | 489,856 |
| West North Central | 14,506 | 174,078 |
| South Atlantic | 19,787 | 237,454 |
| East South Central | 7,832 | 93,988 |
| West South Central | 17,722 | 212,705 |
| Mountain | 7,241 | 86,916 |
| Pacific | 23,349 | 280,186 |
| Totals | 169,538 | 2,034,459 |

**By Parents Living in Small Towns**

| | Monthly | Yearly |
|---|---|---|
| United States | 54,093 | 649,121 |

**By First Births**

| | Monthly | Yearly |
|---|---|---|
| United States | 9,154 | 109,851 |

**By Previous Year Names Updated**

Families with children between the ages of 2 and 12 . . . . . . . . . . . . . . . 8,000,000

Source: "Young Family Index," Market Development Corporation.

If nonwhite population is required, it can be selected. If a proposition appeals only to multi-children families, only their names can be selected. It is this great selectivity, available in most compiled lists, that makes them profitable for many marketers.

Here is one final example of selectivity within a compiled list. One would certainly think that all attorneys are pretty much the same. Of course, they aren't. For instance, of 290,000 attorneys in this country only 45 percent are members of the bar associations. There are 86,000 who go it alone, with one man per office. There are about 26,000 attorneys in government, 32,000 in industry, 4,000 in education, 6,000 patent attorneys, and 13,000 nonpracticing attorneys. It's axiomatic that the closer you can get to matching your customer profile to segments of a list, the better your response is likely to be.

## Working with list brokers and compilers

No one succeeds in direct marketing without working with competent list brokers and compilers.

In most cases, the list broker operates as a direct mail list consultant. He will study your customer's profile and product and then recommend lists along with appropriate selections for testing. The list broker also can supply you with additional information regarding a list's background, such as source, offer, or when the list was last cleaned. He will get list rental clearance for your mailing as well as supply you with a written acknowledgment once the order is placed. Additionally, brokers are responsible for following up the delivery to ensure that the mailing list is where you need it, when you need it, and in the format needed

Whereas a broker acts as a representative of all mailing list owners, a list compiler normally only represents those lists owned and maintained by the company that employs him. They are actually specialists for the compilations they represent.

In many cases a list compiler may only represent one list owner, such as the R. H. Donnelley, Metro-Mail, or R. L. Polk. These files are extremely large. Therefore the list compiler must design test recommendations based on the segmentation of his file. Just as a broker does, the compiler renders order acknowledgments and delivery follow-up services.

Whether dealing with a list broker or list compiler, the more precise the direct marketer can be in providing a profile of his typical customer, the more likely it is he will be provided with good, responsive lists.

## List rental arrangements

Basically, three types of arrangements can be made when renting a list of names, although numerous variations of these arrangements exist.

The *gross name* arrangement is generally used when testing or renting a small quantity of names. This agreement specifies that the mailer will pay for exactly what he orders, no matter how many names he actually mails.

The *net name* arrangement is becoming one of the more used forms of compensating a mailer for nonmailed names. This arrangement is a guarantee of payment to the list owner for a certain portion of names. It is usually applicable only on large volume orders such as one million names or more.

For instance, if you expected to lose 15 percent of a certain list because of duplication with other lists in a mailing program, you would not want to guarantee payment for more than 85 percent of the rented names (85 percent net guarantee). However, if for some reason you were actually able to mail 90 percent of the names, you would be responsible for payment on all names mailed. If you mailed less than 85 percent, you would still be liable for payment for 85 percent of the names ordered.

The *overage* arrangement is an alternate means of renting names. This method is used to simplify bookkeeping and is also normally available only on large orders.

With this method, a certain portion of names are added to the order to compensate the mailer for duplication with other lists in a promotion. If you were anticipating a 15 percent duplication rate, you would ask the list broker to attempt to rent names on a 15 average percent basis. Therefore the number of names you would receive would be inflated by 15 percent allowing you to mail the established quantities after anticipated duplication.

Both the net name and overage arrangements must be negotiated on an individual basis. When applied appropriately, however, they can substantially lower the cost of a mailing and benefit both the mailer and the list owner.

## Lists as a profit center

While the primary purpose of compiling a house list—customers or inquiries—is to generate in-house sales, an important secondary factor is the possible income from the rental of such names to noncompeting advertisers. Indeed, profits from mailing list rentals are without exception at a much higher level than the percentage of profit realized in the sale of goods or services. A list renting for $30 a thousand will gross the advertiser $24 per thousand after payment of 20 percent brokerage commission. So, rental of one million names will produce $24,000 in gross revenue, with a fulfillment cost of approximately 10 percent. Profits derived from mailing list rentals can mean the difference between profit and loss on a direct marketing operation. Also, when a marketer knows his potential revenue from new names, he can use a part or all of this profit for investment in obtaining new customers.

There are different schools of thought about renting mailing lists. One is that it is harmful to the prime business to make customer names available to other advertisers. Another school holds that it is not harmful, providing those who use the list are not in any way competitive. There is yet another school that holds against renting lists only of current or active names. For example, a publisher may not offer current subscriber lists for rental, but he will offer lists of former subscribers.

Most major direct marketers who have assembled large lists of customers or inquiries have come to the conclusion that it is not harmful to their prime business to rent these lists to noncompetitive, reputable firms.

Many direct marketers also exchange lists with both competitors and noncompetitors. When such exchanges are arranged through a mailing list broker, each member of the exchange customarily pays a brokerage commission. For a list that normally rents for $30 a thousand, then, each participant in the exchange would pay only the 20 percent brokerage commission of $6 a thousand.

It is not unusual for two direct competitors to exchange lists, particularly of their older names. For example, two firms sell Christmas greeting cards by mail. Each has a list of about 100,000 customers who have not bought from the firm in three years. These are qualified names for each of the competitors because these customers have previously purchased Christmas greeting cards by mail. But, obviously, they have not chosen to repeat. Therefore, after exchanging lists, each competing firm is mailing to a prime prospect list with a good chance for success, because its proposition may have basic ingredients of appeal that were lacking in that of its competitor.

During the past few years there has been a trend toward list management whereby a given list broker takes over the complete management of a list for rental purposes. Under this arrangement, the list manager performs all or almost all of the following functions:

1. He, rather than the list owner, handles all contacts with all list brokers and processes their orders.
2. He likewise solicits his own list brokerage customers directly.
3. At his own expense, he regularly places advertising in appropriate journals on behalf of the list owner and consistently promotes the list owner's list by mail to prospective users and other list brokers.
4. He and his sales force regularly call on prospects in person and by phone.
5. If the list owner wishes, the broker maintains the list owner's list, either in his own shop or with an experienced computer service organization.
6. He analyzes the results of each mailing when they are available and often makes suggestions for segmented use of the list with a view to increasing profitability.
7. He usually handles all billing to other brokers or his customers, remitting net earnings to the list owner, less commissions.
8. He provides to the list owner a detailed report of list activity, usually on a quarterly basis.

While the normal commission to a list broker is 20 percent of gross, the list manager usually earns a commission of 10 percent of gross when rental is arranged through another broker. He also earns a list brokerage commission plus a management commission when he rents directly to one of his customers.

List rental business is a part-time activity for most list owners. The extra business realized by putting this function into the hands of a competent list manager usually more than warrants the compensation the manager receives for his specialized services.

It should be noted that this extra profit potential exists only when a list is put into the hands of a *competent* list manager. A leading direct marketing consultant, Bob Kestnbaum, recommends that prospective list managers be carefully screened and that the following questions should be asked of each.

**32 questions to ask a prospective list manager**

**Services provided**

1. What method and equipment will be used to maintain the list?
2. Does the manager have the capability of adding demographic data on the basis of ZIP codes or census tracts?
3. Could the list be merged into a larger data base for additional rentals or could it be unduplicated against similar lists being managed by the same organization?
4. What clerical and reporting functions would be assumed? (See order processing and reports.)

**List preparation and maintenance**

5. Is there sufficient flexibility in the system to establish and use all the selection factors appropriate for the particular lists?
6. How are test panels selected and controlled? What system is used to avoid providing names delivered on previous orders?
7. What controls exist to avoid excessive mailing to the same name?
8. In what forms can the list be delivered (label, direct impression, heat transfer, magnetic tape)?
9. What time service would be given on normal orders and rush orders, that is, how rapidly would addressed material be delivered?

**Security procedures**

10. Are magnetic tapes or address masters retained in a safe place which is kept locked?
11. How is access to the locked storage area limited and controlled?
12. Are magnetic tapes or address masters logged out and in when they are removed from the locked storage area?
13. What procedures exist for seeding the list with decoys and for being sure that decoys appear on every test panel or list segment delivered?
14. What procedures are used to identify and mark labels or magnetic tapes shipped out?

**Order processing and reports**

15. What procedures are used to ensure that necessary approvals are secured for each rental order?
16. What records of list rental orders are maintained?
17. What summary counts of names delivered are supplied with each rental order?
18. What types of sales reports and analyses are supplied to the list owner? By month? By offer type? By broker? By user? By industry?
19. What efforts are extended to collect rental accounts receivable and to provide accounts receivable aging reports?

**Sales effort**

20. Does the prospective list manager have special experience and knowledge of and contacts with the most likely types of users of the list in question?

21. Are there salesmen who call on potential list users and brokers? How many? Where located?

22. What types of mailings and advertisements will be used to promote the list? How frequently will they be used?

**Costs and revenue**

23. Will there be a charge for special computer programming?

24. Will there be a charge for generating, inputting, or converting the list?

25. What is the cost of selecting names, producing test panels, or skipping names?

26. How much does it cost to change names, add names, and kill names?

27. What are the charges for running labels or producing magnetic tape?

28. What fees will be charged for managing or promoting the list?

29. If the list is managed on an exclusive basis, how will broker's commission be divided?

**Other considerations**

30. How much experience and knowledge do the employees of the list management firm have?

31. What reputation does the firm have in its field?

32. Are there people in the firm who have the capability to provide sound advice and guidance

**Duplication elimination**

The year 1968 will go down in the history of direct marketing as the year of the breakthrough for overcoming mailing duplication. Before 1968, it was either impossible or impractical to remove duplicate names from mass mailing programs. But in 1968 several computer systems became available for removing duplicate names. The processes employed are commonly known as "merge and purge." Here, very simply, is how merge and purge works.

1. You rent your lists in the usual way through the brokers involved. Almost all lists on magnetic tape or punch cards are suitable.

2. The tapes or punch cards provided for rented lists along with those for the mailer's customer or prospect lists are sent to the service organization designated.

3. The service organization puts the tapes through a computerized matching process which compares the names on each list with every name on every other list, including the mailer's customer list.

4. No matter how many labels may be involved, the mailer receives one set with absolutely no duplication between the rented lists and the customer list.

5. In addition, the mailer receives a second nonduplicating set of labels representing names that appear two or more times on the lists. These names represent known mail order buyers.

Table 4.3 shows the savings possible from the elimination of duplicates. Figures are based on a mailing cost of $100 per thousand for simple computation, although most mailings today cost at least $175 per thousand and more. Looking at Table 4.3, let's take a reduction in duplication of just 15 percent and note the savings as they relate to the quantity mailed. In a one-million-piece mailing you can save $15,000, and in a five-million-piece mailing, $75,000.

**Table 4.3. Savings achievable by eliminating duplicate names from a mailing (amount of savings based on a mailing cost of $100 per thousand pieces).**

| Percent Duplication | Mailing Quantity | | | | | |
|---|---|---|---|---|---|---|
| | 1,000,000 | 2,500,000 | 5,000,000 | 10,000,000 | 25,000,000 | 50,000,000 |
| 10 . . . . . . . . . . . . | $10,000 | $ 25,000 | $ 50,000 | $100,000 | $ 250,000 | $ 500,000 |
| 15 . . . . . . . . . . . . | 15,000 | 37,500 | 75,000 | 150,000 | 375,000 | 750,000 |
| 20 . . . . . . . . . . . . | 20,000 | 50,000 | 100,000 | 200,000 | 500,000 | 1,000,000 |
| 25 . . . . . . . . . . . . | 25,000 | 62,500 | 125,000 | 250,000 | 625,000 | 1,250,000 |
| 30 . . . . . . . . . . . . | 30,000 | 75,000 | 150,000 | 300,000 | 750,000 | 1,500,000 |
| 35 . . . . . . . . . . . . | 35,000 | 87,500 | 175,000 | 350,000 | 875,000 | 1,750,000 |
| 40 . . . . . . . . . . . . | 40,000 | 100,000 | 200,000 | 400,000 | 1,000,000 | 2,000,000 |
| 45 . . . . . . . . . . . . | 45,000 | 112,500 | 225,000 | 450,000 | 1,125,000 | 2,250,000 |
| 50 . . . . . . . . . . . . | 50,000 | 125,000 | 250,000 | 500,000 | 1,250,000 | 2,500,000 |

A case history will demonstrate the dramatic savings possible when the merge and purge system is used. *Southern Living* applied merge and purge to 17 lists totaling 1.4 million names. The publishers found that the duplication rate among the 17 lists was 13.5 percent plus an additional 17.3 percent on their house list. *Southern Living* saved $44,643 on this one mailing. The customer acquisition cost was cut by 25 percent.

In addition to the basic matching process, most merge/purge systems have the following capabilities:

1. *ZIP code elimination.* ZIP codes or states can be dropped at the request of the mailer.

2. *ZIP code select.* ZIP codes or states can be output to a separate file for special tests.

3. *Customer suppression.* By using a tape of customers, it is possible to suppress these names from rented list files. This can be done by type of customer.

4. *Customer select.* Rented names that match the customer file may be generated and held in a separate file.

5. *Multi-buyer drop.* Duplicate names between lists may be held in a separate file for possible special treatment

6. *Multi-buyer kept.* Duplicate names between lists may be produced as a separate list.

7. *Internal duplication.* Names duplicated within a list are dropped and not identified as multi-buyers.

8. *Previous mail suppress.* Names used in a previous mailing may be suppressed.

9. *Mail preference.* The DMMA list of those people not wanting to receive direct mail solicitations can be dropped from all files. This is becoming very important in these times of the "privacy question."

A bonus feature of any merge and purge program is the multi-buyer file. Such names constitute choice prospects. They qualify for follow-up mailings on the same proposition.

A truly unique example of this is the Foster and Gallagher multi-hit program. A large number of lists and names are input into a merge/purge program. The names appearing on more than one list are identified and sorted according to the number of times they appeared. Names are solicited with a mailing only if they appear on multiple lists, and in certain cases they are given special mailing treatment in accordance with how many times they appear.

**Lists age rapidly**  Forgetting the continuous problem of address changes for a moment (such changes on some lists are as high as 25 percent a year), let us note a very important axiom about customer and inquiry lists which should be indelibly imprinted in the memory of every direct marketer. It is this: The longer the period from the time of the last response, the less responsive that customer or prospect is likely to be.

For example, let's say we test a direct response list under three different keys: 1978 buyers, 1977 buyers, and 1976 buyers. Assuming the most recent buyers pulled a 6 percent response, results would probably track something like this: 1978 buyers, 6 percent; 1977 buyers, 3 percent; and 1976 buyers, 1.5 percent.

With attrition rates of 50 percent a year, is it any wonder that "hot line" buyers—those who have purchased within the past three to six months—are the most attractive direct response names available? The sophisticates in mailing list usage consider recency of purchase as only one important criterion; they also take frequency of purchase and monetary value of purchase into account.

Using a scale of 100, most marketers assign values to the three factors as follows: recency of last purchase, 50 percent; frequency of purchase (multiple buyers), 35 percent; and value of purchase (monetary), 15 percent.

We've already seen the value of "hot line" names (most recent buyers), but when we add the multiple-buyer factor (more than one purchase within the season), we can increase the pull of a mailing substantially.

There can be a world of difference between one-time buyers and buyers who have purchased two or more times. In any given list of one-time buyers, there is sure to be a percentage who have bought once, were dissatisfied, and will never buy again. On the other hand, it is safe to assume that multiple buyers are satisfied customers because they have bought more than once.

While astute direct marketers generally give only 15 percent weight to the monetary amount of purchase, this factor in the R-F-M equation should not

**Table 4.4. Merge and purge program illustration.**

| List Number | Total Input | Exclusive List | Multi-buyer | Total Output | Percentage Duplication |
|---|---|---|---|---|---|
| 1 . . . . . . . . . | 48,000 | 47,641 | 30 | 47,671 | 1 |
| 2 . . . . . . . . . | 27,646 | 21,232 | 811 | 22,043 | 18 |
| 3 . . . . . . . . . | 24,837 | 20,016 | 833 | 20,849 | 17 |
| 4 . . . . . . . . . | 43,899 | 33,461 | 1,288 | 34,749 | 19 |
| 5 . . . . . . . . . | 25,220 | 18,647 | 614 | 19,261 | 22 |
| 6 . . . . . . . . . | 12,595 | 11,410 | 206 | 11,616 | 12 |
| 7 . . . . . . . . . | 100,220 | 73,445 | 2,700 | 76,145 | 25 |
| 8 . . . . . . . . . | 58,006 | 43,188 | 1,859 | 45,047 | 23 |
| 9 . . . . . . . . . | 24,527 | 20,435 | 598 | 21,033 | 13 |
| 10 . . . . . . . . | 63,000 | 53,595 | 1,228 | 54,823 | 15 |
| 11 . . . . . . . . | 25,230 | 18,281 | 968 | 19,249 | 24 |
| 12 . . . . . . . . | 23,750 | 19,611 | 524 | 20,135 | 12 |
| 13 . . . . . . . . | 25,272 | 18,158 | 1,319 | 19,477 | 21 |
| 14 . . . . . . . . | 64,460 | 47,904 | 1,812 | 49,716 | 24 |
| 15 . . . . . . . . | 47,480 | 42,621 | 600 | 43,221 | 10 |
| 16 . . . . . . . . | 70,590 | 63,567 | 721 | 64,288 | 9 |
| 17 . . . . . . . . | 16,700 | 15,432 | 203 | 15,635 | 6 |
| 18 . . . . . . . . | 72,000 | 54,720 | 2,251 | 56,971 | 19 |
| 19 . . . . . . . . | 6,000 | 4,544 | 197 | 4,741 | 49 |
| 20 . . . . . . . . | 239,430 | 202,885 | 4,537 | 207,422 | 13 |
| 21 . . . . . . . . | 58,682 | 50,035 | 1,077 | 51,112 | 10 |
| 22 . . . . . . . . | 51,150 | 31,374 | 1,886 | 33,260 | 40 |
| 23 . . . . . . . . | 32,800 | 24,393 | 1,149 | 25,542 | 22 |
| Totals . . . . . . . | 1,161,494 | 936,595 | 27,411 | 964,006 | 16.5 |

The total number of names processed was 1,161,494. Of these, 936,595 names appeared on only one list (exclusive list). There were also 27,411 multibuyers, names appearing on two or more lists. After this list was compiled, it was compared with the mailer's customer list of 1,441,000 names. Another 146,522 names were found to be duplicated, and these also were suppressed, leaving a list of 964,006 unduplicated names for the mailing.

Note: Percent of duplication figures reflect comparisons with the customer list of the mailer as well as with other rented lists.

Source: System Dupli-Match from Alan Drey Co.

be overlooked. Many direct marketers who sell via the catalog method break out their buyers by categories of purchase amounts. For example, $10 to $20; $21 to $30; $31 to $40; and over $40. Catalog distribution by amount of previous purchase has consistently shown a revenue difference of 50 percent to 60 percent between the lower categories of purchase amounts and the higher.

**Analyzing Response by Timing and Locale**

When and where you mail is also a big factor in response. "What are the best mailing months?" is a perennial question at direct marketing seminars. Table 4.5 was provided by Ray Snyder, a direct mail consultant and former sales manager of the Direct Mail Department of *World Book*. The table resulted from a three-year test program for a nonseasonal item. The mailing was made to an equal quantity of like names from a given list every month of the year. The best-pulling month was rated 100 percent.

Table 4.5 is truly meaningful because it closely reflects the experience of most mass mailers. With the exception of seasonal goods such as Christmas items, January is traditionally the month of the year having the greatest response to a wide variety of mail offers.

June is traditionally the worst month. Note the variance of 33 percent on the chart. The theory most often advanced to explain why mail dropped then does so poorly is that this is the start of the vacation season.

It must be emphasized that the chart applies to general offers as opposed to seasonal offers. Rare is the power mower offer that will succeed in January, no matter what the discount! And it's pretty difficult to get the consumer whipped up about Christmas cards in July. But there are sales variations by month for mailers with seasonal offers too. And it is vital that all mailers, those with nonseasonal offers as well as those with seasonal offers, have a performance chart by months.

A performance chart is a key factor in projecting test results. Every mailer is faced with the fact that, if he is to mail in volume in his best month (or months), his test must be made two to three months prior to his best month. He must be able to project accurately how much greater his response will be in his best months over his test months. A performance chart based on experience enables him to make projections with confidence. For example, on the basis of the chart, an offer tested in July will do 16.6 percent better in October. This better performance could well be the difference between profit and loss. Many a test dies at birth because the mailer lacks performance figures by month from which he can make accurate projections.

Just as there is a pattern of best mailing months for each mailer, so there is a pattern of best states. And degrees of responsiveness can be considerable. In addition to a seasonal chart, Snyder also developed a chart (Table 4.6) which shows the response ranking of states. it is based on responses from a total of some 33 million mailing pieces covering 20 different offers of various types of books and merchandise mailed by companies for whom Snyder has worked or acted as a consultant. State rankings vary considerably among marketers, but there is a ranking for every marketer. Later we shall deal with much more sophisticated rankings by ZIP codes within states.

**Determining proper test quantities**

Perhaps one of the most frequently pondered questions about list tests is deciding how big or small a quantity of names should be used. Many rules of thumb for establishing test quantities have been used by mailers for years. Some mailers say, "I always test 10 percent of the list." Others say, "We never test more than 1,000 names on a list." Neither approach is mathematically sound.

**Table 4.5. Typical mail order results by month (base: January = 100).**

| Month | Rating |
|---|---|
| January | 100.0 |
| February | 96.3 |
| March | 71.0 |
| April | 71.5 |
| May | 71.5 |
| June | 67.0 |
| July | 73.3 |
| August | 87.0 |
| September | 79.0 |
| October | 89.9 |
| November | 81.0 |
| December | 79.0 |

**Table 4.6. Sales response rankings based on results of 20 mailings offering various types of books and merchandise.**

| Rank | State or District | Rank | State or District |
|------|-------------------|------|-------------------|
| 1 | Alaska | 27 | Michigan |
| 2 | Washington, D.C. | 28 | Kansas |
| 3 | Hawaii | 29 | Oklahoma |
| 4 | California | 30 | New York |
| 5 | Nevada | 31 | Rhode Island |
| 6 | Arizona | 32 | Georgia |
| 7 | Wyoming | 33 | Ohio |
| 8 | New Mexico | 34 | Delaware |
| 9 | Idaho | 35 | Virginia |
| 10 | Montana | 36 | Pennsylvania |
| 11 | Utah | 37 | Arkansas |
| 12 | Florida | 38 | Missouri |
| 13 | Nebraska | 39 | South Carolina |
| 14 | Louisiana | 40 | Connecticut |
| 15 | Oregon | 41 | North Carolina |
| 16 | Illinois | 42 | New Hampshire |
| 17 | Indiana | 43 | North Dakota |
| 18 | Texas | 44 | Minnesota |
| 19 | Colorado | 45 | Kentucky |
| 20 | Washington | 46 | Vermont |
| 21 | Maryland | 47 | Tennessee |
| 22 | Wisconsin | 48 | Iowa |
| 23 | West Virginia | 49 | Mississippi |
| 24 | South Dakota | 50 | Massachusetts |
| 25 | Maine | 51 | Alabama |
| 26 | New Jersey | | |

Certainly those who follow the rule of 10 percent of the list are not wise in testing a quantity of 100,000 names when the total list is one million. If the test fails, $15,000 to $20,000 could go down the drain. And what confidence can we have about a test of 1,000 names from a universe of one million names? Testing too large a quantity forces us to spend more than is necessary to obtain reliable test results; testing too small a quantity wastes money, since we cannot have much confidence in our results.

Sophisticated mailers today rely on test sizes and results based on the laws of probability. To determine the size of your test, you first need to know three things:

1. What is your anticipated response?

2. What level of confidence do you require? (Must you be right 99 out of 100 times, or can you risk being right 95 out of 100 times?)

3. By how much can you miss the anticipated pull and still be within an acceptable lower response limit? (Can you live with 1 percent plus or minus 0.2 percent, or can you still profit if your mailing pulls 1 percent plus or minus 0.5 percent?)

Because of the time required to compute a probability equation for each individual mailing made or contemplated, it is usually easier to refer to probability tables where calculations have already been made for various percentages of response and limits of error.

Probability tables are made up of four elements: test sample size, level of confidence, response, and limit of error. At the top of each probability table is a notation about the level of confidence on which it is built. Running horizontally across the top of the page are the limits of error, expressed in percentage points. The column headed "R" is the percentage response, or results. Figures within the table where the "response" line and "limit of error" column intersect are the sample sizes required.

To illustrate the use of probability table, let us take an actual sample of a test mailing and determine the limit of error which we could expect on a larger mailing. In this case, we mailed 10,000 pieces and received a 1 percent response. Now we want to find the limits of error for an identical mailing with a 95 percent confidence level. (Statistically, this means that results will be as indicated 95 out of 100 times.)

Using Table 4.7, we would read down the R column until we came to 1 percent response. Then we would read horizontally until we came to the closest figure to our 10,000-piece sample size. Then, reading vertically to that column's heading, we find 0.20 percent as the possible limit of error we could expect on a larger mailing to the same size list under identical circumstances.

**Table 4.7. Size of test mailings required for various response levels and limits of error based on a 95 percent level of confidence.**

| Response Percentage | Limits of Error (Percent of Original Number in Mailing) | | | | |
|---|---|---|---|---|---|
| | 0.16 | 0.18 | 0.20 | 0.25 | 0.30 |
| 0.1 | 1,499 | 1,184 | 958 | 614 | 426 |
| 0.2 | 2,994 | 2,366 | 1,917 | 1,226 | 852 |
| 0.3 | 4,467 | 3,546 | 2,872 | 1,838 | 1,276 |
| 0.4 | 5,977 | 4,723 | 3,826 | 2,448 | 1,700 |
| 0.5 | 7,464 | 5,897 | 4,777 | 3,057 | 2,123 |
| 0.6 | 8,948 | 7,070 | 5,727 | 3,665 | 2,545 |
| 0.7 | 10,429 | 8,240 | 6,675 | 4,272 | 2,966 |
| 0.8 | 11,907 | 9,408 | 7,621 | 4,877 | 3,387 |
| 0.9 | 13,382 | 10,573 | 8,564 | 5,481 | 3,806 |
| 1.0 | 14,854 | 11,736 | 9,506 | 6,084 | 4,225 |
| 1.1 | 16,322 | 12,897 | 10,446 | 6,686 | 4,643 |
| 1.2 | 17,788 | 14,055 | 11,385 | 7,286 | 5,060 |

Source: Alan Drey Co., Chicago.

In like manner, suppose we want to know the number of pieces we should mail to a certain list if we anticipate a 0.8 percent response, cannot afford a limit of error greater than plus or minus 0.25 percent, and want to be sure that 95 of 100 times we will stay within the 0.25 percent limit of error. First we read down the R column until we find the 0.8 percent response figure. Then we read horizontally until we locate the sample size required under the column headed by the 0.25 percent limit of error. We find that we would require a test mailing of 4,877 pieces, or, for convenience, 5,000 names. This means that if the test mailing pulls 0.8 percent response, a larger mailing of identical pieces will produce results falling between 0.55 percent and 1.05 percent—95 out of 100 times.

Included in this chapter are two comprehensive probability tables, one at 99 percent confidence level (Table 4.8), and the other at 95 percent confidence level (Table 4.9).

It must be remembered that probability tables are constructed on a purely statistical basis. Within certain limits of error, they can be used to predict the results that can be expected from a larger mailing *exactly identical* to the test, but only if a good random cross-section has been used in creating the test sample.

It should also be remembered that probabilities work most accurately when your continuation mailing is made under identical circumstances. Any changes in copy, format, or offer to the same list will invalidate the statistical

# Table 4.8. Test sample sizes required for 99 percent confidence level for mailing response levels from 0.1 to 4.0 percent.

LIMITS OF ERROR (EXPRESSED AS PERCENTAGE POINTS)

| R (Response) | .70 | .60 | .50 | .40 | .30 | .20 | .18 | .16 | .14 | .12 | .10 | .08 | .06 | .04 | .02 |
|---|---|---|---|---|---|---|---|---|---|---|---|---|---|---|---|
| .1 | 135 | 184 | 265 | 414 | 736 | 1,657 | 2,046 | 2,589 | 3,381 | 4,603 | 6,628 | 10,357 | 18,412 | 41,427 | 165,709 |
| .2 | 270 | 368 | 529 | 827 | 1,471 | 3,311 | 4,087 | 5,173 | 6,756 | 9,197 | 13,243 | 20,693 | 36,787 | 82,772 | 331,087 |
| .3 | 405 | 551 | 794 | 1,240 | 2,205 | 4,961 | 6,125 | 7,752 | 10,125 | 13,781 | 19,845 | 31,008 | 55,126 | 124,033 | 496,132 |
| .4 | 539 | 734 | 1,057 | 1,652 | 2,937 | 6,608 | 8,158 | 10,325 | 13,486 | 18,356 | 26,434 | 41,303 | 73,427 | 165,212 | 660,846 |
| .5 | 673 | 916 | 1,320 | 2,063 | 3,667 | 8,252 | 10,187 | 12,894 | 16,841 | 22,923 | 33,009 | 51,577 | 91,692 | 206,307 | 825,228 |
| .6 | 807 | 1,099 | 1,582 | 2,473 | 4,396 | 9,893 | 12,213 | 15,457 | 20,189 | 27,480 | 39,571 | 61,830 | 109,919 | 247,320 | 989,279 |
| .7 | 941 | 1,281 | 1,845 | 2,882 | 5,124 | 11,530 | 14,234 | 18,015 | 23,530 | 32,027 | 46,120 | 72,062 | 128,111 | 288,249 | 1,152,997 |
| .8 | 1,074 | 1,462 | 2,106 | 3,291 | 5,850 | 13,164 | 16,251 | 20,569 | 26,864 | 36,565 | 52,655 | 82,274 | 146,265 | 329,096 | 1,316,384 |
| .9 | 1,208 | 1,643 | 2,367 | 3,698 | 6,575 | 14,794 | 18,264 | 23,116 | 30,192 | 41,095 | 59,178 | 92,465 | 164,381 | 369,859 | 1,479,439 |
| 1.0 | 1,340 | 1,825 | 2,627 | 4,105 | 7,299 | 16,422 | 20,273 | 25,658 | 33,513 | 45,616 | 65,687 | 102,635 | 182,463 | 410,541 | 1,642,163 |
| 1.1 | 1,473 | 2,004 | 2,887 | 4,511 | 8,020 | 18,045 | 22,278 | 28,195 | 36,827 | 50,126 | 72,182 | 112,784 | 200,505 | 451,138 | 1,804,554 |
| 1.2 | 1,605 | 2,185 | 3,146 | 4,917 | 8,740 | 19,666 | 24,279 | 30,728 | 40,134 | 54,628 | 78,665 | 122,913 | 218,512 | 491,654 | 1,966,614 |
| 1.3 | 1,737 | 2,365 | 3,405 | 5,321 | 9,459 | 21,283 | 26,275 | 33,255 | 43,435 | 59,121 | 85,134 | 133,021 | 236,482 | 532,085 | 2,128,342 |
| 1.4 | 1,869 | 2,544 | 3,663 | 5,724 | 10,176 | 22,897 | 28,268 | 35,777 | 46,729 | 63,603 | 91,590 | 143,108 | 254,414 | 572,435 | 2,289,739 |
| 1.5 | 2,000 | 2,723 | 3,921 | 6,127 | 10,892 | 24,508 | 30,256 | 38,293 | 50,016 | 68,077 | 98,032 | 153,175 | 272,310 | 612,700 | 2,450,803 |
| 1.6 | 2,132 | 2,901 | 4,178 | 6,529 | 11,607 | 26,115 | 32,241 | 40,805 | 53,296 | 72,542 | 104,461 | 163,221 | 290,170 | 652,884 | 2,611,536 |
| 1.7 | 2,263 | 3,079 | 4,435 | 6,930 | 12,319 | 27,719 | 34,221 | 43,311 | 56,569 | 76,997 | 110,877 | 173,246 | 307,992 | 692,984 | 2,771,937 |
| 1.8 | 2,393 | 3,257 | 4,691 | 7,330 | 13,030 | 29,320 | 36,197 | 45,812 | 59,836 | 81,444 | 117,280 | 183,250 | 325,777 | 733,002 | 2,932,007 |
| 1.9 | 2,523 | 3,435 | 4,946 | 7,729 | 13,741 | 30,917 | 38,169 | 48,308 | 63,096 | 85,881 | 123,670 | 193,234 | 343,527 | 772,936 | 3,091,744 |
| 2.0 | 2,654 | 3,612 | 5,202 | 8,128 | 14,449 | 32,512 | 40,137 | 50,799 | 66,350 | 90,309 | 130,046 | 203,197 | 361,238 | 812,788 | 3,251,150 |
| 2.1 | 2,783 | 3,789 | 5,456 | 8,525 | 15,156 | 34,102 | 42,100 | 53,284 | 69,596 | 94,728 | 136,409 | 213,139 | 378,912 | 852,556 | 3,410,224 |
| 2.2 | 2,913 | 3,965 | 5,710 | 8,922 | 15,862 | 35,690 | 44,061 | 55,765 | 72,836 | 99,138 | 142,759 | 223,060 | 396,551 | 892,242 | 3,568,967 |
| 2.3 | 3,042 | 4,141 | 5,964 | 9,318 | 16,566 | 37,273 | 46,016 | 58,239 | 76,068 | 103,537 | 149,095 | 232,961 | 414,152 | 931,844 | 3,727,377 |
| 2.4 | 3,172 | 4,317 | 6,216 | 9,714 | 17,268 | 38,855 | 47,968 | 60,710 | 79,294 | 107,929 | 155,418 | 242,841 | 431,716 | 971,364 | 3,885,456 |
| 2.5 | 3,300 | 4,492 | 6,469 | 10,108 | 17,970 | 40,432 | 49,915 | 63,174 | 82,513 | 112,311 | 161,728 | 252,700 | 449,245 | 1,010,800 | 4,043,203 |
| 2.6 | 3,429 | 4,667 | 6,721 | 10,501 | 18,669 | 42,006 | 51,859 | 65,634 | 85,726 | 116,682 | 168,025 | 262,538 | 466,734 | 1,050,155 | 4,200,619 |
| 2.7 | 3,557 | 4,842 | 6,972 | 10,894 | 19,367 | 43,577 | 53,798 | 68,088 | 88,932 | 121,046 | 174,308 | 272,356 | 484,187 | 1,089,425 | 4,357,702 |
| 2.8 | 3,685 | 5,016 | 7,223 | 11,286 | 20,064 | 45,145 | 55,734 | 70,538 | 92,131 | 125,402 | 180,578 | 282,153 | 501,606 | 1,128,614 | 4,514,454 |
| 2.9 | 3,812 | 5,189 | 7,473 | 11,677 | 20,759 | 46,708 | 57,664 | 72,982 | 95,324 | 129,745 | 186,835 | 291,929 | 518,984 | 1,167,718 | 4,670,874 |
| 3.0 | 3,940 | 5,363 | 7,723 | 12,067 | 21,453 | 48,270 | 59,591 | 75,421 | 98,508 | 134,081 | 193,079 | 301,685 | 536,327 | 1,206,741 | 4,826,963 |
| 3.1 | 4,067 | 5,536 | 7,972 | 12,457 | 22,145 | 49,827 | 61,514 | 77,854 | 101,687 | 138,409 | 199,309 | 311,420 | 553,635 | 1,245,679 | 4,982,719 |
| 3.2 | 4,194 | 5,709 | 8,221 | 12,845 | 22,836 | 51,381 | 63,433 | 80,284 | 104,858 | 142,725 | 205,526 | 321,134 | 570,903 | 1,284,536 | 5,138,144 |
| 3.3 | 4,321 | 5,881 | 8,469 | 13,233 | 23,525 | 52,932 | 65,348 | 82,706 | 108,024 | 147,034 | 211,729 | 330,827 | 588,135 | 1,323,309 | 5,293,237 |
| 3.4 | 4,447 | 6,053 | 8,716 | 13,620 | 24,213 | 54,480 | 67,258 | 85,124 | 111,183 | 151,333 | 217,920 | 340,500 | 605,333 | 1,362,000 | 5,447,999 |
| 3.5 | 4,573 | 6,224 | 8,964 | 14,006 | 24,899 | 56,024 | 69,165 | 87,537 | 114,334 | 155,621 | 224,097 | 350,152 | 622,490 | 1,400,607 | 5,602,428 |
| 3.6 | 4,699 | 6,395 | 9,210 | 14,391 | 25,584 | 57,565 | 71,067 | 89,945 | 117,479 | 159,903 | 230,261 | 359,783 | 639,611 | 1,439,132 | 5,756,526 |
| 3.7 | 4,824 | 6,567 | 9,456 | 14,775 | 26,268 | 59,103 | 72,966 | 92,347 | 120,616 | 164,174 | 236,412 | 369,393 | 656,699 | 1,477,573 | 5,910,292 |
| 3.8 | 4,949 | 6,737 | 9,702 | 15,159 | 26,949 | 60,637 | 74,860 | 94,745 | 123,749 | 168,435 | 242,549 | 378,983 | 673,746 | 1,515,932 | 6,063,727 |
| 3.9 | 5,074 | 6,907 | 9,947 | 15,542 | 27,629 | 62,168 | 76,750 | 97,137 | 126,872 | 172,688 | 248,673 | 388,552 | 690,756 | 1,554,207 | 6,216,829 |
| 4.0 | 5,199 | 7,077 | 10,191 | 15,924 | 28,309 | 63,696 | 78,636 | 99,525 | 129,991 | 176,933 | 254,784 | 398,100 | 707,733 | 1,592,400 | 6,369,600 |

Table 4.9. Test sample sizes required for 95 percent confidence level for mailing response levels from 0.1 to 4.0 percent.

| R (Response) | LIMITS OF ERROR (EXPRESSED AS PERCENTAGE POINTS) | | | | | | | | | | | | | | |
|---|---|---|---|---|---|---|---|---|---|---|---|---|---|---|---|
| | .02 | .04 | .06 | .08 | .10 | .12 | .14 | .16 | .18 | .20 | .30 | .40 | .50 | .60 | .70 |
| .1 | 95,929 | 23,982 | 10,659 | 5,995 | 3,837 | 2,665 | 1,957 | 1,499 | 1,184 | 959 | 426 | 240 | 153 | 106 | 78 |
| .2 | 191,666 | 47,916 | 21,296 | 11,979 | 7,667 | 5,324 | 3,911 | 2,994 | 2,366 | 1,917 | 852 | 479 | 307 | 213 | 156 |
| .3 | 287,211 | 71,803 | 31,912 | 17,951 | 11,488 | 7,978 | 5,861 | 4,487 | 3,546 | 2,872 | 1,276 | 718 | 459 | 319 | 234 |
| .4 | 382,564 | 95,641 | 42,507 | 23,910 | 15,303 | 10,627 | 7,807 | 5,977 | 4,723 | 3,826 | 1,700 | 956 | 612 | 425 | 312 |
| .5 | 477,724 | 119,431 | 53,080 | 29,858 | 19,109 | 13,270 | 9,749 | 7,464 | 5,987 | 4,777 | 2,123 | 1,194 | 764 | 530 | 390 |
| .6 | 572,693 | 143,173 | 63,632 | 35,793 | 22,908 | 15,908 | 11,687 | 8,948 | 7,070 | 5,727 | 2,545 | 1,432 | 916 | 636 | 467 |
| .7 | 667,470 | 166,867 | 74,163 | 41,717 | 26,699 | 18,541 | 13,622 | 10,429 | 8,240 | 6,675 | 2,966 | 1,669 | 1,068 | 741 | 545 |
| .8 | 762,054 | 190,514 | 84,673 | 47,628 | 30,482 | 21,168 | 15,552 | 11,907 | 9,408 | 7,621 | 3,387 | 1,905 | 1,219 | 847 | 622 |
| .9 | 856,447 | 214,112 | 95,160 | 53,528 | 34,258 | 23,790 | 17,478 | 13,382 | 10,573 | 8,564 | 3,806 | 2,141 | 1,370 | 951 | 699 |
| 1.0 | 950,648 | 237,662 | 105,628 | 59,415 | 38,026 | 26,407 | 19,401 | 14,854 | 11,736 | 9,506 | 4,225 | 2,376 | 1,521 | 1,056 | 776 |
| 1.1 | 1,044,656 | 261,164 | 116,072 | 65,291 | 41,786 | 29,018 | 21,319 | 16,322 | 12,897 | 10,446 | 4,643 | 2,611 | 1,671 | 1,160 | 853 |
| 1.2 | 1,138,472 | 284,618 | 126,496 | 71,155 | 45,539 | 31,624 | 23,234 | 17,788 | 14,055 | 11,385 | 5,060 | 2,846 | 1,821 | 1,265 | 929 |
| 1.3 | 1,232,097 | 308,024 | 136,899 | 77,006 | 49,284 | 34,225 | 25,145 | 19,251 | 15,211 | 12,321 | 5,476 | 3,080 | 1,971 | 1,369 | 1,006 |
| 1.4 | 1,325,529 | 331,382 | 147,280 | 82,845 | 53,021 | 36,820 | 27,051 | 20,711 | 16,364 | 13,255 | 5,891 | 3,314 | 2,121 | 1,473 | 1,082 |
| 1.5 | 1,418,769 | 354,692 | 157,640 | 88,673 | 56,751 | 39,410 | 28,954 | 22,168 | 17,515 | 14,188 | 6,305 | 3,547 | 2,270 | 1,576 | 1,158 |
| 1.6 | 1,511,818 | 377,954 | 167,980 | 94,489 | 60,473 | 41,995 | 30,853 | 23,622 | 18,664 | 15,118 | 6,719 | 3,780 | 2,419 | 1,680 | 1,234 |
| 1.7 | 1,604,674 | 401,168 | 178,297 | 100,292 | 64,187 | 44,574 | 32,748 | 25,073 | 19,811 | 16,047 | 7,132 | 4,012 | 2,567 | 1,783 | 1,310 |
| 1.8 | 1,697,338 | 424,334 | 188,592 | 106,083 | 67,894 | 47,148 | 34,639 | 26,521 | 20,955 | 16,973 | 7,543 | 4,243 | 2,716 | 1,886 | 1,385 |
| 1.9 | 1,789,810 | 447,452 | 198,868 | 111,863 | 71,592 | 49,717 | 36,526 | 27,966 | 22,096 | 17,898 | 7,955 | 4,474 | 2,863 | 1,988 | 1,461 |
| 2.0 | 1,882,090 | 470,523 | 209,121 | 117,631 | 75,284 | 52,280 | 38,410 | 29,407 | 23,235 | 18,821 | 8,365 | 4,705 | 3,011 | 2,091 | 1,536 |
| 2.1 | 1,974,178 | 493,544 | 219,352 | 123,386 | 78,967 | 54,838 | 40,289 | 30,846 | 24,372 | 19,742 | 8,774 | 4,935 | 3,158 | 2,193 | 1,611 |
| 2.2 | 2,066,074 | 516,518 | 229,564 | 129,129 | 82,643 | 57,391 | 42,165 | 32,282 | 25,507 | 20,661 | 9,182 | 5,165 | 3,306 | 2,295 | 1,686 |
| 2.3 | 2,157,778 | 539,444 | 239,753 | 134,861 | 86,311 | 59,938 | 44,036 | 33,715 | 26,638 | 21,578 | 9,590 | 5,394 | 3,452 | 2,397 | 1,761 |
| 2.4 | 2,249,290 | 562,322 | 249,920 | 140,581 | 89,972 | 62,480 | 45,903 | 35,145 | 27,769 | 22,493 | 9,997 | 5,623 | 3,599 | 2,499 | 1,836 |
| 2.5 | 2,340,609 | 585,152 | 260,068 | 146,288 | 93,624 | 65,017 | 47,767 | 36,572 | 28,896 | 23,406 | 10,403 | 5,851 | 3,745 | 2,600 | 1,911 |
| 2.6 | 2,431,737 | 607,934 | 270,192 | 151,983 | 97,269 | 67,547 | 49,627 | 37,996 | 30,021 | 24,317 | 10,807 | 6,079 | 3,891 | 2,702 | 1,985 |
| 2.7 | 2,522,673 | 630,668 | 280,296 | 157,667 | 100,907 | 70,074 | 51,483 | 39,416 | 31,144 | 25,227 | 11,211 | 6,307 | 4,036 | 2,803 | 2,059 |
| 2.8 | 2,613,416 | 653,354 | 290,380 | 163,339 | 104,537 | 72,595 | 53,335 | 40,834 | 32,264 | 26,134 | 11,615 | 6,534 | 4,181 | 2,904 | 2,133 |
| 2.9 | 2,703,968 | 675,992 | 300,440 | 168,998 | 108,159 | 75,110 | 55,183 | 42,249 | 33,382 | 27,039 | 12,017 | 6,760 | 4,326 | 3,004 | 2,207 |
| 3.0 | 2,794,328 | 698,582 | 310,480 | 174,645 | 111,773 | 77,620 | 57,026 | 43,661 | 34,497 | 27,943 | 12,419 | 6,986 | 4,471 | 3,105 | 2,281 |
| 3.1 | 2,884,495 | 721,124 | 320,499 | 180,281 | 115,380 | 80,125 | 58,867 | 45,070 | 35,611 | 28,845 | 12,820 | 7,211 | 4,615 | 3,205 | 2,355 |
| 3.2 | 2,974,470 | 743,618 | 330,496 | 185,904 | 118,979 | 82,623 | 60,702 | 46,476 | 36,721 | 29,745 | 13,220 | 7,436 | 4,759 | 3,305 | 2,428 |
| 3.3 | 3,064,254 | 766,063 | 340,471 | 191,516 | 122,570 | 85,118 | 62,535 | 47,878 | 37,830 | 30,642 | 13,619 | 7,660 | 4,903 | 3,404 | 2,501 |
| 3.4 | 3,153,845 | 788,461 | 350,427 | 197,115 | 126,154 | 87,607 | 64,364 | 49,278 | 38,936 | 31,538 | 14,017 | 7,884 | 5,046 | 3,504 | 2,574 |
| 3.5 | 3,243,244 | 810,811 | 360,360 | 202,703 | 129,730 | 90,089 | 66,188 | 50,675 | 40,040 | 32,432 | 14,414 | 8,108 | 5,189 | 3,603 | 2,647 |
| 3.6 | 3,332,452 | 833,113 | 370,271 | 208,278 | 133,298 | 92,568 | 68,009 | 52,069 | 41,141 | 33,325 | 14,811 | 8,331 | 5,332 | 3,702 | 2,720 |
| 3.7 | 3,421,467 | 855,367 | 380,163 | 213,842 | 136,859 | 95,041 | 69,825 | 53,460 | 42,240 | 34,214 | 15,207 | 8,554 | 5,474 | 3,801 | 2,793 |
| 3.8 | 3,510,290 | 877,572 | 390,031 | 219,393 | 140,412 | 97,507 | 71,638 | 54,848 | 43,336 | 35,103 | 15,601 | 8,776 | 5,616 | 3,900 | 2,865 |
| 3.9 | 3,598,921 | 899,730 | 399,878 | 224,932 | 143,957 | 99,969 | 73,446 | 56,233 | 44,430 | 35,989 | 15,995 | 8,997 | 5,758 | 3,998 | 2,938 |
| 4.0 | 3,687,360 | 921,840 | 409,706 | 230,460 | 147,494 | 102,426 | 75,252 | 57,615 | 45,522 | 36,874 | 16,388 | 9,218 | 5,900 | 4,097 | 3,010 |

study. Seasonal variations in mailing response must also be considered. When a chart of seasonal variations exists, it can be used to weight the figures.

**Problem: high testing costs**

All astute direct marketers today follow the procedure of testing the most-recent buyer names first. They know, with the very rarest of exceptions, that if most-recent buyers don't reach a certain quota, the chances of older names working are remote.

But with all of the sophisticated techniques available today (regression analysis included), direct marketers still face fantastically high testing costs.

Many direct marketers live with three successful list tests out of every ten. This means, for example, that if only 20 lists are tested at a minimum quantity of 5,000 each, at say $175 per thousand in the mail, test costs would be $17,500. And only six of the 20 tests would show "life" under a .300 batting average. The test expense would not end there, however, because continuation tests would be required to confirm test indications.

There's got to be a better way at a lower cost to determine the potential pull of a mailing list. It remains for the list fraternity to find that better way. Some experimentation has been done with testing a list by telephone and correlating the phone response to what can be expected by mail. This is one possibility.

I have another (unproved) theory for a procedure that would cut testing costs about 80 percent. With this procedure, instead of actually mailing to each test list, you'd simply compare the test list with your customer list to determine what percentage of the outside list names are already on your customer list. If the correlation is high (indicating a profile similar to the customer list), the outside list would qualify for a test mailing; a low match rate would indicate that the outside list does not qualify for mailing. The only cost for nonqualifying lists would be list cost, saving all other test mailing costs. I'm waiting for someone to prove the theory.

**Market segmentation**

Market segmentation has long been recognized as a key to maximizing response in relation to promotion expenditures. It is through understanding market segments and developing and applying techniques for isolating the segments that maximizing is reached.

An acknowledged authority on the theories and techniques of market segmentation is Martin Baier, vice-president of marketing of Old American Insurance Company of Kansas City, Missouri. His thoughts and applications merit deep study.

According to Mr. Baier, the increasing complexity of direct marketing activities has brought about an increasing need for segmentation of the heterogeneous total market into smaller and more homogeneous units. Such segmentation can involve either specific, qualified mail response lists or clusters within generally larger compiled lists. Market segmentation frequently has been geographic—by region, state, county, or metropolitan area. Sometimes it has been demographic—by sex, age, marital status, or occupation. Recently it has been psychographic—by habits, attitudes, life styles or behavior patterns of consumers.

To be truly meaningful, too, the resultant market segments should constitute a unit the physical definition of which is not only readily identifiable geographically, but is also one in which its homogeneity enables us to measure it in economic and cultural as well as demographic and psychographic terms.

**Environmental influences**

People with like interests tend to cluster. Their behavior, including their buying habits and attitudes, tends to be influenced by their environment of which, in effect, they themselves are a part. So the need is to be able (a) to identify areas where such groupings occur, (b) to classify them in terms of economic potential, and (c) to measure their cultural pattern—all the effects of their environments on their buying behavior—or, to sum it up in one term, to measure them *culturologically*. Then, once the marketer has determined the common denominator, or *tone*, of one or more of these cultural units in relation to his product, he can apply this indicator to all other units, use it to locate those units with similar characteristics, and expect the same kind of reactions to his marketing moves.

Contrary to general economic theory, purchase decisions are not so much dependent on income as on the buyer's perception of his relative position in his environment or that to which he aspires. The behavior of consumers must thus be related to their environment—to select reference groups, social classes, and cultural influences. Their *ability to buy* must be distinguished from their *proneness to buy*. Such distinctions enable direct marketers to define their best prospects, seek them out, establish sales potentials, predict consumer behavior, and consider penetration in relation to potential in a manner that can be statistically evaluated.

The basic concept of human ecology—that man's behavior relates to environmental influences—tells us that a household with an $8,000 annual income located in an area where the mean household income is $10,000 is prone to emulate the $10,000 level. The reverse also is true—a $12,000 household tends to behave like its $10,000 neighbors. It is this tendency that contributes to the homogeneity of behavior within an area, even though absolute characteristics among individual households vary. Discretionary purchases by households under such circumstances are dependent not simply on the *ability* to buy but also on the *proneness* to buy.

Thorstein Veblen's concept of conspicuous consumption, with its emphasis on the social character of consumption decisions and the interdependence of consumer choices, has proved important and durable. As Veblen put it more than half a century ago, "The accepted standard of expenditure in the community or in the class to which a person belongs largely determines what his standard of living will be."

Many types of face-to-face reference groups exert strong influences on consumer decisions. Such groups include families, social clubs, work associates, church members, and, of course, neighbors. "Keeping up with the Joneses" helps to explain the marketing success that a prestigious magazine is reported to have had when it mailed a subscription offer to the next-door neighbors of its active subscribers. The essence of the invitation was on the order of "Your next-door neighbor reads *National Geographic*. Shouldn't you?" A similar marketing letter from an automobile manufacturer started out with "Have you noticed that new Rambler in your neighbor's driveway. . . ?" So-called referral selling—the use of a third party directly or indirectly to recommend a product or service—is a notable example of reference group influence. A consumer is inclined to respect the judgments of those with whom he associates.

A buyer is strongly influenced, too, by his social class or that to which he aspires, rather than by income alone. Social class has been seen by many as the most meaningful manner of market segmentation. Noting that income level alone does not determine social class, researchers point to such things as educational level and occupation as more important variables for identifying class membership. The beginning plumber and the young lawyer, for instance, may have comparable incomes, but they do not command the same prestige or social class membership.

## ZIP code areas as market segments

Because people with like interests *do* tend to cluster and because their purchase decisions are frequently influenced by their desire to emulate their friends, neighbors, and community innovators, ZIP code areas are now being used by many direct marketers to provide the means to identify meaningful market segments. The homogeneity of ZIP code areas also makes it possible to classify and qualify them in such a manner as to measure the effects of economic and cultural environment on buying behavior within these marketing units.

Generally, geographic units which have heretofore been used in segmenting markets have lacked *homogeneity* as well as ready *identity* with a consumer. The need has been for a marketing unit whose physical boundaries could be defined in terms that were economically meaningful and environmentally measurable. ZIP code areas fulfill the need on both counts.

An obvious convenience of these geographic units—setting them apart from commonly used units such as counties or metropolitan markets—is that each household and business within the unit is easily identifiable by the five-digit number assigned to it as part of its address. The first digit of the code identifies one of ten (0 through 9) geographical areas of the nation. The first three digits combined identify a major city or major distribution point (sectional center) within a state. The full five-digit ZIP code represents either an individual post office for a small town or rural area served from the sectional center or a specific delivery unit of area within a city.

The homogeneity of these units, of special interest for effective and efficient response marketing, results from the fact that each sectional center radiates from a transportation hub. This tends to reflect the economic profile and cultural environment of the area—key factors that in turn influence buying behavior. Within metropolitan areas, the units constitute neighborhood clusters.

This is not to say that there is not considerable spread among households within and between three-digit or five-digit ZIP code areas. There is substantial variation, just as there is among households within and between cities, towns, and counties. The marketer should be aware of this in weighing his relative need for three-digit versus five-digit units or unit groupings. The opportunities for measurement are desirable in either instance—owing, let us repeat, to the ready *identity* and *homogeneity* of ZIP code areas, coupled with a *convenience* heretofore lacking for defining geographic areas.

It is also well to keep in mind that, while we recognize the basic homogeneity of households within a ZIP code area, not all households have the same characteristics. Rather, it is a basic concept of human ecology that clusters of households tend to emulate each other, even though each household has different demographics. As was previously mentioned, both the $8,000 and $12,000 households behave like the households in which the mean household income of ZIP code areas is $10,000. It is the environment which is being measured, not the individual household.

At Old American Insurance Company, a unique data bank stores up to 103 bits of *manifest* (observed) data about each ZIP code area. This information is extracted from Bureau of the Census data as well as other sources. The data bank thus lists potential marketing units (ZIP code areas) in terms of their environmental characterisitics which, when combined into factors, provide the latent (underlying) dimensions of life style and are thus used to explain consumer behavior. These characterisitics (several of which need to be *indexed* to reflect local environment) include:

- Metropolitan type (urban, rural nonfarm, rural farm)
- Race (white, black, Indian, etc.)
- Nativity (foreign born, native of foreign parents, native)
- Origin of foreign born (by selected countries)
- Mother tongue (English, German, Spanish, etc.)
- Age (median)
- Marital status (married, widowed, etc.)
- Education (median years of school completed)
- Occupation (professional, managerial, craftsmen, etc.)
- Industry or work force (construction, manufacturing, etc.)
- Family size (mean)
- Owner-occupancy of residence
- Owner/renter valuation
- Residence structure (median)
- Income (family and individual)
- Automobile valuation (conspicuous consumption)
- Dwelling size (owner or renter)
- Dwelling type (single or multiple)
- Household equipment (dishwasher, freezer, etc.)
- Kitchen facilities
- Structure equipment (air conditioning, multibath, etc.)

**Exhibit 4.1. Life-style market segmentation by ZIP code areas: procedural flow charts.**

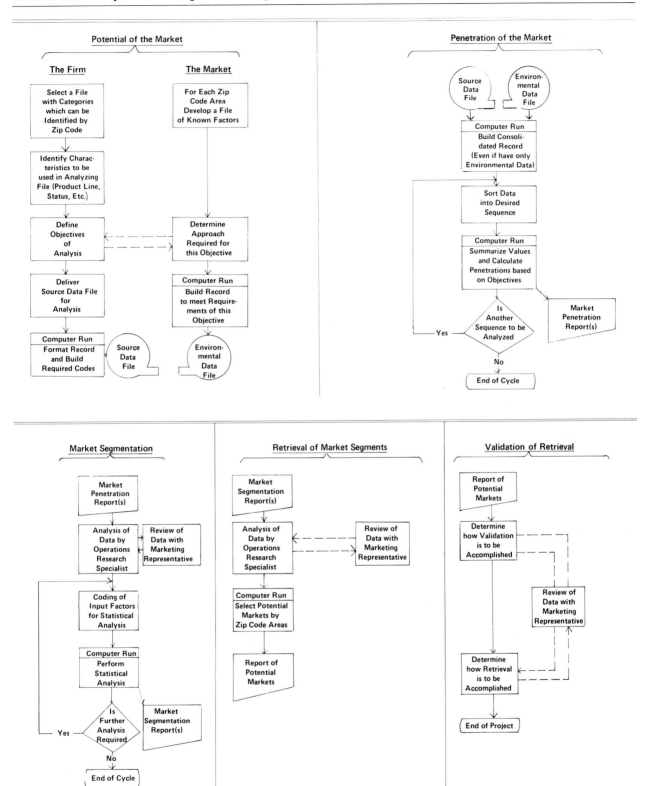

- Automobile ownership (single or multiple)
- Mobility
- Tenure of residence
- Telephone availability
- Direct access to living unit
- Poverty level

The ultimate objective of defining the total potential in this manner is to arrive at an array of market segments manageable in size to the needs of the individual marketer. The key results to be examined will be the number of households (or individual consumers) that qualify as potential buyers. Competitive, economic, and other uncontrollable conditions, of course, should receive due consideration as the total potential—divided into suitable segments—is evaluated.

A broad method for segmenting the total market for measurement, which many direct marketers will find usable and pertinent to their needs, is that of the metropolitan type—which separates central city, urban fringe, and rural areas. A suggested definition for such a division of the total market in terms of ZIP code areas by metropolitan type is this:

> *Central city:* Five-digit ZIP code areas within multicoded cities (those with postal carrier routes) which have a population of more than 50,000 and are within the boundaries of a standard metropolitan statistical area.
>
> *Urban fringe:* Five-digit ZIP code areas within multicoded cities which have a population of less than 50,000 as well as those areas which are not within multicoded cities—both categories being within standard metropolitan statistical areas.

This manner of grouping five-digit areas to evaluate a firm's total potential market results in a fairly even three-way split of all U.S. households. Note, however, that "urban fringe" does not necessarily mean "suburban." A suburban ZIP code area of more than 50,000 population within a standard metropolitan statistical area is regarded as a central city. The broad geographic environs of most standard metropolitan statistical areas put many suburbs as well as more remote small towns into the category of urban fringe.

Three case studies represent the typical value inherent in even such a broad analysis of sales within ZIP code areas when segmented as described above. All entail the direct sale of products or services by mail. Both the exposure of the offers to prospects and the tabulation of sales response were accurately recorded and analyzed. A comparison summary of the results of three cases follows:

| Type of Zip Code Area | Sales Response as a Percent of Mailed Offers (Central City Sales Response = 100) | | |
| --- | --- | --- | --- |
| | Case 1 | Case 2 | Case 3 |
| Central city ............... | 100 | 100 | 100 |
| Urban fringe .............. | 109 | 104 | 89 |
| Rural ................... | 136 | 138 | 142 |

Such division of the total market into segments is purely geographic. A more definitive method of segmenting markets for measurement is also somewhat more complex. It involves identifying, for clusters of five-digit ZIP code areas, a level of response to an individual marketing effort. The environmental characteristics of each ZIP code area (as independent variables) are then related to response (the dependent variable) for determining those characteristics which differentiate the best from lesser levels of response. Having thus defined the relevant factors affecting response, one must then identify other ZIP code areas with similar factors.

The environmental variables—up to 103 of them in the Old American model—are grouped through a statistical process called factor analysis. Using this technique, we can mathematically correlate the 103 environmental variables of the ZIP code areas of interest (many of which inevitably occur with others) with each other and thus condense them into a dozen or more uncorrelated factors, which are much more meaningful and manageable in subsequent analysis. One such factor, for example, may comprise several characteristics which manifest such factors as minimal education, below average income, largely unskilled occupations, low amounts of rent paid, low percentage of homeownership, high nonwhite population, and absence of telephones and household appliances.

Because each factor so defined appears to a greater or lesser degree within each five-digit ZIP code area of interest, these can then be regarded as independent variables to be correlated with penetration, the dependent variable, which is defined as a measure of marketing success in terms of either customers or response. We especially want to observe the *interactions* of the various factors within each individual ZIP code area, that is, a high level of one particular style factor in concert with a relatively low level of another factor.

**Penetration of the market**

The direct marketer, in measuring the penetration of his potential market (the dependent variable) and then searching for correlation with factors defined by environmental characteristics (independent variables), may want to catalog his current customers or measure his direct response within certain broader groupings. Such groupings may be made according to product lines or by degree of sales activity (recency/frequency/monetary). Within each of these subcategories, then, the individual marketer may look at his own penetration (in terms of customers or new buyers) as a percentage of total potential (in terms of households or potential buyers). He can then seek through statistical analysis to establish and explain the correlation between the varying degree of penetration and measurements of the environment within the ZIP code areas in which he now sells or hopes to sell.

Calculating penetration is a relatively simple arithmetical process. Within *clusters* of ZIP code areas, responses are related to mailings or customers are related to households, as follows:

| ZIP Code | Total Mailed | Total Responses | Percent Responses |
|---|---|---|---|
| A .............. | 5,793 | 60 | 1.04 |
| B .............. | 2,735 | 33 | 1.21 |
| C .............. | 6,731 | 138 | 2.05 |
| D ............. | 4,341 | 119 | 2.74 |

As a matter of practical fact, few direct marketers—even those who solicit on a very large scale—can evaluate individual five-digit ZIP code areas with any degree of statistical reliability. There just aren't enough observations within an individual ZIP code to minimize statistical variance at an acceptable level of confidence. For this reason, the Old American model for life style market segmentation employs the technique of *cluster analysis* to combine ZIP code areas which are comparable into large, more measureable clusters of these smaller market segments. Up to 22 characteristics are used in such clustering.

Our concern up to this point primarily has been measuring a firm's penetration of its potential market, that is, its marketing effectiveness in terms of ZIP code areas. When significant differences of penetration are observed, the need for explanation becomes apparent. Explanatory factors (obtained through another statistical technique, *factor analysis*) have been suggested either alone or in combination. Let's turn next to the measurement of the significance of penetration as against potential in terms of the chosen factors.

## Segmentation of the market

Once the direct marketer's most productive market segments have been identified (in terms of percentage penetration of the market) and classified (even so simply as by central city/urban fringe/rural types of areas, or perhaps by the firm's product lines), then qualification and explanatory measurement in terms of factors defining psychographic life styles are necessary. The validity of such measurement is directly related to the homogeneity of the marketing unit used. One reason measurement is needed is that it makes it possible to transfer marketing results—within units which have been productive—to other units where prior experience is lacking but where similar environmental characteristics are observed.

Our objective is to determine the degree of explanation between our factors (clusters of common environmental characteristics, i.e., the independent or explanatory variables) and our penetration percentage (the dependent variable). These coefficients are expressed in decimal form ranging from 0 to 1 (for positive correlation) to 0 to −1 (for negative correlation). In both instances, 1 (positive or negative) indicates perfect correlation and 0 indicates no correlation.

*Regression analysis*, in general, describes a functional (mathematical) relationship between one dependent and one or more independent variables. In our model, stepwise multivariate regression analysis is used. This consists of fitting a line to the observed points (penetration percentages related to potential) in such a way that the sum of the squares of the differences between the observed points and the values estimated by the regression line is minimized. (This technique is also known as the "least-squares" method.)

In using the stepwise analysis, we allow the independent variables (factors defining life style) to enter the regression in the order in which they most explain the penetration variations observed; that is, the more predictive (or explanatory) variable enters first and the least predictive enters last.

Even if the *process* isn't clearly understood, the *result can be* a rank ordering of ZIP code areas from the highest to the lowest *estimated* penetrations along with accumulated availabilities within ZIP code areas with similar factor definitions. Such rank ordering of relevant ZIP code areas on the basis of estimated penetration also permits visualization of the correlation of such ranking with the independent variables. Decide how big a market segment is needed and determine what the over-all penetration would be. Or, set a minimum marketing requirement and determine how big the market segment could be.

**Retrieval of market segments**

Unless the findings from these measurement and evaluation procedures can be applied in some sort of practical mechanism for retrieving the most desirable market segments for the individual marketer, the wisdom of the process can and should be questioned. A firm that sells its products largely through direct marketing has mailing lists of its customers and prospects which are entirely identified by five-digit ZIP codes. It is thus a relatively easy matter to select only those ZIP code areas that have the characteristics desired.

This model is not, of course, limited to direct marketing applications. A knowledge of market segments affording the individual firm its greatest potential for penetration is a prerequisite for any marketer. Such knowledge permits optimum location of dealer outlets, franchises, and salespeople as well as pinpoint distribution of direct mail or other promotional efforts.

A market segment, in our present sense, is a *cluster* of ZIP code areas with *factor* definitions relevant for the individual marketer. When these relevant characteristics have been identified, that segment must be retrieved in terms of ZIP code areas.

Of course, the system cuts across any known characteristics of the prospect as an individual such as age or sex. The process is additive, designed to improve marketing direction. There must be validation, to be sure—test marketing to confirm. This is because no warranties are ever expressed or implied in such a system as this. And it should be remembered that such scientific decision making is an aid to sound executive judgment, not a substitute for it!

**Alternative marketing units**

Certain mailers have found it beneficial to tighten up the geographic boundaries to find a more homogeneous marketing unit. When such smaller units are used, the statistical variance referred to earlier becomes even more severe. And, of course, the means of identifying such units within individual mailing lists is not nearly so universal as is the identification of ZIP code areas.

One alternative to the problem of identification is the use of census tracts. A census tract is a division of a standard metropolitan statistical area (which, in turn, is a grouping of counties) which averages 1,200 to 1,400 households. Census tracts are numerically designated within SMSAs and are outlined to encompass population segments with relatively uniform economic population segments with relatively uniform economic and social characteristics. At even a finer level than the census tract, we have block groups and enumeration districts.

Block groups are actually subdivisions of census tracts. As their name implies, these are combinations of contiguous city blocks and are identified by the first and third digit of the city block number. Each block group number is unique within a census tract. The average census tract has five block groups. The average block group has 200 to 250 residential families.

Enumeration districts are geographic units established and defined by the U.S. Census Bureau for all places outside tracted areas. Enumeration districts also consist of 200 to 250 households. These geographic units, being much smaller in size, are believed to be even more homogeneous.

Demographic information at the census tract, block group or enumeration district level is not as readily available as that for ZIP code areas. However, some of the larger list compilers have this information available for segmentation of their own lists. Also, it is possible to rent a tape containing the demographics of these smaller segments for use in your own mailings. One source of this information is the Zip-O-Data tape produced by Metro Mail.

**AID analysis**  Another analytic tool that can assist in segmenting the heterogeneous market into smaller and more homogeneous units is the AID (automatic interaction detector) program. AID analysis was developed at the University of Michigan for use in the social sciences. This program permits direct marketers to analyze numerous mailing list characteristics and determine which combinations are most relevant to future mailings.

In applying this technique to list segmentation, one finds that the point of each division is that which produces the greatest meaningful difference in percent response (or revenue per thousand pieces mailed) between the two ensuing subgroups. Division ceases when the sample size falls below a specified level or when the statistical significance of the difference between the subgroups that would be created is inadequate. The final subgroups are called "terminal groups." They can be defined in terms of individual ZIP code areas and characteristics and arrayed from high to low according to percent response or revenue per thousand pieces mailed.

Large list compilers such as R. L. Polk use a similar procedure referred to as TREE (total-factor response elaboration and evaluation) analysis for segmentation of their file. This statistical technique is also available through Yuan Liang Marketing Service, an independent direct mail research firm.

## Self-quiz

1. In addition to median age, name five other factors that are significant in establishing a list profile.

   a. _____

   b. _____

   c. _____

   d. _____

   e. _____

2. List the three types of mailing lists in order of expected response.

   a. _____

   b. _____

   c. _____

3. List five principal functions of a list broker.

   a. _____

   b. _____

   c. _____

   d. _____

   e. _____

4. Describe the principal functions of a list manager.

   _____

   _____

   _____

   _____

   _____

   _____

5. Define "merge and purge."

   _____

   _____

   _____

   _____

6. Historically, which is the best month, and which the poorest month, to mail?

   best   month:_____

   poorest  month:_____

7. In order to make probability scales practical, what are the three things you must know to determine the size of your test?

   a. _____

   b. _____

   c. _____

8. Define regression analysis.

   _____

   _____

9. Market segmentation can now be measured by psychographics. Define psychographics.

   _____

   _____

   _____

10. Why do ZIP code areas serve as an ideal means for identifying meaningful market segments?

    _____

    _____

    _____

11. Arrange the following in size order from largest to smallest. (census tract, ZIP code, block group)

    Largest  _____

    Smallest _____

12. Define "enumeration district."

    _____

    _____

    _____

## Pilot project

You are the advertising manager for a publisher of children's books. You have a new set of books for preschool children. You want to test in July to determine if you can mail large quantities in October.

Your assignment: With a total test budget sufficient to mail 50,000 pieces, set up a series of tests.

1. Would you design your tests around house lists, mail response lists, compiled lists, or all of these?

2. What quantity will you have to mail to each test segment with the following assumptions: (a) an anticipated response of 1 percent, (b) a 95 percent confidence level; (c) a margin of error of 20 percent?

3. Taking into consideration your recommended test quantities, would you attempt to rent test lists on a gross, net, or overage basis?

4. Which of the five factors that you supplied in self-quiz question one are most important when analyzing a list profile with regard to this mailing?

5. Would you order a "merge and purge" done?

6. If you were to include the Young Family Index birth list in your tests:

   a. Would you want to test by selected states or selected regions?

   b. Would you want to test by small towns or by large cities?

   c. Would you want to test by income group and, if so, which income groups?

   d. Would you want to test by Nielsen market areas?

   e. Would you want to test by first births, by multi-children families, or by both?

   f. Would you want to test by percentage of nonwhite population?

Note: Your total mailing budget of 50,000 pieces clearly limits the possibility of making all the tests you may want to make. Therefore the tests you do make should be those you consider most important.

# 5

**Where do you go first?**

The advertising pages of magazines are to the direct response advertiser what the retail outlet is to the manufacturer selling through the more traditional channels. A magazine that performs consistently well for a variety of direct response advertisers is like a store in a low-rent, high-traffic location. It's far more profitable than a store selling the same merchandise on the wrong side of town.

Such a magazine just seems to have an atmosphere that is more conducive to the mail response customer. The mail order shopping reader traffic is high in relation to the publication's cost per thousand. Magazines in this category (and this is by no means a complete list) are *National Enquirer*, *Parade*, and the mighty *TV Guide*. Women's publications also doing well for mail order advertisers are *Family Circle*, *Better Homes and Gardens*, *Ladies' Home Journal*, *Cosmopolitan*, *Woman's Day*, *Seventeen*, and *Redbook*. Men's publications include *Mechanix Illustrated*, *Moose*, *Playboy*, and *Penthouse*. (For a comprehensive list of magazines that provide a structured mail order atmosphere, see Table 5.1.)

But just as retail locations come into and go out of favor with each passing decade, so do the trends that determine which publications work well in the mail order marketplace at a particular time. For example, coming into favor right now are *Time*, *Newsweek*, *Family Circle*, and *Smithsonian*. In the '60s there was much greater interest in such publications as *McCall's*, *Ladies' Home Journal*, *House & Garden*, *House Beautiful*, and the *National Observer*.

And I can remember in the '50s looking to *Living for Young Homemakers*, *Harper's/Atlantic*, and *Saturday Review*—and the *Saturday Evening Post* could be counted on for good results.

There are some publications that one might assume at first glance to be just great for the mail order advertiser. But close examination of performance figures for many different advertisers in these publications causes a red flag to be raised for the direct marketing advertiser. Here are a few places to go right now at your own risk: *Reader's Digest*, *National Geographic*, *New York*, and the *New Yorker*. Some of these publications, though, have done well for high ticket items like collectibles.

## Table 5.1. Magazines with shopping advertising pages.

A. D. (Mail Order)
After Dark, The Magazine of Entertainment (Mail Order)
Air Progress (Mail Order)
All Outdoors (Mail Order)
Americana (Mail Order)
American Boating Illustrated (Marketplace)
American Legion Magazine, The (Legion Shopping Section; Mail Order)
Antique Trader Weekly, The (Antiques Directory)
Apartment Life (Mail Order)
Architectural Digest (Mail Order)
Argus (Argus Bazaar)
Army Times Military Group (Mail Order Market)
Astronomy (Astro-Mart)
Audubon (Mail Order)
Auto Racing Digest (Mail Order)
Autoweek (Mail Order)
Baseball Digest (Mail Order)
Basketball Digest (Mail Order)
Bestways (Bazaar)
Better Homes and Gardens (Mail Order)
Better Homes and Gardens Bedroom and Bath Decorating Ideas (Mail Order)
Better Homes and Gardens Christmas Ideas (Mail Order)
Better Homes and Gardens Furnishings and Decorating Ideas (Mail Order)
Better Homes and Gardens Garden Ideas and Outdoor Living (Grower and Mail Order)
Better Homes and Gardens Holiday Cooking & Entertainment Ideas (Mail Order)
Better Homes and Gardens Houseplants (Mail Order)
Better Homes and Gardens How to Grow Fruits and Vegetables (Mail Order)
Better Homes and Gardens 100's of Baking Ideas (Mail Order)
Better Homes and Gardens 100's of Needlework and Crafts Ideas (Mail Order)
Better Homes and Gardens Window and Wall Decorating Ideas (Mail Order)
Big Bike (Mail Order)
Big Eight, The (Mail Order)
Bike World (The Market Place)
Blair & Ketchum's Country Journal (Mail Order)
Bon Appetit (Mail Order)
Boy's Life (Mail Order)
Bride's (Mail Order)
Camera 35 (Spot Shopping)
Capper's Weekly (Arm Chair Shopping Center)
Car Craft (Mail Order)
Car and Driver (Mail Order)
Car and Driver Buyers Guide (Mail Order)
Cat Fancy (The Fancy Shopper)
Charlton Comics Group (Shop-By-Mail)
Chicago Tribune Magazine (Please Send Me)
Choppers Magazine (Mail Order)
Classic (Mail Order)
Columbia (Shopping Section)
Cosmopolitan (The Cosmopolitan Shopper)
Cycle (Mail Order)
Cycle Buyers Guide (Mail Order)
Decorating & Craft Ideas (Mail Order)
Dirt Bike (Mail Order)
Diversion (Mail Order)
Dog Fancy (The Barkin' Basement)
Dogs (Mail Order)
Down East (Mail Order)
Drag News (Mail Order)
Eagle Magazine (Eagle Easy Shopper)
Early American Life (Mail Order)
East/West Inroom Network (Mail Order)
Easyriders (Mail Order)
Elementary Electronics (Hobby Mart)
Elks Magazine, The (Elks Family Shopper)
Ellery Queen's Mystery Magazine (Mail Order)
Equus (Mail Order)

Esquire/Fortnightly (Talking Shop with Esquire)
Essence Magazine (Mail Order)
Family Circle (Everywoman's Shopping Circle)
Family Circle Great Ideas—Barbecue Book (Mail Order)
Family Circle Great Ideas—Christmas Helps (Mail Order)
Family Circle Great Ideas—Decorating Made Easy (Mail Order)
Family Circle Great Ideas—Fashions & Crafts (Mail Order)
Family Circle Great Ideas—One Dish Meals (Mail Order)
Family Food Garden, The (Mail Order)
Family Handyman (Mail Order)
Fate (Mail Order)
Federal Times (Times Shopper)
Field and Stream (Sportsman's Shopper)
Field & Stream Hunting Annual (Mail Order)
Fishing and Hunting News (Outdoor Outlet)
Fishing World (Mail Order)
Flower and Garden Magazine (Shopping with Ed & Betty Jackson)
Fly Fisherman Magazine (Mail Order)
Football Digest (Mail Order)
Formula (Mail Order)
Four Wheeler (Mail Order)
Gambling Times (Mail Order)
Genesis (Mail Order)
Glamour (Shop by Mail)
Golf Digest (Golfers Shopping Guide)
Golf Magazine (Mail Order)
Good Housekeeping (Mail Order)
Good Housekeeping Needlecraft (Mail Order)
Great Lakes Sportsman (Retail/Mail Order)
Hadassah Magazine (Shopping Mart)
Harper's/Atlantic/Natural History (Mail Order)
Harper's Bazaar (Shopping Bazaar)
Harvard Magazine (Mail Order)
Hockey Digest (Mail Order)
Holiday (Mail Order)
Holiday Inn Companion (Mail Order)
Homemaker Of The National Extension Homemakers Council, The (Gift Loft)
Horizon (Mail Order)
Horticulture (The Garden Shop)
Hot Rod Magazine (Mail Order)
Hot Rod Magazine's 4 Wheel & Off-Road (Mail Order)
Hounds and Hunting (Beagler's Shopping Guide)
House Beautiful (Window Shopping)
House Beautiful's Colonial Homes (Mail Order)
House Beautiful's Gardening and Outdoor Living (Mail Order)
House Beautiful's Home Decorating (Mail Order)
House & Garden (Shopping Around)
House and Garden Decorating Guide (Mail Order)
House & Garden Garden Guide (Mail Order)
House & Garden Guide To American Tradition (Mail Order)
Houston Home & Garden (Town Shopper and How To Shopper)
Human Behavior (Mail Order)
Hunting (Mail Order)
I Am (Mail Order)
Kitchen and Bath Improvements (Mail Order)
KMR Women's Group (Mail Order)
Ladies' Home Journal (Journal Store)
Ladies Home Journal Needle & Craft (Mail Order)
Lady's Circle (Shopping Section)
Laufer Youth Publications (Mail Order)
Los Angeles Times Home Magazine (Specialty Shopping)
Mademoiselle (Shop Here Department)
Marvel Comic Group (Mail Order)
McCall's Needlework & Crafts (Gifts and Things)

Mechanix Illustrated (Mail Order)
Mechanix Illustrated Home Improvements You Can Do (Mail Order)
Michigan-Out-Ot-Doors (Trading Post)
Midnight (Mail Order)
Minicycle/BMX Action (Mail Order)
Mobile Living (Mail Order)
Model Railroader (Mail Order)
Modern Bride (Mail Order)
Modern Cycle (Mail Order)
Modern Photography (Mail Order)
Moneysworth (Mail Order)
Montgomery Ward Auto Club News (Mail Order)
Moose Magazine (Moose Home Shopper)
Motocross Action (Mail Order)
Motorcycle Weekly (Mail Order)
Motorcyclist Magazine (Mail Order)
Motorhome Life (Mobile Bazaar)
Motorsports Weekly (Mail Order)
Motor Trend (Mail Order)
Ms. (Mail Order)
National Enquirer (Mail Order)
National Observer (Mail Order)
Natural History (Mail Order)
New England Guide, The (The Gift Page)
New England Sportsman (Retail/Mail Order)
New Republic, The (Mail Order)
New York Times Magazine (Mail Order Marketplace)
Nuestro (Mail Order)
Off-Road (Mail Order)
Ohio Magazine (Mail Order)
101 Home Plans (Mail Order)
1,001 Decorating Ideas (Mail Order and Shopping Section)
Organic Gardening and Farming (Mail Order)
O.R.V. (Mail Order)
Oui (Mail Order)
Our Sunday Visitor (Mail Order)
Outdoor Life (Mail Order)
Palm Springs Life (Shopper's Bazaar)
Parents' Magazine (Shopping Scout)
Penthouse Forum (Mail Order)
Petersen's Photographic Magazine (Mail Order)
Pickup, Van & 4WD (Mail Order)
Pizzazz (Mail Order)
Plants Alive (Garden Center)
Playboy (Mail Order)
Playgirl (Shop by Mail)
Popular Ceramics (Marketplace)
Popular Cycling (Mail Order)
Popular Electronics (Mail Order)
Popular Gardening Indoors (Superthumb Shopping Guide)
Popular Hot Rodding Magazine (Mail Order)
Popular Mechanics (Bargain Hunters)
Popular Photography (Photographic Market Place, Mail Order)
Popular Science (Mail Order)
Presbyterian Survey (Mail Order)
Pro Football Weekly (Mail Order)
Pro Quarterback (Mail Order)
Racquet Club (Classified and Business Directory)
Radio Electronics (Mail Order)
Ramada Reflections (Mail Order)
Reader's Digest, The International Editions, Norwegian (Hilde Kjopetips)
Redbook Magazine (Tops in the Shops)
Retirement Living (Mail Order)
Rider (Mail Order)
Road Test (Mail Order)
Road & Track (Mail Order)
Road & Track's Buyers Guide (Mail Order)
Rod Action (Mail Order)
Rona Barrett Publications (Mail Order)
Rotarian (Sale by Mail Section)
Runner's World (The Market Place)
Safari (Mail Order)
Saturday Evening Post (Shoppers Section)
Saturday Review (Book Mail Order)
Science Digest (Mail Order)
Sea (Mail Order)
Signature (Mail Order)
Skateboard World (Mail Order)

Ski (Ski Shop Section)
Snowmobile News (Mail Order)
Soccer Digest (Mail Order)
Southern Living (Shopper)
Soap Opera Digest (Mail Order)
Spinning Wheel (Antiques Buy-Ways)
Sport Flying (Mail Order)
Sports Afield (Sportsman's Bargain Counter)
Sports Afield Sportsman's Magazine Network (Mail Order)
Street Chopper (Mail Order)
Street Machine (Mail Order)
Street Rodder (Mail Order)
Sunset Christmas Ideas and Answers (Christmas Shopping Center, Christmas Needlework and Crafts Center, Holiday Food Center)
Sunset Joy of Gardening (Special Garden Center)
Sunset Magazine (Shopping Directory)
Super Stock & Drag Illustrated (Mail Order)
'Teen (Mail Order)
Tennis (Shopping Guide)
Texas Outdoor Guide (Texas Sportsman Shopping Mart)
Today's Homes—Plans & Ideas (Mail Order)
Town and Country (Mail Order)
Trailer Boats (Mail Order)
Trailer Life (Mobile Bazaar)
Trails-A-Way (Mail Order)
Truckin' (Mail Order)
Van World (Mail Order)
V.F.W. Magazine (Mail Order)
Western Horseman (Shopper's Corral)
Westways (Mail Order)
Woman's Day (Shopper's Showcase)
Woman's Day Apartment Living (Mail Order)
Woman's Day Beautiful Holiday Handmades (Mail Order)
Woman's Day Best Ideas for Christmas (Mail Order)
Woman's Day Christmas Ideas for Children (Mail Order)
Woman's Day Decorating Guide (Mail Order)
Woman's Day Granny Squares (Mail Order)
Woman's Day Great Holiday Baking Ideas (Mail Order)
Woman's Day Hair Style & Beauty Ideas (Mail Order)
Woman's Day Holiday Party Entertaining (Mail Order)
Woman's Day Home Decorating Ideas (Mail Order)
Woman's Day Kitchen & Bath Guide (Mail Order)
Woman's Day Knit & Stitch (Mail Order)
Woman's Day Needlework and Handicraft Ideas (Mail Order)
Woman's Day 101 Gardening and Outdoor Ideas (Mail Order)
Woman's Day 101 Sweaters You Can Knit & Crochet (Mail Order)
Woman's Day 101 Ways to Lose Weight and Stay Healthy (Mail Order)
Woman's Day 101 Ways to Love, Grow and Care for House Plants (Mail Order)
Woman's Day Outdoor Entertaining (Mail Order)
Woman's Day Remodeling Ideas (Mail Order)
Woman's Day Simply Delicious Meals in Minutes (Mail Order)
Woman's Day Today's Woman Diet & Exercise Guide (Mail Order)
Woman's Day Today's Woman House Plants (Mail Order)
Woman's Day Vegetable Gardening & Home Grown Fruits (Mail Order)
Woodall's Trailer & RV Travel (Mail Order)
Workbasket (Workbasket Shopper)
Workbench (Shopping With Bob Edwards)
World Tennis (Mail Order)
Yankee (Mail Order)

**Regional editions: When is the part bigger than the whole?**

For the buyer of space in magazines today, most publications with circulations of over 1.5 million offer the opportunity to buy a regional portion of the national circulation. But it was not always so.

Although it has been said that the *New Yorker* was the first to publish sectional or regional editions in 1929, it wasn't until the late 1950s that major magazines began selling regional space to all advertisers, not just to those who had distribution limited to a particular section of the circulation area.

The availability of regional editions for everyone opened important opportunities to the mail order advertiser. Here are a few of the things you can do with regional buys:

1. You don't have to invest in the full national cost of a publication to get some indication of its effectiveness for your proposition. In some cases, such as *Time* or *TV Guide*, by running in a single edition you can determine relative response with an investment 20 percent less than what it costs to make a national buy.

2. Some regions traditionally pull better than others for the mail order advertiser. For many mail order products or services, nothing does better than the West Coast or worse than the New England region. You can select the best response area for your particular proposition.

   Remember, in most publications you will be paying a premium for the privilege of buying partial circulation. If you are testing a publication, putting your advertising message in the better-pulling region can offset much of this premium charge.

3. Availability of regional editions makes possible multiple copy testing in a single issue of a publication. Some magazines offer A/B split-run copy testing in each of the regional editions published. For example, in *TV Guide*, you can test one piece of copy against your control in one edition, another against your control in a second edition, another against your control in a third, and so on. As a result, you can learn as much about different pieces of copy in a single issue of one publication as you could discover in several national A/B copy splits in the same publication over a time span of two years or more.

4. When testing regionally, don't make the mistake of testing too small a circulation quantity. It is essential that you test a large enough circulation segment to provide readable results that can be projected accurately for still larger circulations.

Warning: Buying regional space is not all fun and games. You will have to pay for the privilege in a number of ways. As mentioned, regional space costs more. How much more? You can get an idea of what to expect from these representative examples: *Woman's Day* from 19 to 194 percent; *Time* from 7 to 183 percent; *Popular Science* from 33 to 69 percent; *TV Guide* from 10 to 219 percent; and *Reader's Digest* from 62 to 213 percent.

The minimum and maximum figures relate to the number and circulation size of regions you may be buying for any one insertion.

Another factor to keep in mind is the relatively poor position regional ads receive. The regional sections usually appear far back in the magazine or in a "well" or signature of several consecutive pages of advertising with no editorial matter to catch the reader. As you will see later in our discussion of position placement, the poor location of an ad in a magazine can depress results as much as 50 percent below what the same advertisement would pull if it were in the first few pages of the same publication. If you are using regional space for testing, be certain to factor this into your evaluation.

An example of how various factors must be weighed in utilizing regional circulation for test purposes follows.

## Regional test schedule for ABC School of Design

*Redbook*

| | |
|---|---|
| Space: | Full-page four-color insert |
| Position: | Second card position |
| Issue: | May 1978 |
| Space cost: | $11,290 (printing cost not included) |
| Editions used: | National newsstand circulation (1 million) (22.5 percent of total circulation) |
| Regional premium: | 65 percent |

*Family Circle*

| | |
|---|---|
| Space: | Full-page four-color insert |
| Position: | Back of main editorial (regional forms) |
| Issue: | June 1978 |
| Space cost: | $2,894 (printing cost not included) |
| Editions used: | Los Angeles (595,000) San Francisco (386,000) |
| Total test circulation: | 981,000 (12.9 percent of total circulation) |
| Regional premium: | None. This publication offers a special prorated test rate for full-page inserts. |

Since full-page four-color inserts have been extremely profitable for some of the larger mail order advertisers, this size unit was tested for the ABC School of Design to see if such inserts could bring in a lower lead cost than obtained from a black-and-white page and card.

Because women's publications are the most successful media for this advertiser, the school went to two that offered the mechanical capabilities for regional testing of such an insert. Although May and June are not prime mail order months, it was necessary to test then in order to allow turnaround time for the next season's scheduling. Therefore, the following factors would have to be taken into consideration in projecting test results to learn whether this unit would be successful in prime mail order months with full circulation: (1) regional premium, (2) month of insertion, (3) position in book, and (4) relative value of specific media.

When planning your direct marketing media schedule, think about the media universe the way you think about the view of the sky in the evening. If you have no familiarity with the stars, the sky appears to be a jumble of blinking lights with no apparent relationship. But as you begin to study the heavens, you are soon able to pick out clusters of stars which have a relationship to one another in constellations.

You will recognize the stars that make up the Big Dipper in Ursa Major, the Hunter, the Swan, the Bull, and other familiar constellations. If you were to go on to become a professional astronomer, you would eventually recognize 89 distinctly different groups. Once you know the various constellations, a star within a particular grouping inevitably leads your eye to the other related stars.

The magazine universe is no different. There are nearly 400 consumer magazines published with circulations of 100,000 or more. The first step in approaching this vast list is to sort out the universe of magazines into categories. Although this process is somewhat arbitrary, and different experts may not agree entirely as to which magazines fall into which category, we are going to set down a chart of the major publications that you can use

**Table 5.2. Basic consumer magazine categories.**

| Demographic | Category | Sample Publications |
|---|---|---|
| Dual audience | General editorial/ entertainment | Grit, National Enquirer, National Geographic, New York Times Magazine Section, Parade, People, Reader's Digest, TV Guide |
| | News | Time, Newsweek, Sports Illustrated, U.S. News & World Report |
| | Special Interest | Architectural Digest, Business Week, Elks, Foreign Affairs, Hi Fidelity, Modern Photography, Natural History, Ski, Travel & Leisure, Wall St. Journal, Yankee |
| Women | General/service/ shelter (home service) | Better Homes & Gardens, Cosmopolitan, Ebony, Family Circle, Good Housekeeping, House Beautiful, House & Garden, Ladies' Home Journal, McCall's, Redbook, Sunset, Woman's Day |
| | Fashion | Glamour, Harper's Bazaar, Mademoiselle, Vogue |
| | Special interest | Brides, MacFadden's Women's Group, McCall's Needlework & Crafts, Parents |
| Men | General/entertain- ment/fashion | Esquire, Gentlemen's Quarterly, Penthouse, Playboy |
| | Special Interest | Cars, Field & Stream, Mechanix Illustrated, Outdoor Life, Popular Mechanics, Popular Science, Road & Track, Sports Afield |
| Youth | Male | Boy's Life |
| | Female | American Girl, Teen |
| | Dual audience | Exploring, Scholastic Magazines |

like a chart of the skies to map out particular magazine groupings. Once you begin to think of magazines as forming logical groupings within the total magazine universe, you can begin to determine the groupings offering the most likely marketplace for your product or proposition. Table 5.2 is a basic magazine category chart and lists some of the publications currently available for the direct response advertiser.

Within each category there are usually one or more publications that perform particularly well for the direct response advertiser at a lower cost than other publications in the group. We call those magazines the pilot publications for the group. If you use the pilot publications and they produce an acceptable cost per response, you can then proceed to explore the possibility of adding other magazines in that category to your media schedule.

Here is an indication of how women's and shelter publications were used as pilots in a test schedule for Science Research Associates' "Greenhouse" promotion. A logical expansion to other publications within the same categories followed based on the results of the initial tests.

### Science Research Associates Greenhouse promotion

|        | Date           | Type of ad              | Area     | Magazine                |
|--------|----------------|-------------------------|----------|-------------------------|
| Fall   | Sept., 1977    | Full-page insert        | Regional | Redbook                 |
|        | Sept. 20, 1977 | Full-page insert        | Regional | Family Circle           |
| Spring | April 24, 1977 | Full-page insert        | National | Family Circle           |
|        | June 19, 1978  | Full-page insert        | Regional | Woman's Day             |
|        | April, 1978    | Full-page insert        | Regional | Good Housekeeping       |
|        | June, 1978     | Full-page insert        | Regional | Better Homes & Gardens  |
|        |                | Four-color page and card| Regional | Better Homes & Gardens  |
|        |                | Four-color page and card| Regional | Better Homes & Gardens  |
|        | May, 1978      | Four-color page and card| Regional | Sunset                  |
|        | May, 1978      | Four-color page and card| Regional | Southern Living         |

In selecting the pilot publications in a category, keep in mind that you are not dealing with a static situation. As indicated earlier, a publication's mail order advertising viability changes from year to year, and what is a bellwether publication this season may not be the one to use next year. What is important is that you check out your own experience and the experience of others in determining the best places to advertise first in each category, and the next best, and the next best, and so on.

Think of your media buying program as an ever-widening circle, as illustrated in Exhibit 5.1. At the center is a nucleus of pilot publications. Each successively larger ring would include reruns in all profitable pilot publications plus new test books. In the same way, you can expand from campaign

**Exhibit 5.1.
Circle approach
to media selection**

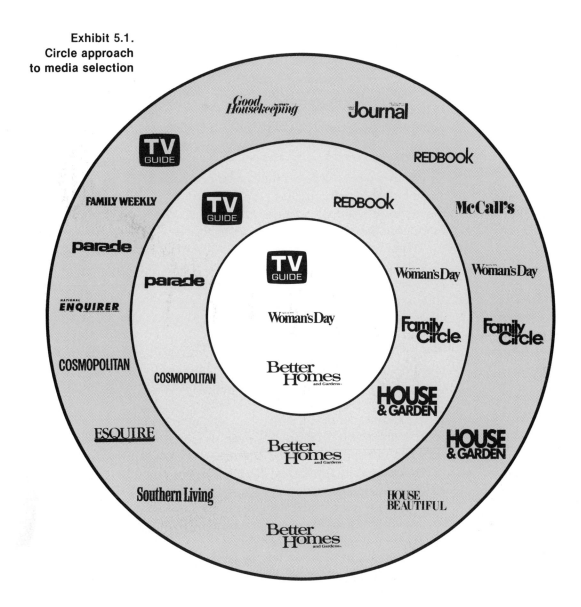

to campaign to cover wider levels of the various media categories until you have reached the widest possible universe.

**Bind-in cards: the big guns of print media advertising**

Today's young media buyer cannot remember a time when preprinted insert cards were not part of the world of print media advertising. It must appear to newcomers to print media advertising that insert cards crop up naturally in publications like weeds in suburban lawns. But it was not always so. Insert cards began to appear in the late 1950s, and magazines at first were slow to accept this radical innovation.

What makes the insert card so commonplace today was the eventual realization that the considerable investment in printing, binding, and space more than paid for itself if the advertiser's goal was getting direct responses from the insertion.

The reason for the success of the insert card is self-evident. Pick up a magazine, thumb through its pages, and see for yourself how effectively the bound-in cards flag down the reader. Each time someone picks up the publication, there is the insert card pointing to your message. Another reason is the ease with which the reader can respond. The business reply card eliminates the trouble of addressing an envelope, providing a stamp, and so on.

Before the development of the insert card, the third and fourth covers of a magazine were the prime mail order positions and were sold at a premium. The bind-in insert card has created a world in which three, four, five, or more direct response advertisers can all have the position impact once reserved for the cover advertisers alone.

When you go to purchase space for a page and an accompanying insert card, you must face the fact that the best things in life are not free. Insert card advertising costs more. You must pay a space charge for the page and the card and sometimes a separate binding charge, and you must then add in the cost of printing the cards. How much you pay, of course, depends on the individual publication, the size of the card, and a number of other factors. There is no rule of thumb to follow in estimating the additional cost for an insert card. Space charges alone for a standard business reply card can be as little as 40 percent of the black-and-white page plus additional binding charges.

When the cost of the insert unit adds up to as much as four times the cost of an ordinary black-and-white page, you will have to receive four times the response to justify the added expense.

For most direct response advertisers, the response is likely to be six to eight times as great when pulling for an order and as much as six to eight times as great in pulling for inquiries. As a result, you can expect to cut your cost per response by 50 percent or more with an insert card as opposed to an ordinary on-page coupon ad.

**Magazine advertising response pattern: What do these early results mean?**

There is a remarkable similarity from one insertion to another in the rate of response over time for most magazines. Monthly publications generally have a similar pattern for the rate of response from week to week. However, the pattern of response for publications in different categories can vary. For example, a mass circulation weekly magazine (*TV Guide* or *Parade*) will pull a higher percentage of the total response in the first few weeks than a shelter book (such as *House & Garden* or *Better Homes & Gardens*). A shelter book has a slower response curve but keeps pulling for a long period of time because it is kept much longer and is not so short lived as a mass circulation magazine.

Also, subscription circulation will pull faster than newsstand circulation. Subscribers usually receive their copies within a few days while newsstand sales are spread out over an entire month. Consequently the response pattern is spread out as well.

If you are running an ad calling for direct response from a monthly magazine, here is a general guide to the likely response flow:

After the first week . . . . . . . .    3-7%
After the second week . . . . . .    20-25%
After the third week . . . . . . .    40-45%

After one month . . . . . . . . . .    50-55%
After two months . . . . . . . . .    75-85%
After three months . . . . . . . .    85-92%
After four months . . . . . . . .    92-95%

From a weekly publication, such as *Time* or *TV Guide*, the curve is entirely different; 50 percent of your response usually comes in the first two weeks.

These expectations, of course, represent the average of many hundreds of response curves for different propositions. You may see variations up or down from the classic curve for any single insertion.

As a general rule for monthlies, you can expect to project the final results within 10 percent accuracy after the third week of counting responses. If you are new to the business, give yourself the experience of entering daily result counts by hand for dozens of ads. Before long you will develop an instinct for projecting how an ad for your particular proposition is doing within the first ten days of measured response.

**Timing and frequency: When should you run? How often should you go back?**

Once you determine where you want to run, timing and frequency are the two crucial factors in putting together an effective print schedule.

Of course, there are some propositions that have a time of the year when they will do best, e.g., novelty items are likely to be purchased in October and November or even as early as late September for Christmas gifts. But for the nonseasonal items, you can look forward to two major print advertising seasons for direct response.

The first and by far the most productive for most propositions is the winter season, which begins with the January issue and runs through the February and March issues. The second season begins with the August issue and runs through the November issue.

The best winter months for most people are January and February. The best fall months are October and November. For schools and book continuity propositions, September frequently does as well or better.

If you have a nonseasonal item and you want to do your initial test at the best possible time, use a February issue with a January sale date or a January issue with a late December or early January sale date of whatever publication makes the most sense for your proposition.

How much of a factor is the particular month in which an ad appears? It could make a difference of 40 percent or even more. Here is an example of what the direct response advertiser may expect to experience during the year if the cost per response (CPR) in February were $2: January, $2.05; February, $2; March, $2.20; April, $2.50; May, $2.60; June, $2.80; July, $2.60; August, $2.40; September, $2.60; October, $2.20; November, $2.20; December, $2.40

These hypothetical relative costs are based on the assumption that the insertion is run one time in any one of the 12 issues of a monthly publication. But, of course, if you are successful you will want to run your copy more than once. So now we are faced with the other crucial question: What will various rates of frequency do to your response? Should you run once a year? Twice? Three times? Or every other month?

The frequency factor is more difficult to formulate than the timing factor. Optimum frequency cannot be generalized for print media advertising. Some propositions can be run month after month in a publication and show very little difference in cost per response. At one time, Doubleday & Company had worked out optimum frequency curves for some of its book club ads that required a 24-month hiatus between insertions.

How, then, do you go about determining ideal frequency of insertions? Try this procedure. The first time your copy appears in a publication, run it at the most likely time of the year for your special appeal. If you have a nonseasonal proposition, use January or February issues.

If the cost per response is in an acceptable range or up to 20 percent better than expected, wait six months and follow with a second insertion. If that insertion produces results within an acceptable range, you probably are a twice-a-year advertiser.

If the first insertion pulls well over 20 percent better than the planned order margin, turn around and repeat within a three or four-month period.

If the response to the test insertion in January or February was marginal, it usually makes sense to wait a full year before returning for another try in that publication.

The best gauge of how quickly you can run the next insertion aimed at the same magazine audience is the strength of the response from the last insertion. What you are reading in the results is a measurement of the saturation factor as it relates to that portion of the circulation that is interested in your selling message.

Of course, like all the other factors that affect response, frequency does not operate in a vacuum. The offer of a particularly advantageous position in a particular month or a breakthrough to better results with improved copy can lead you to set aside whatever carefully worked out frequency you had adopted earlier.

**Determining proper ad size: How much is too much?**

A crucial factor in obtaining an acceptable cost per response is the size of the advertising unit you select. Ordinarily, the bigger the ad the better job the creative people can do in presenting the selling message. But there is one catch. Advertising space costs money. And the more you spend, the greater the response you need to get your money back.

What you want to find is the most efficient size for your particular proposition and for the copy approach you have chosen. Just as with frequency, there is no simple rule of thumb here.

Generally speaking, advertising for leads or prospects or to gain inquiries requires less advertising space than copy that is pulling for orders. Many companies seeking inquiries or running a lead item to get names for catalog follow-up make use of advertising units of less than one column. Only a handful of companies looking for prospects can make effective use of full-page space. Going one step further and using a page and insert card to pull for leads runs the risk of being too effective. This unit can bring in inquiries at very low cost, but there is always the danger that the quality would be very poor. Find out at your own peril.

For example, if you use a black-and-white page with a tear-off coupon that generates leads at $5 each and that convert at a 10 percent rate, then your advertising cost per sale is $50. Take the same insertion and place it as a page and insert card, and the cost per response may be as low as $3. If the conversion rate held up at 10 percent, the advertising cost per sale would be only $30. But it is more likely that the advertiser would experience a sharp conversion rate drop to perhaps 5 percent, with a resultant $60 cost per sale plus the cost of processing the additional leads.

When a direct sale or a future commitment to buy is sought, the dynamics usually are different from those when inquiries are sought. As a general rule, the higher the unit of sale or dollar volume commitment, the larger the unit of space that can be afforded, right up to the double page spread with insert card. However, there are a number of additional factors to be considered as well:

1.  The nature of the product presentation may inherently require a particular space unit. For example, in record club and book club advertising, experience has shown that a maximum number of books and records should be displayed for best results. As a consequence, many of these clubs run a two-page spread as their standard ad unit. And in a small-size publication such as *TV Guide*, they may take six or even eight pages to display the proper number of books and records.

2.  Some propositions, such as Time-Life Books in the continuity bookselling field, require four-color advertising in order to present the beautiful color illustrations which are an important feature of the product being sold.

3.  Usually full-page ads appear at the front of a publication and small-space ads at the back. So going to a full-page unit is often related to the benefits you can expect from a premium, front-of-book position.

4.  If you are successful with a single-page ad with coupon, test using an insert card before you try to add a second page. If the page and insert card work for you, give the spread and card a try.

5.  Most mail order advertising falls into one of three size categories: (a) the spectacular unit—anything from the page and standard card insert to the four-page preprinted insert; (b) the single full-page unit; and (c) the small-space unit less than one column in size.

The awkward sizes in pulling for an order appear to be the one-column and two-column units. These inserts seldom work better than their big-brother pages or little-sister 56-line, 42-line, and 21-line units, although a "square third" (2 columns by 70 lines) can be a very efficient space unit.

Always remember, space costs money. The objective is to take the minimum amount of space you need to express your proposition effectively and to return a profit.

Start by having the creative director at your advertising agency express the proposition in the amount of space needed to convey a powerful selling message. Once you have established the cost per response for this basic unit, you can experiment with other size units.

If you have two publications on your schedule that perform about equally well for the basic unit, try testing the same ad approach expressed in a smaller or larger space size in one of those two publications, while running the basic control unit in the same month in the other publication.

**Four-color, two-color, black-and-white: How colorful should your advertising be?**

All magazines charge extra for adding color to your advertising. And remember there will be additional production expense if you go this route.

Usually the cost of adding a second color to a black-and-white page does not return the added costs charged by the publication for the space and the expense of producing the ad. If the copy is right, the words will do their job without getting an appreciable lift from having headline set in red or blue or green. An exception might be the use of a second color tint as background to provide special impact to your page.

It is with the use of four-color advertising that the direct response advertiser has an opportunity to profit on an investment in color.

A number of publications (for example, *Esquire, Time, Woman's Day, Ladies' Home Journal*) allow you to run a split of four-color vs. black-and-white, in an alternating copy A/B perfect split-run. Test results indicate an increase of anywhere from 30 percent to almost 60 percent where there is appropriate and dramatic utilization of the four-color process.

Given a striking piece of artwork related to the proposition or an inherently colorful product feature to present, you can expect an increase in response when you use four-color advertising. Since you will need more than a 20 percent increase in most publications to make the use of color profitable, it is wise to pretest the value of this factor before scheduling it across the board. Some products such as insurance simply do not require color.

Now just what can you expect the cost of four-color advertising to be? Table 5.3 shows four-color charges from a representative group of consumer publications.

If you plan to use four-color advertising, the increase in publication space cost is only one of the cost factors to be weighed. The cost of the original four-color engravings for a 7 × 10 page runs from $2,000 to $4,000, depending on the copy and artwork being used. This compares with a black-and-white engraving cost which could be from $150 to $250. In addition, any dye transfers or other four-color preparatory work will probably increase mechanical preparation costs by 50 percent or more over a comparable black-and-white insertion.

**The position factor can mean as much as what you say**

Position in life may not be everything, but in direct response it often means the difference between paying out or sudden death. By "position" we mean where your advertisement appears in the publication. There are two rules

**Table 5.3. Four-color rate examples.**

| Publication | Black-and-White Page Rate | Four-Color Page Rate | Percentage Increase for Four-Color |
|---|---|---|---|
| Woman's Day | $39,680 | $47,500 | 19.7 |
| Family Circle | 35,360* | 42,288* | 19.6 |
| Ladies' Home Journal | 28,590 | 36,180 | 26.5 |
| Seventeen | 9,000 | 13,000 | 44.4 |
| Redbook | 22,220 | 29,525 | 32.9 |
| McCall's | 32,825 | 41,600 | 26.7 |
| Good Housekeeping | 22,013* | 27,626* | 25.5 |
| Glamour | 10,875 | 15,300 | 40.7 |
| Newsweek | 26,660 | 41,590 | 56.0 |
| Time | 37,665 | 58,755 | 55.9 |
| Sports Illustrated | 23,870 | 37,235 | 55.9 |
| Popular Mechanics | 7,355* | 12,380* | 68.3 |
| Mechanix Illustrated | 7,450* | 11,175* | 50.0 |
| Reader's Digest | 57,920 | 69,610 | 20.2 |
| Esquire | 6,265* | 9,380* | 49.7 |

*Mail order rates

governing the position factor. First, the closer to the front of the book an ad is placed, the better the response will be. Second, the more visible the position, the better the response will be.

The first rule defies rational analysis. Yet it is as certain as the sun's rising in the morning. Many magazine publishers have offered elaborate research studies demonstrating to the general advertiser that an ad in the editorial matter far back in a publication gets better readership than an ad placed within the first few pages of the publication. This may well be true for the general or institutional advertiser, but it is not true for the direct response advertiser.

Whatever the explanation may be, the fact remains that decades of measured direct response advertising tell the same story over and over again. A position in the first seven pages of the magazine produces a dramatically better response (all other factors being the same) than if the same insertion appeared farther back in the same issue.

How much better? There are as many answers to this question as there are old pros in the business. However, here is about what you might expect the relative response to be from various page positions as measured against the first right-hand page arbitrarily rated at a pull of 100.

| | | | | |
|---|---|---|---|---|
| First right-hand page | 100 | Back of book (following main body of editorial matter) | 50 |
| Second right-hand page | 95 | | |
| Third right-hand page | 90 | | |
| Fourth right-hand page | 85 | Back cover | 100 |
| Back of front of the book (preceding editorial matter) | 70 | Inside third cover | 90 |
| | | Page facing third cover | 85 |

The second rule is more easily explained. An ad must be seen before it can be read or acted on. Right-hand pages pull better than left-hand pages, frequently by as much as 15 percent. Insert cards open the magazine to the advertiser's message, and thereby create their own "cover" position. Of course, the insert card introduces the additional factor of providing a postage-free response vehicle as well. But the response from insert cards, too, is subject to the influence of how far back in the magazine the insertion appears. Here is what you can expect in most publications (assigning a 100 rating to the first card):

> First insert card position . . . . . . . . . . . . . . . . . .100
> Second insert card position . . . . . . . . . . . . . . . . 95
> Third insert card position . . . . . . . . . . . . . . . . . . 85
> Fourth insert card position . . . . . . . . . . . . . . . 75*
> Fifth insert card position . . . . . . . . . . . . . . . . . . 70*
> *If position follows main editorial matter.

The pull of position is as inexorable as the pull of gravity. Well, almost, that is. There are a few exceptions. In the fashion and the mechanics magazines, card positioning seems to make little or no difference. Another exception may involve the placement of an ad opposite a related column or feature article in a publication (for example, a *Home Handyman's Encyclopedia* ad opposite the Home Handyman column). Another exception may involve placement of your ad in a high-readership shopping section at the back of a magazine.

**How to buy space**  Since mail order advertising is always subject to bottom-line analysis, the price you pay for space can mean the difference between profit and loss. Mrs. Florence Peloquin, mail order advertising director for *Woman's Day*, provides some basic questions the advertiser should ask the publisher or his agency before placing space.

1. Is there a special mail order rate? Mail order rates are usually 10 percent to 40 percent lower than general rates.

2. Is there a special mail order section, a shopping section where mail order ads are grouped? Usually the back of the book.

3. Does the book have remnant space available at substantial discounts? Many publishers offer discounts of up to 50 percent off the regular rate.

4. Is there an insertion frequency discount, or dollar volume discount? Is frequency construed as the number of insertions in a time period or consecutive issues? Many publishers credit more than one insertion in an issue towards frequency.

5. Do corporate discounts apply to mail order? Sometimes the corporate discount is better than the mail order discount.

6. Do you have seasonal discounts? Some publishers have low volume advertising months during which they offer substantial discounts.

7. Do you offer spread discounts when running two pages or more in one issue? The discount can run up to 50 percent on the second page.

8. Do you have a publisher's rate? Is this in addition to or in lieu of the mail order rate? It can be additive.

9. Will you accept a per-inquiry (P.I.) deal? Under P.I. deals the advertiser pays the publisher an amount for each inquiry or order, or a minimum flat amount for the space, plus so much per inquiry or order.

10. Do you accept "umbrella contracts?" Some media buying services and agencies own banks or reserves of space with given publications and can offer discounts even for one-time ads.

11. Do you barter for space? Barter usually involves a combination of cash and merchandise.

When bought properly, tested properly, and used properly, magazine advertising represents a vast universe of sales and profit potential for the direct response advertiser.

## Self-quiz

1. Name five magazines which provide a conducive atmosphere for direct response advertisers.

   a. _____

   b. _____

   c. _____

   d. _____

   e. _____

2. Name the four major advantages of using regional editions of magazines.

   a. _____
   _____

   b. _____
   _____

   c. _____
   _____

   d. _____
   _____

3. What are the two negative factors involved in buying regional space?

   a. _____
   _____

   b. _____
   _____

4. Name five basic consumer magazine catagories.

   a. _____

   b. _____

   c. _____

   d. _____

   e. _____

5. Give the definition of a pilot publication.

   _____
   _____
   _____

6. What is the theory of an expanded media buying program based on an ever-widening circle?

   _____
   _____
   _____
   _____

7. What is the principal advantage of an insert card in a magazine?

   _____
   _____
   _____

8. When direct response advertisers use insert cards, the response is likely to be: ____ to ____ times as great when pulling for an order and as much as ____ to ____ times as great in pulling for inquiries.

9. As a general rule, when a direct response advertiser uses a monthly magazine, he or she can usually expect to have about 50 percent of his or her total response after ____ weeks.

10. For weekly publications 50 percent of total response can be expected after ____ weeks.

11. From a timing standpoint, which is the most productive season for most direct response propositions?_____
    _____

12. Which is the second most productive season?
    _____

13. When is the best possible time to test a nonseasonal item? _____
    _____

14. How much is the cost per response (CPR) likely to vary between the best pulling month and the poorest pulling month? ____ percent

15. Provide guidelines for frequency factors in magazine advertising.
    a. If the cost per response is in an acceptable range or up to 20 percent better than expected, wait ____ months and follow up with a second insertion in the second half of the year.
    b. If the first insertion pulls well over 20 percent better than allowed order margin, turn around and repeat within a ____ or ____ month period.
    c. If response to the test insertion in January or February was marginal, it usually makes sense to wait ____ before returning for another try in that publication.

16. Generally speaking, which requires more space for effective direct response advertising?

    ____ Pulling inquiries

    ____ Pulling orders

17. What is the prime advantage of a full page ad vs. a small ad in a magazine?

    _____

    _____

18. If a single page ad with coupon is successful, what is the next logical test?

    _____

    _____

    _____

    _____

    _____

19. What are the three size categories for most mail order advertising?

    a. _____

    _____

    b. _____

    _____

    c. _____

    _____

20. When four-color vs. black and white is tested, results indicate an increase of anywhere from ____ percent to almost ____ percent where there is appropriate and dramatic utilization of the four-color process.

21. What are the two rules governing the "position" factor for the direct response advertiser?

    a. _____

    _____

    b. _____

    _____

22. Right-hand pages pull better than left-hand pages by as much as ____ percent.

23. If a 100 rating is assigned to a first insert card position in a publication having five insert card positions, what would the fifth insert card rate pull? _____

24. Mail order rates are usually ____ percent to ____ percent lower than general rates.

## Pilot project

You are the advertising manager for a publisher of children's books. It is your assignment to test market a new continuity series of ten books written for age levels 6 to 10. Each book in the series will sell for $4.95. Outline a plan for test marketing in magazines.

1. What pilot publications would you schedule for testing?

2. Will you use any regional editions?

3. Do a circle approach to media selection indicating what additional publications you will expand to if the pilot publications prove successful.

4. Prepare a timing schedule, indicating when your pilot ads will break and when your expanded media buying program will take place.

5. What ad size will you use and will the ad be black and white, two-color, or four-color?

# 6

## Newspapers

For sheer circulation in print, there is nothing to compare with the daily and Sunday newspapers. There were 1,762 daily newspapers in the United States with an average daily circulation of 60,977,011, as of January 1, 1978. Thus the circulation available through newspapers offers an exciting opportunity for direct response advertisers. It is significant that many direct response advertisers spend all or a major portion of their budgets in newspapers.

Newspapers are unique in that they can serve as a vehicle for carrying direct response advertising formats foreign to their regular news pages. Remarkable results have been achieved by using these special formats.

**Newspaper preprints**  Use of preprints by direct response advertisers is a phenomenon of this decade. The Newspaper Advertising Bureau of New York estimates that 17.1 billion preprints circulated in 1976. Preprints became a viable method for direct marketers in 1965. In the first five months of that year there was only one preprint mail order advertiser (Time-Life Books) in million-circulation newspapers.

Columbia Record Club followed Time-Life Books in 1965. Wunderman, Ricotta & Kline, the club's agency, first tested preprints in newspapers in six markets (*Akron Beacon, Dallas Times Herald, Des Moines Register, Minneapolis Tribune, Peoria Journal Star,* and *Seattle Times*). Hundreds of millions of preprints have since been run in newspapers by Columbia Record Club. There are two obvious advantages to preprints such as those used by Columbia. First, they provide abundant space for the detailed listing of items available. Second, a perforated postpaid return card may be imprinted, which, because of the weight of the stock used, closely resembles an ordinary post card and can be easily mailed by the respondent.

The dramatic impact of preprints in a newspaper must be measured against the greatly increased cost. Comparing a four-page preprint with a fourth cover in a syndicated Sunday supplement, one finds the preprint costs almost four times as much. The tremendous volume of preprints found in the Sunday newspaper is good evidence that the increased cost often is more than warranted.

## Table 6.1. Facts about newspaper preprint inserts.

| Newspaper | Single-Sheet Insert | | Four-Page Insert | | Six-Page Insert | | Eight-Page Insert | | Sunday Circulation |
|---|---|---|---|---|---|---|---|---|---|
| | Gross Rate | CPM | Gross Rate | CPM | Gross Rate | CPM | Gross Rate | CPM | |
| **Asheville Citizen Times** Asheville, North Carolina (Available daily) | 850 lines or less $1,677 | 24.05 | 850 lines or less $1,718 | 24.63 | 850 lines or less $2,252 | 32.29 | 850 lines or less $2,780 | 39.86 | 70,000 |
| **Atlantic City Press** Atlantic City, New Jersey (CPM based on run of 72,000; no daily) | | 25.00 | | 30.00 | | 30.00 | | 30.00 | 70,000 |
| **Bangor Daily News** Bangor, Maine (CPM based on circulation day of insertion) | | 16.00 | | 18.00 | | 22.00 | | 25.00 | 80,000 |
| **Charleston Gazette Daily Mail** Charleston, W. Va. | $2,365 | 22.45 | $2,365 | 22.45 | $2,365 | 22.45 | $3,935 | 37.35 | 105,000 |
| **Chicago Zone Newspapers** **Aurora Beacon News** Aurora, Ill. | $1,760 | 40.00 | $1,760 | 40.00 | $1,760 | 40.00 | $1,760 | 40.00 | 44,000 |
| **Elgin Courier News Journal & Wheaton Journal** | $1,785 | 41.77 | $1,785 | 41.77 | $1,785 | 41.77 | $1,785 | 41.77 | 38,000 (Elgin) 6,000 (Wh'ton) |
| **Joliet Herald News** Joliet, Illinois | $2,040 | 40.00 | $2,040 | 40.00 | $2,040 | 40.00 | $2,040 | 40.00 | 51,000 |
| **The Cincinnati Enquirer** Cincinnati, Ohio (Available daily; CPM is based on press run day of insertion.) | | 20.50 | | 20.50 | | 20.50 | | 23.50 | 292,000 |
| **Dayton News & Journal Herald,** Dayton, Ohio (Available daily; eight-page minimum) | $4,828 | 21.81 | $5,267 | 23.80 | $5,669 | 25.61 | $6,637 | 29.99 | 222,000 |
| **The Detroit News** Detroit, Michigan (Envelope inserts *not* accepted) | $14,025 | 17.27 | $14,025 | 17.27 | $14,025 | 17.27 | $14,025 | 17.27 | 813,000 |
| **Green Bay Press Gazette,** Green Bay, Wis. (Available daily) | $1,782 | 25.78 | $1,782 | 25.78 | $1,782 | 25.78 | $1,782 | 25.78 | 70,000 |
| **The Record** Hackensack, N.J. (CPM based on circulation day of insertion) | | 22.35 | | 22.35 | | 27.06 | | 30.59 | 200,000 |
| **The Houston Chronicle** Houston, Texas (CPM based on latest publisher's statement; available daily Wed/Thurs) | | 23.90 | | 23.90 | | 23.90 | | 23.90 | 401,000 |
| **The State Journal** Lansing, Mich. (Available daily) | $2,293 | 29.40 | $2,293 | 29.40 | $2,293 | 29.40 | $2,956 | 37.90 | 78,000 |
| **The Arkansas Gazette** Little Rock, Ark. (Available daily) | $3,967 | 27.02 | 3,967 | 27.02 | $3,967 | 27.02 | $3,967 | 27.02 | 147,000 |
| **Manchester Union Leader,** Manchester, N.H. (Available daily) | $1,800 | 27.69 | $1,885 | 29.00 | $1,985 | 30.54 | $2,085 | 32.08 | 65,000 |
| **Newport News Press & Times Herald** (CPM based on actual paid circulation of previous Sunday rounded to nearest thousand.) | | 23.00 | | 27.00 | | 30.00 | | 33.00 | 96,000 |

## Table 6.1. Facts about newspaper preprint inserts (continued).

| Newspaper | Single-Sheet Insert Gross Rate | CPM | Four-Page Insert Gross Rate | CPM | Six-Page Insert Gross Rate | CPM | Eight-Page Insert Gross Rate | CPM | Sunday Circulation |
|---|---|---|---|---|---|---|---|---|---|
| **The Sunday Oklahoman** Oklahoma City, Okla. (Available daily) | $7,245 | 24.86 | $7,245 | 24.86 | $8,840 | 30.34 | $8,840 | 30.34 | 292,000 |
| **The Omaha World Herald,** Omaha, Neb. | $5,320 | 19.05 | $5,320 | 19.05 | $6,399 | 22.92 | $7,544 | 27.02 | 279,000 |
| **Palm Beach Post-Times** W. Palm Beach, Fla. (Available daily) | | 14.88 | | 19.46 | | 20.60 | | 21.75 | 107,000 |
| **Richmond News Leader & Times Dispatch** Richmond, Va. (Available daily) | $3,900 | 18.58 | $4,700 | 22.39 | $5,500 | 26.20 | $6,300 | 30.01 | 210,000 |
| **San Bernardino Sun-Telegram,** San Bernardino, Calif. (CPM based on latest SRDS; available daily) | | 18.00 | | 18.00 | | 23.50 | | 29.50 | 84,000 |
| **San Diego Union Tribune,** San Diego, Calif. (Available daily) | $6,149 | 19.78 | $6,149 | 19.78 | $6,149 | 19.78 | $6,149 | 19.78 | 311,000 |
| **San Francisco Chronicle Examiner,** San Francisco, Calif. (CPM rate based on latest publisher's statement rounded to nearest thousand.) | | 22.00 | | 24.00 | | 24.00 | | 24.00 | 660,000 |
| **The Scranton Times** Scranton, Penna. (Available daily) | | 20.50 | | 20.50 | | 23.50 | | 23.50 | 49,000 |
| **Springfield Sun News** Springfield, Ohio (No daily) | $2,070 | 47.10 | $2,070 | 47.10 | $2,070 | 47.10 | $2,070 | 47.10 | 44,000 |
| **The Tacoma News Tribune,** Tacoma, Wash. (Available daily) | $1,976 | 18.88 | $2,192 | 20.94 | $2,441 | 23.32 | $2,732 | 26.10 | 105,000 |
| **Tampa Tribune & Times** Tampa, Fla. (CPM rate based on press run day of insertion; available daily) | | 23.40 | | 25.24 | | 27.96 | | 29.73 | 197,000 |
| **The Trenton Times** Trenton, N.J. (CPM based on circulation day of insertion; available daily) | | 19.50 | | 19.50 | | 23.92 | | 27.19 | 90,000 |
| **The Washington Post** Washington, D.C. | $16,000 | 20.97 | $16,000 | 20.97 | $16,800 | 22.02 | $17,600 | 23.06 | 763,000 |
| **Winston Salem Journal** Winston Salem, N.C. (Available daily) | $1,485 | 15.42 | $2,200 | 22.84 | $2,750 | 28.56 | $3,300 | 34.27 | 96,000 |
| **The News Tribune** Woodbridge, N.J. (No Sunday; rates are for Saturday and daily) | | 17.65 | | 17.65 | | 30.01 | | 30.01 | 52,000 |

Source: Newspaper Preprint Corporation.

**Exhibit 6.1. First page of a six-page newspaper insert for Columbia House.**

Newpaper Advertising Bureau furnishes the following estimated space costs for inserts for the top 100 markets based on a tabloid size of 10¾×12¾. Two pages plus flap, $25.45 per M; four pages, $26.00 per M; six pages, $27.53 per M; eight pages, $29.32 per M; twelve pages, $34.40 per M; sixteen pages, $39.27 per M; twenty-four pages, $47.43 per M.

It should be noted that these estimated costs in the 100 top markets are for *space only*. Printing costs of the inserts must be added. A breakdown of costs for space, depending on the sizes of preprint, for 39 representative newspapers is given in Table 6.1. Careful note should be taken of the fact that the CPM tends to be lower for large metro papers. Thus, if a direct marketer has a proposition which appeals only to small towns, the chances for successful use of preprints are greatly diminished. Other facts about preprints and their use and trend as provided by Newspaper Preprint Corporation are listed in Table 6.1.

**Acceptable size**

Size depends on the newpaper's policy and equipment, but, generally speaking, minimum sizes are 5½×8⅛. Maximum size is 10¾×14½. These minimum and maximum sizes are folded sizes—unfolded size could be larger. For example, a standard format size of 21½×14½ printed on heavy stock could fold in half to 10¾×14½.

**Sunday vs. weekday inserts**

Figures for 1976 show that weekday preprints have increased to the point that they constitute about 45.5 percent of total preprint circulation in the top 100 markets.

**Card vs. multi-page insert**

A survey shows that 83 percent of total preprints used are of multi-page formats. Because just about all Sunday newspapers accept preprints and between 60 percent and 70 percent of daily newspapers accept inserts, it behooves all direct marketers who have products or services appealing to mass markets to explore this selling vehicle.

**Syndicated newspaper supplements**

Imagine placing three space insertion orders and buying newspaper circulation of 50 million plus! This is indeed possible if you place insertion orders in the three major syndicated newspaper supplements. Branham Newspapers, Inc., major newpaper representative, presents the figures in Table 6.2.

**Table 6.2. Summary of circulation and rates for Sunday newspaper supplements.**

| Publication | Circulation | Four-Color | | Black-and-White | |
|---|---|---|---|---|---|
| | | Page | CPM | Page | CPM |
| Sunday-Metro ........ | 22,300,000 | $162,011 | $7.26 | $135,691 | $6.08 |
| Parade ............ | 20,700,000 | 127,580 | 6.16 | 103,795 | 5.01 |
| Family Weekly ....... | 11,400,000 | 65,430 | 5.73 | 57,450 | 5.03 |
| Totals ............ | 54,400,000 | $355,021 | $6.53 | $296,936 | $5.46 |

Source: Branham Newspapers, Inc.

Distribution of the three syndicated supplements breaks down about this way. *Sunday-Metro* is distributed by about 50 member newspapers. Those carrying *Sunday-Metro* supplements offer a choice of 43 top metro areas for advertising.

*Family Weekly* is generally carried by the newspapers with smaller circulations many of which publish within the top metro areas but basically "C" and "D" counties. The majority of the newspapers distributing *Family Weekly* are outside the top 150 metro areas.

*Parade* is included in some of the *Sunday-Metro* newspapers, but generally it is more evenly distributed among the top 100 metro areas. Obvious advantages of syndicated supplements are their relatively low cost per thousand circulation and the possibility of reaching top metro areas as well as smaller cities, depending on the supplement used.

One thing going for the syndicated supplements is their mail order atmosphere. *Parade*, for instance, points out that 60 percent of its advertising carries some kind of coupon which enables the advertiser to get a measurement of results. For example, four major mail order concerns, Franklin Mint, American Consumer, Haband, and Danbury Mint, are currently spending $1.2 to $1.5 million dollars each on 16 to 20 pages of color advertising in *Parade.*

Among the syndicated supplements, *Parade* and *Family Weekly* offer a mail order booklet inserted on a regular basis. This booklet, commonly called a Dutch Door, usually runs 12 pages. Its page size is one-half that of the supplement. Some issues are taken over entirely by one advertiser. Other issues contain a variety of small mail order ads.

It is obvious that a direct marketer who has not previously placed space in one of the syndicated supplements would not go full run without testing. *Parade*, for example, offers remnant space to mail order advertisers at 36 percent discount. Remnant space is advertising space left over when package goods advertisers buy only in those markets where they have distribution. Second to testing in remnant space is testing in regions.

With about 650 Sunday and weekend magazines, both syndicated and locally edited, a direct response advertiser has an incredible amount of distribution available at low cost.

**Comics as a direct marketing medium**

Perhaps the biggest sleeper as a medium for direct marketers is the comic section of weekend newspapers. Comics are not glamorous, nor are they prestigious. But their total circulation, readership, and demographics constitute an exciting universe for the direct response advertiser. Here are some of the fascinating facts and figures about comics as an advertising medium.

Each week, usually on Sunday, 49.9 million color comics are distributed through 496 different newspapers. These comics literally saturate the major and secondary markets, providing 50 percent or better coverage in 278 of the 300 strategic metropolitan markets of the country. There are two major comic groups—Puck and Metro.

The Puck Group is available through two networks: the National Network and the American Network. The National Network, made up of

**Exhibit 6.2. Comic page ad promoting film processing. Ad calls attention to an envelope inserted loose in newspaper.**

newspapers that almost all have circulations of over 100,000, is distributed through 58 papers in 57 cities. The American Network, made up of newspapers with circulations of under 100,000, is distributed in 65 papers in 63 cities. Also available through Puck are three geographically concentrated editions: the West Coast edition, made up of eleven West Coast newspapers; the California/Nevada/Washington group, with fifteen papers; and the Texas Group of ten papers.

Metro Sunday comics are available on the basis of newspaper networks. There are two networks: a basic network of 56 newspapers, and a selective network of 26 newspapers. Total circulation is 21,976,526 for the two networks, comprising 82 newspapers. Standard Rate and Data Service also lists 17 other smaller comic groups, regionally oriented. The size of these groups ranges from the Texas Sunday Comic Section, with a circulation of 908,865, to the Wyoming Color Comic Group, with a circulation of 37,149. Combined, Metro and Puck have a total circulation of 43,874,245. Metro's cost per thousand for a four-color page is $7.48; Puck's is $6.27.

The demographic characteristics of comic readers are quite a surprise to most advertisers who seem to have ill-conceived ideas about this type of reader. The median age of the adult comic reader is 39.2, slightly younger than the U.S. median age of 41.3.

One of the major misconceptions about comic readership is that the higher one's education, the less likely one is to read the comic pages. Statistics from *Simmons Total Index Study* dispute this as is illustrated in Table 6.3.

Finally, there is the misconception that the higher one's income, the less likely one reads comics. Again, the figures refute this.

Among direct response advertisers, the largest users of comic page advertising in the past have been photo finishers. Huge photo finishing businesses have been started from scratch using comics as a prime advertising medium. The availability of the ad-and-envelope technique in conjunction with comic page advertising serves a genuine need of photo finishers because they are able to provide an envelope in which the prospect can return completed film rolls. The standard charge for a free-standing envelope or for affixing a card or envelope to the ad averages about $3.00 per thousand, plus the cost of printing the response vehicle. With ad-and-envelope, the direct response advertiser pro-

**Table 6.3. Demographic characteristics of readers of comics compared with U.S. population.**

| Characteristic | Comics Readers | U.S. Population |
|---|---|---|
| Age | | |
| 18–24 | 20.1% | 18.4% |
| 25-34 | 22.2 | 21.8 |
| 35-49 | 24.1 | 23.6 |
| 50-64 | 21.9 | 21.5 |
| 65 and above | 11.7 | 14.7 |
| | 100.0% | 100.0% |
| Education | | |
| Graduated from college | 16.1% | 13.5% |
| Attended college | 17.6 | 15.3 |
| Graduated from high school | 40.8 | 38.2 |
| Attended high school | 14.2 | 15.8 |
| Did not attend high school | 11.3 | 17.2 |
| | 100.0% | 100.0% |
| Income | | |
| $25,000 and above | 18.8% | 16.4% |
| $15,000–24,999 | 32.1 | 28.0 |
| $10,000–14,999 | 22.4 | 21.7 |
| $8,000–9,999 | 8.5 | 9.5 |
| $5,000–7,999 | 8.9 | 9.9 |
| $4,999 and under | 9.3 | 14.5 |
| | 100.0% | 100.0% |
| Median income | $15,229 | $13,750 |

vides the same impetus to response with a reply card or reply envelope.

Following the photo finishers with comic page advertising have been insurance companies and land developers. Opportunities obviously are there for a host of other direct response advertisers seeking mass circulation at low cost. Comic page advertising traditionally limits advertising to one advertiser per page. Thus full-page advertising is not essential to gain a dominant position. Comics, not unlike syndicated supplements, should be tested before one goes full run. You can test individual papers among the Metro Group, the Puck Group, and the independent groups.

**ROP advertising**

We have been exploring formats carried by newspapers—preprints, syndicated supplements, and comics. Not to be overlooked, of course, is run-of-paper (ROP) advertising. Generally, direct response advertisers have failed to get the results with ROP advertising that they have obtained from newspaper preprints and syndicated newspaper supplements. One obvious reason is that four-color advertising is not generally available for ROP. Another is that ROP ads don't drop out for individual attention. But many successes can be cited for small-space ROP advertising, small-space ads that have run frequently year after year in hundreds of newspapers. When small-space ads are run over a long period of time with high frequency, the number of reader impressions multiplies rapidly in proportion to the cost.

**Effect of local news on results**

A major difference between newspaper advertising and all other print media is that the newspaper reader is more likely to be influenced by local news events. All newspaper advertising appears within the atmosphere of the local news for a given day. A major scandal in local politics or a catastrophe in a local area such as a tornado can have a devastating effect on the advertising appearing in a given issue. Magazines, on the other hand, do not tie in closely with local events. Magazines are normally put aside to read during hours not taken up by involvement in local events. Because local events have a strong effect on response, positively or negatively, markets with similar demographics don't always respond in the same manner. All newspaper advertising tends to be *local*, even though a schedule may be national.

**Developing a newspaper test program**

When a direct response advertiser first considers testing newspapers as a medium he has a myriad of decisions to make. Should he go ROP, the newspaper preprint route, local Sunday supplements, syndicated supplements, TV program supplements, comics? What papers should he test? Putting ad size and position aside for the moment, we have two initial considerations: the importance of advertising in a mail order climate, and the demographics of markets selected as they relate to the product or service you are offering.

If you had one simple product, say a stamp dispenser, for instance, and a tiny budget, you might place one small ad in one publication. You could run the ad in the mail order section of the *New York Times Sunday Magazine*. Generally if you don't make it there, you won't make it anywhere. Running such an ad would give a "feel." If it works, it would be logical to test similar mail order sections in major cities such as Chicago, Detroit, and Los Angeles.

**Exhibit 6.3. Mail order shopping guide page from the *Chicago Tribune* Sunday magazine.**

Simple items, which are suited to small-space advertising in mail order sections, greatly simplify the testing procedure. But, more often than not, multi-city testing in larger space is required.

Prime direct response test markets in the United States include Atlanta, Buffalo, Cleveland, Dallas-Fort Worth, Denver, Des Moines, Indianapolis, Omaha, and Peoria. In the selection of test markets, you should analyze the newspaper to make certain it has advertising reach and coverage and offers demographics which are suitable to your product. If there are two newspapers in a market, it is worthwhile to evaluate both of them. Let us say that because of budget limitations advertising can be placed in only a limited number of markets. Such criteria as circulation, household penetration, women readers, and advertising linage relating to the product to be advertised should be measured.

A number of sources will provide the data necessary for evaluation. You would begin with SRDS's *Newspaper Rates and Data* for general cost and circulation information. *SRDS Circulation Analysis* would provide information about metro household penetration. *Simmons Total Index Study* could then be used to isolate men or women readers of a particular age group. Other criteria to be measured include retail linage in various classifications and spendable income by metro area.

Demographics are a major consideraton market by market whether you are going ROP, preprints, local supplements, syndicated supplements, or TV program supplements. Once an advertiser develops a test program which closely reflects the demographics for his product or service, expansion to like markets makes possible the rapid acceleration of a full-blown program. But selecting newspapers is tedious, because there are hundreds from which to choose as compared with a relative handful of magazines whose demographics can be more closely related to the proposition. As an example, a test newspaper schedule could be placed in the following markets: Atlanta, preprint; Buffalo (*Courier Express*), *Parade* remnant; Cleveland, Metro comics; Dallas-Fort Worth, ROP; Denver, preprint; Des Moines, ROP; Indianapolis, preprint; Omaha, Metro comics; and, Peoria, *Parade* remnant. If there is more than one newspaper in a test market, the paper with the most promising demographics should be selected.

A test schedule like this would be ambitious in terms of total dollars, but it would have the advantage of simultaneously testing markets and formats. Once a reading has been obtained from the markets and formats, the advertiser can rapidly expand to other markets and will have the advantage of using the most productive formats.

**Advertising seasons**

As in direct mail and magazine direct response advertising, there are two major newspaper direct response advertising seasons. The fall mail order season begins roughly with August and runs through November. (A notable exception is a July insertion which is often useful especially when using a pretested piece.) The winter season begins with January and runs through March.

Exceptions to the two major direct response seasons occur in the sale of seasonal merchandise. Christmas items are usually promoted from

September through the first week of December. A nursery, on the other hand, will start promoting in late December and early January, then again in the early fall. Many nurseries follow the practice of promoting by geographical regions, starting earlier in the south and working up to later promotion in the north.

**Timing of newspaper insertions**

Beyond the seasonal factor of direct response advertising in newspapers, timing is important as it relates to days of the week. According to the *E&P Yearbook, Bureau of Advertising Circulation Analysis*, the number of copies of a newspaper sold per day is remarkably constant month after month—despite such events as summer vacations and Christmas holidays. And people buy the newspaper to read not only the editorial matter but also the ads. According to an *Audits & Surveys Study*, the percentage of people opening an average ad page any week day, Monday through Friday, varies less than 3 percent, with Tuesday ranking the highest at 84 percent.

There is no question that the local newspaper is an integral part of practically everyone's daily life. While magazines may be set aside for reading at a convenient time, newspapers are read the day they are delivered or purchased or are not read at all. Monday through Thursday are favorite choices of many direct response advertisers for their ROP advertising. Many direct response advertisers judiciously avoid the weekday issue containing grocery advertising.

As we have seen, more and more newspapers are accepting preprints for weekday insertions. This can be a major advantage considering the larger number of preprints appearing in most big Sunday newspapers.

**Newspaper response patterns**

Newspapers have the shortest time lapse from closing date to appearance date of all print media. In most cases, ads can appear in the newspaper within 48 hours after placement. Depending on the format used, up to 90 percent or more of responses will be reached for a typical direct response newspaper ad within these time frames: ROP, after the second week; preprints, after the third week; syndicated newspaper supplements, after the third week; and comics, after the second week.

Naturally, response patterns vary according to the proposition. Thus, it is important for each advertiser to develop his own response pattern. But the nature of newspaper advertising permits a quick turnaround. *Dow Theory Forecasts*, for instance has run ads in hundreds of newspapers. Dow is able to project results, giving you the option of deciding whether to repeat an ad, within a week after the first orders are received.

**Determining proper ad size**

In direct response newspaper advertising, as in retail or national newspaper ads, few people dispute the claim that the larger advertisement generally will get more attention than a smaller one. But whether the full-page ad gets twice the attention of the half-page ad or four times the attention of the quarter-page ad is debatable. It is cost per response that counts. Just as in magazine advertising, less space is usually indicated for inquiry advertising and more space is dictated for a direct order ad.

According to a study conducted by the Bureau of Advertising in 1971 relating to mail-back newspaper coupons, the size of the space seems to be a factor in reader response only to the extent that it is a factor in initial reader attention. In this study, 85 percent of newspaper inserts ran ads of 1,000 lines or more. Only half used fewer than 1,000 lines, with a minimum of 500 lines per ad.

A low-budget advertiser often must choose between a single full-page ad and several small ads over an extended time. The proper guide to follow in determining the initial size of ads is to base the size on the space required to tell the *complete story*.

Trying to sell membership in a record and tape club in a small space would be ludicrous. Experience shows that one must offer a wide selection of records in the ad to get memberships. The same is true for a book club. On the other hand, if you are selling a single item at a low price—say a cigarette lighter for $4.95—the complete story can be told in a small space. Where small-space advertising can tell the whole story, consistency and repetition often prove to be keys to success.

Aside from the obvious requirement of using a full page or more for a proposition, constant testing of ad sizes will establish the proper size to produce the most efficient cost per inquiry or per order.

## The position factor

Newspapers and magazines have many similarities in respect to the importance of position in direct response advertising. Research has demonstrated high readership of newspaper ads, whatever the position. However, direct response advertisers still prefer right-hand pages. Generally, such advertisers find that ads are more effective if they appear in the front of the newspaper than in the back. And placement of coupon ads in the gutter of any newspaper page is almost always avoided.

All newspapers are printed in sections. Special consideration should be given to the reading habits of men and women as they relate to specific sections of a newspaper. Three major sections of any given newspaper are sports, women's pages, and general news. Table 6.4 shows results of a study by *Million Market Newspapers* of 32,000 ads. What this study obviously shows is that any appeals to sports-minded men will get high readership on the sports pages. If you have a product that appeals to women, you will get high readership in the women's section. A product that appeals to both men and women calls for running the ad in the general news section.

**Table 6.4. Newspaper advertisements featuring products of interest to men or women by section placement.**

| Section Placement | Median Performance | |
| --- | --- | --- |
| | Men | Women |
| Sports . . . . . . . . . . . . . | 114 | 49 |
| Women's . . . . . . . . . . | 63 | 101 |
| General news . . . . . . . . | 100 | 101 |

Source: "Million Market Newspapers," Starch studies of 32,000 ads (1961–63).

## Color vs. black and white

The possibilities of using color in newspaper advertising may be regarded as similar to those for magazine advertising with one major exception. If you plan to use one or more colors other than black in an ROP ad, you simply can't get the quality that you can in a color magazine ad. This does not mean that ROP color should not be tested. A majority of newspapers that offer color will allow A/B splits of color vs. black and white.

According to a December 1977 Bureau of Advertising Study (1969 cost figures), using the top 100 markets as a group, two-color ROP costs 17 percent more than the same full page in black and white. Four-color ROP costs 29 percent more than the same full page in black and white. In both cases, these comparisons are based on cost per thousand copies of the newspaper. Based on the same cost per thousand copies (in the same market), Preprint Corporation estimates that hi-fi and spectacolor cost about twice as much as black-and-white space and production. In other words, for every $100 spent in the top 100 markets to buy a full page in black and white, it costs $117 to buy the same full page in two-color ROP; $129 to buy it in four-color ROP; and $200 to buy it in hi-fi or spectacolor.

Studies have been made via split-runs and the recognition method to test the attention-getting power of both two-color and full-color ROP. Such studies have shown increases of 58 percent for two color and 78 percent for full color above the level of results for black-and white versions of the same ads. Comparable cost differences are 17 percent and 23 percent.

When Starch "noting score" norms are used to estimate the same attention-getting differential, a different conclusion is reached. The differences are about 10 percent and about 30 percent (when size and product category are held constant). Using norms means comparing a black-and-white ad for one product in another city at another time. These variables inevitably blur the significance of comparisons.

For the direct response advertiser, these studies are interesting. However, you should remember that genuine controlled testing is the only way to get true figures.

## Self-quiz

1. Name the two obvious advantages of preprints.

   a. _____

   b. _____

2. Which is the most popular format for a preprint?

   ☐ Card          ☐ Multi-page

3. Name the three major syndicated newspaper supplements.

   a. _____

   b. _____

   c. _____

4. Indicate major market penetration for each of the supplements.

   *Sunday Metro*     Top 43 metros        _____

                      C & D counties       _____

                      Below top 150 metros _____

   *Parade*           Top 43 metros        _____

                      C & D counties       _____

                      Below top 150 metros _____

   *Family Weekly*    Top 43 metros        _____

                      C & D counties       _____

                      Below top 150 metros _____

5. Define a Dutch Door.

   _____

   _____

   _____

   _____

6. What is remnant space?

   _____

   _____

   _____

   _____

7. What are the names of the two major comic groups?

   a. _____

   b. _____

8. The higher one's education, the less likely one will read the comic pages.

   ☐ True      ☐ False

9. The higher one's income, the less likely one will read the comic pages.

   ☐ True      ☐ False

10. What is the advantage of the ad-and-card and ad-and-envelope for comic page advertisers?

    _____

    _____

    _____

11. How many advertisers will comics groups allow per page? _____

12. What major advantage to direct response advertisers is offered by preprints and supplements over ROP advertising?

    _____

    _____

    _____

13. What is the major difference between newspaper advertising and all other print advertising as related to potential results?

    _____

    _____

    _____

14. What are the two initial considerations in the development of a newspaper test program?

    a. _____

    b. _____

15. If you have a single item which is suitable for advertising in a small space and a limited budget for testing, which publication would you test first?_____

16. Name nine prime test markets for newspaper direct response advertising:

    a. _____

    b. _____

    c. _____

    d. _____

    e. _____

    f. _____

    g. _____

    h. _____

    i. _____

17. What are the two main seasons for newspaper direct response advertising?

    a. _____

    b. _____

18. Give the preferred weekdays for ROP advertising:

    _____   _____   _____

19. Depending on the format used, up to 90 percent or more of responses will be reached for a typical direct response newspaper ad within these time frames:

    ROP . . . . . . . . . . . .after _____week(s)

    Preprints . . . . . . . . .after _____week(s)

    Supplements . . . . . .after _____week(s)

    Comics . . . . . . . . . .after _____week(s)

20. The size of newspaper space seems to be a factor in reader response only to the extent it is a factor in:

    _____   _____   _____

21. When running ROP, direct response advertisers should specify:

    ☐ Left-hand page     ☐ Right-hand page

22. What is the major disadvantage of running color ROP?

    _____

    _____

    _____

    _____

## Pilot project

You are the advertising manager of a mail order operation selling collectibles. You have been successful in magazines offering a series of historic plates. You have never used newspapers, but now you have a $75,000 budget to test the medium.

Outline a newspaper test plan.

1. Select your test cities.

2. Will your tests run in the Sunday edition or the weekday edition, or both?

3. What formats will you test—preprints, supplements, comics, local TV books, ROP?

4. What size preprints or ads will you test?

5. At what time of the year will you run your tests?

Note: Remember that if you use preprints, your total space budget should cover printing costs.

# 7

## Broadcast

The use of broadcast media—television and radio—as direct response media has grown dramatically in recent years. This chapter will discuss how to use direct response television and radio to solicit orders or inquiries and to support other media to increase over-all response.

**Direct response television**

Direct response television is most easily recognized by direct marketers. We've all seen the record offers and the commercials selling household implements, services, schools, and hotels. You name it and someone is probably offering it to you on television. As a matter of fact, this type of advertising has increased from a reported $22.5 million in 1969 to $105.6 million in 1973—a 469 percent increase—and has grown to the point where the Television Bureau of Advertising can no longer keep up with the statistics.

The primary objective of direct response television is to *sell your product!* There are two ways to sell that product on television, direct sales and leads and conversions.

**Direct sale**

This method is best utilized by those who offer low or moderately priced merchandise. The commercial may suggest ordering by mail and phone. Optional payment terms might be cash in advance, C.O.D., or a credit-card charge.

**Leads/conversions**

Not all products can be sold by the direct method. You cannot expect the viewer to order a very high-priced item by phone or mail, nor will he enroll in a school or sign up for such offers as career development courses, which represent a substantial investment. Sale, in this case, becomes a two-step process.

1. Use your commercial to offer informational material to develop leads for future sales.
2. Actual conversion from inquiry to order is handled through follow-up by a salesperson (in person or by telephone), or a descriptive brochure, or a combination of both.

Ratings   Direct response advertisers who solicit direct sales or inquiries have found that programs with low ratings are, surprisingly, to their advantage. Two reasons are given for this: commercials on programs with lower ratings cost less; and viewers of lower-rated programs, such as old movies, seem to be more responsive to direct offers.

Ratings are a measurement of household viewing. One rating point equals 1 percent of households in the market. A 20 rating means that 20 percent of households are viewing that program.

Gross rating points   Gross rating points (GRP) are the simple total of the ratings attributed to each of the programs or time periods that make up a broadcast schedule. For planning purposes, GRPs are used to denote advertising weight in terms of gross exposure opportunities. For example, 100 household GRP means that your schedule will reach the equivalent of 100 percent of households in the market.

Attentiveness   Attentiveness in viewing varies during the broadcast day. It ranges from a low level during daytime to peak highs in the prime-time night viewing hours. Also, we know that certain types of programs have a more attentive audience than others (see Table 7.1).

Generally, the higher the rating, the higher the attentiveness level. Conversely, the lower the rating, the lower the viewer attentiveness.

When a viewer is watching a program he enjoys, his interest in that program is high. During the commercial break, that viewer will not run to the telephone or grab a pencil and paper to write down a phone number or address. He's too involved with the programming to react to a direct response commercial. But when the viewer is watching the thirty-ninth rerun of a situation comedy or movie, his attentiveness is low. Because the program doesn't really hold his total interest, your commercial has a better chance of reaching him. He won't care enough about missing part of the program to resist taking action to order your product or service.

The television day has four parts, called *dayparts:* daytime

### Table 7.1. Viewer attention levels by program type.

| | Men | | Women | |
| | Total Audience | Ages 18–49 | Total Audience | Ages 18–49 |
|---|---|---|---|---|
| **Weekday daytime** | | | | |
| "Today Show" | 50 | 35 | 40 | 30 |
| Serials | 80 | 70 | 75 | 75 |
| Quiz/game shows | 75 | 60 | 65 | 60 |
| Situation comedies | 70 | 60 | 55 | 45 |
| **Early evening** | | | | |
| Situation comedies | 60 | 50 | 55 | 45 |
| Action/adventure | 70 | 65 | 65 | 60 |
| Talk shows | 70 | 60 | 65 | 55 |
| News | 70 | 60 | 65 | 55 |
| **Prime time** | | | | |
| Movies | 80 | 80 | 75 | 75 |
| Variety | 75 | 70 | 70 | 65 |
| Drama | 75 | 75 | 75 | 75 |
| Situation comedies | 70 | 65 | 70 | 65 |
| Sports | 80 | 80 | 50 | 50 |
| **Late night** | | | | |
| News | 75 | 70 | 70 | 65 |
| Talk shows | 65 | 55 | 65 | 60 |
| Movies | 75 | 75 | 75 | 75 |

*Percent at Full Attention*

Source: W. R. Simmons, 1973

(sign-on to 4:00 P.M.); early fringe (4:00 P.M. to 8:00 P.M. daily, and weekend daytime); prime time (8:00 P.M. to 11:00 P.M.); and late fringe (11:00 P.M. to sign-off).

Prime time usually has the highest attentiveness level, followed by late fringe, early fringe, and daytime. Because much of the programming of independent stations consists of syndicated reruns and movies, a lower level of attentiveness prevails for those as opposed to that for first-run programs on the network stations. Avoid "news" and other high-interest programming.

Cost The less you pay for your television time, the fewer responses you'll need to make your schedule pay out. Television is a supply-and-demand medium and costs are based on audience delivery. High-rated programs carry a higher price tag. By purchasing the lower-rated programs, the direct response advertiser can usually negotiate a package of low-cost announcements that will provide high frequency in the low attentiveness areas. Stations, particularly independents, will also sell ROS packages at low rates. ROS—run of station—allows the station to schedule the spots wherever free time is available. These are areas the station has been unable to sell at regular rates, but these are also areas that will produce good response for the direct marketer.

P.I. and bonus-to-payout When television was in its infancy, these two methods of buying time were highly prevalent. Today, with the high demand for television time, very few stations will accept this type of deal. However, for those who might be able to negotiate such packages, we will define them.

*P.I. (per inquiry)* allows the *station* to run as many commercials as it wishes, whenever and wherever the managers wish. The station is not paid by the spot, but it receives a pre-determined amount for every inquiry received by the advertiser.

*Bonus-to-payout* is a guaranteed schedule. The advertiser negotiates a package and stipulates the number of inquiries the schedule must deliver. If, at the conclusion of the schedule, the goal has not been reached, the station must continue to run spots until the requirement has been fulfilled.

Commercial length The 60-second commercial is now the most generally accepted commercial length for direct response. You can adequately show and describe your product and have sufficient time to "super" (superimpose) the phone number and address. If you have a product that requires a more-involved presentation, you may have to use a two-minute commercial which gives you the time to present your product in a more leisurely manner or provide more description. However, this commercial length can be difficult to clear, especially in a high-demand period. Some stations will not sell 120-second spots when limited inventory is available. Some direct marketers have successfully adopted the compromise—a 90-second commercial. This length allows for a more detailed presentation and generally has been made available by stations. The 30-second commercial, widely used by general advertisers, is not recommended for direct response because time limitations will not enable you to adequately present your product, telephone number, and address.

Copy Writing TV copy calls for considerable discipline to keep the copy short, direct, clear, and uncomplicated. For the direct response practitioner accustomed to the luxury of such devices as four-page brochures, two-page letters, and order cards, compressing an effective sales message into the relatively few words that can be fitted into a 60- or 120-second commercial can be a mind-boggling challenge. But, obviously, it can be done. Indeed, a number of direct response advertisers are able to use 60-second spots effectively at half the cost of 120s. It would take a complete chapter in this book to begin to cover all the do's and don'ts and some of the more complex facts of TV commercial writing. The basic rules for writing good direct response TV copy, however, are simple:

1. Don't set up creative restrictions because you think 60 or even 120 seconds isn't enough time to tell your story properly. First create, *then* cut.

2. Keep your message believable and uncomplicated.

3. Don't try to convey too many ideas or different images. Make as many copy points as you want or can. But be sure that all the copy has a central theme or idea that viewers can easily grasp and follow and *act* upon.

4. Make sure your action imperatives are clear. When you ask for the order, don't pussyfoot. Don't be afraid to be corny or repetitive. Be sure to leave enough time in your tag to repeat your ordering instructions at least twice.

5. Remember that information reinforced by a video super *and* an audio mention is at least twice as effective as either alone and that a super *without an audio backup* has relatively little value.

The necessity for longer spots for more-involved presentations can best be illustrated by this script for a commercial written to sell a set of knives.

| Video | Audio |
|---|---|
| 1. *Open on MCU of professional demonstrator in kitchen, hacking at wooden block.* | DEMONSTRATOR: I'm purposely chopping this hardwood block to smithereens to demonstrate an amazing new product: Miracle Mac Knives! |
| 2. *Zoom to ECU of demonstrator still hacking at block. Super card 1 (flashing: warning).* | DEM. *(VO):* Ladies and gentlemen, please don't try this on the knives in your kitchen drawer. Miracle Mac Knives are the *only* knives in the world that can take this kind of punishment, |
| 3. *Cut to demonstrator cutting paper into strips.* | and keep coming back for more!! |

| Video | Audio |
|---|---|
| 4. *Cut to ECU of demonstrator: gestures to blade.* | The secret is space-age, chrome molybdenum steel—the hardest steel ever made—that stays sharp, for *life*, without any grinding or sharpening tools! |
| 5. *Hands demonstrate sharpening.* | Imagine! Just a simple pass over the back of a china plate restores the original cutting edge. |
| 6. *Pull back for MCU of demonstrator.* | DEMONSTRATOR: Grab a pencil and paper folks because I want to send you a set of these amazing Mac Knives for 30 days *free!* But first, watch. |
| 7. *Demonstrate tomato.* | *(VO)* You can cut a tomato paper-thin slice after slice, and never lose a drop of juice; |
| 8. *Demonstrate roast.* | carve meat from the bone as clean as a whistle; |
| 9. *Demonstrate radishes.* | decorate radishes like an expert; |
| 10. *Demonstrate bread in mid-air.* | cut bread a sixteenth of an inch thin; |
| 11. *Demonstrate turkey.* | carve a turkey clear down to the bone in seconds; |
| 12. *Demonstrate potato.* | even take an eye out of a potato so easy you won't believe it! |
| 13. *Cut to ECU of hands demonstrating blade.* | And just look at this: Each knife is scientifically designed to keep your fingers away from the cutting board, |
| 14. *Hands demonstrate tips.* | with safe rounded tips, |
| 15. *Hands demonstrate hole.* | and handy hanging hole, |
| 16. *Hands demonstrate handles.* | plus teak handles that are permanently bonded to the steel for super strength. |
| 17. *Pull back to demonstrator who displays knives one at a time.* | DEMONSTRATOR: And now, during this special TV offer, you can own one, two, three, four Miracle Mac Knives for just $19.95. |
| 18. *Dissolve to knives and box. Super card 2: 30-day free trial.* | DEM. *(VO):* But first, try them at home for 30 days free! No need to send any money! |
| 19. *Cut to knife rack demonstration. Super card 3: Free! When you send $19.95 plus one dollar shipping and handling.* | However, if you use your credit card or include payment with your order, we'll include this handsome hardwood knife rack at no extra cost! If not fully satisfied, return the knife set, keep the knife rack, and we'll refund your purchase price of $19.95. |
| 20. *Demonstrator assembles sandwich and cuts it.* | Try the knives that are so hard, so sharp, they slice through a Dagwood sandwich in one stroke! |

**Video**

21. *Cut to slide of phone number and address. Super card 4: offer for cable TV viewers only.*

**Audio**

DEMONSTRATOR: Order your set today. Give the knives a real workout for 30 days. Here's how: Call 000-0000 right now or write Mac Knives, care of Station OOO, Charleston, West Virginia. Send only $19.95 plus one dollar shipping and handling. That's Mac Knives, care of Station OOO, Charleston, West Virginia, or call 000-0000 now.

**Seasonality**    As in traditional direct response print media, the time of year is an important factor in direct response television. Television costs are also based on viewing levels according to the time of year. These levels vary from month to month and season to season. Viewing levels by daypart also vary. These are illustrated in Table 7.2.

Television costs are higher when viewing levels are higher. You can expect to pay more for television from October through April. Costs are lower from May through September. In addition, there are certain times of year when demand is light and costs will be lower. Beginning with the lowest and in ascending order, these periods are: December 26 to January 15, January 16 to March 1, July 1 to August 31, and September 1 to the start of new fall programming.

**Table 7.2. Index of seasonality of viewing, by daypart (annual average = 100).**

|  | Day | Early Evening | Prime | Late Evening | Sat. & Sun. Morning |
|---|---|---|---|---|---|
| Households |  |  |  |  |  |
| January-March | 108 | 112 | 113 | 105 | 111 |
| April-June | 92 | 91 | 98 | 99 | 93 |
| July-September | 98 | 82 | 83 | 98 | 81 |
| October-December | 102 | 115 | 107 | 97 | 115 |
| Men |  |  |  |  |  |
| January-March | 113 | 115 | 113 | 109 | 104 |
| April-June | 89 | 87 | 96 | 101 | 85 |
| July-September | 90 | 77 | 80 | 91 | 74 |
| October-December | 107 | 120 | 111 | 98 | 132 |
| Women |  |  |  |  |  |
| January-March | 106 | 107 | 113 | 105 | 103 |
| April-June | 96 | 93 | 96 | 99 | 86 |
| July-September | 91 | 82 | 80 | 98 | 86 |
| October-December | 105 | 118 | 111 | 98 | 122 |

Note: Levels in medium-face type are 10 percent or more above the average viewing index.

Source: A. C. Nielsen Audience Demographic Report, 1974.

You will, therefore, achieve a lower cost per order if you can minimize your television costs by buying in low-demand periods. These are the times, as well, when stations will be most receptive to negotiating low-cost packages. Certain low-cost periods coincide with what is considered the best times of year for direct response—notably January through March.

**Markets and station selections**  Some markets will work successfully; others are simply not receptive to some products or offers. Do your homework before you make that leap into television. Begin by analyzing where your best response came from when you used mail or print media. Hit these markets first.

Try a one-week schedule on one or two stations in the market. If you are using telephone response, you'll have an indication of how well the offer is pulling after the first two or three days. Mail takes longer. If you're getting good response, extend your schedule to a second week and a third week if it is still pulling strongly. As soon as response starts to taper off—STOP. Don't try to get an order from every potential customer. Your television schedule won't pay out if you run beyond the point where you've achieved maximum response and have hit the downside. When you have had a successful run, give your commercial a rest. Stay out of that market for a while, or use the time period for a different offer. Twice a year for most offers is maximum.

**Analyzing results**

$$\text{Television cost} \div \text{orders} = \text{cost per order}$$

Look at that equation carefully. Those stations that produce an acceptable CPO (cost per order) should be used again. Analyze your schedules on the nonprofitable CPO stations to compare costs and schedule times with the better-producing stations. Were costs too high? Were the spots placed in the right areas? Next time, try to negotiate lower costs or better positioning, or omit the station from the schedule.

**Support television**  Making the transition from direct response television to support television for most direct marketers requires a totally new perspective. Unlike conventional direct response television advertising, broadcast support is an advertising medium that requires utilization of different techniques and a totally different understanding of how television works. You must consider the medium as if you were a package-goods or general-consumer advertiser and not a traditional direct marketer. Support advertising draws on all the techniques used by package-goods advertisers and applies these principles within the context of support-advertising requirements.

A "do-it-yourself" manual for support television deserves a volume of its own. However, these highlights will give you enough information to consider whether support television has application for your product.

The purpose of support television is to *call attention to another medium.* That medium can be newspaper inserts, direct mail, newspaper, consumer-magazine advertising, or some combination of any or all of these.

**Market penetration**  Before you can consider using support television, examine the penetration of the market you will achieve with your primary medium. (Print *is* measurable in terms of television market circulation.) The area a TV market covers is called an area of dominant influence (ADI). Newspapers and major print media break out their circulation by ADI areas. Mail can easily be assigned ZIP codes to ADI areas.

Your primary medium must have enough penetration of the televison market to make television cost efficient. Consider as effective only that newspaper circulation or mail which falls within the television coverage area. If your mail-and-print coverage of the TV area is very low, you might consider adding a second newspaper or adding more mail to achieve higher penetration. You can combine newspaper and magazine circulation plus mail to achieve the necessary market penetration and use television to support the combination of media.

**Your primary medium**

Before testing television support, you must know how well your primary medium works. Don't consider using television support of newspaper inserts if you've never used them before. Establish a group of control markets where you have a track record of the results achieved with your primary medium so that you can compare the results that television support provides with those control markets where TV was omitted. Support only pretested material with television.

**Target audiences**

Television, like the other media, is an extension of marketing. Identify your best prospects in terms of age, sex, education, and income. There is research data available on viewing habits in all the categories listed in the maximum reach potential rundown shown in Table 7.3. By knowing your target audience and using the research materials available, you can construct a television plan and ultimately a schedule with which you will be able to select those areas where you can best reach that target. The more you know about the consumer of your product, the more efficiently you can use television.

**Where and when to advertise**

Define your market. Are your sales best in large urban areas? Rural areas? Or do you have a flat national pattern? Does one region of the country account for the bulk of your sales? Do you have greater mail or newspaper penetration in the winter or the summer? January? July?

**Competition**

Learn as much as you can about your competitors' television activities. Where and how are they advertising? Use this knowledge to counter competitive efforts with your television schedule.

**Creative contribution**

The way you plan your creative strategy will have a bearing on your television plan. Exclusive use of 60-second commercials limits the amount of prime time you can schedule. Can you tell your story with a thirty? Will a combination of thirties and sixties do the job best?

**Reach/frequency**

All the information mentioned in the preceding sections is combined to put together a television plan that will give you the most effective reach and

**Table 7.3. Maximum reach potential of television advertising to various demographic groups.**

| Demographic Description | Day | Prime | Early Evening | Late Evening | Early/Late Evening | Sat./Sun. Morning |
|---|---|---|---|---|---|---|
| Households ......... | 78 | 96 | 91 | 81 | 96 | 60 |
| Women 18 and above . | 65 | 92 | 76 | 71 | 88 | 33 |
| Women 18–49 ....... | 64 | 92 | 73 | 72 | 88 | 35 |
| Women 50 and above . | 66 | 92 | 81 | 67 | 89 | 30 |
| Men 18 and above .... | 38 | 90 | 72 | 69 | 88 | 33 |
| Men 18–49 .......... | 31 | 89 | 66 | 72 | 86 | 33 |
| Men 50 and above .... | 50 | 92 | 81 | 65 | 91 | 33 |
| Female teens ........ | 60 | 90 | 76 | 58 | 85 | 41 |
| Male teens .......... | 54 | 86 | 70 | 60 | 80 | 43 |
| Children 2–5 ........ | 84 | 90 | 88 | 19 | 90 | 83 |
| Children 6–11 ....... | 73 | 96 | 90 | 34 | 93 | 82 |

Example of how to read: A maximum of 78 percent of total homes with television is exposed to daytime television at least once in the course of a week.

Source: A. C. Nielsen; O&M Estimates.

frequency against your primary consumer. Reach and frequency are the key factors in support television.

*Reach.* This refers to the number of different homes (or individuals) exposed to a medium within a given period of time, usually one week or four weeks.

*Frequency.* This refers to the average number of messages to which a home (or individuals) reached by a schedule is exposed within a given period of time (one week, four weeks).

The following script for a short TV spot was used to support inserts in selected Sunday newspapers.

**Video**

1. *Announcer in front of rear-projection screen, footage of crowded expressway traffic scene.*

2. *Chroma-key of letter insert.*

3. *Chroma-key: Old American Insurance Company.*

4. *Chroma-key on right: $25,000 traffic and travel accident protection.*

5. *Change chroma-key: Just 25¢ for the first month.*

6. *Slide of letter insert and newspaper logo.*

**Audio**

ANNOUNCER: Ever stop to think how dangerous it is to drive today? That's why I hope you'll take a few minutes this weekend to read this very important letter. It's from Old American Insurance Company, and you'll find it right in your weekend newspaper. Old American tells how you can apply for twenty-five thousand dollars worth of protection against the crippling costs of death or dismemberment from a fatal traffic accident. And the premium for the first month is just twenty-five cents!

*(Tag)* It's an offer that's too good to pass up. So be sure to look for this letter in the (name of paper)!

Each daypart has a maximum reach potential. No matter how many spots you run, you can't achieve reach higher than that maximum. Reach potential is illustrated in Table 7.3.

By predetermining your reach and frequency objectives, that is, how much of the market you want to reach and how often you reach them, and using your knowledge of reach potential, you can construct a plan that will be best suited to meeting your objectives. You should then compare different combinations of dayparts to determine which combination best fulfills those objectives (see Table 7.4).

**Table 7.4. Comparison of television advertising plans budgeted at $100,000 and designed to maximize reach and frequency of messages to television households.**

|  | Day | Early Fringe | Prime | Late Fringe | Total |
|---|---|---|---|---|---|
| Cost per gross rating point (GRP) | $150 | $165 | $400 | $325 | |
| **Plan A** | | | | | |
| Daypart dispersion | 25% | 25% | 25% | 25% | 100% |
| GRP by daypart | 96 | 96 | 96 | 96 | 384 |
| Budget by daypart | $14,400 | $15,840 | $38,400 | $31,200 | $99,840 |
| Reach | 42 | 51 | 56 | 42 | 78 |
| Frequency | 2.3 | 1.9 | 1.7 | 2.3 | 4.9 |
| **Plan B** | | | | | |
| Daypart dispersion | 40% | 10% | 40% | 10% | 100% |
| GRP by daypart | 150 | 36 | 150 | 36 | 372 |
| Budget by daypart | $22,500 | $5,940 | $60,000 | $11,700 | $100,140 |
| Reach | 50 | 28 | 68 | 21 | 80 |
| Frequency | 3.0 | 1.3 | 2.2 | 1.7 | 4.7 |
| **Plan C** | | | | | |
| Daypart dispersion | 34% | 33% | — | 33% | 100% |
| GRP by daypart | 158 | 156 | — | 156 | 470 |
| Budget by daypart | $23,700 | $25,740 | — | $50,700 | $100,140 |
| Reach | 51 | 62 | — | 53 | 78 |
| Frequency | 3.1 | 2.5 | — | 2.9 | 6.0 |
| **Plan D** | | | | | |
| Daypart dispersion | — | 25% | 50% | 25% | 100% |
| GRP by daypart | — | 78 | 156 | 78 | 312 |
| Budget by daypart | — | $12,870 | $62,400 | $25,350 | $100,620 |
| Reach | — | 46 | 68 | 37 | 78 |
| Frequency | — | 1.7 | 2.3 | 2.1 | 4.0 |

*Evaluation.* The outlined plan B and plan C deliver the highest reach ("B") and frequency ("C") of the plans considered. Plan B at 372 GRPs delivers the highest reach of the four plans with frequency equivalent to that delivered by plan A. However, plan A requires 384 GRPs, yet has lowest reach. Therefore, plan B is more efficient. The daypart mix of plan C delivers a very high level of frequency with reach equivalent to that of plans A and

D. While it achieves slightly less reach than plan B, this daypart combination delivers the highest frequency of all four plans. Therefore, plan C should be tested against plan B to determine which combination produces greater results.

**Testing support television**

Every advertiser must determine through testing what GRP level will provide the greatest response for his particular product. There is no special formula that will apply to every advertiser. However, certain procedures basic to all testing should be followed:

1. Those markets that represent a significant sample of your over-all universe should be utilized. If your product has national potential, your test markets should represent 5 percent or more of the total United States. This provides you with a large enough base from which to project a national operation.

2. Along with the test markets, you must have a set of control markets of like size representing the same sample of your sales universe. You then compare test market results with results in the control markets which have no television support.

The initial GRP level you test will be determined by the medium you are supporting. Support of a newspaper insert will require a level different from mail support, which is stretched over a longer period of time. To some extent, the amount of dollars you are willing to commit to television support will also dictate your GRP level, but this should not be a prime criterion.

Once you have tested that initial level and compared the results with those of your control markets, you can test higher or lower GRP levels. It is important to test in increments of 50 percent or more of the initial level. Slight differences of GRP levels will not be significant enough to enable you to clearly measure the results. For example, if your initial test is 300 GRP, then your subsequent tests should reach a high level of 450 GRP (+50 percent) and a low level of 150 GRP (−50 percent).

In addition to testing GRP levels, you can construct tests to determine whether a different length of flight or the way you schedule your GRPs within the flight will produce a significant increase in results.

Numerous tests can be set up to maximize the efficiency of your television advertising. Keep testing variations, but remember to control your tests carefully so that you are testing only one variable at a time. And *always* test that variable against control markets (without the variable) so your results can be easily interpreted.

**Attentiveness**

We have previously explained how lack of attentiveness works for the direct response advertiser. Support advertising, on the other hand, requires high attentiveness. We are not asking the viewer to act now. We want that person to become aware of something arriving in the mail or in his Sunday newspaper, *TV Guide*, or any other medium you are supporting. Like the package-goods or general advertisers, you want the viewer to become familiar with and aware of the product so it is easily recognizable and accepted when the consumer encounters it. You want to precondition the viewer with your advertising message. Knowledge of high attentiveness levels will enable you to determine where to best place your advertising. By using attentiveness patterns in program selection, you ensure greater value and impact for your television dollars.

**Analysis**

It is extremely important to evaluate carefully what has been estimated in terms of rating points and audience delivery when you buy your schedule. This is called pre-buy analysis. And you must just as carefully evaluate what your schedule actually achieved after it has run with a post-buy analysis. With direct response, analysis is relatively simple. Effectiveness is measured in terms of final cost per order.

Support television schedules are bought on a fixed-position basis and evaluated by rating point and audience delivery. In most spot markets, rating surveys are published only three or four times a year. Thus, you will buy your schedule on the data available at that time (pre-buy analysis) and evaluate your schedule and actual delivery according to the rating data available after your schedule has run (post-buy analysis).

This analysis process is invaluable in determining the level of success of your support campaign. If your plan called for a 200 rating point schedule, your post-buy analysis might show that you actually achieved 150 points in one market and 250 in another. Without the post-buy analysis, you would be drawing uninformed conclusions with regard to the success or failure of your support program. Only with accurate pre- and post-buy analysis can you clearly interpret the results of your campaign. The analysis provides a firm, reliable basis for future testing and future campaigns.

**Television commercial testing procedures**

Most general advertisers pretest commercials before airing them. Direct marketers can use the same techniques. Here we discuss the pretesting methods most commonly employed. Questions arise before there can be adoption of a method for testing TV commercials. These questions are important and should be answered before one can put any suggested methodology in perspective.

The major questions are:

1. What is the connection between persuasion and recall? What techniques should be used to measure one or the other?

2. What kind of information is required for the evaluation of alternative commercials?

**Persuasion vs. recall**

There is no definite relationship between persuasion and recall. A high-recall commercial may not be persuasive, or a highly persuasive commercial may not have high recall. A commercial, however, that has high recall values as well as persuasion will do better than a commercial with only one strong factor. Therefore, relying on a rating for on-air recall without having some measure of the persuasive values of a commercial may be misleading. Given the alternative, it would be better to have a commercial with low recall and high persuasion rather than the reverse.

Advertisers who use recall as a measure of advertising do so after they have determined what will most likely persuade people to buy their product. This information is developed by each advertiser through market research among users and nonusers of the product (or brand).

**The kind of information required**

Information gained from the various research techniques available can be separated into that which indicates *why* something happened and that which indicates what *has* happened. For example, in the broadest sense, focus groups or in-depth interviews provide the most information about what could or might happen. On-air testing, in-market awareness studies, and sales measurements indicate what *did* happen. An interim step, pretesting, is required to give you an indication of what will probably happen and why. This interim step should provide a numerical measurement of the various goals of a commercial.

Specifically, a commercial must do several things:

1. It must communicate to the listener what the advertiser is trying to tell him about the product.
2. It must provide an advertising vehicle that involves the listener.
3. It must encourage a more positive attitude from the listener toward the brand or advertiser.
4. It must convince the listener that the total value of buying, using, or owning the product is greater than the cost.
5. It must motivate the prospect to take positive action.

Most ad pretesting is done to measure how well different commercial approaches achieve these objectives. Advertisers have found that there is no better way to reduce the chances of running an ineffetive campaign and to increase the chances of producing a good one than to pretest. Several companies provide commercial testing services to help you evaluate tentative approaches.

**Potential for two-way response TV**

As a direct response medium, television entered a dramatic new phase in December 1977 when QUBE was introduced in Columbus, Ohio.

QUBE, developed by Warner Communications, can best be described as a new "two-way response medium." It makes use of the great signal-carrying capacity of cable television. It allows the home viewer to communicate directly with the station by means of an on-line computer hookup. By means of a small console selector, the subscriber can respond immediately to a commercial or program by pushing appropriate buttons. In the test market, 30 channels were available for interaction and immediate response by the home viewer.

Advertisers—especially direct response advertisers—will be able to achieve results never before possible through the medium of television:

- Direct selling of merchandise
- Procuring qualified prospects for salesmen to follow up
- Sampling of new products by mailing a sample directly to the homes of viewers who request it

- Building traffic through mailing discount coupons to homes
- Carrying out research through the use of interactive questions and answers
- Testing the effectiveness of two or more commercials simultaneously in the same market

At this writing, Warner Communications is making plans to extend the QUBE two-way TV system to more of its cable operations nationwide and to other cable systems. The implications of this new technology for direct response advertisers are exciting, to say the least. When implemented nationwide, QUBE will achieve virtually the ultimate effectiveness in advertising communications.

**Radio**  Unlike television, all radio-audience measurement is based on demographics. Households are not measured. People are. While radio listenership has declined slightly, audiences are still tuned in for an average of three hours daily. This is shown in Table 7.5.

**Table 7.5. Average daily hours of radio listening per person (Monday through Sunday, 6:00 A.M. to midnight).**

|  | 1972 | 1973 | 1974 | 1975 | 1976 | Index* |
|---|---|---|---|---|---|---|
| Persons 12 and above | 3.17 | 3.20 | 3.12 | 3.24 | 3.08 | 97 |
| Persons 18 and above | 3.24 | 3.27 | 3.18 | 3.29 | 3.16 | 98 |
| Men | 3.07 | 2.94 | 3.01 | 3.22 | 3.01 | 98 |
| Women | 3.38 | 3.56 | 3.33 | 3.36 | 3.29 | 97 |
| Persons 18–24 | 3.21 | 3.54 | 3.44 | 3.57 | 3.54 | 110 |
| Men | 3.37 | 3.36 | 3.42 | 3.58 | 3.51 | 104 |
| Women | 3.08 | 3.69 | 3.46 | 3.56 | 3.57 | 116 |
| Persons 25–34 | 3.43 | 3.33 | 3.25 | 3.49 | 3.32 | 97 |
| Men | 3.31 | 3.22 | 3.13 | 3.75 | 3.19 | 96 |
| Women | 3.55 | 3.44 | 3.36 | 3.23 | 3.44 | 97 |
| Persons 35–49 | 3.43 | 3.42 | 3.40 | 3.54 | 3.46 | 101 |
| Men | 3.25 | 2.95 | 3.16 | 3.28 | 3.11 | 96 |
| Women | 3.60 | 3.87 | 3.63 | 3.79 | 3.78 | 105 |
| Persons 50 and above | 3.00 | 3.00 | 2.86 | 2.88 | 2.67 | 89 |
| Men | 2.65 | 2.56 | 2.61 | 2.64 | 2.56 | 97 |
| Women | 3.28 | 3.37 | 3.06 | 3.06 | 2.76 | 84 |
| Teens 12–17 | 2.80 | 2.78 | 2.81 | 2.91 | 2.65 | 95 |

*Index 1972 = 100

Source: Television Radio Age, 1977.

When you are using radio for either direct response or support advertising, you should know your target audience. Find out which of the demographic categories listed in Table 7.6 are most closely related to your product. Radio is an extremely fragmented medium, offering a variety of formats. Each format tends to appeal to a specific audience segment. Unless you know what format is most compatible with your target audience, you could be spending your radio dollars ineffectively. Table 7.6 shows radio listening by station format according to age segments. In addition to demographic variations by format, each format tends to be skewed toward specific income levels. Table 7.7 relates typical formats to income levels.

### Table 7.6. Radio listening by station format.

| Format | Age Groups | | | |
|---|---|---|---|---|
| | 18–24 | 25–34 | 35–49 | 50 + |
| **Men** | | | | |
| Heavy rock | 304 | 127 | 38 | 19 |
| Top 40 | 209 | 154 | 68 | 26 |
| Black | 145 | 117 | 94 | 48 |
| Golden oldies | 123 | 143 | 83 | 58 |
| Popular music | 98 | 119 | 124 | 71 |
| Sports | 73 | 77 | 114 | 110 |
| Classical/semiclassical | 62 | 83 | 124 | 94 |
| Talk | 61 | 67 | 125 | 116 |
| Modern country | 54 | 113 | 141 | 81 |
| Standards | 50 | 83 | 144 | 94 |
| Instrumentals | 48 | 90 | 146 | 93 |
| News | 26 | 49 | 111 | 148 |
| **Women** | | | | |
| Heavy rock | 328 | 97 | 56 | 19 |
| Top 40 | 228 | 153 | 73 | 29 |
| Black | 181 | 122 | 103 | 64 |
| Golden oldies | 146 | 137 | 88 | 60 |
| Popular music | 117 | 124 | 121 | 68 |
| Sports | 88 | 66 | 87 | 124 |
| Classical/semiclassical | 84 | 89 | 112 | 103 |
| Talk | 47 | 76 | 112 | 133 |
| Modern country | 78 | 133 | 122 | 79 |
| Standards | 66 | 98 | 140 | 85 |
| Instrumentals | 73 | 104 | 135 | 81 |
| News | 34 | 50 | 100 | 154 |

Note: Significant indices are shown in medium-face type.

Source: Target Group Index, 1976.

Most formats are suitable for support advertising. Instrumental and good music stations, however, are not ordinarily effective for direct response advertising. In general, the more commercial interruptions there are, the more attentive is the listener.

**Dayparts** As in television, certain dayparts have larger audiences than others. Radio listening varies by age group during the broadcast day (see Table 7.8).

**Table 7.7. Relationship of income level to choice of radio formats by adults.**

| Format | Household Income Level | | | | |
| --- | --- | --- | --- | --- | --- |
| | Under $5,000 | $5,000–7,999 | $8,000–9,999 | $10,000–14,999 | $15,000 and Above |
| Contemporary/total . . . . . . . . | 68 | 108 | 112 | 108 | 120 |
| Middle of the road . . . . . . . . . | 75 | 93 | 115 | 116 | 118 |
| Standard . . . . . . . . . . . . . . . | 64 | 89 | 106 | 119 | 151 |
| Good music . . . . . . . . . . . . . | 46 | 66 | 117 | 146 | 172 |
| Classical/semiclassical . . . . . | 47 | 69 | 105 | 135 | 196 |
| Country/western . . . . . . . . . . | 93 | 120 | 120 | 89 | 72 |
| Talk . . . . . . . . . . . . . . . . . . . | 91 | 83 | 93 | 114 | 134 |
| News . . . . . . . . . . . . . . . . . . | 79 | 84 | 95 | 111 | 158 |
| Black . . . . . . . . . . . . . . . . . . | 169 | 120 | 69 | 55 | 40 |
| Index base . . . . . . . . . . . . . . | 100 | 100 | 100 | 100 | 100 |

Note: Indices more than 10 percent above their respective bases are in medium-face type.

Source: O&M Estimates, 1976.

With most formats, the largest radio audiences are to be found in morning auto driving time (6:00 A.M. to 10:00 A.M.) and evening driving time (3:00 P.M. to 7:00 P.M.). These are the dayparts in which the highest percentage of out-of-home listeners is reached. The hours when people are concerned with getting to and from the office or preparing breakfast and dinner are the most advantageous times for positive reaction to a direct response commercial. Again, the largest audience does not necessarily produce the best response. Conversely, the support advertiser should use these times heavily for his commercial message; they do provide higher reach than the other dayparts.

**Reach and frequency**

Radio is a low-reach/high-frequency medium. This is because radio is such a fragmented medium where people tend to listen to the same station every day and where the audience is divided among numerous stations. Maximum reach potential is 60 percent, and it is necessary to buy several stations to achieve maximum reach. Reach builds very slowly in radio. In the course of one week, 50 GRPs in daytime television will achieve a 30 percent reach and a 1.7 frequency. With radio, it takes four weeks at 50 GRPs to achieve a 31 percent reach, but the frequency climbs to 6.5.

This means that the support advertiser using radio will have to buy very heavily in all dayparts to obtain the desired reach, while the direct marketer will easily achieve the frequency necessary for good response.

The support advertiser should consider using radio as an adjunct to television support, building reach via television and using radio in a supplementary way as a frequency-building vehicle.

**Commercial length**

The 60-second commercial is the one most widely used. This unit is the most economical. Most station rate cards are based on the 60-second unit. Thirty-

**Table 7.8. Radio listening by daypart.**

| Daypart | Age Groups | | | | |
|---|---|---|---|---|---|
| | 18–24 | 25–34 | 35–49 | 50–64 | 65 + |
| **Men** | | | | | |
| Weekday | | | | | |
| 6:00 to 10:00 A.M. . . . . . . . | 103 | 103 | 102 | 101 | 83 |
| 10:00 A.M. to 3:00 P.M. . . . | 142 | 109 | 93 | 77 | 73 |
| 3:00 to 7:00 P.M. . . . . . . . . | 147 | 115 | 95 | 72 | 60 |
| 7:00 P.M. to Midnight . . . . . | 173 | 107 | 81 | 70 | 67 |
| Midnight to 6:00 A.M. . . . . . | 198 | 113 | 78 | 61 | 40 |
| Weekend | | | | | |
| 6:00 to 10:00 A.M. . . . . . . . | 107 | 71 | 100 | 105 | 98 |
| 10:00 A.M. to 3:00 P.M. . . . | 138 | 119 | 95 | 78 | 56 |
| 3:00 to 7:00 P.M. . . . . . . . . | 163 | 114 | 89 | 69 | 55 |
| 7:00 P.M. to Midnight . . . . . | 187 | 110 | 79 | 62 | 56 |
| Midnight to 6:00 A.M. . . . . . | 221 | 116 | 72 | 39 | 49 |
| **Women** | | | | | |
| Weekday | | | | | |
| 6:00 to 10:00 A.M. . . . . . . . | 95 | 103 | 109 | 106 | 81 |
| 10:00 A.M. to 3:00 P.M. . . . | 129 | 113 | 104 | 91 | 58 |
| 3:00 to 7:00 P.M. . . . . . . . . | 162 | 112 | 96 | 80 | 49 |
| 7:00 P.M. to Midnight . . . . . | 188 | 91 | 76 | 87 | 66 |
| Midnight to 6:00 A.M. . . . . . | 192 | 105 | 67 | 80 | 66 |
| Weekend | | | | | |
| 6:00 to 10:00 A.M. . . . . . . . | 96 | 97 | 102 | 109 | 92 |
| 10:00 A.M. to 3:00 P.M. . . . | 149 | 119 | 96 | 86 | 47 |
| 3:00 to 7:00 P.M. . . . . . . . . | 181 | 118 | 90 | 70 | 43 |
| 7:00 P.M. to Midnight . . . . . | 213 | 99 | 77 | 67 | 54 |
| Midnight to 6:00 A.M. . . . . . | 225 | 107 | 59 | 72 | 49 |

Highest daypart for each age group is shown in medium-face type.

Source: Target Group Index, 1976.

second spots are priced at 75 percent of the 60-second rate. Therefore, you are paying a 25 percent premium for 30 seconds less commercial time. (The radio networks are now basing rates on a 30-second unit, but it will be some time before the independent stations make this adjustment.)

**Creative strategy**

Structure your copy to the format you are using. Your copy should be phrased in the appropriate vernacular as in the following examples:

**Format A
Rock station**

*(Hypothetical product: Warren's Widgets)*

*Copy:* Hey you beautiful people listening out there. You know what's the greatest? Well, when it comes to widgets—it's Warren's. Yes, Warren's Widgets really lay it on. They're mean widgets—they stay alive and never quit. You can count on Warren's Widgets to hang in there year after year. And when you need a widget, you need it bad, it's no time to start waiting around. So get your widgets now. Call 212/068-4432. If you call right now, you'll not only get your three-pack of Warren's Widgets for only $8.98, but you'll get an additional $4.98 value piggyback pack of three refills absolutely free. How about that? Here's the straight scam. Call 212/068-4432. Get your Warren's Widgets like now, cause Warren's Widgets are like wow! We're waiting.

**Format B**
**Country station**

*(Hypothetical product: Warren's Widgets)*

*Copy:* Hi cousins. All you good old boys and girls will want to know about Warren's Widgets. When it comes to widgets, they just don't come any better. Use 'em, abuse 'em—Warren's just won't quit. Go right on working year after year. Why, back home we've got a Warren's Widget that Warren put in when he wasn't higher than a one-legged frog can jump. A Warren in your widget cup is like money in your mattress. Something you can always count on. To get your Warren's Widgets, call 212/068-4432. And here's real down-home country value. Call right now and get the three-pack of Warren's Widgets for $8.98 plus absolutely free a piggyback pack of three refills worth $4.98. Write that old number down, 212/068-4432, and call your cousin now. I'm awaitin' and awishin' for your call.

The script for the following 60-second commercial was prepared for an all-news format.

| | |
|---|---|
| *Sound effects:* | *Phone ring, receiver lift.* |
| *Live voice:* | Hello, Bill Johnson here. |
| *Phone voice:* | Johnson, I need a favor. |
| *Live voice:* | *(Aside)* Not again. |
| | *(Upbeat)* Yes, Mr. Willoughby. |
| *Phone voice:* | Could you lend me your copy of the preview issue of *Crain's Chicago Business?* |
| *Live voice:* | Sure, Mr. Willoughby. You've borrowed it dozens of times. |
| *Phone voice:* | Of course I have. In my position, I have to stay up-to-date in what's affecting business here in Chicago. I need to know what's happening now, why it's happening, and what's most likely to happen next. And it's all there in *Crain's Chicago Business.* |
| *Live voice:* | I agree, Mr. Willoughby and that's because it's published by the people who know business *and* Chicago best, Crain Communications, publishers of *Advertising Age, Automotive News,* and lots more. This publisher's 75 correspondents in key business centers here and abroad report anything that might affect any Chicago business. |
| *Phone voice:* | I know, Johnson. Now will you lend me your copy. |
| *Live voice:* | No. |
| *Phone voice:* | *(Astonished)* No???! |
| *Live voice:* | No, because you can get your own copy of the *second free* preview issue of *Crain's Chicago Business* on May twenty-second at Union, Chicago Northwestern, or La Salle Street Stations. Or just call 000-0000. |

## Self-quiz

1. Define GRP (gross rating points).

_____

_____

_____

_____

2. Name the four parts of the television day.

a. _____

b. _____

c. _____

d. _____

3. Define these terms:

a. "P.I." _____

_____

b. "bonus-to-payout"_____

_____

_____

4. Which commercial length is best for an involved TV persentation?

☐ 30 seconds ☐ 60 seconds

☐ 90 seconds ☐120 seconds

5. When are TV commercial costs likely to be at their lowest?

☐ 12/26–1/15 ☐ 1/16–3/1

☐ 7/1–8/31 ☐ 9/1–(new fall programming)

6. When should use of a TV commercial be suspended?

_____

_____

7. How does the target audience for support TV differ from the target audience for direct response TV?

_____

_____

_____

_____

8. Define the terms "reach" and "frequency."

Reach:_____

_____

Frequency:_____

_____

9. Which is more important in measuring the effect of a TV commercial, persuasion or recall?

_____

_____

_____

10. Name three distinctive radio "formats."

a. _____

b. _____

c. _____

11. What is the most common length for a radio commercial?

☐ 30 seconds ☐ 60 seconds

☐ 90 seconds ☐ 120 seconds

## Pilot project

It is your assignment to sell an album of rock music by a "hot" group for $9.95. The medium you are to use is radio. Prepare a 60-second commercial for a rock station format.

# 8

## Co-ops

Few people think of the technique of issuing coupons as a form of direct marketing, but it is, in fact, a classic example. For decades now package-goods firms have used coupon co-ops to introduce new products through retail stores and to hypo sales of existing products. The trend in mail distribution of cents-off coupons has been steadily upward. Why?

As in all business, manufacturers would not be issuing these billions of cents-off coupons if the marketplace were not receptive. Studies of consumer attitudes toward coupons reveal that two out of every three households in the United States now use coupons as an integral part of their regular shopping habits because consumers say:

- Coupons save money
- They inform consumers about products and provide encouragement to try new products
- They reduce the cost of the products

Marketers use them:

- To improve competitive penetration in a market
- To move out-of-balance inventories
- To stimulate product demand at the retail level as a means of obtaining retailer agreements to stock a product
- To accelerate the introduction and widespread use of a new product
- To obtain new users for an old product

**Table 8.1. Growth of coupon distribution (excludes in-ad coupons).**

| Year | Number (Billions) |
|------|-------------------|
| 1971 | 20.3 |
| 1972 | 23.4 |
| 1973 | 27.6 |
| 1974 | 29.8 |
| 1975 | 35.7 |
| 1976 | 45.8 |

**What types of consumers use coupons?**

Interestingly, it is not only the low-income family that is using coupons. A survey conducted by A. C. Nielsen in 1975 showed that 78 percent of families with an annual income of $15,000 and up used coupons compared to only 51 percent of families with an annual income under $5,000. The Nielsen Clearing House is one of the major handlers of retailer redemption of manufacturers' coupons and is also the source of most statistical data concerning them.

As might be expected, families with seven or more members were the highest users—78 percent. Those with one or two members had a 60 percent usage; three to four members—70 percent; five to six members—73 percent.

While the cost of distributing co-op coupons via direct mail is by far the highest, it also produces the highest redemption rate. The better pull per thousand distribution makes up for the higher front-end cost and results in one of the lower costs per coupon redeemed. Table 8.2 gives comparative statistics.

**Table 8.2. Cost of coupon redemption for different circulation methods.**

| Circulation Method | Cost per M Printing/ Delivery | Average Redemption | Distribution Cost[1] | Total Number of Redemptions | Total Redemption Costs[2] | Program Cost | Cost per Coupon Redeemed |
|---|---|---|---|---|---|---|---|
| Direct mail | | | | | | | |
| Co-op | $14.00 | 10.2% | $350,000 | 2,555,000 | $485,450 | $835,450 | 32.6¢ |
| Magazine | | | | | | | |
| Solo | 6.00 | 3.0 | 150,000 | 750,000 | 142,500 | 292,500 | 39.0 |
| Page plus pop-up | 12.00 | 5.4 | 300,000 | 1,350,000 | 256,500 | 556,500 | 41.2 |
| Newspaper | | | | | | | |
| Solo r.o.p. | 3.75 | 2.8 | 93,750 | 700,000 | 133,000 | 226,750 | 32.4 |
| Co-op r.o.p. | 1.00 | 3.2 | 25,000 | 800,000 | 152,000 | 177,000 | 22.1 |
| Sunday supplements | | | | | | | |
| Solo | 6.00 | 2.4 | 150,000 | 600,000 | 114,000 | 264,000 | 44.0 |
| Free-standing insert | 2.25 | 5.3 | 56,250 | 1,325,000 | 251,175 | 307,425 | 23.2 |

1. Distribution cost based on 25 million circulation; some programs have more, others less. Also, rates vary with circulation selected.

2. Redemption costs based on 14-cent face value plus 5-cent handling charge and 1-cent international handling charge.

Source: Redemption rates based on A. C. Nielsen Co. figures; distribution costs based on published rates and industry estimates. Reprinted from the June 13, 1977, issue of *Advertising Age* with permission.

The vast majority of coupons are issued for food items, with household products, toiletry items, and drug products following in that order. Ninety-nine percent of food manufacturers issue coupons, as do 90 percent of household product makers, 73 percent of toiletry firms, and 37 percent of drug product companies.

**Newspaper inserts**

Newspapers are the prime medium for couponing—56.0 percent of the total. This figure relates to on-page ads and ads in Sunday supplements. It is to be noted that the cost per coupon redeemed for free-standing inserts averages 23.2 cents, which is less than direct mail (32.6-cents-per-coupon average).

- Usage of preprinted inserts has grown from 8 billion in 1970 to 20 billion in 1977.
- Insert revenue in 1976 amounted to $846,462,000.
- More than 1,400 newspapers with a total circulation of over 50 million distribute them. About 90 percent of these newspapers are now distributing inserts on weekdays as well as Sundays.

**Table 8.3. Distribution of coupons by media, 1977.**

| Media | Percent |
|---|---|
| Newspapers | 56.0 |
| Magazines | 12.4 |
| Direct mail | 3.0 |
| In/on packs | 8.2 |
| Sunday supplements | 8.5 |
| Free-standing inserts | 11.8 |

Space costs for co-op newspaper inserts vary tremendously by markets. (Space costs are over and above the cost of printing the insert.) Prices in large metro markets tend to be far lower than in C and D markets. There is a trend, however, toward newspaper insert co-ops in non-metro markets, and it is expected that this trend will continue to grow.

**Kinds of co-ops**  The use of co-ops is by no means limited to distribution of cents-off coupons. Phillip Dresden, manager of mail order sales for the Reuben H. Donnelley Corporation in Stamford, Connecticut, is an authority on co-ops. In addition to newspaper co-ops, he lists four other basic co-ops that are in vogue with direct marketers today.

1. *Mail order co-ops.* These are co-op mailings to a company's list of mail order buyers. A company will periodically mail to its recent buyers' list, usually with a covering letter. Some other co-ops gather several lists of mail order buyers' names, remove duplicate names, and offer the co-op mailing to participating advertisers.

2. *Magazine co-ops.* These are co-ops that mail to a magazine subscription list, the magazine itself being the entrepreneur. This is becoming a less frequently used mechanism.

3. *Specialty co-ops.* These are aimed at a specific age or demographic group. An example would be a young family co-op mailed to the new mothers' list. Other examples are co-ops to college students, businessmen, and so forth. Mailings can vary in size from just a few thousand pieces to four or five million.

4. *Mass consumer co-ops.* These are co-ops compiled from auto registration and telephone lists. They usually contain a combination of grocery cents-off coupons and mail order offers. The R. H. Donnelley/Carol Wright Co-op, the only large mass-compiled co-op in the field currently, reaches about 18,000,000 households seven or eight times a year.

Standard Rate & Data Service (SRDS) has an entire section devoted to co-op mailings in its periodic directory called *Direct Mail List Rates and Data.* The listings contain much valuable information.

**Co-op formats**  Direct marketers have two basic formats available to them: postcard and "loose" inserts. Most postcard publications carry three postcards to the page, the reply card unit size measuring approximately 6 × 3⅝. An advertiser can purchase a single card, or two or three adjacent cards.

Sponsors determine the size and weight limitations for loose inserts. Typically the weight limitation is one-quarter ounce, and the size limitation is 5 × 8. If the advertiser exceeds the weight limitation he is usually subject to a surcharge.

**Getting co-ops read**  Participants in co-ops face fierce readership competition. You can greatly improve your chances for getting your piece read and acted on by knowing the behavior patterns of people who receive co-ops. Phil Dresden provides a valuable insight:

I have witnessed a number of focus group research interview sessions through a one-way mirror. Different groups of housewives were brought in and handed co-op envelopes filled with coupons and offers. There was an amazingly consistent behavior pattern. The participants, without exception, sorted each envelope's contents into two piles. Later when they were asked what was the basis for the two piles, they answered: 'Interesting–not interesting; like–dislike; value–no value.' Your offer must find its way to the right pile during that initial sorting.

The way to get into the first pile is to have a simple message clearly stated with effective graphics. The more alternatives you offer, the less your response will be. In a phrase, don't get sorted out; keep it simple. You only have a few seconds to make an impact. Inserts in direct mail co-ops are more like ads in a magazine then like regular direct mail. If the offer appears to be too much trouble, if it appears that the message is going to take some time and effort to get at, the housewife goes to the next offer.

Before you release your final mechanical to the printer, write two questions down on a piece of paper and see if you can answer them honestly: (1) Have you given the potential respondent an opportunity for dialog with you? (2) What precisely are you asking the potential respondent to believe and to do?

Generally, in co-op direct marketing advertising the recipient sees little and remembers less. Any purchase is basically made on impulse, and response levels can be seriously impacted if the potential respondent does not act within a short time span. The products and services should fall into the pattern of something wanted or needed *now*.

**Testing a co-op**   As Phil Dresden points out, testing co-ops is a tricky business. When you test an insert in a co-op you are doing so with one group of partners; when you "roll out," you are likely to be participating with a different group of partners. So you must live with this variable. Here are a few simple rules for testing co-ops based on the Dresden experience:

1. Because testing is a trial for a subsequent major promotion, it is important to ensure conditions such that the major promotion will be as close to the original as possible.

2. Know what your break-even point is and test a sample large enough so your result can be acted upon.

3. Test the co-op first and leave the segments for later unless your product clearly suggests a particular segment. For example, if your product is aimed entirely at a female market, test only the female portion of a co-op mailing.

4. Test a cross section of the complete co-op list. If no "nth" sample is available, request distribution in several different markets—all widely dispersed.

5. Don't let too much time elapse between your test and your continuation, especially if the item you are testing is of a seasonal nature.

**Economics of co-ops**   The prime appeal of co-ops for direct marketers is in their economy. And, not unlike other media, a wide range of circulation costs exists.

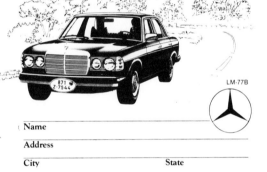

Exhibit 8.1. A page of postcards from Lawyers Market Place—a postcard publication beamed at special interests of lawyers.

Perhaps the most common method of charging for a co-op is in dollars per thousand. A loose insert might run $12.00 to $15.00 per thousand for moderate distribution (the advertiser provides the insert). Substantial discounts are available for multi-million circulation. Postcard circulation can range anywhere from $5.50 per thousand to $25.00 per thousand (including printing costs).

Many co-op sponsors will negotiate P. I. arrangements (an agreed upon charge per inquiry or per order with or without a guaranteed minimum). P. I. arrangements, when available, give the direct marketer good protection against an unusually poor response.

What response might one expect from a co-op mailing vs. a solo mailing or a newspaper insert? You can be fairly sure that a co-op mailing will pull much less per thousand circulation than a solo mailing and somewhat more than a newspaper insert. Phil Dresden ponts out that, not unlike solo mailings, co-op response is dependent on such factors as the offer, list, and time of distribution. Where solo direct mail might have a response range of 1 percent to 10 percent, that same offer in a co-op might only pull from 0.1 percent to 2 percent.

## Package inserts

The never-ending quest for reducing selling costs has led many major direct marketers to offer package insert programs to noncompeting advertisers. Fingerhut, for example, of Minnetonka, Minnesota, offers an extensive package insert program. The firm averages 20,000 inserts every day, 100,000 per week, or a total of 5.2 million inserts yearly.

Jack Oldstein, president of Dependable Lists, Inc., states, "Package inserts offer immediacy, guaranteed mail order buyers, with no waste circulation, the understood endorsement by the mailer of your product to his loyal customer, and the names used are fresher than the next update."

Virgil D. Angerman, formerly sales promotion manager of Boise Cascade Envelope Division, gives this sage advice about package insert programs. "The planning of a package insert program is much like planning a direct mail campaign. The advertiser should evaluate the type of person who will receive the package insert. The advertiser should ask if he or she is the logical prospect for a particular merchandise or service. The question should be raised, will the insert do a thorough selling job? Is the offer attractive? Have you made it easy to send an inquiry or order?" Just as with mailing lists, best results are realized when you match your offer to the market. If you are selling insurance to older people, using package inserts with vitamin shipments makes sense. If you are selling sports apparel, using package inserts with shipments going to fishermen and hunters makes sense, and so forth.

Professional mailing list brokers will provide list cards of firms who accept package inserts just as they supply list cards of direct marketers who make their mailing lists available for rental.

## Other co-ops

While special interest, package insert, and newspaper co-ops offer mass distribution opportunities to direct marketers at low cost, there are also several off-beat co-ops available. A special type of co-op is the program offered by Montgomery Ward that allows selected advertisers to run advertising in various editions of their merchandise catalogs.

Many paperback book publishers make card inserts available to direct response advertisers. Circulation can run into the millions. Direct response advertisers can select distribution by title. Thus, the advertiser can fairly well estimate the demographic profile of readers by the type of book they are buying. *Gone with the Wind* would probably be a good distribution channel for an offer to women, *The Day of the Jackal* for an offer to men, and so forth.

One of the more recent developments is co-op distribution via grocery stores. Producers of grocery bags have devised manufacturing facilities whereby inserts can be pre-inserted in grocery bags. Thus, when the housewife empties her grocery bag, one or more direct response offers are included. Another medium available through retail grocery stores is what is commonly called the "supermarket rack." Shoppers are exposed to a variety of literature in racks adjacent to check-out counters. Distribution of rack material is handled by a number of firms specializing in this activity.

Perhaps the most unusual of co-ops is what might be called a "reverse co-op." Major mailers have made arrangements with package-goods firms to distribute cents-off coupons in mailings that solicit mail orders for completely unrelated merchandise. For example, the direct marketer is offering an AM/FM radio direct to the consumer for $49.95. The teaser copy on the outside envelope says "Free Coupons Enclosed." The consumer opens the envelope and finds a major offer for an AM/FM radio but enclosed, as well, are cents-off coupons. One advertiser I know who tested this technique found that he got more orders per thousand mailed for the radio when he enclosed coupons than when he did not.

Co-ops are a major tool for direct response advertisers when used correctly. Co-ops are not suitable for selling a $400 calculator, but are excellent for getting inquiries about a $400 calculator. Co-ops are highly preferred for in-store coupon redemptions and for scores of direct response offers requiring a minimum of information for a targeted audience.

## Self-quiz

1. Give the three prime reasons consumers use coupons as an integral part of their regular shopping habits.

   a. _____

   b. _____

   c. _____

2. What type of family is more likely to redeem coupons?

   ☐ Families with annual income under $5,000

   ☐ Families with income over $15,000

3. What is the average cost per coupon redeemed?

   For direct mail co-op: ____cents

   For Sunday supplement free-standing inserts: ____cents

4. Name four types of co-ops.

   a. _____

   b. _____

   c. _____

   d. _____

5. What is the difference between "loose" insert co-ops and postcard co-ops?

   _____

   _____

   _____

   _____

   _____

6. Describe how housewives tend to sort out the contents of co-op envelopes.

   _____

   _____

   _____

   _____

7. What are the two questions you should ask yourself before you release a co-op insert for printing?

   a. _____

   _____

   b. _____

   _____

8. What is the one variable you must live with in scheduling the continuation of a co-op that you tested previously?

   _____

   _____

   _____

   _____

   _____

9. What is the general range of cost for a postcard co-op? From $5.50 per thousand to $____ per thousand.

10. What is a P.I. arrangement?

    _____

    _____

    _____

    _____

11. If a solo direct mail effort pulled from 1 to 10 percent, you would expect that same offer in a co-op to pull from ____percent to ____percent.

12. Name five advantages of package inserts.

    a. _____

    b. _____

    c. _____

    d. _____

    e. _____

## Pilot project

You are a manufacturer of pocket calculators. You have a low-end pocket calculator that sells for $9.95 and a top-of-the-line calculator that sells for $99.95.

You have determined that the $9.95 calculator has broad consumer appeal. The $99.95 calculator, on the other hand, appeals primarily to the business market. You have selected the R. H. Donnelley/Carol Wright Co-op to reach the mass consumer market and *Business Market Place* to reach the business market. Your assignment is:

1. Prepare copy for a loose insert slip-size 5 × 8—for the Carol Wright Co-op, designed to produce orders for the $9.95 pocket calculator.

2. Prepare copy for a single postcard—size 5⅞ × 3¾ —for the *Business Market Place* postcard publication, designed to produce inquiries for the $99.95 pocket calculator.

# 9

## Telephone Marketing

Within the past few years, the use and, more important, the general acceptance of the telephone as a marketing medium has grown and developed at a rate that no practitioner of this specialized technique would have dreamed possible.

In the United States, 2.5 billion calls are made each year by marketers. Of $3.25 billion in sales derived from its catalog, Sears, Roebuck and Company receives over $2 billion via phone order, nearly ten times the volume that comes in through the mail! Marketers offer $8.50 magazine subscriptions, $200 sculptures, $6,000 automobiles, and $125,000 earth-moving machines. They complete orders on the spot; they make appointments for their salespeople; they screen prospects for literature distribution; they jog slow paying customers.

This chapter not only analyzes new developments in the field but discusses in detail the factors that should go into the planning and implementation of an effective telemarketing program. The bulk of the material has been prepared by Murray Roman, a pioneer in the development of the telephone as a major marketing medium. Author of *Telephone Marketing: How to Build Your Business by Telephone,* Roman is Chairman of Campaign Communications Institute of America, Inc., an organization that specializes in developing and carrying out telemarketing programs for business and industrial clients, political campaigns, and fund-raising organizations. He has set many of the standards that are today accepted as doctrine by many major telephone marketers. Roman was the originator of the "production line" concept to standardize and control telephone programs. He also pioneered the concept of using taped messages from prominent and authoritative persons as a part of the telemarketing sales approach.

Telephone marketing as a way of life in the United States has burgeoned in recent years because, by taking advantage of dramatic technological breakthroughs, it functions as the only selective, targeted, "person-to-person mass medium" existing today. Print media, radio, and television, of course, are outstanding examples of mass media, while direct mail offers the marketer pinpoint selectivity, and the personal sales visit remains the number one person-to-person approach. But only telephone combines all of these attributes, enabling the marketer to select his area of operations, test quickly and economically, and indulge in a direct personal interactive conversation with his prospect. Yet, it is entirely compatible with all other media.

Like every other development that has impact on a complex society, the growth of telemarketing has brought problems in its wake and has raised some questions. There are those, for example, who are concerned that the marketer's access to the citizen's home at any hour constitutes an invasion of privacy. Others express vehement opposition to the relatively recent introduction of automatic sequential dialing, in which a caller can ring telephone numbers in numerical order without knowing or caring about the called person's location, interests, or demographic or psychographic characteristics or even whether he is calling a residential or a business number.

Invasion of privacy? In 1976, AT&T received a total of 1.3 million complaints. Of these, only 2,190 related to telephone marketing. Automatic sequential dialing? Any competent direct marketing executive knows that the key to successful, cost-effective promotion is *selectivity*, the carefully planned approach directed only to those prospects whose history, status, location, age, income, and related characteristics indicate their potential interest in the offered product or service.

The fact is that generally customers don't object to calls: most actually welcome them. Retailers like Sears, Roebuck and Montgomery Ward have employees whose sole function is calling charge customers to tell them about special promotions. They report that customers await such calls, tend to establish a personal relationship with the communicators, and talk to them as they would to family and friends. And, of course, the alert business prospect is almost always ready to accept calls that might help him cut costs or improve the level of his own sales.

To keep the telemarketing medium problem-free, it is essential that calls be made only to consumers with a demonstrated interest in the offer being made. Telephone marketers themselves recognize the high cost and lowered production of results for nonselective calls made straight out of the white pages of a local directory. For this reason alone, it seems predictable that sequentially (nonselective) dialed calls will ultimately prove their lack of feasibility, through a consistent prohibitively negative relationship between costs and results.

**Varied uses**  Direct marketers have recognized that it is this key ratio of sales costs to sales income that marks the telephone as by far the best tool to be used for a wide variety of purposes. Today, the telephone when properly planned and controlled is successfully being used to:

- Take an order for virtually any amount
- Prospect for qualified leads
- Make marginal accounts profitable

- Motivate delinquent accounts
- Follow up on and reinforce direct mail
- Receive direct response inquiries to TV, radio, or print-media advertising
- Convert inquiries into sales
- Make an appointment for a sales visit
- Reactivate or upgrade old customers
- Promote special merchandising to generate store traffic
- Find and screen new business
- Solicit qualified credit applications
- Introduce a new product to a distribution network
- Deliver a taped message to a select audience
- Raise funds for institutions or public causes
- "Get out the vote" in key election districts
- Gain a reaction or develop information through survey techniques
- Determine campaign, brand penetration, price testing
- Cover distant customers economically
- Reach more customers in less time

Yet, the unique aspects that mark the telephone make it possible for each of these things to be done economically and promptly. With the telephone, there is no need to prepare a printed package, distribute it widely and then sit back and wait, perhaps for several weeks, before evaluating a test operation. As few as 500 calls, made in a matter of hours, will produce immediate, low-cost results that will help determine the viability of any offer.

**Telephone as a test medium**
In connection with the important direct marketing factor of testing, telephone's flexibility makes it possible to call sample names from a number of lists to determine how effective an offering will prove to be. When testing a program, the best lists should be tested first under the premise that, if the best list doesn't produce, there is small likelihood for success with lesser lists. The best lists, you will recall, are inquiries, past and present customers, and prospects within a target group having a high response to other direct selling approaches for the same or similar offers. With the telephone, all this can be quickly and accurately tested—and with only token investment.

While a test is being conducted, necessary changes can be made—in the offer, the price, the terms, and the copy approach. Changes can be made even as such problem areas become evident through prospect reaction to the test calls. All the while, the marketer has the satisfaction of realizing he is using the one medium whose costs have actually been fairly stable over the years. The longer the distance the less it costs per mile! In 1950, for example, a three-minute station-to-station daytime call from New York to Philadelphia cost 45 cents, today that call costs $1.01.

Yet, in 1952 it cost $2.50 to call San Francisco from New York; now it's only $1.30. And if you wait until after 5:00 P.M., which is only 2:00 P.M. in

California, the cost per station-to-station call drops to only 83 cents for the first three minutes.

**Ingredients for success**

What are the considerations you must investigate before finding yourself in a position to reap the benefits offered by the telephone?

First, it is well to remember that oral communication is an art that few people take the time to master. Effective use of the telephone as a marketing instrument requires far more than merely seating your star salespeople at telephones and asking them to dial some numbers. It has frequently been demonstrated that a person who is an absolute whiz at face-to-face, eyeball-to-eyeball selling can prove to be a dismal failure when it comes to using the telephone.

That is because effective face-to-face salesmanship grows out of such esoteric factors as personal relationships, a look of pleasure or surprise, a wink, a grin, a handshake. But, successful telephone sales spring from a "voice that smiles," a carefully prepared script, effective cost control procedures, and rigidly controlled record-keeping.

Verbal speed rate is another important factor. Facial expressions, plus a natural tendency to do a little lipreading from time to time, usually enable people to understand one another more easily during face-to-face sessions. But, when the telephone is employed, the voice is the only influence at work. Talking too fast will often lead to distrust at the other end of the line. The listener may develop suspicions that he or she is being double-talked into something. Conversely, speaking too slowly creates impatience, loss of interest on the part of the listener, and a desire to hang up before the sales message is completed.

Cultivating the proper speech rate is just one of several things that must be taught to those chosen to serve as your telephone communicators. *Proper training* of those who will sit at the phone four or five hours daily to represent you thus becomes a primary consideration in planning effective telephone operations.

The number of calls made per hour is a key element in the costs of your program. Therefore it is important that your communicators be trained to get through to the decision maker on each call. He should not waste time talking to a secretary or an assistant, i.e., going through an entire sales talk with someone who has no authority to buy. When a business executive is called, it is to be expected that a good secretary will challenge your right to talk to him. But training in the need for immediate proper identification plus a pretested script will help your communicator get through quickly and effectively.

Communication is a two-way affair. A properly prepared script will include a series of questions and objections the prospect might be expected to raise and, of course, the effective answers to them. (These can be ascertained through the results from the original test program.) Your communicators, therefore, must be trained not only to read their scripts in the most persuasive way possible, but also to listen to what the person on the other end of the line is saying. When an order is actually placed or an appointment made, details of quantity, price, style, date, address, and the like should be read back immediately to eliminate—or at least minimize—the possibility of error. And when a complex offer is being made, there is nothing wrong with instructing your people to throw in a "Do you follow me?" or a "Is that clear?" once in a while.

**Taped messages**
One of the most effective recent developments in the increasingly successful use of the telephone as a marketing tool has been the inclusion of a previously taped message as part of the sales procedure. Here is the technique. The live communicator makes a brief introduction and gives a statement as to the reason for the call. He then tells the prospect that a prominent, authoritative, or notable person—whose name, of course, is clearly mentioned—has prepared a special taped message. The caller emphasizes that the taped message will take no more than two minutes to play.

In this approach, the call is being taken out of the level of a salesperson approach. The prospect personally is asked to listen. He then gives permission to hear someone he has heard of, relates to, perhaps respects or even idolizes. Many notable persons have made such tapes in support of business interests or to help nonprofit, philanthropic organizations raise funds. The list of those whose tapes have helped in selling is long. It includes, to name but a few, movie star Charlton Heston, editor Norman Cousins, civic leader Bess Myerson, broadcaster Betty Furness, investment counselor Gustave Levy, President Richard Cremer of the Montgomery Ward Auto Club, Vice-President Robert Meyers of American Express, and Dr. Jerry Caulder for Monsanto.

On a business-to-business sales level, the effect of the personal call plus the taped message can be maximized when it is made by a national sales manager, a board chairman, or an industry-recognized consultant.

This peer relationship between a calling executive and a called decision maker, gives the prospect a feeling that he is talking with a knowledgeable authority rather than simply with an order taker. The technique serves also to function like the printed or broadcast endorsement, even when the tape maker simply talks about the virtue of the product, service, or cause without specifically saying, "I use it."

Here is an actual example of a script which has been used successfully. It opens with the communicator's introduction, followed by the taped message, and closes with the communicator's return to the line for the purpose of obtaining the order:

Hello. This is David Jones, of the Bell & Howell Business Equipment Group. I'm using this special telephone message approach because I'd like to bring to your attention, as directly as I can, an important new breakthrough in automated banking systems.

Over the years, we at Bell & Howell have been concerned with the needs of many banks that cannot justify the cost of large and elaborate equipment to handle statement rendering and mailing efficiently, accurately, and economically. I believe, based on our sales to banks of smaller or similar size, that our new Matchmaker 2, specially designed to handle your volume of demand deposit accounts, can provide just this type of streamlined statement handling at a cost that may well be significantly lower than what you can incur in your present manual system. Here's how it works:

The new Matchmaker 2 and one operator are all that you need to automate your statement rendering and mailing system. In a fraction of the time that the costly hand method takes, the Matchmaker 2 automatically counts the number of transactions and matches checks, deposit slips, statements, and special inserts, then stuffs and seals envelopes, ready for mailing. Designed to handle an average of three to four hundred statements per hour, the Matchmaker 2 gets statements in the mail on time every month. And because it's from Bell & Howell, any user is assured of continuous, efficient performance and dependable service.

So that you may judge its value and application for your bank's special requirements, our telephone communicator will be happy to arrange to have one of our representatives call on you at a time that is convenient. I hope you'll take this opportunity to consider the new Matchmaker 2 but, in any case, thank you for taking the time to listen.

An important advantage of the taped message approach is its facility for maintaining quality control, a familiar element in the preparation of materials for print or broadcast purposes. Once a final version of the copy has been agreed upon, making a tape ensures that every prospect will hear the message in exactly the same words, tone of voice, inflections, and pace. No matter how well trained your communicators may be, continual variations will appear in their approaches—from one to the next and from each as the day wears on. But with the taped message, delivery is identical every time, no matter how large the ultimate total volume of your calls.

It might be thought that neither consumers nor business executives would react happily to the notion that they are getting only the taped voice of a popular, well-known individual.

Surprisingly, people seem to understand and to accept the fact that well-known personalities or top-level business executives can't spend their whole day calling people personally. Many tests and surveys clearly indicate that most people prefer to hear from a famous person or from someone in a peer relationship with whom they can identify. People prefer to hear someone who tells a completely authentic sales story, rather than listen to a caller whose name and voice are totally unfamiliar to them.

The use of a standardized, quality-controlled tape represents something more than just a technique suitable for use via telephone. It epitomizes the entire concept of the vital distinction between modern telephone marketing as a science and mere "selling over the telephone."

**Production-line approach**

As was pointed out in *Telephone Marketing: How to Build Your Business by Telephone,* a structured, production-line approach is essential if a telephone program is to be rendered effective and successful. A series of practical steps must be planned and carefully implemented to encompass:

- Planning a fundamental marketing strategy using supportive integrated research;

- Creating materials for communicator use in accordance with professional advertising, marketing, and sales practices;
- Organizing logistical operations to obtain maximum efficiency per call and maximum calls per hour;
- Selecting and training personnel in a planned and careful manner;
- Maintaining up-to-the-minute records of reactions and results, to provide the basis for ongoing evaluation of cost effectiveness.

The definition and analysis of the telephone marketing operation retain their validity only to the extent that the individual marketer adheres strictly to the concept of the structured production-line technique.

Murray Roman writes: "The telephone is an electronic tool that is available to every marketer for use as a rigidly controlled, sophisticated, immediately measurable production-line base for a sales or sales-related operation that meets the requirements of the contemporary market.

"It's unique person-to-person attributes, when carefully combined with manufacturing-type controls, provide for a productive and profitable marriage of uniform message presentation and alert reaction to the needs of an individual prospect. The telephone makes it possible to approach every potential customer with a prepared, predetermined, standard copy message while, at the same time, permitting reasonable flexibility in response to each individual prospect's requirements. In no other form of promotional communication does the medium so profoundly influence the message."

**Do-it-yourself or buy**    This fundamental matter of production-line technique and rigid operational controls raises the question of whether a marketer should organize and implement his own in-house telemarketing program or seek the professional services of a specialized organization geared solely to the agency approach.

One factor to be taken into account is that of continuity and intensity. If the marketer's sales operation is limited to a relatively few seasonal high peaks each year, the questions of available phone room space, acquiring and training temporarily engaged communicator personnel, and switching staff supervisors and executives away from their normal duties for a few weeks at a time must be considered. These and other problems inherent in the higher costs of any specialized but temporary operation must be given full weight before a decision is made.

In this type of situation, contracting for the services of a specialized telemarketing agency operation might be a wise decision for both saving on costs and obtaining better results more promptly and expeditiously. Where a marketer's effort is an ongoing one, however, such investment factors as space, personnel, training, and phone line availability, might readily indicate the advantages of an in-house operation, with its concomitant benefits of continuous and immediate controls, long-range budgeting, and prompt, on-the-spot reporting or reactions to test offers and test lists.

Before you decide to "do-it-yourself," consider the requirements: Is there an internal base of experience and expertise in the telephone marketing you can draw upon? Do you have personnel available who can design a specific telephone sales approach to maximize the impact of your sales message, can they train, supervise, and motivate telephone sales people to deliver the message in the best possible way and coordinate all support media needed for the campaign? Whether your plan calls for pre- or post-mailings, cooperating advertisements, follow-up contacts by salesmen, credit-screening, order fulfillment, or invoicing, careful preparation is necessary to ensure satisfactory returns.

Will you have to recruit telephone sales people? Anyone who represents your company by telephone should be trained, supervised, and experienced both in what you're offering and how best to use the telephone as your communication device. Also, how are they to be paid? By salary, commissions, incentives, or bonuses? Professional agencies know the advantages and pitfalls of each compensation method; you may not.

What types of telephone equipment can most efficiently reach your market? Here the services now placed in your hands by the telephone company can become a bewildering and expensive set of tools unless you know the advantages and limitations of each. Should calls be placed directly, or is the extra impact of "person-to-person" contact worth the cost? Is *Wide Area Telephone Service* (WATS) feasible? If WATS, what type of coverage do you need—national or partial, full-time, or measured-time? Would an "800" number (inbound WATS) or the collect-calls method better serve a call-in campaign? How many phone lines do you need? Should only one type of service be used, or is a mix of different calling modes better suited to your specific needs?

How long will the campaign run? Is it better to call your prospects during the day, in the evening, at their offices, or in their homes? Do you have their phone numbers?

Finally, are there any legal requirements affecting your campaign? Many states require licensing for real estate, insurance, and investment brokerage telephone solicitors. If you have any doubts, it's best to check with your company lawyer and state licensing board before you place your first call.

Many marketers find the services of professional telephone sales agencies preferable to internal operations. The professional telephone marketer can help implement a campaign and assist in structuring initial goals in the same way an advertising agency applies its experience to guide a client.

An outside telephone sales operation should be examined in the same manner you'd consider the services of the advertising agency, direct-mail supplier, or media consultant. Ask the same questions and set the same standards for that company's personnel as you would apply to your own people. Has the company shown a creative talent and expertise in telephone selling? How much help are they willing to give? Will they merely pick up the phone and say what you tell them to say? Or will they come up with worthwhile suggestions for profiting on the investment that telephone selling requires?

A list of past clients is always a good indication of just how effective any telephone marketing agency will be. Is their experience broad based? Have they completed projects for well-known, reputable clients? Do they know *your business* and how best to reach *your audience?*

What are the limitations of their calling capacity? Will the company be able to meet time, location, and volume requirements? And, does the service this agency offers meet your needs effectively and at a cost-effective level? Many professional telephone marketing companies utilize a network of homeworkers, housewives, and other part-time personnel who make calls from their home phones. While this type of call operation can be less expensive, fully staffed central workshops with local WATS lines often produce higher response rates that offset incremental costs.

**Multimedia application** Despite its unique and exclusive marketing features, the telephone represents a tool that is effectively used as an integral part of a carefully planned multimedia mix. Consistently, this technique demonstrates an ability to pull substantial numbers of orders from recipients of mailings who have not responded to the mailed offer. As an example of such a multimedia approach, here is a summary of a mail and telephone campaign for a positive option offer of four $200 sculptures from the Card Division of the American Express Company.

The campaign was particularly effective at the crucial point when a high order rate for the second sculpture was necessary. Telephone sales alone resulted in a 77.7 percent order rate for the fourth sculpture after the "cream" of the list was skimmed by the mail campaign.

"This was the first time that we used telephone to supplement direct mail," said Henry S. Y. Wee, Director of Marketing, Merchandising Sales for the American Express Card Division. "We're convinced that telephone adds a vital plus to a positive option program. In this campaign the return on investment for telephone was tremendous."

The telephone marketing campaign began *after direct mail for the second sculpture* had produced the maximum number of orders anticipated.

The script incorporated the playing of a "tape within a tape." The communicator played a tape in which Robert Meyers, vice-president of the Card Division, introduced the sculptor, Philip Kraczkowski, who described the series. The artist's portion of the tape stated:

> To recreate the saga of the early West with integrity, the artist must achieve unerring realism. I see the history of America's West as a monumental era. The taming of this rugged land signifies the spirit and determination which has characterized our people for nearly 200 years.
>
> The four figures that together comprise my commemorative sculpture collection attempt to recreate classic scenes from frontier life. If I have, indeed, created a collection that depicts the story of the American West with real and lasting value, then its production by Royal Worchester in pewter—the sculptor's medium—enhances this value for its excellence and high standard of craftsmanship.

Communicators asked for orders, using the precise language of the script. Prospects' questions were answered with scripted answers. The communicators were successful in securing orders for the second sculpture from 22 percent of the persons called. Pre-order cost for this phase of the campaign was $16.14, for an expense/sales ratio of 8.1 percent. This is an impressive return considering that the list had already been creamed.

A telephone campaign was also used to follow up on purchasers of the second statue who had failed to respond to the mail offer of statue number three. A final telephone campaign followed up purchasers of the third statue who failed to respond to the mail offer for statue number four. As might be expected, the percentage of conversions rose in both these campaigns. The rate of increase, however, was higher than might be anticipated.

The phone campaign for the third sculpture yielded an order rate of 34 percent. Its per-order cost was $10.17, compared with $16.14 on the second statue, for an expense/sales ratio of 5.0 percent, compared with 8.1 percent for the second.

The phone campaign for the fourth sculpture resulted in an order rate of 88.7 percent, compared with 34 percent for the third sculpture. Its per-order cost was $5.25, for a 2.6 percent expense/sales ratio.

In all, the phone program produced more than $200,000 in orders at an expense/sales ratio of less than 8 percent.

Telephone is suitable for multimedia use with promotional efforts involving print and broadcast media as well as direct mail. For example, it has proved an effective means of following up coupon returns from newspaper and magazine advertising, particularly in setting up appointments in the homes of consumer prospects for demonstrations of such products or services as learning courses, alterations to the home, insurance interviews, and isotonic excercising aids.

**Use of 800 numbers**     The easy availability of the telephone in about 95 percent of the nation's households makes it possible also for a marketer to elicit calls from the interested prospect via the "800" line procedure. Through other general media such as print or broadcast, the advertiser stimulates the consumer to call him in response to an offer. To effect proper cost controls, however, great care must be exercised in the timing and scheduling of the advertising asking for these "800" calls. Because a rental fee is paid for each such line by the marketer, it is obviously in his interest to make sure that the line is properly used—that there are neither long hours for which he is paying without adequate usage nor peak times in which the line or lines are so overloaded that constant busy signals result in discouraged prospects who finally stop trying altogether.

The files of telemarketing agencies such as CCI as well as the records of substantial numbers of marketing organizations that have run their own in-house operations, are replete with success stories similar to the American Express experience. But telephone is not a panacea from which one can automatically expect fabulous results without knowledge or effort. There are the failures, too. But they can almost invariably be attributed to an inability to follow standard, logical procedures somewhere along the line, such as poor selection of lists, failure to test before investing significant money in mass calls, lack of communicator training, failure to research the level of the appeal of the offer, ignoring the signals revealed by test results, and not keeping adequate records.

**Summary**    Despite these pitfalls against which the alert marketer must constantly guard, success has been the rule for most telemarketing operations. Here is a summary of the basic considerations that must be taken into account in the planning and execution of an effective and successful telemarketing program.

**The "do-it-yourself" or "buy" decision**    Any company intending to implement its own telephone program must possess the necessary creativity and expertise. Proper implementation of a telephone program requires careful planning and constant monitoring to ensure maximum results. There must be labor intensiveness which will enable a company to quickly shift into high gear on completion of the pretesting phase. Moreover, the most appropriate telephone equipment should be utilized to maximize production at minimum costs. There are also certain legal requirements—especially at the state level—and these can be particularly restrictive in such businesses as insurance, real estate, and mutual funds.

A company deciding to retain an external organization for a telephone program should carefully review the capabilities and experience of the agency being considered. Certain organizations specialize in such areas as market research and validations and are not necessarily equipped to implement telephone as a medium for selling. Ask for the names of other clients represented by the organization, and make sure there are control mechanisms that will reflect at any given time the status of the ongoing program.

**Organizational responsibilities and assignments**    As with any facet of a total marketing program, the positioning and implementation are better accomplished with reinforcement by senior executive support. Telephone, more than certain other media, requires a well conceived plan of coordination because of the speed with which the program is conducted.

A squad of five telephone operators working an eight-hour day will quickly bring measurable results and must be monitored on a daily basis to ensure proper results and best list utilization.

Lead-time factors must be determined concerning telephone's relationship to other media. Are you calling before or after a mail drop? Are "cold" prospects being called? Did coupon response cream the market first?

**Lists and reporting systems**    A telephone program is only as good as the universe to which it is directed. And in telephone marketing the universe is determined by the list of names compiled, rented, or purchased.

It is rare to obtain a list on which more than 85 percent of the names are current. On most lists, one-quarter of the names cannot be reached. They have either unlisted or unpublished numbers. When business executives are called, an even higher percentage have either left the company or changed positions.

When you are acquiring lists, you should consider the manner in which telephone numbers will be obtained. When you hire someone to look up the telephone numbers, the normal charges can range from 10 to 20 cents per name. And you are billed for a name regardless of whether the telephone number is obtainable. Various telephone companies provide a free look-up service on a time availability basis. But strong pressure is being exerted by the telephone company to eliminate this service. Without ZIP codes, look-up costs are higher, and every list should be pretested before being implemented. The best lists should always be used first—at the beginning of the program—on the theory that, if the best will not work, the program is destined to fail. National computer lists that provide consumer phone numbers for an additional charge are now available.

**The message**  The first question in developing the telephone message is whether a live telephone communicator is to be used alone or in a service capacity as a control mechanism to introduce a tape.

The use of a tape alone (i.e. without live telephone operators) has limited applications and is recommended only for "call-in" programs in instances where the person called will not be offended.

In many programs, a tape used with live telephone operators is preferable to using operators alone. The relevance of the "voice" on tape to the "list" being called is the key. Norman Cousins to his prospects, or Alistair Cooke to listeners of "Masterpiece Theatre" is better, more effective, and more personal than any anonymous communicator.

Tape provides a uniform standard of quality that can be measured and controlled through program modifications. This uniform standard is impossible to achieve when live communicators are used to deliver the sales message. There are, however, certain controls that can be applied to maximize quality by formulating highly structured parameters for programs in which live operators are used exclusively.

Operators should be thoroughly briefed before implementing any telephone program, and an easy-to-present script should be provided that clearly outlines the purpose of the call.

Key questions from the person called should be anticipated as well as objections to whatever it is the operator is selling. Suitable answers and explanations should be provided beforehand.

A checklist system for categorizing calls will simplify the operator's task. This will minimize time spent doing paperwork and maximize time spent on the telephone.

The most common form of checklist where a simple buy/no buy decision is involved will normally include:

- Orders
- Literature/information requests
- Not interested
- Request call back
- Not available (particularly in business)
- Didn't answer/busy (try four or five times)

**Fulfillment**  A verbal "yes" on the telephone is often quickly forgotten unless written verification is received by the prospect within a few days. Telephone operators would always reinforce the prospect's affirmative response by repeating whatever the person has agreed to.

Telephone marketing has become a way of life in the United States and is making rapid progress in other nations as well. Businessmen and consumers alike have become accustomed to the practice of being called, and most give every indication that they welcome such contact. Major users of phone calls include banks, insurance companies, publishers, and retailers—all of whom are necessarily sensitive to consumer complaints and who would rapidly bring such programs to a close if they were convinced that such calls are not welcomed.

Carefully measured in surveys, consumer attitudes toward telephone marketing, however, tend to reflect a high degree of acceptance. For example, one such study conducted on behalf of a major casualty insurance company showed that 90 percent of the respondents rated the method of solicitation as "good" in calls they had actually received. Only 6 percent said it was "fair," and only a tiny 1 percent styled it as "poor." Asked to comment on the politeness of the communicators, 90 percent of the respondents found them "very polite," while all the remainder characterized them as "reasonably polite."

It would appear that continued acceptable (therefore, fruitful and profitable) use of the telephone as an important marketing tool thus depends on the manner in which marketers employ this powerful medium. Calls must offer real benefits. They must be short, truthful, polite. They must be made at reasonable times, taking into account occupational, cultural, ethnic, and religious practices of the prospects.

It is important that scripts be created in such a manner as to enable a communicator to terminate a call promptly and courteously when response indicates antagonism or even lack of reasonable interest. This means, in turn, that communicators must be trained to pay attention equally to what they hear and to what they say and that their scripts furnish them with logical responses to anticipated questions and objections.

In short, continued and expanded use of the telephone as a marketing medium depends not only on the commercial successes that it can attain through strict adherence to proved procedures and techniques, but also on strict attention to approaches and methods that will generate a substantial measure of goodwill on the part of prospective customers toward those who use the telephone to solicit business from them.

## Self-quiz

1. List ten of the varied uses of telephone.

   a. _____

   b. _____

   c. _____

   d. _____

   e. _____

   f. _____

   g. _____

   h. _____

   i. _____

   j. _____

2. When testing a proposition by telephone, which lists should be tested first?

   ☐ Best list      ☐ Cross section of lists

3. Why have taped messages proved successful?

   _____

   _____

   _____

   _____

4. What are the five steps necessary to the production-line approach to telephone marketing?

   a. _____

   b. _____

   c. _____

   d. _____

   e. _____

5. What are the disadvantages of a do-it-yourself sales function?

   _____

   _____

   _____

   _____

6. What are the advantages of using an outside telephone sales operation?

   _____

   _____

   _____

   _____

7. Give an example of how the telephone might be used as part of a multimedia program.

   _____

   _____

   _____

   _____

8. What is the greatest appeal of using the "800" number procedure?

   _____

   _____

   _____

   _____

9. The most common form of checklist where a simple buy/no buy decision is involved will normally include:

   a. _____

   b. _____

   c. _____

   d. _____

   e. _____

   f. _____

## Pilot project

You are in the public relations department of a major corporation. The chairman of the board of your corporation (a very influential man) has accepted the chairmanship of the cancer drive for your city.

A list of major potential donors has been compiled for a telephone campaign. You have been asked to do a script for a taped message.

Develop a plan that will answer the following questions:

1. What is the time limit for your tape?
2. You have been given the option of selecting any person you want to induce people to contribute to the cancer fund. Whom would you select—in addition to your chairman?

Write the script.

# Section III

# Creating
# and Producing
# Direct Marketing

# 10

## Techniques of Creating Direct Mail Packages

Direct mail is an expensive advertising medium. It costs you 15 to 20 times as much to reach a person with a direct mail package as it does to reach him with a 60-second TV commercial or a full-page ad in a newspaper. But, direct mail has certain unique advantages that more than compensate for its higher cost. If you understand what these advantages are and use them properly, you will be able to bring in orders or responses at a cost equal to or below that of space or broadcast. And, as a general rule, customers acquired by direct mail are usually better customers in terms of repeat business than those acquired by space or broadcast advertising.

**The advantages of direct mail**

Through careful list selections and segmentation, direct mail can give you pinpoint selectivity unmatched by any other advertising medium. You can literally pick out households one by one, mailing only to those that are the best prospects for your offer. The fundamentals of list selection and segmentation are discussed in chapter 4. Review these carefully. In addition to its capacity for pinpoint selectivity, direct mail can do a better selling job than any other advertising medium. There are several reasons for this.

**Virtually unlimited choice of formats**

In direct mail, you are not restricted to 60 seconds of time or a 7 × 10 page. You can use large, lavishly illustrated brochures. You can have any number of inserts. You can use pop-ups, fold-outs, swatches—even enclose a phonograph record. What you can do is limited only by your imagination and the budget constraints. For example, one enterprising mailer used a unique response device: he mailed a carrier pigeon to each prospect. The respondent taped his reply to the pigeon's leg and released the pigeon. The mailer didn't even have to pay a return postage charge!

**Personal character**

Even though you mail in the millions, you are still mailing individual pieces to individually addressed human beings. Every recipient knows that an ad or TV commercial was not created specifically for him but for a mass audience. Direct mail approaches the prospect on a personal level which, with

**191**

computer-produced letters, even extends to a personal greeting by name. As any salesman will agree, you can sell much better when you are talking to an individual rather than people en masse.

**No competition**  In most advertising media, the advertising is an adjunct, not the main reason the person is watching the TV station or reading the magazine. In direct mail, advertising arrives all by itself to be opened and read at the recipient's leisure. When it is read, there is nothing to compete with it for your prospect's attention.

**Most testable medium**  With direct mail you can virtually simulate laboratory conditions for testing. You control exactly when the mail is dropped; you control exactly who gets which test package. Many magazines and newspapers can give you an A/B split; direct mail will give you as many "splits" as you care to have.

**Unique capability to involve the recipient**  Direct mail offers a wide choice of devices that involve the recipient, such as tokens, stamps, questionnaires, and quizzes. And with direct mail, you can literally get the recipient to "talk back" to you—to open a dialogue—by asking him questions and giving him space to respond on the reply device.

**Selecting the format**  Because direct mail offers an unlimited choice of format, a good place to start is deciding which *basic* format you wish to use. There are three basic formats to choose from:

*The classic format* utilizes a separate outer or mailing envelope. The size of that envelope, the material from which it is made (paper, plastic, foil), and the number of colors in which it is printed can vary widely. And what goes inside that envelope can vary even more widely. "Classic" formats range from simple, dignified, businesslike letters to lavish packages stuffed with brochures, inserts, gift circulars—even pop-ups and phonograph records. The classic format is the most personal of the direct mail formats. For this reason, it almost always includes a separate letter, either preprinted or computerized.

*The self-mailer* does not have an outer envelope. These mailers vary from a single sheet of paper folded once for mailing to wonderfully complex pieces with multiple sheets and preformed reply envelopes. Generally, a self-mailer comes off the press complete, ready to address and mail. As a rule, self-mailers are less expensive than "classic" mailing packages. There is only one component to produce and no inserting needed since the piece is completed on press.

*The catalog* is literally a magazine, up to many hundreds of pages, stitched, glued, or perfect-bound. Catalogs require a highly specialized format, and their use is subject to many important guidelines. Catalogs are discussed in detail in chapter 11.

No discussion of direct mail formats would be complete without mentioning some of the specialized devices that are used regularly in direct mail:

*Involvement devices* include stamps, tokens, rub-offs, sealed envelopes—one company even used a jigsaw puzzle which the recipient had to put together! (See Exhibit 10.1.) Regardless of the format you use, reader involvement can make it dramatically more effective. If you get the reader involved with your offer and message, you're well on your way to a sale. The most effective way to get the reader involved is to include a product sample or swatch in the mailing. Obviously this device is not suitable for all types of merchandise, but nothing beats letting somebody touch, feel, and try what you're selling.

*Specialized devices* include die-cut shapes, tip-ons, and pop-ups. These can be great attention-getters. But be careful: you don't want to let the "gimmick" take the reader's attention from your basic sales message. One company tested an elaborate (and expensive) pop-up device and found that the mailing actually pulled better without it! The pop-up was stealing attention from the mailer's message.

In connection with formats, there are several tried-and-true variations you should consider for your mailing package.

The *second letter*, or "publisher's letter" (Exhibit 10.2), has become almost a "must" in direct mail today. Repeated testing indicates that such a letter boosts response 10 percent or more. This is either a folded letter or a letter in a separate sealed envelope which warns sternly: "Open this letter *only* if you have decided not to respond to this offer." Of course everybody opens it immediately. This gives you the chance to do a little extra selling, primarily in reassuring the prospect that he really has nothing to lose and everything to gain in accepting your offer.

The *illustrated letter* has one big thing going for it: a picture can quickly grab the reader's interest before he makes that split-second decision to read on or to pitch it (Exhibit 10.3). Illustrations can be cartoons, line art, or photographs. But the illustrations must be relevant to your product or service and help to dramatize the key benefit you are trying to get across. So reserve the picture of your building for your annual report.

*Invitation formats* have been around for a long time (see Exhibit 10.4). But they are very effective, especially for publishers, club memberships, and credit card solicitations. The format simulates a formal invitation ("You are invited to accept . . ."). The outside of the invitation usually carries a letter explaining the offer. Naturally, an RSVP—a call to action—is included in the mailing.

The *simulated telegram* is less formal but carries a lot of urgency (see Exhibit 10.4). It's popular as a follow-up mailing or part of a renewal series and has worked well for credit card solicitation and loans-by-mail offers. The simulated telegram is usually printed on yellow stock and, more often than not, is computer-filled. (Caution: the basic telegram format is copyrighted by Western Union. You are not allowed to "lift" it.)

*Personalization*, regardless of what format you use, has become common today. Personalization is done by computer, by ink-jet imaging, or by the new technique of laser printing. Still most common is computer personalizing. You will be printing continuous forms, then running the forms through a computer printer, which either "types" the entire letter or fills in the salutation and certain lines of the letter that contain variable information. (See

**Exhibit 10.1. A unique involvement device: the recipient was asked to punch out the pieces of a jigsaw puzzle and reassemble them correctly.**

Here's all you
have to do to
enter the Lanier
**Secretary Sweepstakes**

Punch out puzzle,
put it together
the right way
and tell us
which secretary's
boss uses
Lanier dictating
equipment.

*Write your answer
on one of the
entry cards
provided and mail
it today!*

**Exhibit 10.2. The "publisher's letter" or "second letter" has become a proven results booster in direct mail today.**

Amoco Oil Compa[ny]

*Please open this note only if you have decided not to apply for an Amoco Oil Credit Card*

ctoa/sl                                                          5-017963-000

Dear Motorist:

If you have decided <u>not</u> to accept our credit card offer, I think
I can guess why.

Probably you're thinking that this special invitation to join our
"family" as a new credit card holder "must have some kind of catch
to it."

Well, let me reassure you:  <u>there isn't</u>.

Our credit card will be issued just as soon as your application
is approved.  There are no gimmicks, no hidden charges, and
nothing you have to buy -- now or ever.

Of course, there is a great deal you <u>can</u> buy with an Amoco Oil
Credit Card...including two of the finest lead-free gasolines on
the market today.  And we certainly hope you will want to take
advantage of the very wide credit privileges it confers.  But
there is no obligation to do so.

On the contrary, we feel it is <u>our</u> obligation to prove that we
mean it when we say, "You expect more from Amoco, and you get it."

I do hope you will give us the opportunity of proving it by taking
us up on this offer.  It will be a pleasure to welcome you to our
nationwide family of credit card holders.


Sincerely yours,

H.G. McAuley
for Amoco Oil


HGM:ctoa/sl

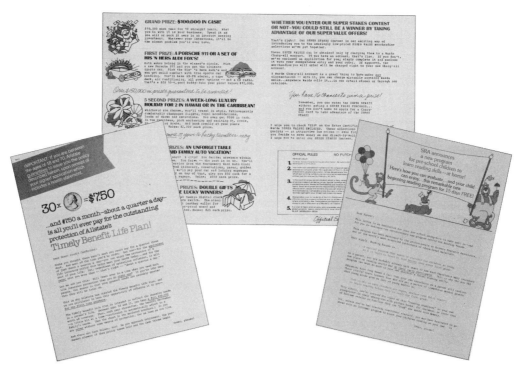

**Exhibit 10.3. Illustrated letters use pictures to grab the reader's attention and get him into—and through—the letter.**

Exhibit 10.5.) Remember: a computer can print only one typeface and size for a given piece and in only one color. Ink-jet imaging is more flexible in that it can vary the typeface and type size within a single piece (see Exhibit 10.5). Laser personalizing, which can personalize anything—even up to "signing" letters with individual signatures—is the most flexible of all.

When you run into somebody who tells you that personalized letters "always" outpull nonpersonalized ones, be skeptical. In my experience, personalized letters *usually* outpull nonpersonalized ones, but not always. Also, they have to outpull by enough to pay for the extra cost of personalization. When you use personalization, use all the information you can. But don't scatter the person's name indiscriminately throughout the letter. A good rule to follow is to write a personalized letter as you would write a letter to any person you know fairly well.

*Which format for your mailing piece?* That depends. It depends on your budget. It depends on whom you're trying to reach. Do you want a package that will stand out on the businessman's desk? Or is it something designed for leisurely reading by the consumer at home? If you're not sure, you should use the "classic" format with a separate outer envelope and a separate letter. The great preponderance of direct mail today uses this format and, while it is more expensive than a self-mailer, it will usually pull better.

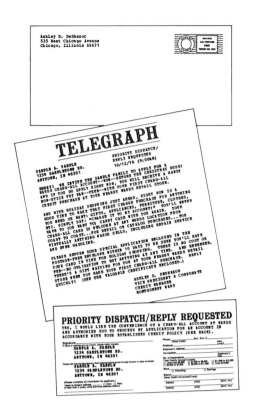

**Exhibit 10.4. Two specialized formats in direct mail: the "telegraph" format (left), which simulates the urgency and "news appeal" of a telegram, and the "invitation" format (right), which builds an aura of exclusivity in the mailing.**

One further caution on formats: postal regulations, which govern the mailability of any given piece, change regularly. You are well advised to check the layout of your mailing piece with your local post office before you produce it. There are few things in life more disheartening than a phone call that begins: "This is the post office, and we're holding your mail because...."

## The creative process

Now that we have the product or service, our offer (proposition), and our format, we're ready to create the mailing piece. Right? Wrong. And therein lies a basic failing in a lot of direct mail produced today. The writer is too anxious to dash to his typewriter, and the artist is too anxious to get to his drawing board. Why does this occur? Marketing is "work," but creative effort is *fun*, and we all tend to do what we like to do. But unless the creative work is grounded in good, solid marketing, it is not going to work—or at least, not as well as it should. Therefore, at Stone & Adler, we have instituted two procedures that precede any creative work. I highly recommend them to you, even if your entire creative department is one person: you.

## The creative strategy

First, we insist on a *written* creative strategy. This is a document that expresses the following:

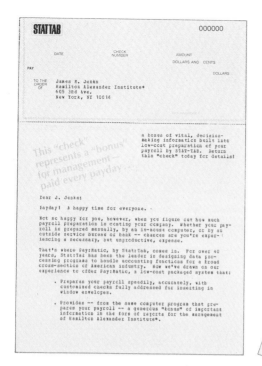

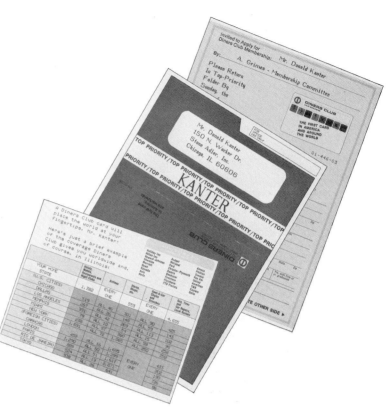

**Exhibit 10.5. The computer can be used to personalize letters (left) so that they look individually typed. The newer technique of ink-jet imaging (right) permits the use of varied typefaces and sizes.**

1. *The product.* What it is, what it does, how it works, what it costs, what its features are, what its *benefits* are, what makes it different, what makes it better—even what its weaknesses are.

2. *Competitive products.* How they compare with ours in terms of features, benefits, and price.

3. *The market.* How big is it and what share of it do we have? Who buys the product today and why? Who else *should* buy it and why? Who are our present customers and future prospects in terms of demographic characteristics, such as age, sex, marital status, income, and education. Who are they in psychographic terms? Are they liberal or conservative, hip or square?

4. *The media.* What's going to carry our message? If space or broadcast media are to be used, which ones, how often, and in what space of time units? If direct mail is the only medium, what lists will we be using—specifically or in general? What do we know or assume about quantities, formats, colors?

5. *The budget.* What limitations should govern our creative thinking in terms of creative staff time, layout costs, photography, illustrations, production costs?

6. *Objectives.* As specifically as possible, what are we trying to *do*, in terms of over-all goals and specific goals, in accordance with the total program, and in line with specific components within the program? Among all possible goals, what are our priorities? Which ones are primary and vital; which are secondary and merely desirable; which are nice but expendable?

7. *Creative implementation.* How do we propose to organize what we know or assume about the product, the competition, and the market to achieve our stated objectives? How will we position the product? What relative emphasis will we give to product features and product benefits? What do we anticipate as our central copy theme? How will it be executed visually? And how will it be orchestrated among various elements of the program? Most important of all from a response standpoint, what will our offer be and how will it be dramatized?

How your creative strategy document addresses these questions, the order in which you address them, and the format in which you cast them are all minor matters. They can be varied according to circumstances. When the creative strategy is thoroughly digested by both the writer and the artist, they both have a good idea of what the mailing package should accomplish, how, and why. We're now ready to move to the second "pre-creative" document: *the hypothesis statement.*

**The hypothesis theory** Frequently the decision is made to prepare "two or three" test variations of copy appeals or creative themes, and the creative people dutifully and proudly produce the required two or three variations. Only after they're done is it apparent that these "creative variations" are really expressing the same basic hypothesis in different ways. In other words, they are really testing nothing.

The hypothesis theory is a way to avoid this expensive method of testing. The people concerned ask themselves: "What are the different reasons a person would want to buy this product or service." At this point—never mind copy—the idea is to think of different selling hypotheses.

For Old American Insurance Company, for example, the assignment was to create a mailing package to sell that company's Guaranteed Acceptance Life Policy, a guaranteed policy for persons between 40 and 80 that pays death benefits of $1,000 to $3,000. Here are three hypotheses (three "reasons for buying") that were developed:

*Hypothesis one:* The strongest appeal of the policy lies in three specific guarantees offered to the buyer: (1) to issue the policy regardless of the applicant's health; (2) never to increase the premium; and (3) never to cancel the policy. (This is how the policy had been sold for years. This hypothesis was the control against which the other hypotheses were tested.)

*Hypothesis two:* Older people know they need more life insurance but hesitate to apply for it because they are afraid of being turned down.

*Hypothesis three:* Older people do not realize that they need more life insurance because they think that Social Security will take care of final expenses. They don't realize how small the Social Security death benefit is.

Exhibit 10.6. Shown here and on page 201 are three mailings prepared by Old American Insurance Company to test three different creative hypotheses. In the mailing above, guaranteed issue, fixed premium and non-cancellability are the strongest appeals. The package below speaks to the fear of being turned down that stops many old people from applying. The mailing on the facing page addresses the fact that many older people do not realize how small the Social Security death benefit is.

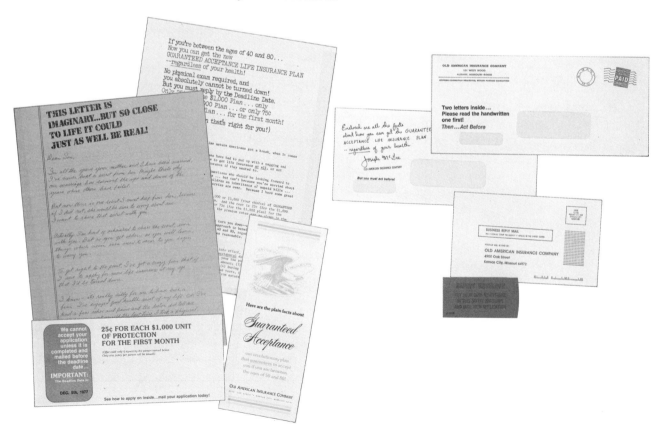

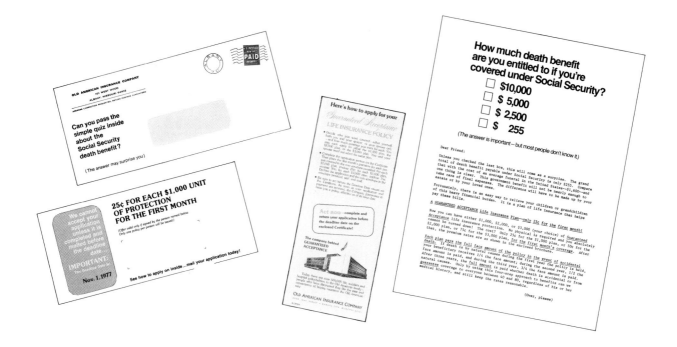

These three hypotheses were the basis for the three mailing packages illustrated in Exhibit 10.6. The winner substantially outpulled the control package and became the new control package for this particular product. What was the winner? The package based on Hypothesis three.

Now we're ready to create a mailing piece.

**The interdependence of copy and art**

The copywriter has traditionally played the basic role in creating direct mail pieces. And the copywriter is still the key man or woman in most creative shops.

The role of the art director is growing more and more important, because it is the art director who brings the concept to life, the one who illustrates it properly and dramatically, who devises graphics that command the reader's attention and who (this is most important) leads the reader through the various pieces of the mailing package so the copywriter's words will have the greatest possible impact.

The direct marketing art director is different from those found in general advertising agencies. And nowhere is this better illustrated than in typography. To the art director in many large general agencies, typography is too often a question of what new typeface is "hot" at the Art Director's Club this month. The result can be something that is beautiful to look at but almost impossible to read or follow.

The direct marketing art director knows better. She or he knows that typography can "talk" for any advertiser. Type sets moods, expresses character. Type can scream or whisper, attract or detract, build confidence or suspicion, express dignity or crudeness, be masculine or feminine, bold or refined. Type can motivate or repel. Type makes an image good or bad every time.

Virgil D. Angerman, sales promotion manager of Boise Cascade Envelopes, has investigated the subject of typefaces in depth. In the course of his research, he has selected 20 representative typefaces, each of which expresses a basic image (see Exhibit 10.7).

**The copywriter as salesperson**

Don Kanter, executive vice president of Stone & Adler, has a unique way of describing some copywriters. "The trouble with many copywriters," he says, "is that they think their job is to write copy." Kanter quickly explains this by adding, "That is equivalent to a salesperson saying, 'My job is to talk.' The job is not to 'talk.' For a writer, the job is not to 'write.' For both, the job is to *sell*. Selling is the end result; writing is merely the means a copywriter uses to reach that end. This is true of all advertising copywriting; it is especially true of direct response copywriting because the writer is usually the only salesperson with whom the prospect will ever come in contact. If he or she doesn't make the sale, there is nobody else to do it."

**The benefit/price/ value equation**

To sell effectively, the direct response writer must know why people buy. They buy, essentially, when they consider something to be a value. This is often expressed in a simple equation: Benefit divided by Price equals Value. In other words, every time a person is confronted with a buying decision, he subconsciously assigns a worth to the benefits he perceives. At the same time, he assigns a worth to the price he must pay. And subjectively, very subconsciously, he divides one into the other to reach his buying decision. If, in his mind, the benefits outweigh the price, he will buy. If the price outweighs the benefits, he will not buy.

**What is price?**

To most people, *price* is the monetary amount asked for the goods or services being sold: the $29.95, or $39.95, or $5.00 per month, or whatever. But there is more to price than that. There's time. We are asking the customer to wait before he or she can enjoy the benefits of what he or she buys. There's the factor of buying the product sight unseen (unlike retail purchasing, where you can see, touch, and often try what you are buying). There's a factor of buying from a company the customer may not know. There's the risk that the product or service may not deliver the benefits that have been promised. In direct marketing, all of these are part of the price that must be paid. While we may not be able to do much about the actual price (the $29.95, or $39.95, or $5.00 a month), we can (and we must) do everything possible to reduce the other factors of price to the minimum.

How? By using the proven techniques that direct marketing has pioneered:

- Testimonials
- Guarantees
- Free trial offers or cancellation privileges
- Reassurance about the stature and reliability of the selling company

**Exhibit 10.7. Note how typefaces can literally "talk"—can express clear and different images or feelings.**

| | | | |
|---|---|---|---|
| **Antiquity** | Delicate | Firmness | *Oriental* |
| INLAND COPPERPLATE | BERNHARD MODERN | CENTURY NOVA | REINER SCRIPT |
| **Boldness** | Dependability | **Gaiety** | **PATRIOTIC** |
| FRANKLIN GOTHIC | GARAMOND BOLD | P. T. BARNUM | SAPHIR |
| Character | Dignity | Luxury | Progressive |
| CRAW MODERN | MELIOR | CASLON OPEN FACE | AMERICANA BOLD |
| Conservatism | Ecclesiastical | **Masculinity** | Reliable |
| EUROSTYLE | OLD ENGLISH | FORTUNE EXTRA BOLD | GOUDY OLD STYLE |
| *Continental* | Femininity | *Movement* | **Strength** |
| BERNHARD TANGO | FUTURA LIGHT | BRUSH | COOPER BLACK |

---

ACME FAST FREIGHT, Inc.
525 WEST 47TH STREET
CHICAGO, ILLINOIS 60609

Italic type indicates movement

MOSER
*Secretarial School*
308 NORTH MICHIGAN AVENUE
CHICAGO, ILL. 60601 • PHONE 329-0954

Feminity reflected in typeface

J. C. JEWELERS
7566 MILWAUKEE AVENUE
NILES, ILLINOIS 60648

Hand-tooled type
signifies luxury

**FRUEHAUF**
CORPORATION
P. O. BOX 8170
DETROIT, MICHIGAN 48213

Forceful type suggests strength

COMPUTER BUSINESS
SERVICES, INC.
6400 N. CENTRAL EXPRESSWAY, DALLAS, TEXAS 75206

Discloses type of business

CONTINENTAL ILLINOIS NATIONAL BANK
AND TRUST COMPANY OF CHICAGO
231 S. LA SALLE STREET
CHICAGO, ILLINOIS 60690

Conservatism expressed in type

A-B-C Business Forms, Inc.
5481 MILWAUKEE AVE. — CHICAGO, ILLINOIS 60630

Type used implies progressive firm

---

**Allstate**
Allstate Plaza
Northbrook, Ill. 60062

**Mobil**
150 EAST 42ND STREET
NEW YORK, NEW YORK 10017

The Swiss Colony
MONROE WISCONSIN
53566

**GraybaR**
ELECTRIC COMPANY, INC.
2045 North Cornell Avenue
MELROSE PARK, ILL. 60160

*Sunset*
Lane Magazine & Book Company
Menlo Park, California 94025

Intext
Scranton, Pennsylvania 18515

STOR DOR
*FORWARDING COMPANY*
1601 S. Western Avenue
CHICAGO, ILLINOIS 60608

ALDENS
5000 WEST ROOSEVELT ROAD
CHICAGO, ILLINOIS 60607

**What is a benefit?** Let's assume we are selling a stereo system. This system has two three-way speakers, each with a big "woofer" and "tweeter" and a mid-range. That's a benefit. Right? Wrong. That's a selling point or product feature. It's a distinction that every writer must recognize and keep in mind. A benefit is something that affects the customer personally. It exists apart from the merchandise or service itself. A selling point or product feature is something in the product or service that makes possible and supports the benefit. Our stereo system with two three-way speaker systems is a selling point. It is a quality in the product itself. That I can enjoy lifelike, three-dimensional sound is the benefit. It is this benefit that affects me personally. This benefit is made possible by the fact that this stereo system has two three-way speakers. Remember, it is the benefit that the customer really wants to have. It is the selling point that proves to him that he can really have it.

**Translate selling points into benefits** Before you write any copy, therefore, it is very important to dig out every selling point you can and translate each selling point into a customer benefit. The more benefits the customer perceives (i.e., the more benefits you can point out to him), the more likely he will buy. Here's an example. Suppose you're writing copy to sell a portable counter-top dishwasher. These are some of the selling points in this merchandise. And alongside each is the benefit which that selling point makes possible:

| Selling Point | Benefit |
| --- | --- |
| 1. Has a 10-minute operating cycle. | 1. Does a load of dishes in 10 minutes; gets you out of the kitchen faster. |
| 2. Measures 18 inches in diameter. | 2. Small enough to fit on a counter-top; doesn't take up valuable floor space. |
| 3. Transparent plastic top. | 3. Lets you watch the washing cycle; you know when the dishes are done. |
| 4. Has universal hose coupling. | 4. Fits any standard kitchen faucet; attaches and detaches in seconds. |

**Copy strategy and basic human wants** With your benefits down on paper, you now have to decide on the copy strategy or the appeals that will do the best selling job. Creative people refer to this in different ways. Some talk about how you "position" the product in the prospect's mind. Others refer to "coming up with the big idea" behind the copy. What is it about your offer and benefit story that is most appealing? When you stop to think about it, people respond to any given proposition for one of two reasons: to gain something they do not have or to avoid losing something they now possess. As you can see from the accompanying chart, basic human wants can be divided into these two categories. The professional copywriter carefully sifts and weighs the list of basic human wants to determine the main appeal of his proposition. (In chapter 12 you'll see how the same product can be slanted to employ many different appeals just by changing your headline.)

**Basic human wants**

The desire to gain:
To make money
To save time
To avoid effort
To achieve comfort
To have health
To be popular
To enjoy pleasure
To be clean
To be praised
To be in style
To gratify curiosity
To satisfy an appetite
To have beautiful possessions
To attract the opposite sex
To be an individual
To emulate others
To take advantage of opportunities

The desire to avoid loss:
To avoid criticism
To keep possessions
To avoid physical pain
To avoid loss of reputation
To avoid loss of money
To avoid trouble

Does your proposition offer the promise of saving time and avoiding hard or disagreeable work? Most people like to avoid work. Saving time is almost a fetish of the American people. Appeal to this basic want, if you can.

Does your proposition help people feel important? People like to keep up with the Joneses. People like to be made to feel that they are part of a select group. A tremendous number of people are susceptible to snob appeal. Perhaps you can offer a terrific bargain by mail and capitalize on the appeal of saving money. The desire to "get it wholesale" is very strong.

**Eleven guidelines to good copy**

Don Kanter uses these guidelines as checkpoints for good, professional copy:

1. Does the writer know his product? Has he or she dug out every selling point and benefit?

2. Does the writer know his market? Is he or she aiming the copy at the most likely prospects rather than at the world in general?

3. Is the writer talking to the prospect in language that he will understand?

4. Does the writer make a promise to the prospect, then prove that he or she can deliver what was promised?

5. Does the writer get to the point at once? Does he or she make that all-important promise right away?

6. Is the copy, especially the headlines and lead paragraphs, germane and specific to the selling proposition?

7. Is the copy concise? There is a great temptation to overwrite, especially in direct mail.

8. Is the copy logical and clear? Does it "flow" from point to point?

9. Is the copy enthusiastic? Does the writer obviously believe in what he or she is selling?

10. Is the copy complete? Are all questions answered, especially obvious ones like size and color?

11. Is the copy designed to sell. Or is it designed to impress the reader with the writer's ability? If somebody says "that's a great mailing," you've got the wrong reaction. What you want to hear is, "That's a great product (or service). I'd love to have it."

**Creating the classic mailing package**

Now that we've looked at formats and discussed copy, let's turn to the individual pieces in a so-called classic mailing package.

**The brochure**

As noted, most mailing packages require a good brochure or circular in addition to a letter. It can be a small, two-color affair. Or a beautiful, giant circular that's almost as big as a tablecloth. But the job it has to do is the same, and it deserves your best creative effort.

One way or another your circular has to do a complete selling job. To give yourself every chance for success, review the appearance, content, and preparation of your circulars. The following is a handy checklist for this purpose.

*Appearance*

1. Is the circular designed for the market you are trying to reach?

2. Is the presentation suited to the product or service you are offering?

3. Is the circular consistent with the rest of the mailing package?

*Content*

4. Is there a big idea behind your circular?

5. Do your headlines stick to the key offer?

6. Is your product or service dramatized to its best advantage by format and/or presentation?

7. Do you show broadly adaptable examples of your product or service in use?

8. Does your entire presentation follow a logical sequence and tell a complete story—including price, offer, and guarantee?

*Preparation*

9. Can the circular be cut out of regular size paper stock?

10. Is the quality of paper stock in keeping with the presentation?

11. Is color employed judiciously to show the product or service in its best light?

**The order form**

If Ernest Hemingway had been a direct response writer, he probably would have dubbed the order form "the moment of truth." Many prospects make a final decision on whether to respond after reading it. Some even read the order form before anything else in the envelope because they know it's the easiest way to find out what's being offered at what price. The best advice I can offer on order forms comes from Henry Cowen, a direct marketing specialist. He says, "There are direct mail manuals around that recommend simple, easy-to-read order forms, but my experience indicates the mailer is far better off with a busy, rather jumbled appearance and plenty of copy. Formal and legal-looking forms that appear valuable, too valuable to throw away, are good." The key words in Cowen's statement are "too valuable to throw away." The order form or reply form that appears valuable induces readership. It impels the reader to do something with it, to take advantage of the offer. High on the list of devices and techniques that make order forms look valuable are certificate borders, safety paper backgrounds, simulated rubber stamps, eagles, blue handwriting, seals, serial numbers, receipt stubs, and so on. And sheer size alone can greatly add to the valuable appearance of a response form. (You've seen examples of many of these techniques on the order forms shown in chapter 2.)

By all means, don't call your reply device an order form. Call it a Reservation Certificate, Free Gift Check, Trial Membership Application, or some other benefit heading. It automatically seems more valuable to the reader.

Getting back more inquiry and order forms starts with making them appear too valuable to throw away. But to put frosting on the cake, add the dimension of personal involvement. Give the reader something to do with the order form. Ask him to put a token in a "yes" or "no" slot. Get him to affix a gummed stamp. Have him tear off a stub that has your guarantee on it. Once you have prodded the prospect into action, there is a good chance you will receive an order.

Finally, the order form should restate your offer and benefits. If a prospect loses the letter or circular, a good order form should be able to stand alone and do a complete selling job. And if it's designed to be mailed back on its own (without an envelope), it's usually worthwhile to prepay the postage.

Gift slips and other enclosures
In addition to the letter, brochure, and order form, one of the most common enclosures is a free gift slip. If you have a free gift offer, you'll normally get much better results by putting that offer on a separate slip rather than building it into your circular.

If you insert an extra enclosure, make sure it stands out from the rest of the mailing and gets attention. You can often accomplish this by printing the enclosure on a colored stock and making it a different size from the other mailing components. Most free gifts, for example, can be adequately played up on a small slip that's 3½ × 8½ or 5½ × 8½.

Another enclosure that's often used is a business reply envelope. This isn't essential if the order form can be designed as a self-mailer. But, if you have an offer that the reader might consider to be of a private nature, an envelope is usually better. Buying a self-improvement book, for example. Or applying for an insurance policy, where the application asks some personal

**Exhibit 10.8.** Order forms (which should never be called "order forms") are the moment of truth in a direct mail package. Principal rule: make them look too valuable to throw away.

**Exhibit 10.9.** If you have a free gift with your offer, you'll usually get better results by highlighting it with a separate slip.

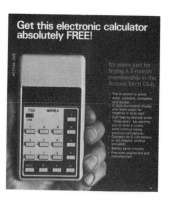

questions. Also, the extra expense of a reply envelope is often justified if you want to encourage more cash-with-order replies.

**Writing a winning letter**

Now we're ready to write a letter, one of the key elements in any successful mailing package. As suggested earlier, we've thought about the objective. We've decided on our offer. We know the market—the people we're writing to. We have a complete list of product benefits. And we've chosen the right copy strategy.

The first task is to decide on the lead for our letter. Nothing is more important. Numerous tests have shown that one lead in a letter can pull substantially better than another. Let's look at six of the most common types of leads used in sales letters. To help you compare them, let's take a sample product and write six different leads for that product. The product we'll use is a businessmen's self-improvement book, which includes biographical sketches of a dozen prominent business leaders.

1. *News.* If you have a product or service that is really news, you have the makings of an effective lead. There is nothing more effective than news. If you have a product or service that's been around a while, perhaps you can zero in on one aspect of it that's timely or newsworthy.
   Example: Now you can discover the same success secrets that helped a dozen famous business leaders reach the top!

2. *How/what/why.* Any beginning newspaper reporter is taught that a good story should start out by answering the main questions that go through a reader's mind—who, what, when, where, why, and how. You can build an effective lead by promising to answer one of these questions and then immediately enlarging on it in your opening paragraphs.
   Examples: How successful people really get ahead;
   [or]
   What it takes to survive in the executive jungle;
   [or]
   Why some people always get singled out for promotions and salary increases.

3. *Numbered ways.* This is often an effective lead because it sets the stage for an organized selling story. If you use a specific number, it will attract curiosity and usually make the reader want to find out what they are.
   Example: Seventeen little-known ways to improve your on-the-job performance—and one big way to make it pay off!

4. *Command.* If you can use a lead which will command with authority and without offense, you have taken a big step toward getting the reader to do what you want.
   Example: Don't let the lack of education hold you back any longer!

5. *Narrative.* This is one of the most difficult types of leads to write, but it can prove to be one of the most effective. It capitalizes on people's interest in stories. To be effective, a narrative lead must lead into the sales story in a natural way and still hold the reader's interest. Ideally, the lead should also give the reader some clue to where the story is going or

why he or she should be interested.

Example: When he started in the stock room at IBM, nobody ever thought Tom Watson would some day be president of this multibillion dollar corporation.

6. *Question.* If you start with the right type of question, you can immediately put your reader in the proper frame of mind for your message. But be sure the question is provocative. Make it a specific question, promising benefits—one that's sure to be answered in the affirmative.

Example: If I can show you a proven way to get a better job, without any obligation on your part—will you give me a few minutes of your time?

It is impossible to put too much emphasis on the importance of working on your leads. The lead is the first thing your reader sees. Usually he or she makes a decision to read or not read at this point. I always write out at least three or four different leads, then choose the one I think will do the best job of appealing to the reader's basic wants.

**Seven-step formula**　　Here's a letter-writing formula that has served me well. I believe it follows a more detailed route than most formulas. And, used wisely, it should not stifle your creativity.

*Promise a benefit in your headline or first paragraph—your most important benefit.* You simply can't go wrong by leading off with the most important benefit to the reader. Some writers believe in the slow buildup. But, most experienced writers I know favor making the important point first.

*Immediately enlarge on your most important benefit.* This step is crucial. Many writers come up with a great lead, then fail to follow through. Or they catch attention with their heading, but then take two or three paragraphs to warm up to their subject. The reader's attention is gone! Try hard to elaborate on your most important benefit right away, and you'll build up interest fast.

*Tell the reader specifically what he or she is going to get.* It's amazing how many letters lack details on such basic product features as size, color, weight, and sales terms. Perhaps the writer is so close to his proposition he assumes the reader knows all about it. A dangerous assumption! And when you tell the reader what he or she's going to get, don't overlook the intangibles that go along with your product or service. For example, he's getting smart appearance in addition to a pair of slacks, knowledge in addition to a 340-page book.

*Back up your statements with proof and endorsements.* Most prospects are somewhat skeptical about advertising. They know it sometimes gets a little overenthusiastic about a product. So they accept it only with a grain of salt. If you can back up your own statements with third-party testimonials or a list of satisfied users, everything you say becomes more believable.

*Tell the reader what she might lose if she doesn't act.* As noted, people respond affirmatively either to gain something they do not possess or to avoid losing something they already have. Here's a good spot in your letter to overcome human inertia—imply what may be lost if action is postponed. People don't like to be left out. A skillful writer can use this human trait as a powerful influence in his or her message.

*Re-phrase your prominent benefits in your closing offer.* As a good salesperson does, sum up the benefits to the prospect in your closing offer. This is the proper prelude to asking for action. This is where you can intensify the prospect's desire to have the product. The stronger the benefits you can persuade the reader to recall, the easier it will be for him or her to justify an affirmative decision.

*Incite action,* **Now.** This is the spot where you win or lose the battle with inertia. Experienced advertisers know once a letter is put aside or tossed into that file, you're out of luck. So wind up with a call for action and a logical reason for acting now. Too many letters close with a statement like "supplies are limited." That argument lacks credibility. Today's consumer knows you probably have a warehouse full of merchandise. So make your reason a believable one. For example, "It may be many months before we go back to press on this book." Or "Orders are shipped on a first-come basis. The sooner yours is received, the sooner you can be enjoying your new widget."

**Make a letter look inviting**

Here's a final, very important tip from top professional writers. They try to make their letters look attractive, inviting, and easy to read (see Exhibit 10.10). The pros keep paragraphs down to six or seven lines. They use subheads and indented paragraphs to break up long copy. They emphasize pertinent thoughts, knowing that many readers will scan indented paragraphs before they decide whether to read a letter clear through. They use underscoring, CAPITAL LETTERS, and a second ink color to make key words and sentences stand out. And they skillfully use leader dots and dashes to break up long sentences.

Scan the two versions of the *Playboy* letter in Exhibit 10.11. Notice how much more inviting the letter on the left is compared to the original typewritten version. Same copy, but one letter encourages reading and the other doesn't.

**Letter length and the postscript**

"Do people read long copy?" The answer is Yes! People will read something for as long as it interests them. An uninteresting one-page letter can be too long. A skillfully woven four-pager can hold the reader until the end. Thus, a letter should be long enough to cover the subject adequately and short enough to retain interest. Don't be afraid of long copy. If you have something to say and can say it well, it will probably do better than short copy. After all, the longer you hold a prospect's interest, the more sales points you can get across and the more likely you are to win an order.

Regardless of letter length, however, it usually pays to tack on a postscript. The PS is one of the most effective parts of any letter. Many prospects will first glance through a letter. The eye will pick up an indented paragraph here, stop on an underlined statement there, and finally come to rest on the PS. If you can express an important idea in the PS, the reader may go back and read the whole letter. This makes the PS worthy of your best

# THE KIPLINGER WASHINGTON EDITORS, INC.

1729 H STREET, NORTHWEST, WASHINGTON, D. C. 20006   TELEPHONE: 298-6400

THE KIPLINGER WASHINGTON LETTER  THE KIPLINGER TAX LETTER
THE KIPLINGER AGRICULTURAL LETTER  THE KIPLINGER FLORIDA LETTER
THE KIPLINGER CALIFORNIA LETTER  THE KIPLINGER EUROPEAN LETTER
CHANGING TIMES MAGAZINE

Will There Be BOOM and More INFLATION Ahead?

The next few years will see business climb to the highest level this country has ever known.  And with it...inflation.  Not a boom, but steady growth accompanied by rising prices.

Those who prepare NOW for the growth and inflation that lies ahead will reap big dividends for their foresight...and avoid the blunders others will make.

You'll get the information you need for this type of planning in the Kiplinger Washington Letter... and the enclosed form will bring you the next 26 issues of this helpful service on a "Try-out" basis. The fee:  Only $21 for the six months just ahead.

During the depression, in 1935, Kiplinger warned of inflation and told what to do about it.  Those who heeded his advice were ready when prices began to rise.

Again, in January of 1946, Kiplinger renounced the widely-held view that a severe post-war depression was inevitable.  Instead he predicted shortages, rising wages and prices, a high level of business.  And again, those who heeded his advice were able to avoid losses, to cash in on the surging economy of the late 40's, early 50's and mid-60's.

Now Kiplinger not only foresees expansion ahead, but also continuing inflation, and in his weekly Letter to clients he points out profit opportunities in the future...and also dangers.

The Kiplinger Letter not only keeps you informed of present trends and developments, but gives you advance notice of new government policies...political moves and their real meaning...money policy... foreign affairs...taxes...prices...union plans and tactics... employment...wages...anything that will have an effect on you, your job, your personal finances, your family.

To take advantage of this opportunity to try the Letter and benefit from its keen judgments and helpful advice during the fast-

(Over, please)

1. Most prominent benefit

2. Enlarging upon benefit

3. Telling reader specifically what he is going to get

4. Proving the value with past experience

5. Tell the prospect what he will lose if he doesn't act

6. Summarizing prominent benefits in closing offer

7. Inciting action NOW

**Exhibit 10.10. Shown here and on the facing page is the Kiplinger letter, one of the most famous letters in direct mail. With minor changes, it's been running (and working) for 30 years! Notice how it follows the "seven-step formula" for writing sales letters.**

**7. Inciting action NOW**

changing months ahead...fill in and return the enclosed form along with your $21 payment. And do it with this guarantee: That you may cancel the service and get a prompt refund of the unused part of your payment, any time you feel it is not worth far more to you than it costs.

I'll start your service as soon as I hear from you, and you'll have each weekly issue on your desk every Monday morning thereafter.

Sincerely,

Stanley Mayes
Assistant to the President

SM:kbi

P.S.   More than half of all new subscribers sign up for a full year. In appreciation, we'll send you FREE an important Kiplinger Special Report if you decide to take a full year's service, too. Details are spelled out on the enclosed slip.

# Playboy Clubs International, Inc.

*You've just picked up the keys to a new place. Now let a Playboy Club Key help you feel at home. (You'll save 40% on your Key with this get-acquainted invitation.)*

Dear Friend:

Welcome to your new neighborhood!

The first few months in a new home are always busy, exciting times.  So
many new places to explore . . . so many things to buy . . . and, of course,
a whole new set of friends to make.

      Chances are you could use a little help getting settled, getting
      acquainted.  And you can get that help from your friends at The Playboy
      Club with a Playboy Club Key.

There are so many ways a Playboy Club Key can help you get a handle on
your new territory.  Ways you might never have imagined.

- A Playboy Club Key can help you meet some of the finest people in
  town . . . your fellow keyholders.
- A Playboy Club Key can introduce you to many of the best restaurants
  and entertainment spots in your area.  Restaurants that are willing
  to give you two-for-one prices on meals just because you're a
  keyholder.

*Over please...*

**Exhibit 10.11. Notice how much more inviting the letter on the left is, even though both letters have identical copy.**

# Playboy Clubs International, Inc.

You've just picked up the keys to a new place.  Now let a Playboy Club Key help you feel at home.  (You'll save 40% on your Key with this get-acquainted invitation.)

Dear Friend:

Welcome to your new neighborhood!

The first few months in a new home are always busy, exciting times.  So many new places to explore . . . so many things to buy . . . and, of course, a whole new set of friends to make.

Chances are you could use a little help getting settled, getting acquainted. And you can get that help from your friends at The Playboy Club with a Playboy Club Key.

There are so many ways a Playboy Club Key can help you get a handle on your new territory.  Ways you might never have imagined.

A Playboy Club Key can help you meet some of the finest people in town . . . your fellow keyholders.

A Playboy Club Key can introduce you to many of the best restaurants and entertainment spots in your area.  Restaurants that are willing to give you two-for-one prices on meals just because you're a keyholder.

A Playboy Club Key can help you shop for the many things you find you need in your new home -- at discounts of 10% to 40% off manufacturers' suggested list prices.  And we're talking about nationally advertised brand-name merchandise.  Big-ticket items like appliances, home furnishings, carpeting, TV's, radios and audio systems.  Even cars!

Over please...

efforts. Use it to restate a key benefit. Or to offer an added inducement, like a free gift. Even when somebody has read the rest of the letter, the PS can make the difference between whether the prospect places an order. Use the PS to close on a strong note, to sign off with the strongest appeal you have.

## The value of versioned copy

Suppose, just suppose, that instead of sending exactly the same letter to all your prospects, you could create a number of versions for each major segment of your market. And rather than talking about all the advantages and benefits of the product, you could simply zero in on those that fit each market segment. Sounds like a logical idea that should increase response, doesn't it.

Yet my own experience with versioned or segmented copy has been mixed. Sometimes I've seen this technique work very effectively; other times it's a bomb. So I suggest that you test it for yourself. If your product story should be substantially different for certain audience segments—and you can identify and select them on the lists you're using—develop special versions of your regular copy and give the technique a try.

One type of versioned copy that generally does pay off is special copy slanted to your *previous* buyers. Customers like to think a firm remembers them and will give them special treatment. In going back to your satisfied buyers, there's less need to resell your company. You can concentrate on the product or the service being offered.

## How to improve a good mailing package

So far we've been talking about how to create a new mailing package. Let's suppose you've done that, and you want to make it better. Or you've got a successful mailing package you've been using for a couple of years (your control) and you want to beat it. How do you go about it? One of the best ways I know is to come up with an entirely different appeal for your letter. For instance, suppose you're selling an income tax guide and your present letter is built around saving money. That's probably a tough appeal to beat. But to develop a new approach you might write a letter around a negative appeal, something people want to avoid. Experience with many propositions has proved that a negative appeal is often stronger than a positive one. Yet it's frequently overlooked by copywriters. An appropriate negative copy appeal for our example might be something like, "How to avoid costly mistakes that can get you in trouble with the Internal Revenue Service." Or, "Are you taking advantage of these six commonly overlooked tax deductions?"

Another good technique is to change the type of lead on your letter. Review the examples of six common types of leads given earlier. If you're using a news lead, try one built around the narrative approach. Or develop a provocative question as the lead. Usually a new lead will require you to rewrite the first few paragraphs of copy to fit the lead, but then you can often pick up the balance of the letter from your control copy. A top creative man who has a well-organized approach for coming up with new ideas is Sol Blumenfeld, a veteran direct mail professional. Here are some of the approaches Blumenfeld uses:

**The additive approach**    This means adding something to a control package that can increase its efficiency in such as way as to justify the extra cost involved. Usually, this entails using inserts. Inserts that can be used to heighten response include testimonial slips, extra discounts, a free gift for cash with order, and a news flash or bulletin. Other additive ideas include building stamps or tokens into the response device. And, if you have a logical reason to justify it, add an expiration date to your offer.

**The extractive approach**    This copy exercise requires a careful review of your existing mailing package copy. You often can find a potential winning lead buried somewhere in the body copy.

**The innovative approach**    Unlike the extractive approach, this is designed to produce completely new ideas. If you are testing three or four new copy approaches, at least one of them should represent a potential breakthrough, something that's highly original, perhaps even a little wild. I encourage writers to let themselves go, because I've seen them produce real breakthroughs this way—dramatic new formats, exciting copy approaches, and offers that have really shellacked the old control!

**Summary**    In direct mail, copy is still king. What you say, how you phrase it, the appeals you use, and your copy style all affect the results you can achieve. The successful writer doesn't write a word until he or she has thought about the objective, the offer, and the market. The writer then translates product features into benefits and develops the right copy strategy, the strategy that will sell the most people.

From a copy standpoint, the lead is the most important part of every letter. Test your leads. Take advantage of the letter-writing techniques the pros use to make their copy more readable. And don't be afraid of long copy. When you come to circulars, envelopes, and order forms, don't neglect the importance of graphics and typography. All such pieces should be inviting to the eye and should visually support your selling copy. Use color to advantage. Stick with typefaces that are easy to read and avoid using too many different faces on the same page.

To keep your mailing pieces on target, see the 28-point creative checklist in chapter 12 developed by Tom Collins. The checklist will help you put your thinking into focus and eliminate the weak areas that can often make the difference between success and failure. The best way to improve your copywriting is by continual writing and testing. If your market is too small to test, or if you're just getting started in direct mail, here are some safe bets. These basic principles work for most mailers most of the time and, if applied by a good copywriter, will produce better-than-average results.

*Mailing format*
- The letter ranks first in importance.
- The most effective mailing package consists of outside envelope, letter, circular, response form, and business reply envelope.

*Letters*

- Form letters using indented paragraphs will usually outpull those in which paragraphs are not indented.
- Underlining important phrases and sentences usually increases results slightly.
- A separate letter with a separate circular will generally do better than a combination letter and circular.
- A form letter with an effective running headline will ordinarily do as well as a filled-in letter.
- Authentic testimonials in a sales letter ordinarily increase the pull.
- A two-page letter ordinarily outpulls a one-page letter.

*Circulars*

- A circular that deals specifically with the proposition presented in the letter will be more effective than a circular of an institutional character.
- A combination of art and photography will usually produce a better circular than one employing either art or photography alone.
- A circular usually proves to be ineffective in selling news magazines and news services.
- In selling big-ticket products, deluxe large-size, color circulars virtually always warrant the extra cost over circulars 11 × 17 or smaller.

*Outside envelopes*

- Illustrated envelopes increase response if their message is tied into the offer.
- Variety in types and sizes of envelopes pays, especially in a series of mailing.

*Reply forms*

- Reply cards with receipt stubs will usually increase response over cards with no stub.
- "Busy" order or request forms that look important will usually produce a larger response than neat, clean-looking forms.
- Postage-free business reply cards will generally bring more responses than those to which the respondent must affix postage.

*Reply envelopes*

- A reply envelope increases cash-with-order response.
- A reply envelope increases responses to collection letters.

*Color*

- Two-color letters usually outpull one-color letters.
- An order or reply form printed in colored ink or on colored stock usually outpulls one printed in black ink on white stock.
- A two-color curcular generally proves to be more effective than a one-color circular.

- Full color is warranted in the promotion of such items as food items, apparel, furniture, and other merchandise if the fidelity of color reproduction is good.

*Postage*

- Third-class mail ordinarily pulls as well as first-class mail.
- Postage-metered envelopes usually pull better than affixing postage stamps (and you can meter third-class postage).
- A "designed" printed permit on the envelope usually does as well as postage metered mail.

**Self-quiz**

1. What unique advantages permit direct mail to do a better selling job than any other advertising medium?

   a. _____

   b. _____

   c. _____

   d. _____

   e. _____

2. What are the three basic formats of direct mail?

   a. _____

   b. _____

   c. _____

3. Complete the following true-false quiz:

   a. Personalized letters will always outpull non-personalized ones. _____

   b. A "publisher's letter" will usually boost response 10 percent or more. _____

   c. A pop-up device is a sure-fire way to increase response. _____

   d. Simulated telegrams are "passe." _____

4. What are the two procedures that should be completed before any creative work is started?

   a. _____

   b. _____

5. Complete this equation for making a sale:

   Benefit *divided by* _____ *equals* _____

6. What is the difference between a benefit and a selling point?

   _____

   _____

   _____

   _____

7. What are some of the basic wants inherent in most people?

   a. _____

   b. _____

   c. _____

   d. _____

   e. _____

   f. _____

   g. _____

   h. _____

   i. _____

   j. _____

8. What do most people desire to avoid?

   a. _____

   b. _____

   c. _____

   d. _____

   e. _____

   f. _____

9. Name eleven guidelines to good direct mail copy:

   a. _____

   b. _____

   c. _____

   d. _____

   e. _____

   f. _____

   g. _____

   h. _____

   i. _____

   j. _____

   k. _____

10. What is the key objective in preparing an order form? Make order forms look _____

_____

11. Name four typical involvement devices.

    a. _____

    b. _____

    c. _____

    d. _____

12. Name the six most common types of leads used in sales letters.

    a. _____

    b. _____

    c. _____

    d. _____

    e. _____

    f. _____

13. List the points in the seven-step letter writing formula in sequence:

    a. _____

    b. _____

    c. _____

    d. _____

    e. _____

    f. _____

    g. _____

14. What are the two best applications of a P.S.?

    a. To restate _____

    b. To offer an added_____

15. Define each of these approaches for improving a good mailing package:

    a. The additive approach _____

    _____

    _____

    b. The extractive approach _____

    _____

    _____

    c. The innovative approach _____

    _____

    _____

## Pilot project

You are the advertising manager of a major national oil company. Your company wants to get more of its credit cards in the hands of qualified persons. Your assignment: prepare a direct mail package to "sell" your company's credit card.

*Assumptions.* The credit card is free; there is no yearly charge or fee to have one. It is honored at your company's service stations from coast to coast for anything sold in those stations (gasoline, oil, tires, batteries, repair work). Your company's service stations do not honor any other credit card.

The objective of your direct mail package is to get credit-worthy persons to fill out an application for the card. They will be credit-checked, and a certain number of persons will be turned down. Another obvious objective is that, when a person has applied and been approved for the card, you want him or her to *use* it.

Here are questions to guide you through the decisions you will have to make:

1. What format would you select, "classic" or self-mailer? Why?

2. Write a creative strategy.

3. Come up with at least three "selling hypotheses"—three reasons a person would want to have (and use) your company's credit card.

4. Here are some selling points (or product features) of the card. Below each one, list the *customer benefit* made possible by that selling point. (To get you started, the first one is filled in.) Note: more than one benefit can usually be derived from a single selling point.
   a. Lets you charge purchases.
      *You don't need to carry cash.*
   b. Card is good nationwide.

      _____

   c. Card is good for anything sold at our service stations.

      _____

   d. No other card is accepted at our stations.

      _____

5. What is the "big idea" behind your mailing package? How will you implement this theme in the letter? Circular? Outer envelope? Order form (application)?

6. Are you going to use any additional pieces, such as gift slips or a publisher's letter?

7. Write your sales letter. Pay particular attention to the "seven-step formula."

8. How could you use versioned copy in your letter?

# 11

## Techniques of Creating Catalogs

There's hardly an American today who isn't within a mile or two of a shopping center. "Logic" says catalog buying should be as passe as the buggy whip. Quite the contrary, catalogs are in a tremendous period of growth.

America "loves" catalogs. According to an A.C. Nielsen survey, nearly 8 out of 10 consumers (77 percent) have nothing against catalogs generally, and 6 out of 10 like to receive them.

Readership of catalogs is tremendous: more than three out of four consumers read them thoroughly or at least thumb through them. Thorough readership is very high, 64 percent. But the real payoff is that 66 percent of those receiving catalogs make purchases at least some of the time.

These statistics are interesting, to be sure. But statistics reveal only what transpires, not why. What is it that causes a woman in Chicago who can't feel or try on a particular dress to order that dress from a Neiman-Marcus catalog and await shipment from Dallas? Certainly this lady could find a similar dress in the scores of women's specialty stores in the Chicago trading area. As a matter of fact, there is a Neiman-Marcus store in a Chicago area shopping center! Yet she orders that dress by mail.

The mail order buyer is a unique person. Even conservative estimates indicate at least half of the buying public—and even larger proportions of the more affluent market segments—feel comfortable today purchasing from mail order catalogs.

**Changing life styles**  A major factor in the boom in catalog selling has to be attributed to changing life styles. According to the IBM Corporation, catalog shopping will account for 30 percent of all U.S. retail sales by 1980. Contrast this with the situation only a few years ago when shopping was a form of recreation for the average person. It provided an excuse to get out of the house and socialize. Today, half the married women work. These women and their unmarried working sisters do not have the desire or the time to shop as much as they did. Furthermore, they have the independence and the income to pursue other social activities.

Therefore, instead of competing for parking space and counter positioning, many prefer to shop at home. In essence, they do not go to the store: the store comes to them.

Arthur Cohen, former vice-president for marketing at Bloomingdale's, New York, tells how the U.S. consumer profile has changed in the past few years: "Income and education are on the way up. People are now secure enough to deal with an abstract seller—a person they can't talk to or see. A working woman comes home at night, disappointed that she didn't have time to shop at her favorite store. Then she sees that the store has come to her through the mail. She can sit down, thumb through, order what she likes, and be secure in the fact that if it's not right, the store will return her money and take it back."

This change in life style has caused not only the growth in catalogs, but also a change in manner of product presentation. "The presentation is all important," states Robert Sakowitz, president of the famous Houston retail chain. "And it had better be clear. If you make a product look too good, too romantic with wispy backgrounds or whatever, the percentage of returned goods is appreciably higher. Another reason for a straightforward presentation, rather than a story theme gimmick, is that our customers are increasingly turning to catalogs as just another way to shop and they don't need to be entertained and romanced."

This emerging and changing life style of Americans (and that of other nations too) has led to dramatic changes in the makeup and distribution of catalogs. Successful catalogs today are developed to meet the needs and wants of well defined markets. Graphics reflect the life styles of these identified markets.

**Catalogs offer six consumer benefits**

The reasons catalog sales continue to grow can best be identified by detailing the six basic services provided by successful catalog merchants:

1. *Saves time.* Not only does the consumer want to save time today, but so does the business person. The consumer catalog allows the consumer to shop from home; the business catalog allows the business person to shop from the office. The antithesis of saving time in ordering is lost time in getting merchandise delivered. Ease of ordering has been accelerated by many catalog firms who allow telephone ordering via an 800 number. But speed of delivery is the other side of the coin.

   Many catalog firms have put the purchaser's mind at ease by promising shipment within 24 to 36 hours.

   Should QUBE (see chapter 7) progress with its plan to develop catalog shopping via TV, the ease of ordering and speed of shipping will take another giant step forward.

2. *Offer more complete selections.* Part of the explanation of the tremendous growth of specialty catalogs over the past decade has been the wide selection of merchandise they offer in their specialization. Warshawsky and Company of Chicago, for example, offers automotive parts for all makes of cars—domestic and foreign—going back to the oldest models

on the road. No individual automotive parts store could come close to matching the Warshawsky selection.

LeeWards, the craft company of Elgin, Illinois, offers a selection of some 10,000 items available to the consumer. The Brookstone Company in Peterborough, New Hampshire, is famous the country over for "hard to find tools." Catalog buyers feel secure in ordering from catalog firms which offer a wide selection of merchandise in their specialty.

3. *Lower price (usually).* It is not at all true that catalog merchandise is always available at a lower price than the same or similar merchandise in a retail store. But because of the volume of sales on given items, the catalog merchant often can offer a savings over retail prices.

4. *Credit availability.* Certainly one of the reasons for the continued growth of catalog selling has been the availability of credit. Most catalogs today offer charge privileges through bank cards and in many cases through travel-and-entertainment cards such as American Express, Carte Blanche, and Diners Club. This availability of credit has made it possible for "big ticket" sales via the catalog method.

5. *Better product description.* The disciplines of catalog selling make it essential that catalog copywriters give precise descriptions of each item offered in a catalog—size, color, weight, everything the potential purchaser needs to know to make a buying decision. These precise product descriptions give the catalog seller an advantage over retail stores where clerks may not have adequate product information. Good catalog descriptions give not only details about a product but also the selling features. Precise descriptions are *exactly* the same for everyone shopping the catalog.

6. *Iron-clad guarantees.* It can be safely said that no successful catalog ever succeeded without an iron-clad guarantee. Sears built its business on its guarantee of satisfaction. An iron-clad guarantee is even more important for a catalog seller who does not enjoy the reputation of a Sears. Consider, for example, this guarantee from Ambassador Leather Company of Tempe, Arizona:

> If for any reason (or no reason at all) you are not completely satisfied with the design, color, workmanship, size or material of any product you buy from Ambassador, simply return it to us within 30 days of receiving it, and we will refund the purchase price promptly—or, if you desire, replace the product you bought free of charge. What's more . . . if you should feel, at any time, that your purchase is not giving you the service you expected it to, just send it back to us and we will either refund the price you paid for it, or replace the product without charge . . . whichever you prefer.

Everyone who sells via the catalog method has an opportunity to offer the six consumer benefits. From the seller's standpoint these six consumer benefits should be construed as six commitments.

**How consumers perceive successful catalogs**

Dick Hodgson, a noted direct marketing consultant and catalog specialist, points out that there are four key perceptions that must be held by the consumer in order for the catalog operation to be successful.

1. *Perceived availability.* Mr. Hodgson points out that while the product or service being sold may be available from a neighborhood merchant, this becomes a major competitive issue only if the potential buyer is aware of this fact and thus determines it would be easier to purchase from a nearby source.

   The Brookstone Company, mentioned earlier, offers a catalog which carries the slogan: "Hard To Find Tools." Actually, many of the tools Brookstone sells—or similar tools that will do the same jobs—are available through local hardware merchants. But they're the type of articles merchants keep in those bins under their counters or in the stockroom, "just in case somebody asks for them." Thus, the reader of a Brookstone catalog perceives such tools to be truly "hard to find." Brookstone has had steady and profitable growth serving buyers who have come to depend on its catalog rather than the local merchants as a source for tools and, as Brookstone puts it, "Other Fine Things."

   Direct marketers have developed many special techniques to encourage their customers to perceive their products or services as being unique and thus not easily available elsewhere. Marketers emphasize their exclusive colors, designs, and packaging; special combinations of products; attractive and easily understood credit plans; early introductions of new or improved products; and a variety of other effective techniques that traditional retailers have been reluctant to adopt.

2. *Perceived authority.* The second of Dick Hodgson's benchmarks for a successful catalog is *perceived authority.* Successful catalog operations, Dick points out, either trade on an area of established authority or go to great lengths to build a base of authority from which to sell. Take, for example, those successful airline seatback catalogs. Note how much space they devote to luggage and other travel-related items. With their years of experience in handling luggage, airlines are perceived by the consumer as having clearly established themselves as authorities on the durability of luggage. And when the airline says a bag is durable, the consumer has got to believe it knows what it is talking about.

   One sometimes wonders why so many catalogs seem to waste so much space on seemingly ego-centered editorial material about the facilities and the people of the companies behind them. It's not just an ego trip in most cases, but rather its a carefully calculated effort to build authority in the minds of customers and prospects to encourage buying with confidence. And such space is far from wasted when it eliminates the need for a lot of back-up copy for each item in the book.

3. *Perceived value.* The third of Dick Hodgson's points is perceived value. Suppose that you are a consumer interested in a jade necklace. You go to the leading department store in your city and look at a small assortment of jade necklaces. Then you "shop" the Gump's catalog which is pro-

duced twice a year by the famous Gump's store in San Francisco. You know the reputation of Gump's for its precious items from the Far East, including jade. If you are typical, your perception of value would be heavily swayed toward Gump's because of its "authority" with respect to jade.

4. *Perceived satisfaction.* As previously mentioned, a guarantee of satisfaction is a key in catalog selling. The American consumer has been trained in the perception that if he is unhappy with his purchase he can return it for replacement, full credit, or full refund.

The customer's perceived satisfaction doesn't start and end with the guarantee. Smart direct marketers are very selective in the merchandise they offer to forestall potential fears customers might have about dissatisfaction. In fashions, for example, direct marketers often purposely select styles that don't involve critical fits. They select colors that reproduce well and are easily visualized from printed illustrations. And they prepare copy which not only romances the product, but carefully spells out details which, if misunderstood, could result in dissatisfaction.

**Four types of catalogs**

The function of catalogs can be better understood by categorizing the types of catalogs and examining the characteristics of each. There are four general types of catalogs: retail catalogs, full-line catalogs, industrial specialty catalogs, and consumer specialty catalogs. Each type bears special considerations.

**Retail catalogs**

A recent phenomenon on the marketing scene has been the interest in catalogs by retailers. Some stores, most notably Neiman-Marcus, have been famous for their catalogs for decades. For most stores, the principal objective has been to build in-store traffic. Now, however, emphasis is shifting to other objectives. A major new goal is generation of mail and phone orders from customers outside the retailers' trading area.

According to John Pellegrene, vice-president of Dayton's, that store's catalog objectives are now 65 percent to promote in-store traffic and 35 percent to generate phone and mail orders. Cleveland's May Company orients its catalog mainly to promote store traffic sales. On the other hand, Sakowitz's John Cadenhead states the majority of his catalog response is outside of his store's Houston marketplace.

So the objectives of the retailer are not necessarily similar to those of the mail order catalog entrepreneur who does not have a retail store. The retailer usually wants store traffic inside his trading area and mail order sales outside it. Also, the retailer can opt for a catalog largely underwritten by vendor money, vendors considering such funds to be "advertising allowances." But the store pays a price when the vendor pays to "advertise" an item in the store's catalog.

*The vendor catalog.* Some time ago, someone got the idea that the "smart" way for a retail catalog operation to go was to sell "advertising" in the catalog to vendors, with vendors underwriting all, or most, of the cost. You can't argue with the arithmetic. But with each "ad" a retailer accepts, he compromises mail order principles. Vendors dictate the catalog makeup. Retailers don't. Art Cohen, former vice-president of marketing at Bloomingdale's (estimated annual catalog expenditures about $13,000,000), told members of the Hundred Million Club (a direct marketing club) that anywhere from 70 to 90 cents on the dollar of their catalog costs are covered by vendor money.

Referring to the dictates of the vendors, Mr. Cohen stated, "The number of choices you have is limited. For example, a deal has been made with Estee Lauder for a full page or for a back cover or for a one-eighth page. (The advertiser decides what it's going to be.) So the way you paginate your book is not as free flowing as it might be if you were running a completely controlled catalog division."

Contrast the restraints of a vendor-sponsored catalog with a controlled catalog. Susan Edmondson of Kaleidoscope and Roger Horchow of Horchow have the absolute freedom to decide whether they will offer any cosmetics in their catalogs at all, and if they do, how much space they will allot and where. What's more, if they do offer cosmetics in their catalogs, and they bomb out, no one will be able to pressure them to run cosmetics again. Vendor-sponsored catalogs run in the face of mail order principles; lure of vendor money isn't all it appears to be.

A giant step closer to a true mail order catalog is the well-executed "store traffic" catalog. Many stores produce such catalogs and mail them to charge customers in their trading areas. The prime objective is to produce store traffic; a secondary objective is to produce mail order sales.

This creates a dilemma. For example, a store might be a leader in the sale of sterling silver in its trading area so it features sterling silver in its catalog. The result might be big in-store sales, but zero mail order sales. For another example, a department store that is a leader in "high fashion" apparel finds that only staple apparel sells in its catalog. Dilemma: Should it leave "high fashion" out of its catalog and risk losing some of its big in-store sales?

The problem isn't severe if the retailer restricts distribution to his trading area with building store traffic being the prime objective. But suppose the retailer decides to mail the catalog outside his trading area, soliciting "pure" mail orders? His mail order sales are certain to be diluted to the extent he has violated sound mail order principles.

**Prospect lists**  The Waterloo of most retailers who try to build a mail order customer list is their concept of mail order prospects. To paraphrase Bob Ingalls, a catalog specialist with Stone & Adler, a retail prospect is not a mail order prospect per se. A mail order prospect has the propensity to buy without having physical contact with the merchandise.

The first evidence of this difference appears when the retailer tests his charge list against mail order buyer lists. The retailer is usually amazed to find his precious charge list doesn't pull as many orders per thousand as lists of people who have purchased by mail or phone from others.

Some retailers have made the grievous error of mailing to lists compiled to match the profile of their charge list, using such demographics as income, education, and home ownership. They've found, with practically no exception, that such lists don't even come close to the pull of mail order buyer lists.

The extent to which retailers build healthy mail order operations in the future will be dependent upon two basics: the application of sound mail order principles and long-term commitment.

Vendor-sponsored catalogs can be marginally successful depending upon the percentage of underwriting. Store traffic catalogs can be marginally successful, depending on the dominant percentage of traffic building items versus mail order items. But neither vendor-sponsored catalogs nor traffic building catalogs can ever achieve the success of pure mail order catalogs.

Well-known retailers have the inherent advantages of recognition and reputation. But the advantages end there. The Kaleidoscopes and the Horchows of this world didn't see black ink the first year, nor will the typical retailer, even if he follows most of the disciplines. Black ink in three to five years is more likely.

Instant success is unlikely because of an irrefutable mail order principle: your profits come from your customer list. A customer list isn't built cheaply. A substantial investment is required to build a good-size customer list in a short period. And to extract maximum profits from a customer list, all the mail order sophistication of a Kaleidoscope or Horchow is needed. The mail order marketer must develop a sophisticated R-F-M (recency-frequency-monetary) system with catalog frequency geared to customer buying habits.

**The shorter route**  The retailer willing to make the necessary commitment to a mail order catalog operation can follow a shorter, more profitable route if his commitment includes the employment of personnel with mail order expertise, either in-house personnel or outside mail order talent, or both. Basic needs include:

1. A mail order merchandise manager who will select the right merchandise using the services of retail buyers to secure merchandise at the right price.

2. Graphic arts talent with the ability to produce a mail order catalog with the right image.

3. Circulation/promotion talent with the ability to maximize the size of and profit from the customer list.

**Full-line merchandise**
**catalogs**  In the purest sense there are only a handful of full-line merchandise catalogs in this country, catalogs that, in effect, are complete department stores. Among these are Sears, Ward, Alden, Spiegel, and J. C. Penney.

The chances of seeing many new entries in the full-line merchandise catalog business are remote, except in the case of existing retail chains. K mart, for example, is a prime candidate to follow in the footsteps of J. C. Penney which decided to launch a full-scale catalog operation after decades in the retail business.

Among the sub-categories of full-line merchandise catalogs is the "wholesale" catalog, which features selections of merchandise such as appliances, electronics, and jewelry. Most such catalogs are backed by vendor money, the vendors paying all or a portion of the cost for running catalog pages featuring their merchandise.

## Industrial specialty catalogs

A real phenomenon of the past decade has been the growth of industrial catalogs through which business sells to business. But in spite of phenomenal growth during the past decade, the potential in this area has hardly been scratched.

It might be said that the growth of the industrial catalog has been in close ratio to the ever ascending cost of the industrial salesman's call. Because it costs so much for a company to maintain a salesman on the road, he must necessarily limit his calls to prospects with the greatest sales potential. Consequently, salesmen must purposely pass up many prospects simply because they can't afford the cost of the call. This leaves a tremendous void to be filled by the industrial catalog.

Consider the Fortune 500 company which learned through research that its salesmen couldn't afford to call on any customer who purchased less than $200 in supplies a year. This giant corporation had several hundred thousand prospects who failed to meet the minimum annual purchase requirement. To overcome the problem this corporation developed a full scale selling catalog to use in conjunction with a telephone program. The results were remarkable. Fourteen percent of all prospects contacted by mail and phone placed orders, orders which the sales force could not afford to take in person.

The industrial catalog has proved to be the ideal vehicle for servicing the aftermarket for companies that sell capital goods equipment through sales forces. Consider the visual products division of a major corporation like Minnesota Mining and Manufacturing. Its salespeople in one division derive a major share of their income from the sale of overhead projectors. The aftermarket for these products consists of transparencies and other supplies. It is worthwhile for the salesperson to sell the overhead projector, but in most cases he can't afford to go back to sell $25 to $35 worth of supplies. The supplier catalog performs this function.

The industrial specialty catalog is not limited to aftermarkets, of course. There are scores of industrial specialty catalog operations that sell only through catalogs. There are catalogs for office forms, computer supplies, office supplies, maintenance supplies, advertising specialties, business gifts, and many other products.

To succeed with an industrial specialty catalog, it is essential that you follow the same disciplines as for a consumer catalog. It's a mistake to assume that a "salesman's catalog" that simply lists specifications will succeed as a selling catalog on its own.

## Consumer specialty catalogs

The most dramatic growth over the past decade has occurred in the area of consumer specialty catalogs—catalogs that fill special needs or cater to identifiable life styles. The great Sears, Roebuck and Company, for example, in addition to its basic full-line merchandise catalog now publishes some 20 special-interest catalogs offering auto parts, western apparel, tall men's clothing, winter sporting goods, convalescent products, and similar groups of products for market segments.

There has been tremendous growth in up-scale specialty merchandise catalogs. Some of these operations have come from nowhere. Take the case of Susan Edmondson of Atlanta, Georgia. Starting her catalog operation called Kaleidoscope, in January 1974, by the end of 1976 she was reportedly doing $12 million in business. It is estimated that sales for the year 1978 exceeded $18 million.* The Horchow Collection in Dallas, Texas, is reputed to be doing in excess of $20 million annually. Both the Kaleidoscope and Horchow Collection catalogs are distinguished by their unique selections of merchandise and their smashing graphics.

The granddaddies of special interest catalogs are unquestionably the seed and nursery catalogs. Many a gardener keeps happy during the cold winter months thumbing through his nursery catalog, anticipating "the flowers that bloom in the springtime." W. Atlee Burpee Company, one of the old-timers, has been issuing catalogs for about 100 years. Its catalogs average 184 pages in length, and Burpee distributes approximately 2.5 million copies a year. Another pioneer in the field of nursery catalogs is Henry Field Seeds & Nursery Company of Shenandoah, Iowa.

But for sheer volume of customers in the specialty field, nothing compares with gift and gadget specialty merchandise firms. Here are the customer counts for some of the leaders:

*Note: Kaleidoscope, in spite of its rapid sales growth, encountered severe financial difficulties following the 1978 selling season. According to trade sources, inability to fill orders satisfactorily was the principal reason given.

**Table 11.1. Size of customer lists for selected consumer specialty catalog firms.**

| Firm | Total Customers | Period |
|------|-----------------|--------|
| Foster & Gallagher | 2,750,000 | 1976-78 |
| Hanover House | 1,046,964 | 1976-77 |
| Miles Kimball | 2,200,000 | 1976-78 |
| Spencer Gifts | 4,100,000 | 1976-78 |
| Sunset House | 3,496,518 | 1976-78 |

The world is not your oyster if you plan a consumer specialty catalog operation. To the contrary, your chance of failure is great unless you are skilled at identifying and segmenting markets. Hanover House Industries, Inc., one of the more successful specialty catalog operations considers market segmentation to be a key ingredient of success. Hanover House publishes nine different catalogs, each slanted to a different income bracket. Hanover believes the trend is for marketers to "position" catalogs according to demographics, income, age, ethnic background, and life style. Certain markets find specific types of specialty items most saleable. While the market determines the kind of products for a catalog, each catalog in turn has an ideal market.

**The basics of a successful catalog**

It is an understatement to say that "successful catalogs don't happen by accident." Successful catalogs are created by following certain basic principles outlined in these ten general areas: positioning, merchandise selection, merchandise positioning and grouping, graphics, use of color, size, copy, sales stimulators, order forms, and analysis.

**Right positioning**

Every catalog must be positioned properly, have a reason for being. Every catalog must justify its existence on its own. When Len Carlson, founder of Sunset House, started his mail order operation on the West Coast, he determined through small-space advertising that there was a big market for gifts and gadgets—particularly if he assembled hundreds of them in one interesting catalog. He offered a convenient way for the consumer, particularly the housewife, to shop for gifts and gadgets at home. There were few retail stores offering such a wide assortment of items all in one department. The wisdom of Carlson's thinking is proved by the fact that, 15 years after the launching of Sunset House, sales volume was pushing $30 million.

A careful study of successful catalogs will verify that each has an underlying theme. "Everything in office supplies," "maintenance supplies at direct-to-you prices," "useful and entertaining hobbies," "executive gift guide," "wholesale auto parts for all makes"—these are but a sampling of the expressed purposes and themes for catalogs destined to do the complete selling job. Prime requirements of a catalog are economy, selection, and ease of ordering. Themes that incorporate these requirements operate within a favorable climate.

## Right merchandise selection

The theme, the positioning, the reason for being, dictates the type of merchandise to be offered in a catalog. But there is good merchandise and bad merchandise. The right merchandise selection is essential to success. The established mail order catalog operation determines the proper merchandise for its market through a process of evolution. For a firm starting cold, the right merchandise selection is particularly difficult.

There are several guidelines for the beginner to follow in selecting merchandise for his catalog:

1. Obtain copies of all catalogs that may be considered competitive in any way. Cut out descriptions and illustrations of all items that you feel may fit the theme of your catalog.

2. Note carefully the items carried in more than one catalog. This indicates the item has better than average sales appeal.

3. Obtain copies of all publications offering merchandise fitting your merchandise categories.

4. Using a directory like *Thomas Register*, look up and list available manufacturers for each of the merchandise categories you have selected for your catalog.

5. Write to every manufacturer and spell out the theme of your catalog. Ask each manufacturer, for example, to specify his three most popular items that fit the quality image to be established.

6. Ask each manufacturer to specify the following:
   a. What is its discount (should be 50 percent or better)?
   b. Does it drop ship and what is the charge?
   c. What is the policy on returned goods (any refurbishing charge)?
   d. What is the minimum order for the maximum discount?
   e. How fast and in what quantities can it fill repeat orders?
   f. Can a special model be developed which is not available in retail stores?

7. Have your merchandise buyer attend all major consumer and dealer shows that display the categories of merchandise being sought for the catalog.

These are some of the courses to follow in selecting merchandise for a catalog. The process requires digging, organization, ingenuity, determination, and plain hard work!

It is easiest and safest for a mail order operator to "grow" into a catalog operation through space advertising. Using this process, a mail order operator continuously runs small space ads for a variety of items. Response to these space ads creates an audience, and the winners in space become featured items in the catalogs. Then it is a simple task to expand the line.

Many a mail order operator has built a very large customer list through such methods as solo mailings, merchandise offers in space, or broadcast ads. It becomes a simple process to convert the winning offers into a catalog. For example, here is a list of solo items later combined into a successful catalog: AM/FM radio, sewing machine, color TV set, power saw, ladies' and men's wristwatches, and socket wrench set.

When you have *proved* sellers to offer a customer list through a catalog, you can hardly miss. The item that sells best through a solo offer will almost always be the biggest seller when offered in a catalog. The success of the strategy of using only proved winners in a catalog is explained by the fact that if you are offering 15 proved items, it is a cinch that no one on the customer list has purchased all 15. But they have been satisfied with one or more of the items. This technique hasn't been used by very many mail order firms, but it offers a vast profit potential if developed correctly.

Right positioning and grouping of merchandise
The merchandise has been selected. How do you decide what goes where? How much space do you allot to each item? These are tough questions, particularly when you are producing a maiden catalog. The answers are easier after you have done several catalogs.

Especially for the beginner, it's important to know what most professionals in catalog selling have experienced. With rare exceptions, they've found that the best way to position merchandise is by popularity of the category, starting a category with the most popular position and working toward the back.

An example of the wisdom of leading with your best comes from the analysis of a large nursery catalog. Sales analysis showed that the placement of the best-selling category of nursery stock was in the back of the catalog. In the following season, this category was moved to the front of the catalog. Not only did sales in it increase over the previous season, but all other categories benefited as well. The theory here is that if you attract readership in the front of the catalog with your most popular items, a higher percentage will shop the balance of the catalog. One drawback of this procedure is that the first category could run several pages with diminishing effectiveness on each succeeding page.

A refinement of the technique of locating the best selling merchandise up front is to cater to the seven "hot spots" in a catalog. These hot spots have been identified by professionals in the catalog field as the front cover, back cover, inside front cover, page three, four, and five, inside back cover, center spread, and the page facing the order form.

Some professionals arrange their catalogs by groupings of merchandise in categories such as "party games," "kitchen aids," "space savers," and so forth. And then there are those who disregard categories completely, "mixing" items throughout the catalog. (The theory here is that the reader will go through the entire catalog to find items of particular interest.) Roy Hedberg, president of Sunset House, is against arranging catalogs by categories. His opposition is based on careful tests conducted by his firm. He feels his readers are more likely to shop the entire book if they are not "turned off" by specific category sections that they consider uninteresting.

Allotting space for individual items of merchandise is a tricky business, especially where previous sales data do not exist. However, you can follow these guidelines.

1. When you select items that are carried in other catalogs, pattern your space allotment after theirs.

2. When you have a firm cost estimate for your entire catalog, determine your advertising cost per catalog page and per unit of space. Then determine how many of the given items you must sell in order to break even on the cost of space you plan to allocate. If this sales quota seems too high to you, reduce the allotted space.

3. If you have great confidence in an item but a considerable amount of space must be used for illustrating it properly, don't cut the space. Either use sufficient space or drop the item.

4. When you are offering more than one model of the same item, feature the model that you feel offers the greatest sales potential and sublist the additional model or models. For example, say you have two digital clock radios, an AM and the other AM/FM. You could list the AM digital clock radio and describe it, listing the price next to the item number. Beneath this item number, you would show the price and item number for the AM/FM digital clock radio. Just one line gives you an opportunity to offer another item for sale.

These guidelines certainly aren't foolproof, but they are useful until results from a maiden catalog are available.

Right graphics    A catalog that must sell on its own can ride or fall on graphics. By graphics, we mean the total visual presentation that your printed piece displays, including design, layout, photography, and typography. If you or persons on your company's staff do not have experience in producing all elements of your catalog graphic presentation, you should look for expert help. You should consider using the services of an art studio or direct marketing agency that has had extensive experience in producing catalogs.

Your graphic presentation starts with the cover. Covers register positive or negative impressions with readers. Positive impressions encourage the prospect to get into the catalog; negative impressions turn the reader off.

Having a theme helps you decide what your catalog cover should look like. Let's say you are producing a sporting goods catalog with top-of-the-line equipment and apparel. The theme of the catalog could be "the finest in

MONTGOMERY
WARD
1978
Suburban
Farm
& Garden

Index . . . . . . . . . . . page 74     Ordering Information . . page 76      Credit Terms . . . . . page 77

Twin-cylinder 16-HP
tractors, pgs. 2-3

Rear-tine
tillers,
pg. 49

Hole diggers, pgs. 136-137

Log splitters, pg. 30

The Right Equipment Makes the Job Easy

**Exhibit 11.2.** The back cover of this Kaleidoscope catalog uses valuable selling space to feature a high-fashion item plus three unique "impulse" items.

740M8

ROBERT STONE
606 LAUREL AVE
WILMETTE      IL 60091

PEEL OFF LABEL AND PLACE ON ORDER FORM IN SPACE PROVIDED

**Kaleidoscope**
2201 Faulkner Rd., NE
Atlanta, Georgia 30324

Member: Direct Mail Marketing Association
and New England Mail Order Association

ELEPHANT POWER. No more tilted books with these heavyweights on hand. Italian elephant bookends are sculptured from a thick block of red travertine — solid enough to support your largest volumes. A Kaleidoscope exclusive.
**Travertine bookends, #6262**, 38.00 (4.50)

QUITE A QUARTET. Your dinner table comes alive with a gathering of India's most exotic animals. Each is painstakingly crafted of *papier maché* and wood, handpainted in brilliant detail. A fascinating collection of napkin rings or towel holders. Set of 4.
**Napkin rings, #6101**, 45.00 (1.85)

THE FEMININE SPIRIT lives in a 2-piece ensemble that's guaranteed to turn heads! Ivory 100% cotton crochet looks great on sun-kissed skin, keeps its cool even in the tropics. Tunic top doubles as a terrific beach cover-up — with scoop neck, full sleeves and front patch pockets. Pants feature discreet close weave from top of leg to elasticized waistband. Perfect for travel. Sizes S,M,L.
**Crocheted suit, #6323**, 140.00 (2.25)

WINGS OF GOLD. The Russian aristocracy commissioned this original butterfly jewelry in the 18th Century. Now its fragile beauty returns in carefully executed reproductions. Every detail has been captured, from the precious bits of lapis lazuli to the rich tone of antique Russian gold. 14K gold necklace and matching earings.
**Butterfly necklace, # 6133**, 80.00 (1.65)
**Butterfly earrings**, 110.00 (1.85)
**Pierced, #6131; Clip, #6132.**

**Exhibit 11.3. This page from an industrial catalog caters to the needs of the industrial buyer: it has an 8½ × 11 size to fit catalog files; specifications and uses for each item; and prices for varying quantities.**

**Safety Aids**            **Revere Chemical Corporation**

| Revere **REV-GRIP** Non Skid Surfacing | **Surfaces** Metal Concrete Wood | **Uses** Non-slip abrasive surface. Eliminate slippery floors. |

**LESS THAN 34¢ per sq. ft.**

## Revere **REV-GRIP**
### Eliminate Slippery Floors

**Rev-Grip** combines a heavy-bodied plastic with wear resisting, mineral aggregate. Troweled over metal, wood, or concrete, it bonds permanently. It becomes an abrasive, non-toxic, fire-retardant coating. **Rev-Grip** resists water, gasoline, oil, alcohol, fats, grease, mild acids. Wears 40 to 60 times longer than floor varnish or paint. Resistant to shock, traffic, weathering, corrosion, and rust.

**Application**
Ready to use. Just trowel it on. Overnight dry. Surface preparation: none.

**Coverage**
One gallon covers approximately 50 square feet.

**IMPORTANT HELPS MEET OSHA STANDARDS**

| REV-GRIP No. M20470 | |
|---|---|
| 5 gallon pail | $16.95/gal. |
| 4 gallons (1 gallon pails) | $17.57/gal. |
| 2 gallons (1 gallon pails) | $18.10/gal. |

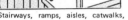

Stairways, ramps, aisles, catwalks, in showers and swimming pools.

| Revere **SAF-TRED** Non-Skid | **Surfaces** Stairs Steps Ladder Rungs | **Uses** Provides friction surface even when wet, oily, or greasy. |

**AS LOW AS 40¢ each**

## Revere **SAF-TRED**
### Prevent Slips and Falls

**Saf-Tred** is a tough fabric coated with diamond-hard mineral grains to provide a long-wearing, friction surface. **Saf-Tred** stays in place for years, is unaffected by moisture, grease, oil, or changes in temperature.

**Application**
Strip off protective backing and press adhesive-coated surface in place.

**Coverage**
Available in 2 sizes — ¾" wide x 24" long
                               6" wide x 24" long

**Color:** Dark Grey

- Safe, sure footing — even when wet, oily or greasy
- Unaffected by moisture, grease, oil or temperature changes
- Easily applied in seconds
- Stays in place for years

**IMPORTANT HELPS MEET OSHA STANDARDS**

| SAF-TRED No. M20260 | |
|---|---|
| ¾" x 24" 200 per carton | $ .40/ea. |
| ¾" x 24" 100 per carton | $ .43/ea. |
| 6" x 24" 50 per carton | $2.27/ea. |
| 6" x 24" 25 per carton | $2.49/ea. |

accessories and apparel for major participation sports." This theme almost automatically dictates a sport scene in deluxe surroundings. For example, if the catalog is released prior to the skiing season, a shot of two attractive people skiing down a slope at a fashionable resort would certainly seem to illustrate the catalog theme. And it goes without saying that it would be appropriate to have the models use equipment and clothing offered in the catalog.

Let's turn now to other aspects of catalog covers. The decision must always be made whether products should be offered for sale on the front and back covers of a catalog. Most professionals agree that you should practically always do so on the back cover, nearly always *not* on the front cover. The back cover is choice selling space, an excellent location for hot items. But the front cover tends to steal from the opportunity to set the theme. (Displaying merchandise in use on the front cover and referring to page numbers for full information is not to be confused with attempting to sell from the front cover.)

Since the theme is so important, the cover of a special *sale catalog* can be extremely appropriate for the direct sale of merchandise. The sale becomes the theme, especially for established customers. And the catalog cover brings the big news into immediate focus.

The most serious mistake made by most neophytes who produce their own catalogs is believing that manufacturer's stock photos of merchandise will do the job. Using such photos will save money, but they will rarely do the selling job. The number-one problem of using stock photos is that the catalog will almost certainly end up a visual hodgepodge, with a multiplicity of photo techniques, varying degrees of sharpness, straight product shots, and in-use photos. And many stock photos can't be reduced in size and still be effective in the space allotted.

An art studio experienced in catalog production will gang-shoot many items, shooting in proper perspective and showing items in their best light. Most important, a house experienced in catalog production will put human interest into the visuals, putting sell into photography with lots of in-use shots. Many catalogs become sterile and monotonous, with page after page laid out the same way. But good graphic layouts should reflect the opposite of monotony. Each page should be interesting, a new adventure. A variety of layouts should be employed for the same size units. Exhibit 11.4 shows two facing pages from a Sunset House catalog. There are a total of 18 space units on the two pages. Fourteen items are given one unit of space each and two items are given double units of space. The two double units serve as "stoppers" and win attention for the balance of each page.

This is but one layout arrangement within the 94-page Sunset House catalog. Other layouts include a page having six units of equal size facing a page with four units of equal size and one double unit; and a page with six units of equal size facing a six-unit page with three units of equal size and one triple unit. Interspersed are some one- and two-item pages.

Working with a unit-space layout system offers a tremendous economic advantage not apparent to the neophyte. Take the nine-item right-hand page

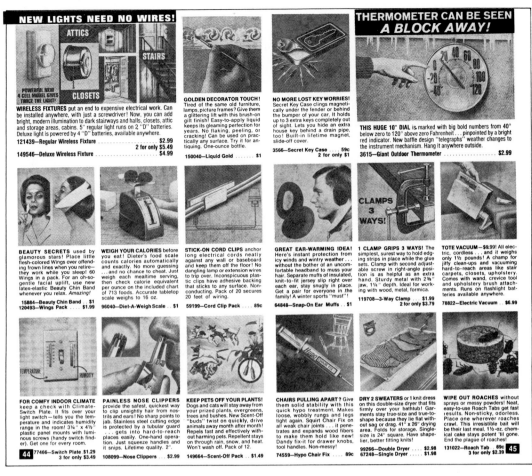

**Exhibit 11.4. Two facing pages from a Sunset House catalog.**

as an example. Let's say that six of these nine items were profitable. Following good catalog principles, Sunset House would want to drop the three losing items and repeat the six winning items for the next catalog. With unit spaces, the company doesn't need to make up a new page. It simply removes the losing items and drops in three new items in the same units of space.

Choosing the right paper stock is part and parcel of your graphic presentation. The finest of art and photography can be ruined by the wrong paper. Here it is important to check with your printer and to examine samples of what the finished product will look like.

**Right use of color**

When should you use one color, when two colors, when four colors? These are agonizing questions, particularly when there are no results to use as guidelines. Usually, the big question is between one color and four colors. Cost of photography and engravings is substantial where four colors are used.

Certain guidelines should be considered before deciding between one color and four colors:

1. When a catalog is divided between one- or two-color pages and four-color pages, it is nearly always true the four-color pages will "steal"

some of the business that would have come from the one- or two-color pages if they hadn't been competing with four-color pages. Therefore, a proper analysis must consider the *total* pull of the book rather than the business secured from the four-color pages separately.

2. If any four-color printing is used in the book, it makes good sense to set the theme by using it on the front and back cover.

3. Four-color work increases sales of some items tremendously and has little or no effect on the sale of others. A good question to ask is, "Is it essential to use full color to show the merchandise?" Full color is an obvious advantage when showing apparel, home furnishings, and food. On the other hand, a beautiful one-color photo of sterling silver may do more for the display of the merchandise than adding other colors for background purposes.

4. Finally, the use of full color must be related to the total production run, as a practical matter. Since full color photography and plates constitute a major cost item, there is a real possibility that increased sales can never cover the increased cost if the production run is too small. For instance, if full color work for a catalog comes to $20,000 and the run is only 100,000 copies, then the cost of color is $200 additional for each 1,000 catalogs. Obviously, a prohibitive amount. The same expenditure—$20,000—amortized over one million catalogs brings the cost down to only $20 additional per thousand catalogs, and this is a very realistic additional cost.

**Right size**  Another major consideration in producing a catalog is deciding on the right size—not only page size, but also number of pages. First, let's consider some fundamentals of right page size.

1. Economics dictates that the page size be selected so that your catalog can be cut out of standard sized sheets or rolls and be printed most economically on high-speed presses.

2. If yours is an industrial catalog, you should consider producing a standard size catalog which fits into catalog files maintained by most manufacturing firms.

3. Most statisticians in the catalog field can prove the thickness of a catalog does have a relationship to sales. If a catalog is too thin, it takes on the complexion of a "flyer" to be scanned and tossed away rather than kept for future reference. Therefore, when the total number of items to be offered through a catalog is scant, wisdom dictates that you use a smaller page size such as 5½ × 8½ instead of 8½ × 11. Twelve pages size 8½ × 11 are the space equivalent of 24 pages of 5½ × 8½.

4. Another consideration is the nature of the merchandise being offered for sale. Some items, such as a complete cookware set or a complete tool set, require a great deal more display space than other items, such as kitchen utensils, vitamins, and so forth.

5. Many catalog professionals have found that a change of pace in catalog size is an aid to increased sales. Two of the leading firms in the specialty

merchandise field, Spencer Gifts of Atlantic City, New Jersey, and Sunset House of Los Angeles, California, customarily produce several editions of a small-size catalog during the year. Then they switch to an 8½ × 11 catalog for Christmas.

Finally, many professionals will tell you that the total response from a catalog will increase as you increase the total number of pages. An example would be going from 86 to 94 pages. The theory is that, as you increase the number of offerings, you increase the opportunity for attracting more customers. Naturally there is a point of no return for this theory. Just adding "any old items" won't do. Items added must be of appeal equal to those in the rest of the book. And naturally, one must take the additional cost into consideration.

**Right copy**  Because a mail order catalog must *sell on its own*, copy is a major factor in the success or failure of any catalog. You can have the best of themes, excellent product selection, and good graphics, but if your copy is dull, sales will suffer. Maxwell C. Ross, a direct mail consultant, points out that there are not enough action verbs used in headlines in catalogs. Too many catalogs simply apply labels like "peach trees," "apple trees," and so forth, instead of saying "You can grow peaches like those in only three years."

Precise description is vital in mail order selling. You must give the size, weight, color selection, materials, and so forth. But the pro also uses a mixture of selling copy along with the specifications.

Sunset House is a master at using end-use selling headlines under their in-use photographs. Consider some of these headlines: "Dust high spots easily!" "Chase away silverfish," "Hang your ironing board," "No-slip ironing!" and "One wipe cleans your iron!"

Still another technique is to use headlines that are labels along with subheads that are selling headlines. WinCraft of Winona, Minnesota, a firm that sells fund-raising and promotional items to schools, follows the technique of using labels plus selling headlines throughout its catalog. Here are a few examples.

**MINI-PEP POM POMS**
Ideal for Pep Clubs, Drill Teams, Marching Units of All Kinds!

**ECOLOGY BUTTONS**
Help Fight Pollution!

**MASCOT BUTTONS**
Add "Booster Power" to Your School's Spirit!

One of the most important pieces of copy in any catalog is the *guarantee*. A review of guarantees in hundreds of catalogs discloses that, while there is general recognition that guarantees are essential, there is little agreement that they should be clear and simple. Many guarantees are garbled, with confusing legal terms. A clear-cut guarantee is essential to every good mail order catalog and, indeed, provides an incentive for ordering.

An equal or even stronger incentive for ordering is knowing that your peers like what they buy, and the best way to provide this assurance is to spread *testimonials* throughout the catalog. It is amazing how few firms that sell via the catalog method make good use of testimonials. Too often, the president of a catalog sales company keeps testimonials securely locked in his desk, a secret from his prospects and customers.

**Right sales stimulators** It can't be said too often: A catalog must sell on its own. Many catalogs just arrive and lie there. Other catalogs are live, vibrant, exciting. Careful analysis usually indicates that sales stimulators make the difference. How do you stimulate readership and action? There are many great techniques. Here are some of the basics.

1. *Overwraps.* Perhaps the greatest spur to catalog readership over the past decade has been the development of the overwrap. This is a sheet wrapped around a catalog and stapled to it providing two pages for extra copy at both front and back of the mailing piece. Traditionally, scores of firms marketing through mail order carried a printed letter on the first inside page of the catalog. Research showed though, that that letter is the least read piece of copy in the catalog. But when the letters are carried as an overwrap, readership has increased dramatically. There is something about a printed letter on top of the catalog which induces the prospect to read it to determine what the catalog is all about.

   The overwrap is the ideal device for featuring special incentives to order. And, you can use specific pieces of copy to allude to specific customer and prospect categories without altering your basic catalog. For instance, you can address a letter for your best customers as "Dear Preferred Customer." Or you can make a special appeal to customers about to be taken off of your mailing list by warning that this is the last catalog to be sent unless an order is received.

   The flexibility of the overwrap also allows you to alert the recipient to pass the catalog to others in the organization. Say you are sending a catalog to a school. Through overwrap letters, you can allude to the special interest of the principal, the Parent-Teacher Association, the director of language, the director of the mathematics department, and the director of the science department.

   Because all overwraps are four pages, there are additional promotional opportunities. The overwrap usually runs two pages for the letter, the first outside page and first inside page. This leaves space for offering merchandise on the back inside page that often pays more than the full cost of the overwrap. There is still another opportunity for page three: it enables the marketer to test new items at low cost without making basic changes in his catalog.

   Finally, there is page four, which is best used as an additional order form. Since the order form is also used for addressing puposes, the label is affixed directly above the order form. This helps tremendously in processing, since the label with the list key is right on the order form. Statistics show that the order form which becomes page four of the overwrap is more often than not the first order form used.

There is little question that overwraps for catalogs are here to stay. This excellent idea has time and again resulted in order increases of 50 percent and more.

2. *Incentives for early orders.* Because so many catalogs are seasonal in nature, it is to the advantage of the mail order firm to get as many early orders as possible. In order to do this, it must provide incentives to the customer.

Sunset House solved this problem by designing a sweepstakes with a built-in incentive to order early. Daily drawings gave the customer 30 opportunities to win if he or she responded immediately. If a prospect responded three days after the first deadline, for instance, he or she had 27 opportunities to win; if a prospect responded ten days later, he or she had 20 opportunities to win and so forth.

3. *Telephone orders.* In-WATS telephone service has proved a boon to catalog merchandisers. Major catalog firms like Sears have for years done a very substantial portion of their business by telephone. But it is only in the past several years that other catalog merchandisers have latched on to the tremendous appeal of the opportunity to order by telephone.

The convenience of toll-free service is a strong appeal in itself. But particularly exciting to the mail order firm is that it provides the opportunity to increase the size of the average order. Time after time we have seen an average order increase from 20 to 30 percent when phone-in privileges are offered. The well-disciplined telephone operator will take the basic order a customer phones in and then suggest add-ons.

4. *Bank cards.* Offering bank card charge privileges is similar in effect to offering phone-in order privileges. The result is that the average order is larger. Offering bank card privileges is particularly attractive to firms that normally sell for cash. Bank cards give the marketer the opportunity to offer charge privileges without having an accounts receivable problem.

Ambassador Leather Goods offers customers the opportunity to use phone-in order and bank charge privileges by stating, "If you have a Master Charge or Visa account, you don't even need pen and check book. Just pick up your telephone and call your order in to us, toll free!"

5. *Free trial periods.* It's ironic that some direct marketers who offer a 15-day trial period in solo mailings offer no free trial period when selling via the catalog method. Yet the chances for increased sales with a free trial period are well known.

Where practical, consideration should be given to this technique. It's hard to beat the appeal of this headline: "Everything in this catalog offered for 15 days' free trial!"

6. *Free gifts, or discounts tied to size of order.* Increasing the size of the average order can mean the difference between profit and loss, especially for specialty catalogs where the average order is traditionally small.

Many catalogs for businesses offer free gifts of varying value tied to the dollar amount of the total order. For example, a catalog might offer a free coffee mug for any order between $10.00 and $25.00, a free transistor radio for any order $25.01 to $50.00; and a free digital clock radio for any order for $50.01 or more.

Many specialty merchandise firms increase the average order by grouping merchandise and applying discounts based on the number of items purchased from a given page, a given spread, or a given number of pages. For instance, if a customer buys ten or more $1 items, he or she pays only 88 cents each.

These are some of the basic sales stimulators used by profitable catalog operations.

**Right order forms**    In the final analysis, the one thing you want to get back from your catalog is the order form. No one can possibly compute the amount of business lost annually due to confusing order forms, but the figure must be staggering. Nothing can be left to chance where the order form is concerned.

What are the basics of an effective order form?

1. Is there space to indicate quantity, item number or style number, name of item, color if there is a choice, size if there is a choice, imprinting if offered, and the dollar amount.

2. Consistent with the total number of items called for on the average order, is there a sufficient number of lines for listing the items desired? (It is always desirable to leave space for more than the average number as an incentive for ordering more items.)

3. Are the terms perfectly clear? If postage, insurance, and handling charges are extra, is the chart clear? If there are taxes to be added, is the percentage specified? If charge card privileges are offered, is there space to give the required identification numbers? If interest charges are applied to installment accounts, does the explanation comply with the Truth in Lending Law?

4. If drop shipments are solicited, is space allocated to provide for instructions?

5. If a discount is offered for exceeding a minimum order requirement, is it clearly spelled out?

The Kaleidoscope form illustrated here is a good example of a well-structured catalog order form. It takes the prospect through all the necessary steps in logical sequence. A key question to be asked when developing a mail order catalog is: Should we use a bind-in order form, or should we print an order form as a page and require the prospect to tear out the page and mail it in his or her own envelope? The overwhelming vote among the pros is for a bind-in order form. It increases results in most cases; it also affords an opportunity to feature one or more additional items on the flap. In many cases, the additional business secured with this added exposure more than pays for the additional cost of the combination bind-in order form and reply envelope.

**Exhibit 11.5.** This model order form, while uncluttered, makes it easy to order. Toll-free ordering privileges are featured, special instructions are high-lighted, the guarantee is stated clearly, and the customer is urged to provide the names of up to three friends.

**Kaleidoscope** 2201 Faulkner Road NE, Atlanta, Georgia 30324

PLACE PEEL-OFF ADDRESS LABEL HERE (MAKE ANY CORRECTIONS) OR PRINT INFORMATION

NAME

ADDRESS

CITY _____ ZIP

STATE

PHONE:
PLEASE INCLUDE AREA CODE

☐ Check or money order enclosed

Charge: ☐ Master Charge, ☐ VISA (BankAmericard), ☐ American Express, ☐ Diners Club

Account number (All digits, please):

InterBank Number
(Master Charge only)

Expiration Date _____

(Required for charge orders only)

SIGNATURE _____

| ITEM NO. | DESCRIPTION OF ITEM | SIZE | QTY. | ITEM PRICE | POST. HDLG. & INS. | TOTAL CHARGE |
|---|---|---|---|---|---|---|
| | | | | | | |
| | | | | | | |
| | | | | | | |
| | | | | | | |
| | | | | | | |
| | | | | | | |
| | | | | | | |
| | | | | | | |
| | | | | | | |

SPECIAL INSTRUCTIONS ✱

M8

(Ga. residents add sales tax)
TOTAL ORDER $ _____

**Thank you for your order!**

**FOR FASTEST SERVICE** on charge orders, call us *toll-free* at 800.241.0508 (Alternate number 800.241.0504.) Georgia residents call 404.321.5734 collect. You'll be served by a Kaleidoscope staff member who will be happy to help with your shopping.

✱ **SPECIAL INSTRUCTIONS.** Please let us know your special requirements – different shipping addresses, gift wrapping (add 1.00), card enclosures, etc. You name it and we'll do our best to comply.

**GUARANTEE**
Your complete satisfaction is absolutely guaranteed. If, for *any* reason, you're dissatisfied with a purchase from Kaleidoscope, your money will be promptly and cheerfully refunded.

We'd be pleased to send our catalog to:

Name _____
Address _____
City _____
State _____ Zip _____

Name _____
Address _____
City _____
State _____ Zip _____

Right analysis    Every catalog sales manager worth his or her salt is in reality a financial analyst. If the sales manager is good, he or she is a ruthless analyst. The professional catalog sales manager is never satisfied simply to learn that the total catalog distribution was profitable. He or she wants to know which items were the winners and losers; he or she wants all the facts and figures.

The Bible is undoubtedly the most purchased book ever published. But to every sales manager, the second most valuable book is a marked-up copy of his or her last catalog. This was brought home to me during a meeting with the catalog sales manager of one of the world's largest mail order firms. He had one book on his desk. It was his latest catalog, in excess of 800 pages. Written in grease pencil on every single page was the total sales of that page! There is no more dramatic way to see visually how products moved or didn't move.

The catalog sales manager looks at item exposure in a catalog the same way an advertising manager looks at space advertising in print media. Every inch of space you use in a catalog costs a certain amount of money. The cost of space is charged to the item being advertised.

Table 11.2 illustrates the importance of analyzing by item and by page. Let's examine these pages, starting with page 23. Note that three items are offered, one getting a space allocation of a half page and the other two each getting one-fourth page. Note the half-page allocation has an advertising cost of $968 as compared to an advertising cost of $484 for the quarter-page units.

It is significant that item #1618, with a space allocation of one-half page,

**Table 11.2. Analysis of sales results for selected pages from a typical catalog.**

| Page Number | Item Number | Space Allocation | Dollar Volume | Advert. Cost | Product Cost | Total of Costs | Item Profit | Loss | Page Profit(Loss) |
|---|---|---|---|---|---|---|---|---|---|
| 23 | 1618 | ½ page | $6,699 | $ 968 | $1,608 | $2,576 | $4,123 | | |
| | 1619 | ¼ page | 556 | 484 | 133 | 617 | | $ 61 | |
| | 1620 | ¼ page | 1,004 | 484 | 241 | 725 | 279 | | |
| Totals for page . . . . . . . . . | | | $8,259 | $1,936 | $1,982 | $3,918 | $4,402 | $ 61 | $4,341 |
| 47 | 2612 | ⅔ page | $8,592 | $1,291 | $3,007 | $4,298 | $4,294 | | |
| | 2613 | ⅙ page | 386 | 323 | 135 | 458 | | 72 | |
| | 2614 | ⅙ page | 193 | 323 | 68 | 391 | | 198 | |
| Totals for page . . . . . . . . . | | | $9,171 | $1,937 | $3,210 | $5,147 | $4,294 | $ 270 | $4,024 |
| 67 | 3499 | ½ page | $ 817 | $ 968 | $ 531 | $1,499 | | $ 682 | |
| | 3500 | ¼ page | 925 | 484 | 426 | 910 | $ 15 | | |
| | 3501 | ¼ page | 316 | 484 | 205 | 689 | | 373 | |
| Totals for page . . . . . . . . . | | | $2,058 | $1,936 | $1,162 | $3,098 | $ 15 | $1,055 | ($1,040) |
| 69 | 4621 | ¾ page | $3,226 | $1,452 | $1,484 | $2,936 | $290 | | |
| | 4622 | ¼ page | 1,689 | 484 | 777 | 1,261 | 428 | | |
| Totals for page . . . . . . . . . | | | $4,915 | $1,936 | $2,261 | $4,197 | $ 718 | | $ 718 |

Source: Stone & Adler

did $6,699 in sales, over 80 percent of the total sales for the page. Item #1619 lost a small amount of money. Item #1620 made a minimum profit. If profits were calculated for the total page, ignoring the contribution of each item, then item #1619 would not show up as a loser and item #1620 would not show up as a minimum profit item.

Page 47 is also a profit maker. But note that only item #2612 shows a profit, whereas the other two items are losers.

Page 67 is a bad page. Two of the items lost money and the other just broke even. Total loss for the page was $1,040.

Finally let's look at page 69. Both items were profitable. But take careful note that the item allocated three-fourths of a page produced $290 in profit, whereas item #4622, which was allocated only one-fourth of a page, produced $428 in profit.

Let's take a closer look at these figures through the eyes of the catalog sales manager. The first thing he will do is to look at his big winners. From the four pages he has two big winners: items #1618 and #2612. He allocated one-half page to item #1618. For the next edition of his catalog, he well may consider increasing the space to three-fourths of a page or even a full page. He allocated two-thirds of a page to item #2612. For the next edition, he may consider going to one full page.

Now let's look at the losers. Item #1619 was a small loser. He may consider dropping this to one-sixth of a page or eliminating it entirely. On page 47 he had two losers: items #2613 and #2614. Since he allocated only the minimum one-sixth of a page, he can go one of two ways: either eliminate the items entirely or give them more space with the hope that additional space will put them in the profit column.

On page 67 he also had two losers: items #3499 and #3501. He gave one-half page to item #3499. Now he must decide whether it should be eliminated entirely. Since he gave only one-fourth page to item #3501, it is a moot question whether he can put it in the profit column by reducing the space further. These are difficult decisions to make.

One factor that will influence a catalog sales manager's decision is whether the catalog features full-line selection or not. The general merchandise house with full-line selections often must live with losers, whereas the specialty merchandise house (like Miles Kimball, Foster & Gallagher, and Sunset House) is rarely confronted with the problem.

The sophisticated catalog sales manager sees things in numerical results that the neophyte rarely sees. For the sake of illustration, let's assume item #1618, a big winner, was a sport sweater. The catalog sales manager asks himself, "If sport sweaters sell so well, why shouldn't we test sport jackets, sweatshirts, and jacket emblems?" Thus, he builds on a winner.

A few final comments can be made of the importance of space allocation. The amount of space allocated is first determined by the minimum amount of space required to describe and illustrate an item properly. Beyond this, increasing a one-half page allocation to one page will not necessarily double sales, although in some cases it can more than double sales. Conversely, decreasing a space allocation from a half page to one-fourth page, for instance, will not necessarily cut sales in half.

## HAVE PLENTY OF YOUR FAVORITE FLAVORINGS ON HAND WITH WATKINS' CONVENIENT 6-OZ. SIZE

# Everyday Extracts

From that day back in 1868 when the first bottle of Watkins Vanilla Extract was sold, the "Watkins Philosophy" has never changed: Search the world for the best and purest ingredients . . . process them with utmost care . . . and always keep looking for ways to improve, but never compromise on quality.

All our extracts and flavorings are made in this same tradition. Our Almond Extract, for example, comes from the oil of the bitter Almond. It's carefully pressed, distilled and fermented until it's full bodied and fragrant. Our Lemon Extract, too, is made only from finest natural ingredients. And where natural oils don't make the best, longest-lasting flavors, or when there are no natural oils to extract, Watkins carefully selects other fine ingredients to exactly match original flavors, as in our Butter, Coconut and Maple flavors. Our five most frequently used extracts come in convenient 6-oz. sizes, so you can rely on them every day to add rich, full flavor to main dishes, desserts, and beverages.

*"My flavoring shelf wouldn't be complete without your Lemon Extract. It measures up to high standards of old-fashioned quality and good taste."*

Mrs. Clara Roberts
Summit, Illinois

6

## Lemon

When you add Watkins Extract of Lemon to your favorite recipes you're adding a little bit of sunshine. A few drops in seafood or vegetable dishes bring out their full flavor, make them taste really special. And everyone loves the tangy taste of lemon in salad dressings and desserts. No lemons to squeeze!

**No. 1089   6 oz. Extract of Lemon   $1.99**

### Lemon Jelly Roll

| | |
|---|---|
| 4 eggs, separated | 1 c. cake flour |
| 1 c. sugar | 1/2 tsp. baking powder |
| 1/2 tsp. Watkins | 2 tbsp. boiling water |
| Lemon Extract | |

Beat egg yolks until very light in color. Add sugar and beat thoroughly. Add Watkins Lemon Extract and stiffly-beaten egg whites. Sift flour with baking powder and fold into egg mixture. Add boiling water and bake in a greased jelly roll pan or large flat pan in a 1/4 inch layer or less, about 8 minutes in 375°F. oven. Turn out onto wet cloth or board dusted with powdered sugar. Trim dry edges, spread with lemon filling and roll.

#### Lemon Jelly Filling:

2/3 c. granulated sugar, 2 tsp. flour or cornstarch, 1 tsp. butter, 1 egg, grated rind and juice of 1 lemon (at least 2 tbsp.). Mix and cook in a double boiler until thick, stirring constantly. Jelly may be used instead of lemon filling.

**Two-step catalog program** The cost of getting new catalog customers is major. Especially when first starting out, many marketers are inclined to mail the catalog directly to "logical" prospects. The cost of this procedure, however, often is far in excess of the margin of profit on each order.

A better approach is to use other media to get catalog requests. A classic use of the two-step method is illustrated in the case of the Watkins Company of Winona, Minnesota. That firm was founded in 1868 and built its business through dealers and agents who sold the firms's spices, extracts, and home remedies door to door. As the years went by, the number of Watkins' dealers diminished. Competition in the form of gourmet food stores and gourmet food departments in chain stores increased and threatened Watkins' very existence. The time had arrived for Watkins to explore another method of selling—mail order.

After examining available research data, the Watkins agency determined that several hundred thousand women in this country knew the Watkins name favorably, either because they, their mothers, or their grandmothers had purchased Watkins products from Watkins dealers. The question was, "How can we find these women and get them to send for a catalog of Watkins' products?" The best answer, they decided, was to use space advertising to solicit catalog requests, particularly in small town and rural markets.

Seven test ads of 45 lines each were prepared and run in a single edition of *TV Guide*. The ads are shown on the following pages. The rationale applied to the seven ads warrants study.

Ad A, the control ad, parlayed three strategies: (1) get "FREE" into the headline (a basic mail order strategy); (2) offer its most popular product, vanilla extract, as the freebie; and (3) give the product free only with a purchase to spur catalog sales.

Strategy for ad B was that if Watkins spices are highly regarded, why not provide five simple packets for 25 cents? Such an offer should produce a high front-end response (catalog requests) and spur catalog sales after sampling the spices. Ad B also included a kicker, a free spice recipe book to encourage an even bigger response.

Ad C was conceived as a blockbuster. The strategy was based on the premise that vanilla extract is the company's most renowned product. Therefore, make an "irresistible" offer of a $2.69 bottle of Watkins vanilla for $1.00, "the same price it was in the year 1868!" Front-end pull was expected to be great. And a strong back-end pull seemed like a logical expectation. To hypo front-end response ad C also included a kicker, an extract recipe book.

Ad D was another bargain offer, the $4.25 "Old Watkins Cookbook" for only $2. There were great expectations for the back-end pull. After all, what good would it do a woman to have "recipes that go back over 100 years" if she didn't purchase the specified Watkins ingredients to make these great recipes?

Ad E, "Get $4 Off!" played on the principle that cents-off coupons are great order incentives. Ask any package goods manufacturer.

**Exhibit 11.7. Telescopic test of ads for Watkins products shown on these facing pages.**

## Yours Free!
with your first by-mail purchase from **Watkins** catalog of world-famous spices, extracts and home remedies

**Send now for your Free Catalog**

*FREE BONUS if you act now:* $1.25 bottle of *double-strength* Vanilla with your first by-mail purchase from our new catalog that abounds with over 140 delicious & delightful items made in the Watkins tradition!

SPECIAL OFFER EXPIRES 5/31/76

Clip coupon *now* and mail with your name & address to:

**Watkins** Dept. VS-55, Winona, Minn. 55987

*Serving you from the comfort of your home since 1868*

**Control Ad A**

---

Sample 5 of **Watkins** world-famous **SPICES** ONLY 25¢

**Cinnamon • Black Pepper • Spiced Salt • Ground Beef Seasoning • Soup & Vegetable Seasoning**

Only first quality raw spices — full of natural oils — go into Watkins spices. For this they were awarded *Grand Prize* at the Paris Exposition. Sample the best the world has to offer in *your* recipes! You'll soon see . . .

**A little goes a long way with Watkins!**

**FREE BONUS!** 52 pages of recipes that reveal the "mysteries" of spice cookery.

LIMIT: ONE PER CUSTOMER. OFFER EXPIRES 5/31/76

Clip coupon *now* and mail with your name & address plus 25¢ to:

**Watkins** Dept. S-5 Winona, Minn. 55987

*Serving you from the comfort of your home since 1868*

**Ad B**

---

BIG 11 oz. SIZE REG. $2.69 now just $1

## Watkins all-time famous Vanilla
back at the same price it was in the year 1868!

LIMIT: ONE PER CUSTOMER. OFFER EXPIRES 5/31/76

Watkins Vanilla still *is* what it *was* 108 years ago: a flavor specially concentrated to give over *twice* the strength of standard vanilla extracts. Now it's back at 1868 prices!

**PLUS 52-page Recipe Book FREE!** Abounds with recipes using our secret flavoring touches.

Clip coupon *now* and mail with your name and address plus $1 to:

**Watkins** Dept. V-5 Winona, Minn. 55987

*Serving you from the comfort of your home since 1868*

**Ad C**

---

Now . . . from J. R. Watkins, world-famous for their spices & extracts . . .

## Recipes that go back over 100 years
ONLY $2.00

**YOURS . . . IN A LIMITED EDITION FOR LESS THAN HALF PRICE!**

Boston Brown Bread . . . Stuffed Apple Salad . . . Quickly-Made Cake — *plus* over 200 more delectable recipes — including many favorites from the "Old Watkins Cookbook." Sections on seasoning secrets, household hints and more! Reg. $4.25, now only $2 (including postage)!

LIMIT: ONE PER CUSTOMER. OFFER EXPIRES 5/31/76

Clip coupon *now* and mail with your name and address plus $2 to:

**Watkins** Dept. R-5 Winona, Minn. 55987

*Serving you from the comfort of your home since 1868*

**Ad D**

# Get $4 Off!

Send now for Watkins' FREE catalog of world-famous spices, extracts & home remedies... and we'll include $4.00 worth of discount coupons... FREE!

Quantities of our new catalog – with over 140 delicious & delightful items – are limited! *FREE BONUS* if you act now: $4 worth of catalog discount coupons! No obligation to buy!

SPECIAL OFFER
EXPIRES 5/31/76

Clip coupon *now* and mail with your name & address to:

**Watkins** Dept. C-5
Winona, Minn. 55987

*Serving you from the comfort of your home since 1868*

Ad E

Your mother and grandmother before her knew the Watkins reputation for extra strength and extra flavor in our spices & extracts.

NOW WE'D LIKE TO SHARE IT WITH YOU. SEND NOW FOR OUR **FREE CATALOG**

Over 140 delicious & delightful items... from award-winning spices to the world's largest selling liniment & home remedies... all made of a quality hard to come by nowadays.

For free catalog, clip coupon *now* and mail with your name and address to:

**Watkins** Dept. FC-5
Winona, Minn. 55987

*Serving you from the comfort of your home since 1868*

Ad F

# Watkins all-time famous Liniment

back at the same price it was in the year 1868!

BIG 12 oz. SIZE
REG. $2.79
now just $1

LIMIT: ONE PER CUSTOMER. OFFER EXPIRES 5/31/76

People must like how our Liniment helps to reduce the discomfort of muscular aches, pains and soreness because nobody in the world sells as much liniment as Watkins. And now it's back at the same price it was *108 years ago* during this special by-mail offer!

**Plus Watkins latest by-mail catalog – FREE!**

Clip coupon *now* and mail with your name and address plus $1 to:

**Watkins** Dept. L-5
Winona, Minn. 55987

*Serving you from the comfort of your home since 1868*

Ad G

## WATKINS: 'TV GUIDE' TELESCOPIC TEST RESULT SUMMARY

| Ads | Inquiries per M circulation | % of orders per M inquiries |
|---|---|---|
| Ad A .... | 0.9 | 20.39% |
| Ad B .... | 1.20 | 3.21 |
| Ad C .... | 2.49 | 3.06 |
| Ad D .... | .06 | 2.66 |
| Ad E .... | .05 | 9.14 |
| Ad F .... | .04 | 12.08 |
| Ad G .... | .07 | 7.85 |

Ad F played upon nostalgia, "Your mother and grandmother before her. . . ." Research was replete with statements such as, "My mother and grandmother always had Watkins extracts and spices on hand."

The thinking for the final ad was that if Watkins vanilla (its most popular product) at $1 was an attractive value, perhaps the old man will again call out, "Don't forget the liniment."

*The results.* How did Watkins do with their telescopic test? Lots of surprises. Strong possibilities. Fascinating. A look at the result summary underscores again the wisdom of telescopic testing and the dramatic contrasts that occur between front-end and back-end results.

Examination of front-end results (inquiries) reveals one runaway winner, ad C, the full-size bottle of vanilla for $1. This ad drew 2.49 inquiries per 1,000 circulation. The only other ad to draw more than one inquiry per 1,000 was ad B. Control ad A received slightly less than one inquiry per 1,000.

High in the disappointment column was ad D, the bargain recipe book offer. Cents-off coupons, ad E, didn't cause a stampede to the mail box. Nostalgia, ad F, didn't come out as a mandate for "the good old days." And apparently the old man forgot to tell the little woman, "Don't forget the liniment," ad G.

But looking at back-end results (the payoff) shows a different story. Ad C, the big front-end winner, fell on its back-end. Only 3.06 percent ordered from the catalog they received with their vanilla. Bargain hunters, perhaps?

Ad A, the control ad, saved the day. Look at those back-end results: an order from better than one out of every five who received the free catalog. Closest contender is ad F based on the nostalgia theme. But it's not very close, drawing only half the inquiries and slightly more than half the orders per thousand.

Having determined the winning appeal, the agency then proceeded to run similar ads in scores of publications, including such mass circulation magazines as *Woman's Day* and *Family Circle.* Within eighteen months, Watkins had received a quarter of a million inquiries and had converted over 20 percent of these to mail order customers.

But this remarkable success story doesn't end here. Having proved that Watkins could get catalog requests economically and convert them to mail order customers at a profit, the agency asked itself, "Suppose we were to take a group of the best selling products from the Watkins catalog, offer them for direct sales in space advertising, and use the complete catalog as a bounce-back in the shipment?" To test the validity of this concept, the seven top-selling items in the catalog were offered in a space ad, using publications that had previously proved successful in drawing catalog requests. Every single insertion of this direct sell ad made a front-end profit! Then 10 percent or more of those who received the catalog with their shipment ordered additional merchandise from Watkins. So Watkins now has two ways to apply the two-step method, both highly profitable.

**Exhibit 11.8. Coupon from space ad for Watkins products.**

## The name your grandparents grew up with...

### SENSATIONAL OFFER!
**SAVE $1.00**
First order only! Take $1.00 discount if order totals $8 or more!

## Stock up with these WORLD-FAMOUS spices and home remedies from
# THE WATKINS COMPANY

Watkins
**DOUBLE-STRENGTH**
# VANILLA
Rich, true flavor literally goes twice as far in cooking and baking. Freezeproof, too for ices. This is how real vanilla used to taste!

( ) 1022 11-oz. bottle. ea. $2.99
( ) 1022-2 2 bottles. ea. $2.89

**Watkins MENTHOL CAMPHOR OINTMENT**
Cool, soothing relief for colds and coughs. Just rub it on. Also relieves minor cuts, burns, chapped skin. Clear and non staining!

2358 4¾ oz tin ea $2.99
2358-2 2 tins ea $2.89

**Watkins PETRO-CARBO SALVE**
for sores and chafing

Cool protective dressing stays moist on the skin, aids healing

2372 5 oz tin ea $2.99
2372-2 2 tins ea $2.89

Watkins
**FRESH GRANULATED PEPPER**
Not ground it's granulated – you can taste the peppery difference!

1140 6 oz canister ea $2.99
1140 2 2 canisters ea $2.89

Watkins
**PURE GROUND CINNAMON**
Old fashioned flavor you've almost forgotten!

1115 6 oz canister ea $3.89
1115 2 2 canisters ea $3.79

**WORLD-FAMOUS**
Watkins **LINIMENT**
for aches and pains
Deep penetration helps reduce minor muscular pain, relieves neuralgia, stiff necks, sore backs.

2303 12 oz bottle ea $2.99
2303-2 2 bottles ea $2.89

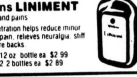

Rub away pain
Watkins **CREAM OF CAMPHOR LINIMENT**
Penetrates quickly without burning with a glowing warmth that stimulates circulation and provides soothing comfort

2302 12 oz bottle ea $2.99
2302-2 2 bottles ea $2.89

**SAVE $1.00**
First order only! Take $1.00 discount if order totals $8 or more!

**OUR GUARANTEE: You must be satisfied or your money back!**
**TO: WATKINS PRODUCTS, INC., Winona, Minn. 55987.**

Name
Address
City                State                Zip
Check    or charge Master Charge    BankAmericard    Total Amount $
Card No                    Exp Date

**CHECK WHAT YOU WANT, TEAR OUT AND MAIL TODAY**

A88G

**Self-quiz**

1. A major factor in the boom in catalog sales is

   _____

   _____

2. List the six consumer benefits for catalogs.

   a. _____

   b. _____

   c. _____

   d. _____

   e. _____

   f. _____

3. List the four key perceptions which must be held by the consumer in order for a catalog to be successful.

   a. _____

   b. _____

   c. _____

   d. _____

4. Name the four types of catalogs.

   a. _____

   b. _____

   c. _____

   d. _____

5. List the 10 basics of a successful catalog.

   a. _____

   b. _____

   c. _____

   d. _____

   e. _____

   f. _____

   g. _____

   h. _____

   i. _____

   j. _____

6. Describe the advantages of an overwrap.

   _____

   _____

   _____

   _____

   _____

7. What is the formula for deciding whether items carried in a catalog are profitable?

   _____

   _____

   _____

   _____

   _____

8. If an item in a catalog is marginally profitable, should more or less space be alloted the next time it is run?

   ☐ More        ☐ Less

9. What is a two-step catalog program?

   _____

   _____

   _____

10. Give a clear definition of "front-end/back-end" results.

    _____

    _____

    _____

    _____

## Pilot project

You have surveyed the "older age market" and have determined that you can reach more than 20 million people between the ages of 55 and 80 through existing mailing lists.

Your company, at present, sells prescription drugs to 750,000 people in the identified market. You would like to expand your operation to sell not only prescription drugs but also other items to older people. At present you have a 24-page prescription drug catalog. Average order from your existing catalog is $14.80.

Develop a marketing plan that will include the following:

1. A list of 25 items you consider typical of those you propose to offer in your expanded catalog.

2. How you propose to position this expanded catalog.

3. What margin of profit you plan to set as a minimum.

4. Whether you would use space advertising in addition to direct mail and, if so, what publications you would use to solicit catalog requests.

# 12

## Techniques of Creating Print Advertising

Many of the creative techniques needed for creating a successful direct mail package (chapter 10) are also necessary in creating productive direct response ads in magazines and newspapers. But the space available for words and pictures is much more severely limited, and most of the gimmicks, gadgets, showmanship, and personal tone of direct mail do not apply here. This throws a heavy load of responsibility for the success of the ad on a carefully worded headline, a compelling opening, tightly structured copy, and appropriate visual emphasis.

Before the actual work of creating an ad begins, two important questions should be answered: Who is the prospect? and What are the outstanding product advantages or customer benefits?

Often there is no single clear answer but, rather, several distinct possibilities. Then the profitable course of action is to prepare ads embodying all your most promising hypotheses and split-test as many of them as your budget permits.

**Visualizing the prospect** Every good mail order or direct mail piece should attract the most attention from the likeliest prospects, and every good creator of direct response advertising visualizes his prospect with varying degrees of precision when he sits down at his typewriter or drawing board.

Good direct response advertising makes its strongest appeal to its best prospects and then gathers in as many additional prospects as possible.

And who are the prospects? They are the ones with the strongest desire for what you're selling. You must look for the common denominators.

For instance, let's say you are selling a book on the American Revolution. Here are some of the relevant common denominators that would be shared by many people in your total audience.

1. An interest in the American Revolution in particular.
2. An interest in American history in general.
3. A patriotic interest in America.

4. An interest in history.
5. An interest in big, beautiful coffee table books.
6. An interest in impressing friends with historical lore.
7. A love of bargains.
8. An interest in seeing children in the family become adults with high achievement.

Now, out of the total audience of 1,000, some readers would possess all eight denominators, some would possess some combination of six, some a different combination of six, some just one of the eight, and so on.

If you could know the secret hearts of all 1,000 people and rank them on a scale of relative desire to buy, you would place at the very top of the list those who possessed all eight denominators, then just below them those who possessed just seven, and so on down to the bottom of the scale, where you would place people who possess none.

Obviously, you should make as many sales as possible among your hottest prospects first, for that is where your sales will be easiest. Then you want to reach down the scale to sell as many of the others as you can. By the time you get down to the people possessing only one of the denominators, you will probably find interest so faint that it would almost be impossible to make your sales effort pay unless it were fantastically appealing.

Obvious? Yes, to mail order professionals who learned the hard way. But to the tenderfoot, it is not so obvious. In his eagerness to sell everybody, he may muff his easiest sales by using a curiosity-only appeal that conceals what is really being offered.

On the other hand, the veteran but uninspired pro may gather up all the easy sales lying on the surface but, through lack of creative imagination, fail to reach deeper into the market. For instance, let's say that of 1,000 readers, 50 possess all eight denominators. A crude omnibus appeal that could scoop up many of them would be something like, "At last—for every liberty-loving American family, especially those with children, whose friends are amazed by their understanding of American history, here is a big, beautiful book about the American Revolution you will display with pride—yours for only one-fifth of what you'd expect to pay!" A terrible headline, but at least one that those possessing the eight denominators of interest would stop to look at and consider. You may get only 5 percent readership, but it will be the right 5 percent.

Now, on the other hand, suppose you want to do something terribly creative to reach a wider market. So you do a beautiful advertising message headed "The Impossible Dream," in which you somehow work your way from that starting point to what it is you're selling. Again, you may get only 5 percent readership, but these readers will be scattered along the entire length of your scale of interest. Of the 50 people who stopped to read your message, only two or three may be prime prospects possessing all eight denominators. Many people really interested in books on the American Revolution, in inspiring their children with patriotic sentiments, and in acquiring big impressive books at big savings will have hurried past unaware.

The point: don't let prime prospects get away. In mail order you can't afford to. Some people out there don't have to be sold; they already want what you have, and if you tell them that you have it, they will buy it. Alone they may not constitute enough of a market to make your selling effort pay, but without them you haven't got a chance. So, through your clarity and directness, you gather in these prime prospects; then through your creative imagination you reach beyond them to awaken and excite mild prospects as well.

Once the prospect is clearly visualized, a good headline almost writes itself. For example, here is an effective and successful headline from an ad by Quadrangle/The New York Times Book Company. It simply defines the prospect so clearly and accurately that the interested reader feels an instant tug:

### For people who are almost (but not quite) satisfied with their house plants . . . and can't figure out what they're doing wrong

Our most successful ad for Washington School of Art, offering a correspondence course, resulted from our bringing the psychographic profile of our prime prospect into sharp focus. We began to confront the fact that the prospect was someone who had been drawing pictures better than the rest of us since the first grade. Such people are filled with a rare combination of pride in their talent and shame at their lack of perfection. And their goal is not necessarily fame or fortune, but simply to become a "real artist," a phrase that has different meanings to different people. So the winning headline simply reached out to the right people and offered them the right benefit:

### If you can draw fairly well (but still not good enough) we'll turn you into a real artist

Of course, a good headline does not necessarily present an explicit definition of the prospect, but it is always implied. Here are some classic headlines and the prospects whom the writer undoubtedly visualized:

### Can a man or woman my age become a hotel executive?

The prospect is—probably—a middle-aged man or woman who needs, for whatever reason, an interesting, pleasant, not too technically demanding occupational skill such as hotel management, and is eager for reassurance that you *can* teach an old dog new tricks. Note, however, how wide the net is cast. No one is excluded. Even a person fearing he may be too young to be a hotel executive can theoretically read himself into this headline:

### Don't envy the plumber—be one

The prospect is a poorly paid worker, probably blue-collar, who is looking for a way to improve his lot and who has looked with both indignation and envy at the plumber, who appears not much more skilled but earns several times as much per hour.

### How to stumble upon a fortune in gems

The prospect is everybody, all of us, who all our lives have daydreamed of gaining sudden wealth without extreme sacrifice.

### Is your home picture-poor?

The prospect is someone, probably a woman, with a home, who has a number of bare or inadequately decorated walls, and who feels not only a personal lack but also, perhaps more important, a vague underlying sense of social shame at this conspicuous cultural "poverty." Whether she appreciates it or not, she recognizes that art, books, and music are regarded as part of the "good life" and are supposed to add a certain richness to life.

### Be a "non-degree" engineer

This is really a modern version of "don't envy the plumber." The prospect is an unskilled or semiskilled factory worker who looks with a mixture of resentment and grudging envy on the aristocracy in his midst, the fair-haired boys who earn much more, dress better, and enjoy special privileges because they are graduate engineers. The prospect would like to enjoy at least some of their job status but is unwilling or unable to go to college and get an engineering degree.

### Are you tired of cooking with odds and ends?

The prospect is Everywoman who has accumulated over the years an enameled pan here, an aluminum pot there, an iron skillet elsewhere, and to whom a matched set of anything represents neatness, order, and elegance.

### Can you call a man a failure at 30?

The prospect is a young white-collar worker between 25 and 32 who is deeply concerned that life isn't turning out the way he dreamed and that he is on the verge of failing to "make it"—permanently.

**Selecting advantages and benefits**

Advantages belong to the product. Benefits belong to the consumer. If the product or service is unique or unfamiliar to the prospect, stressing benefits is important. But if it is simply a new, improved model in a highly competitive field where there already exists an established demand, the product advantage or advantages become important.

Thus, when pocket electronic calculators were first introduced, such benefits as *pride, power,* and *profit* were important attributes. But, as the market became flooded with competing types and brands, product advantages such as the floating decimal became more important.

There are two kinds of benefits, the immediate or obvious benefit and the not so obvious ultimate benefit—the real potential meaning for the customer's life of the product or service being sold. The ultimate benefit often proves to have a greater effect, for it reaches deeper into the prospect's feelings.

For a girl who is a prospect for a course in Speedwriting shorthand, the obvious benefit is "a good job with more pay." But a strong possible ultimate benefit was expressed in the headline:

### Catch yourself a new boss, etc.

Needless to say, the "etc." could easily be interpreted to mean "husband."

Exhibit 12.1. Classic direct response ad written by John Caples, a member of the Advertising Hall of Fame.

"Can he really play?" a girl whispered. "Heavens no!" Arthur exclaimed. "He never played a note in his life."

# They Laughed When I Sat Down At the Piano But When I Started to Play!~

ARTHUR had just played "The Rosary." The room rang with applause. I decided that this would be a dramatic moment for me to make my debut. To the amazement of all my friends, I strode confidently over to the piano and sat down.

"Jack is up to his old tricks," somebody chuckled. The crowd laughed. They were all certain that I couldn't play a single note.

"Can he really play?" I heard a girl whisper to Arthur.

"Heavens, no!" Arthur exclaimed· "He never played a note in all his life. . . But just you watch him. This is going to be good."

I decided to make the most of the situation. With mock dignity I drew out a silk handkerchief and lightly dusted off the piano keys. Then I rose and gave the revolving piano stool a quarter of a turn, just as I had seen an imitator of Paderewski do in a vaudeville sketch.

"What do you think of his execution?" called a voice from the rear.

"We're in favor of it!" came back the answer, and the crowd rocked with laughter.

## Then I Started to Play

Instantly a tense silence fell on the guests. The laughter died on their lips as if by magic. I played through the first few bars of Beethoven's immortal Moonlight Sonata. I heard gasps of amazement. My friends sat breathless — spellbound!

I played on and as I played I forgot the people around me. I forgot the hour, the place, the breathless listeners. The little world I lived in seemed to fade — seemed to grow dim—unreal. Only the music was real. Only the music and visions it brought me. Visions as beautiful and as changing as the wind blown clouds and drifting moonlight that long ago inspired the master composer. It seemed as if the master

### Pick Your Instrument

| | |
|---|---|
| Piano | 'Cello |
| Organ | Harmony and |
| Violin | Composition |
| Drums and | Sight Singing |
| Traps | Ukulele |
| Banjo | Guitar |
| Tenor | Hawaiian |
| Banjo | Steel Guitar |
| Mandolin | Harp |
| Clarinet | Cornet |
| Flute | Piccolo |
| Saxophone | Trombone |
| Voice and Speech Culture | |
| Automatic Finger Control | |
| Piano Accordion | |

musician himself were speaking to me—speaking through the medium of music—not in words but in chords. Not in sentences but in exquisite melodies!

#### A Complete Triumph!

As the last notes of the Moonlight Sonata died away, the room resounded with a sudden roar of applause. I found myself surrounded by excited faces. How my friends carried on! Men shook my hand — wildly congratulating me— pounded me on the back in their enthusiasm! Everybody was exclaiming with delight—plying me with rapid questions. . . "Jack! Why didn't you tell us you could play like that?". . . "Where did you learn?"—"How long have you studied?"— "Who was your teacher?"

"I have never even seen my teacher," I replied. "And just a short while ago I couldn't play a note.',

"Quit your kidding," laughed Arthur, himself an accomplished pianist. "You've been studying for years. I can tell."

"I have been studying only a short while," I insisted. "I decided to keep it a secret so that I could surprise all you folks."

Then I told them the whole story.

"Have you ever heard of the U. S. School of Music?" I asked.

A few of my friends nodded. "That's a correspondence school, isn't it?" they exclaimed.

"Exactly," I replied. "They have a new simplified method that can teach you to play any instrument by mail in just a few months."

#### How I Learned to Play Without a Teacher

And then I explained how for years I had longed to play the piano.

"A few months ago," I continued, "I saw an interesting ad for the U. S. School of Music—a new method of learning to play which only cost a few cents a day! The ad told how a woman had mastered the piano in her spare time at home—and without a teacher! Best of all, the wonderful new method she used, required no laborious scales— no heartless exercises — no tiresome practising. It sounded so convincing that I filled out the coupon requesting the Free Demonstration Lesson.

"The free book arrived promptly and I started in that very night to study the Demonstration Lesson. I was amazed to see how easy it was to play this new way. Then I sent for the course.

"When the course arrived I found it was just as the ad said — as easy as A.B.C! And, as

the lessons continued they got easier and easier. Before I knew it I was playing all the pieces I liked best. Nothing stopped me. I could play ballads or classical numbers or jazz, all with equal ease! And I never did have any special talent for music!"

#### Play Any Instrument

You too, can now teach yourself to be an accomplished musician—right at home—in half the usual time. You can't go wrong with this simple new method which has already shown 350,000 people how to play their favorite instruments. Forget that old-fashioned idea that you need special "talent." Just read the list of instruments in the panel, decide which one you want to play and the U. S. School will do the rest. And bear in mind no matter which instrument you choose, the cost in each case will be the same—just a few cents a day. No matter whether you are a mere beginner or already a good performer, you will be interested in learning about this new and wonderful method.

#### Send for Our Free Booklet and Demonstration Lesson

Thousands of successful students never dreamed they possessed musical ability until it was revealed to them by a remarkable "Musical Ability Test" which we send entirely without cost with our interesting free booklet.

If you are in earnest about wanting to play your favorite instrument—if you really want to gain happiness and increase your popularity—send at once for the free booklet and Demonstration Lesson. No cost — no obligation. Right now we are making a Special Offer for a limited number of new students. Sign and send the convenient coupon now — before it's too late to gain the benefits of this offer. Instruments supplied when needed, cash or credit. U. S. School of Music, 1631 Brunswick Bldg., New York City.

- - - - - - - - - - - -

U. S. School of Music,
1631 Brunswick Bldg., New York City.
Please send me your free book, "Music Lessons in Your Own Home", with introduction by Dr. Frank Crane, Demonstration Lesson and particulars of your Special Offer. I am interested in the following course:

...........................................

Have you above instrument?.................

Name........
(Please write plainly)

Address.....................................

City.................................State...........

Victor Schwab, one of the great mail order pioneers, was fond of quoting Dr. Samuel Johnson's approach to auctioning off the contents of a brewery: "We are not here to sell boilers and vats, but the potentiality of growing rich beyond the dreams of avarice."

It pays to ask yourself over and over again, "What am I selling? Yes, I know it's a book or a steak knife, or a home study course in upholstering—but what am I *really* selling? What human values are at stake?"

For example, suppose you have the job of selling a correspondence course in advertising. Here is a list of ultimate benefits and the way they may be expressed in headlines for the course. Some of the headlines are patently absurd, but they illustrate the mind-stretching process involved in looking for the ultimate benefit in your product or service.

*Health:* "Successful ad men are healthier and happier than you think—and now you can be one of them."

*Money:* "What's your best chance of earning $50,000 a year by the time you are 30?"

*Security:* "You are always in demand when you can write advertising that sells."

*Pride:* "Imagine your pride when you can coin a slogan repeated by 50 million people."

*Approval:* "Did you write that ad? Why I've seen it everywhere."

*Enjoyment:* "Get more fun out of your daily job. Become a successful ad writer!"

*Excitement:* "Imagine working until 4:00 A.M.—and loving every minute of it!"

*Power:* "The heads of giant corporations will listen to your advice—when you've mastered the secrets of advertising that works." (Just a wee bit of exaggeration there, perhaps.)

*Fulfillment:* "Are you wasting a natural talent for advertising?"

*Freedom:* "People who can get million dollar advertising ideas don't have to worry about punching a time clock."

*Identity:* "Join the top advertising professionals who keep the wheels of our economy turning."

*Relaxation:* "How some people succeed in advertising without getting ulcers."

*Escape:* "Hate going to work in the morning? Get a job you'll love—in advertising!"

*Curiosity:* "Now go behind the scenes of America's top advertising agencies—and find out how multimillion dollar campaigns are born!"

*Possessions:* "I took your course five years ago—today I own two homes, two cars, and a Chris-Craft."

*Sex:* "Join the guys and gals who've made good in the swinging advertising scene."

*Hunger:* "A really good ad man always knows where his next meal is coming from."

**Harnessing the powers of semantics**

A single word is a whole bundle—a nucleus, you might say—of thoughts and feelings. And when different nuclei are joined together, the result is nuclear fusion, generating enough power to move the earth.

A whole new semi-science, semantics, has been founded on this unique property of words. The newspaper columnist, Sydney Harris, has popularized it with his occasional feature, "Antics with Semantics." A typical antic goes something like this: "I am sensible in the face of danger. You are a bit overcautious. He is a coward." The factual content may be the same, but the semantic implications vary widely.

Semantics is the hydrogen bomb of persuasion. In politics, for example, entire election campaigns sometimes hinge on the single word "boss." If one side manages to convince the public that the other side is controlled by a boss or bosses, but that the first side has only "party leaders," it will probably win the election.

In direct marketing, clear understanding and skillful use of semantics can make a powerful contribution to ad headlines. Here are a few examples.

What do you think when you read the word "Europe"? Perhaps there are certain negative connotations—constant military squabbles, lack of Yankee know-how, and so on. But far more important in the psyche of most Americans are the romantic implications—castles, colorful peasants, awesome relics of the past, charming sidewalk cafes, all merging into the lifelong dream of making the Grand Tour of Europe.

Another semantically rich word is "shoestring." A man is a fool to start a business of his own with inadequate capital. But if he succeeds, he is a "wizard," and his inadequate capital is seen in retrospect as a "shoestring." Harian Publications got the idea of linking these two words with a couple of modest connectives and achieved verbal nuclear fusion that sold thousands of books on low-cost travel: *Europe on a Shoestring.*

Because there is no copyright on semantic discoveries, Simon and Schuster could capitalize on Harian's discovery and publish their *$1 Complete Guide to Florida.* In fact, they were so successful they broke the mail order "rule" that a product selling for only $1.00 cannot be profitably sold in print ads.

For the word "Europe" they simply substituted another semantically rich word, "Florida," and came up with another powerful winner. A one-inch advertisement using this headline drew thousands of responses at a profitable cost per order, even when this tiny ad appeared to be completely lost on a 2,400-line page filled with larger ads screaming for attention.

The fascinating thing about this kind of verbal nuclear fusion is that once it has been adhieved it can be repeated almost endlessly—not only in the same form but in other forms as well.

For example, a real breakthrough in selling *Motor's Auto Repair Manual* was achieved many years ago with the headline, "Now You Can Lick Any Auto Repair Job." Every single word made a contribution to the power of the headline, as indeed each word always does in an effective headline. "Now" made the ad a news event, even after it had been running for years. "You," perhaps the sweetest word ever sounded to the ears, made it clear that the

**Exhibit 12.2. A classic ad.** This ad, appearing in scores of publications over a period of years, consistently outpulled all ads tested against it. Its success may well be attributed to the strong appeal to parental pride in the major headline.

benefit included the reader and not just professional auto mechanics. "Can," another great word, promises power, achievement. "Lick" promises not only sure mastery but sweet triumph. Notice how much richer it is than "do." "Any" increases the breadth of the promise to the outermost limit. "Auto" selects the prospect and defines the field of interest. "Repair" defines the proposition, and "Job" emphasizes the completeness of its scope.

Once this breakthrough had been achieved, it was possible to make the same statement in many different ways with equal success. "Now Any Auto Repair Job Can Be 'Duck Soup' for You," "Now Any Auto Repair Job Can Be Your 'Meat,' " and so on.

"Engineer" is a rich, many-faceted word. To an artist or a writer, the word may connote a literal-minded square. To an engineer's prospective mother-in-law, it may connote a good provider. To an engineer, it means a degree in engineering and professional standing earned by hard study at college.

But to the manual and semiskilled workers in an electronics plant, our agency reasoned, in developing appeals for the Cleveland Institute of Electronics, the word "engineer" suggests the college-educated wise guy who is the fair-haired boy in the plant—an object both of envy on the part of the workers and of secret derision born of envy. We couldn't promise "You too can be an engineer," because "engineer" by itself is taken to mean a graduate engineer, and completion of CIE courses doesn't provide college credits or a college degree. However, many of the job titles in our promotion, such as "broadcast engineer," "field engineer," or "sales engineer," have the word "engineer" in them without requiring a college degree. So we were legitimately able to promise prospective enrollees the prestige and other rewards of being an engineer in an ad headed, "Be a Non-Degree Engineer." (See Exhibit 12.3.)

Semantic considerations like these cause mail order people to spend hours discussing and tinkering with a single headline or even a single word in the headline. It will pay you to study the mail order headlines you see used over and over again and try to analyze and apply the semantic secret of their success.

**Building in the "hook"**

A successful direct marketing ad must compete fiercely for the reader's time and attention. No matter how great the copy is, it will be wasted if the headline does not compel reading. So most successful headlines have a "hook" to catch the reader and pull him in. The most common hooks are such words as *why, how, new, now, this, what*. They make the reader want to know the answer. *Why* is it? *How* does it? *What* is it?

Consider the flat statement:

**Increasing your vocabulary can help you get ahead in life**

This is merely an argumentative, pontifical claim. It doesn't lead anywhere. But notice how the addition of just one word changes the whole meaning and the mood;

**How increasing your vocabulary can help you get ahead in life.**

This unstylish, uncreative headline, and the copy that followed sold hundreds of thousands of copies of a vocabulary book. It selected the prospect (people who were interested in larger vocabularies), it promised an ultimate benefit (*success*), and it built in a hook (*how*).

Of course, the hook can be merely implied. There is no hook word in the headline, "Be a Non-Degree Engineer." But there is a clear implication that the copy is going to tell you how to achieve this.

# How to Become a "Non-Degree" Engineer in the Booming World of Electronics

**Thousands of real engineering jobs are being filled by men without engineering degrees. The pay is good, the future bright. Here's how to qualify...**

### By G. O. ALLEN

*President, Cleveland Institute of Electronics*

THE BIG BOOM IN ELECTRONICS—and the resulting shortage of graduate engineers—has created a new breed of professional man: the "non-degree" engineer. He has an income and prestige few men achieve without going to college. Depending on the branch of electronics he's in, he may "ride herd" over a flock of computers, run a powerful TV transmitter, supervise a service department, or work side by side with distinguished scientists designing and testing new electronic miracles.

According to one recent survey, in military-connected work alone 80% of the civilian field engineers are not college graduates. Yet they enjoy officer status and get generous *per diem* allowances in addition to their excellent salaries.

In TV and radio, you qualify for the key job of Broadcast Engineer if you have an FCC License, whether you've gone to college or not.

### Now You Can Learn at Home

To qualify, however, you do need to know more than soldering, testing circuits, and replacing components. You need to really know your electronics theory—and to prove it by getting an FCC Commercial License.

Now you can master electronics theory at home, in your spare time. Over the last 30 years, here at Cleveland Institute of Electronics, we've perfected AUTO-PROGRAMMED™ lessons that make learning at home easy, even if you once had trouble studying. To help you even more, your instructor gives the homework you send in his undivided personal attention—it's like being the only student in his "class." He even mails back his corrections and comments the

same day he gets your work, so you hear from him while everything is still fresh in your mind.

Does it work? I'll say! Better than 9 out of 10 CIE men who take the U.S. Government's tough FCC licensing exam *pass it on their very first try.* (Among non-CIE men, 2 out of 3 who take the exam *fail.*) That's why we can promise in writing to refund your tuition in full if you complete one of our FCC courses and fail to pass the licensing exam.

Students who have taken other courses often comment on how much more they learn from us. Says Mark E. Newland of Santa Maria, Calif.:

"Of 11 different correspondence courses I've taken, CIE's was the best prepared, most interesting, and easiest to understand. I passed my 1st Class FCC exam after completing my course, and have increased my earnings by $120 a month."

### Mail Coupon for 2 Free Books

Thousands of today's "non-degree" engineers started by reading our 2 free books: (1) Our school catalog "How to Succeed in Electronics," describing opportunities in electronics, our teaching methods, and our courses, and (2) our special booklet, "How to Get a Commercial FCC License." To receive both without cost or obligation, mail coupon below.

**CIE** Cleveland Institute of Electronics
1776 E. 17th St. Dept. PS-6, Cleveland, Ohio 44114

---

Cleveland Institute of Electronics
1776 East 17th Street, Dept. PS-6, Cleveland, Ohio 44114

  Please send me without cost or obligation:
1. Your 40-page booklet describing the job opportunities in Electronics today, how your courses can prepare me for them, your methods of instruction, and your special student services.
2. Your booklet on "How to Get a Commercial FCC License."

I am especially interested in:
☐ Electronics Technology    ☐ Electronic Communications
☐ First Class FCC License   ☐ Industrial Electronics
☐ Broadcast Engineering     ☐ Advanced Engineering

Name....................................Age......
  (Please print)

Address...................................................

City....................State..........Zip.......

Present Job Title.................................

Accredited Member National Home Study Council
A Leader in Electronics Training...Since 1934

**Writing the lead**  Perhaps the most troublesome and important part of any piece of mail order copy is the lead, or opening. A lead that "grabs" the reader doesn't guarantee that he will read the rest of the copy. But one that fails to grab him does practically guarantee that he *won't* read the rest.

Always remember in writing or judging a lead that your reader has better things to do than sit around and read your advertising. He doesn't really want to read your copy—until you make him want to. And your lead has got to make him want to.

A common error in writing leads is failure to get to the point immediately—or at least to *point* to the point. Haven't you had the experience of listening to a friend or associate or public speaker who is trying to tell you something but not able to get to the point? Remember how impatient you felt as you fumed inwardly, "Get to the point!" Your readers feel that same way about copy—and can very easily yawn and turn away. A good roundabout lead is not impossible, but it takes a brilliant writer.

A good principle to follow is that the copy should proceed from the headline. That is, if your headline announces what you are there to talk about, then you should get down to business and talk about it. Although it is true that some successful advertising merely *continues* the message started by the headline or display copy, there is far less danger of confusion if the copy *repeats* and *expands* the headline message, exactly the way a good news item does.

Notice how marvelously these leads from the *Wall Street Journal* news columns form a bridge between the headlines and the rest of the stories:

### New postage-stamp ink to speed mail processing

NEW YORK—U.S. postage stamps will soon be tagged with a special luminescent ink that will permit automatic locating and cancelling of the stamps to speed processing of the mail.

### Affluent Americans awash in documents snap up home safes

NEW YORK—There's a popular new home appliance that won't wash a dish, dry a diaper, or keep a steak on ice. It's a safe. And it's being propelled into prominence by a paper work explosion.

Notice, too, that although the lead restates the thought of the headline, it does it in a different way, recapping the thought but also advancing the story.

**Classic copy structure**  In a classic mail order copy argument, a good lead should be visualized as the first step in a straight path of feeling and logic from the headline or display theme to the concluding call for action. In that all-important first step, the reader should be able to see clearly where the path is taking him. Otherwise he may not want to go. (This is the huge error of ads that seek to pique your curiosity with something irrelevant and then make a tie-in to the real point. Who's got time for satisfying that much curiosity these days?)

The sections of a classic copy argument may be labeled *problem, promise of solution, explanation of promise, proof, call to action.* However, if you're going to start with the problem, it seems like a good idea at least to hint right away at the forthcoming solution. Then the reader won't mind your not getting to the point right away, as long as he knows where you're going. A generation ago, when the pace of life was slower, a brilliant copywriter could get away with spending the first third of his copy leisurely outlining the problem before finally getting around to the solution. But in today's more hectic times, it's riskier.

Here is an ad seeking Duraclean dealers in which the problem lead contains the promise of solution.

### I found the easy way to escape from being a "wage slave"

I kept my job while my customer list grew . . . then found myself in a high-profit business. Five years ago, I wouldn't have believed that I could be where I am today.

I was deeply in debt. My self-confidence had been shaken by a disastrous business setback. Having nobody behind me, I had floundered and failed for lack of experience, help, and guidance.

Now the copy could have simply started out, "Five years ago, I was deeply in debt," and so on. But the promise of happier days to come provides a carrot on a stick, drawing us down the garden path. You could argue that the headline had already announced the promise. But in most cases, good copy should be able to stand alone and make a complete argument even if all the display type were removed.

Here, from an ad for isometric exercises, is an example of the flashback technique referred to above:

[Starts with the promise]

Imagine a 6-second exercise that helps you keep fit better than 24 push-ups. Or another that's capable of doubling muscular strength in 3 weeks!

Both of these "quickie" exercises are part of a fantastically simple body-building method developed by Donald J. Salls, Alabama Doctor of Education, fitness expert and coach. His own trim physique, his family's vigorous health and the nail-hard brawn of his teams are dramatic proof of the results he gets—not to mention the steady stream of reports from housewives, athletes, even school children who have discovered Dr. Salls' remarkable exercises.

[Flashback to problem]

Most Americans find exercise a tedious chore. Yet we all recognize the urgent personal and social needs for keeping our bodies strong, shapely, and healthy. What man wouldn't take secret pride in displaying a more muscular figure? What woman doesn't long for a slimmer, more attractive figure?
The endless time and trouble required to get such results has been a major, if not impossible hurdle for so many of us. But now [return to the promise] doctors, trainers, and physical educators are beginning to recommend the easy new approach to body fitness and contour control that Dr. Salls has distilled down to his wonderfully simple set of 10 exercises.

Of course a really strong, exciting promise doesn't necessarily need a statement of the problem at all. If you're selling a "New Tree that Grows a Foot a Month," it could be argued that you don't actually have to spell out how frustrating it is to spend years wating for ordinary trees to grow up; this is well known and implied.

**Other ways to structure copy**

There are as many different ways to structure a piece of advertising copy as there are to build a house.

But response advertising, whether in publication or direct mail, has special requirements. The general advertiser is satisifed with making an impression, but the response advertiser must stimulate immediate action. Your copy must pile up in your reader's mind argument after argument, sales point after sales point, until his resistance collapses under the sheer weight of your persuasiveness, and he does what you ask.

One of the greatest faults in the copy of writers who are not wise in the ways of response is failure to apply this steadily increasing pressure. This may sound like old-fashioned "hard sell," but, ideally, the impression your copy makes should be just the opposite. The best copy, like the best salesperson does not appear to be selling at all, but simply to be sharing information or proposals of mutual benefit to the buyer and seller.

Of course, in selling certain kinds of staple merchandise, copy structuring may not be important. There the advertising may be compared to a painting in that the aim is to convey as much as possible at first glance and then convey more and more with each repeated look. You wouldn't sell a 35-piece electric drill set with a 1,000-word essay but, rather, by spreading out the set in glowing full-color illustrations richly studded with "feature call-outs."

But where you are engaged in selling intangibles, an idea or ideas instead of familiar merchandise, the way you structure your copy can be vitally important.

In addition to the classic form mentioned above, here are some other ways to structure copy.

With the "cluster-of-diamonds" technique, you assemble a great many precious details of what you are selling and present them to the reader in an appropriate setting. A good example is the "67 Reasons Why" subscription advertising of *U.S. News & World Report*, listing 67 capsule descriptions of typical recent news articles in the magazine. Note that the "setting"—the surrounding copy containing general information and argumentation—is as important as the specific jewels in the cluster. Neither would be sufficiently attractive without the other technique.

The "string-of-pearls" technique is similar but not quite the same. Each "pearl" is a complete little gem of selling, and a number of them are simply strung together in almost any sequence to make a chain. David Ogilvy's "Surprising Amsterdam" series of ads is like this. Each surprising fact about Amsterdam is like a small-space ad for the city, but only when all these little ads are strung together do you feel compelled to get up from your easy chair and send for those KLM brochures. This technique is especially useful, by the way, when you have a vast subject like an encyclopedia to discuss. You have not one but many stories to tell. And, if you simply ramble on and on, most readers won't stay with you. So make a little list of the stories you want to tell, write a tight little one-paragraph essay on each point, announce the subject to each essay in a boldface subhead, and then string them all together like pearls, with an appropriate beginning and ending.

The "fan dancers" technique is like a line of chorus girls equipped with

Sally Rand fans. The dancers are always about to reveal their secret charms, but they never quite do. You've seen this kind of copy many times. One of the best examples is the circular received in answer to an irresistible classified ad in *Popular Mechanics*. The ad simply said "505 odd, successful enterprises. Expect something odd." The circular described the entire contents of a book of money-making ideas in maddening fashion. Something like: "No. 24. Here's an idea that requires nothing but old coat hangers. A retired couple on a Kansas farm nets $240 weekly with this one." "No. 25. All you need is a telephone—and you don't call them, they call you to give their orders. A bedridden woman in Montpelier nets $70.00 a week this way." And so on.

With the "machine gun" technique, you simply spray facts and arguments in the general direction of the reader, in the hope that at least some of them will hit. This may be called the no-structure structure, and it is the first refuge of the amateur. If you have a great product and manage to convey your enthusiasm for it through the sheer exuberance of your copy, you will succeed, not because of your technique, but despite it. And the higher the levels of taste and education of your readers, the less chance you will have.

**Establishing the uniqueness of your product or service**

What is the unique claim to fame of the product or service you are selling? This could be one of your strongest selling points. The word "only" is one of the greatest advertising words. If what you offer is "better" or "best," this is merely a claim in support of your argument that the reader *should* come to you for the product or services offered. But, if what you are offering is the "only" one of its kind, then the reader *must* come to you if he or she wants the benefits that only you can offer.

Here are some ways in which you may be able to stake out a unique position in the marketplace for the product or service you are selling: "We're the largest." People respect bigness in a company or a sales total—they reason that, if a product leads the others in its field, it must be good. Thus "No. 1 Best-Seller" is always a potent phrase, for it is not just an airy claim but a hard fact that proves some kind of merit.

But what if you're *not* the largest? Perhaps you can still establish a unique position. . . . "We're the largest of our kind." By simply defining your identity more sharply, you may still be able to claim some kind of size superiority. For example, there was the Trenton merchant who used to boast that he had "the largest clothing store in the world in a garage!"

A mail order photo finisher decided that one benefit it had to sell was the sheer bigness of it operation. It wasn't the biggest—that distinction belonged, of course, to Eastman Kodak. But it was second. And Eastman Kodak was involved in selling a lot of other things too, such as film and cameras and chemicals. Their photo finishing service was only one of many divisions. So the advertiser was able to fashion a unique claim: "America's Largest *Independent* Photo Finisher."

"We're the fastest-growing." If you're on the way to *becoming* the largest, that's about as impressive a proof of merit as being the largest—in fact, it may be even *more* impressive, because it adds the excitement of the underdog coming up fast. *U.S. News & World Report* used this to good effect during the 1950s while its circulation was growing from approximately 400,000 to about three times that figure: "America's Fastest-Growing Newsmagazine." Later, the same claim was used effectively for Capitol Record Club, "America's Fastest-Growing Record Club."

"We offer a unique combination of advantages." It may be that no one claim you can make is unique, but that none of your competitors is able to equal your claim that you have *all* of a certain number of advantages.

In the early 1960s, the Literary Guild began to compete in earnest with the Book-of-the-Month Club. They started offering books that compared very favorably with those offered by BOMC. But the latter had a couple of unique claims that the Guild couldn't match—BOMC's distinguished board of judges and its book-dividend system, with a history of having distributed $375 million worth of books to members.

How to compete? The Guild couldn't claim the greatest savings; one of Doubleday's other clubs actually saved the subscriber more off the publisher's price. It couldn't claim that it had books offered by no other club; some of Doubleday's other clubs were offering some of the same books, and even BOMC would sometimes make special arrangements to offer a book being featured by the Guild.

But the Guild was able to feature a unique *set* of advantages that undoubtedly played a part in the success it has enjoyed: "Only the Literary Guild saves you 40 percent to 60 percent on books like these as soon as they are published." Other clubs could make either of these two claims, but only the Guild could claim both.

"We have a uniquely advantageous location." A classic of this was James Webb Young's great ad for "Old Jim Young's Mountain Grown Apples—Every Bite Crackles, and the Juice Runs Down Your Lips." In it Jim Young, trader, tells how the natives snickered when his pappy bought himself an abandoned homestead in a little valley high up in the Jemes Mountains. But "Pappy" Young, one of the slickest farmers ever to come out of Madison Avenue, knew that "this little mountain valley is just a natural apple spot—as they say some hillsides are in France for certain wine grapes. The summer sun beats down into this valley all day, to color and ripen apples perfectly; but the cold mountain air drains down through it at night to make them crisp and firm. Then it turns out that the soil there is full of volcanic ash, and for some reason that seems to produce apples with a flavor that is really something."

Haband Ties used to make a big thing out of being located in Paterson, New Jersey, the silk center of the nation. Even though most of the company's ties and other apparel were made of synthetic fibers, somehow the idea of buying ties from the silk center made the reader feel he was buying ties at the very source. In the same way, maple syrup from Vermont should be a lot easier to sell than maple syrup from Arizona.

Finally, suppose you believe that you have something unique to sell but you hesitate to start an argument with your competitors by making a flat claim that they may challenge. In that case you can *imply your uniqueness* by the way in which you word the claim. "Here's one mouthwash that keeps your mouth sweet and fresh all day long" doesn't flatly claim that it's the only one. It simply says, "at least *we've* got this desirable quality, whether any other product does or not." *Newsweek* identified itself as "the news magazine that separates fact from opinion"—a powerful use of that innocent word "the" which devastates the competition.

## Effective use of testimonials

If you have a great product or service, you have an almost inexhaustible source of great copy practically free—written by your own customers. They will come up with selling phrases straight from the heart that no copywriter, no matter how brilliant, would ever think of. They will write with a depth of conviction that the best copywriters will find hard to equal.

The value of testimonials in mail order advertising has been recognized for nearly 100 years, is generally taken for granted, and nonetheless is frequently overlooked. If a survey were conducted of companies dependent on responses by mail the survey would undoubtedly reveal that a shockingly high percentage of those companies have no regular, methodical system of soliciting, filing, and using good testimonials. Yet a direct marketing enterprise may often stand or fall on whether it makes good use of testimonials.

Many years ago the Merlite Company was founded to sell the Presto midget fire extinguisher, entirely through agents. The advertising job was to pull inquiries from prospective agents, who were then converted to active salespeople by the follow-up direct mail package. One of the first efforts for Merlite was the creation of a testimonial-soliciting letter. From this letter, which was mailed to a fair number of their best agents, came the story which formed the basis for a successful small space ad which ran for years and resulted in the sale of thousands of units. The headline: "I'm Making $1,000 a Month—and Haven't Touched Bottom Yet!" In those days, $1,000 a month was big money—it represented just about the top limit of the wildest dreams of people of modest means. If the ad had claimed, "Make $1,000 a month selling this amazing little device," it would have sounded like a hard-to-believe get-rich-quick scheme. But the fact that an actual agent said it (his name and picture appeared in every ad) made the possibility a fact, not a claim. And the "haven't touched bottom yet" was a homey additional promise that probably no city slicker copywriter would have thought of if he were creating a fictional testimonial.

Many U.S. School of Music ads in the past were built around testimonials. Being able to play a musical instrument has a deep meaning for people that could best be expressed by the students themselves. One ad bore a headline extracted from an ecstatic student's comments: "I Can't Believe My Ears—I'm Playing Music! My friends all think it's me, but I keep telling them it's your wonderful course."

One of the most appealing and effective stories used in art school advertising was that of a Florida mother who enrolled in the course and became one of the state's best-known painters. Her story was filled with more joy of fulfillment, credible praise for the course, and identification for other women than could be used in the ad. For instance, the day her textbooks arrived, she felt like a "child with a new toy." Her instructors were "just wonderful. I actually came to feel they were my friends." But what if you're a homemaker tied down with housework and babies? Isn't it hard to find time to paint? "It's not as hard as it sounds. When you have something exciting to look forward to, the housework flies. It's like when you're expecting a guest. You seem to get through the chores easily because you're looking forward to the visit." But won't hubby and kids be resentful if Mom spends a lot of time painting? Not her family. "They're so enthusiastic. Everytime I complete a painting, it's like a wonderful family party at our home." Isn't this reassuring? Isn't this what every creative woman would enjoy? And doesn't she make it all sound wonderfully possible and attainable?

You may have received some unsolicited testimonials that you have gotten permission to use and are already using. But, if you expand this by setting up a methodical testimonial-soliciting program, you can increase tenfold your effective use of testimonials. Because the quality and usefulness of testimonials vary widely, the more testimonials you pull in, the more pure gold you should be able to pan from the ore. Of course, it's important to get the testimonial donor's signature on some kind of release giving you permission to use his comments, name, and photo, if any. The wording of the releases varies. Some companies are content with a very simple "You have my permission" sentence; others use a more elaborately foolproof legal form. You should consult your attorney about the kind you choose to use.

Your testimonial-soliciting letter should drop a few gentle hints about your interest in hearing of actual benefits and improvements from your product. Otherwise you'll get too many customers writing similar lines of empty praise such as "it's the greatest" and "it's the finest."

**Justify the price**   "Why Such a Bargain? The Answer Is Simple." These eight magic words constitute one of the most important building blocks in the mail order sale. They have been expressed hundreds of different ways in the past, and will appear in hundreds of new forms in the future. But whether in the mail order ads of magazines and direct mail yesterday and today, or the televised home-printed facsimile transmission of tomorrow, the *price justification argument* will always be with us. It does an important job of making the low price seem believable and the high price not really so high.

Here are a number of examples of price justification from the past. As you read through them, ask yourself if it isn't likely that similar arguments will still be used in the year 2000.

*Doubleday Subscription Service:* "How can the Doubleday Subscription Service offer these extremely low prices? The answer is really quite simple. Not everyone wants the same magazines. By getting all the publishers to allow us to make their offers in one mailing, each subscriber has a chance to pick and choose; each magazine gets its most interested readers at the lowest possible cost. The savings are passed on to you in the lowest possible prices for new, introductory subscriptions."

*Reader's Digest (Music of the World's Great Composers):* "How is this low price possible? Without the great resources of RCA and the large 'audience' of *Reader's Digest*, such a collection would have to cost about $60.00. This sum would be needed to cover royalties to musicians, the cost of recording, transferring sound from tape to records, manufacturing and packaging. But because a single large pressing of records brings down the cost of manufacturing, and because the entire edition is reserved in advance for *Digest* subscribers, you can have these luxury-class records now at a fraction of the usual price for records of such outstanding quality!"

*Singer (socket wrench and tool set):* "This set is not available in stores—but sets like these sell regularly in stores at a much higher price. You save the difference because—unlike the usual store which sells just a few sets at a time, we sell many hundreds, thus enabling us to purchase large quantities at big savings which we pass on to you."

*American Heritage (History of the Civil War):* "The post-publication price of the standard edition will be $19.95; it can be kept down to this level because of the exceptionally large first printing. But if you reserve a copy before publication (a great help with shipping, storage, inventory, etc.) we shall be glad to reduce the $19.95 price by 25 percent." (Notice the double whammy here. First the value of the post-publication edition is justified, and then the even greater value of the pre-publication edition is justified.)

*Book-of-the-Month Club (Pre-Publication Society):* "Like the 'limited edition'—a very old custom in publishing—'pre-publication' offerings are designed to help *underwrite* the costs of any publishing project where there is an exceptionally high risk and heavy investment. Under modern printing conditions, if a publisher can be assured of a relatively large edition, the per-copy cost is reduced with almost every extra thousand copies printed. In recent years the usual procedure has been for the publisher, himself, to print an elaborate circular announcing the 'pre-publication offer' (similar to the one enclosed) and to permit booksellers, at a slight cost, to mail these announcements to select good customers. Rarely, however, do more than a few hundred booksellers over the country participate in this kind of promotion, with the result that comparatively few book lovers ever learn of it, and usually only in large cities. The efforts of the Pre-Publication Society will be far more thorough and widespread."

**Visual reinforcement of words and ideas**

All our powers of comprehension are built on our earliest sensations and associations. First comes touch, but that won't be much held to advertising till Aldous Huxley's "Feelyvision" is invented. Next, when we are several months old, comes image, as we learn to associate Mama's smiling face with getting fed, burped, and changed. Then comes the spoken word, when we learn to call Mama by name. This early experience with the image and the spoken word is what makes television such a potent advertising force.

Our earliest experience with the printed word is usually in our heavily illustrated first reader (or preschool picture book). It is printed in large clear serif type, in lowercase—which is why serif body types seem more readable than sans serif, and lowercase more comfortable than upper. And when the book says, "Oh! See the boy!" sure enough, there is usually a picture of a boy. This makes it less likely that we would stand up in class and read aloud, "Oh! See the doy!"

Advertising has seized on this fact of human development and developed it into an astonishingly effective tool of communication. It has learned, probably far more than ever before in human history, to team words and pictures for greater impact than either alone can achieve. Sometimes it's a *rebus*, in which a picture is substituted for some of the words. For instance, instead of saying *"(a summons, a will, a deed, a mortgage, a lease) are a few of the reasons why every family should have a lawyer," an ad for New York Life Insurance Company substituted a picture of such documents as a will and a mortgage, for the words in parentheses.*

*Sometimes it's a pantomime,* with the words providing only the necessary minimum of explanation. An Itkin Brothers office furniture ad showed in four pictures what the subhead promised: "In less than 45 minutes you can have four new offices without changing your address, increasing rent, or interrupting work." The pictures were the headline, and the four captions under the photos of the partitions being installed simply read: "8:45 . . . 8:50 . . . 9:15 . . . and 9:25."

Sometimes it's a *visual literalism*. For instance, our small-space ad for U.S. School of Music, headed "Are You Missing Half the Fun of Playing the Guitar?" showed only half a guitar. The instrument was literally sawed in half.

Sometimes it's an *abstract picture*. How the devil can you picture the abstract concept "two," for instance? Avis made it literal with a photo of two fingers.

Also, the over-all appearance of the ad provides visual reinforcement. Even if there are no illustrations, which is often true, the typography and design can convey a great deal about what kind of company is behind the advertising. For decades most mail order advertising was notorious for being less attractive than general advertising; much of it still is. Whether this helps or hurts results is hotly debated. It may be that a certain homey or buckeye look adds an air of unsophisticated honesty and sincerity. But for any company involved in starting an *ongoing relationship with a customer*, the appearance of its direct marketing advertising should convey that it is a responsible, tasteful, and orderly company with which to do business.

**The response device**  Most direct response ads carry a reply coupon or card for ease of responding. The significant exception is small-space ads. A two-inch ad would have to be about twice as big to accommodate a coupon. Many advertisers find that it does not produce twice as many results.

A black-and-white page with an insert card (a postpaid reply post card inserted next to the ad) costs about two and a half times more than a black-and-white page alone but usually pulls at least four times as much as a page with coupon. (Advantages of insert cards were explored in chapter 5).

There are many variations of the postpaid reply envelope, depending on cost and publication policy: oversize card insert, full-page insert with detachable card, four-page card stock insert with detachable card, eight-page newspaper advertising supplement with bound-in or stuck-on card or envelope, loose envelope (such as for film processing) inserted in Sunday newspapers, and so on.

The creative problem in preparing coupon or card copy is to summarize the message from the advertiser to the prospect as clearly, succinctly, and attractively as possible. Many readers tear out a card or coupon and leave it in a pocket or drawer for days or even weeks before deciding to send it in. At that point, the reader wants to know what this minicontract entails. It is important to provide as much resell and reassurance as possible.

If the advertiser is a club, the coupon copy should clearly spell out terms of membership.

Check boxes, numbers to be circled, and other aids to make completing the form easy should be provided wherever possible.

Any money-back guarantee, whether already mentioned in the adjoining copy or not, should be clearly stated.

## "Telescopic" testing

Standard practice in direct mail for many years is to test simultaneously as many as five or six or even ten or twelve different copy appeals, formats, or offers. Giving each package equal exposure over a representative variety of lists is probably the most scientifically precise research method in advertising. But this practice has *not* been so common in publication advertising. There, for a long time, advertisers were limited to the simple *A-B split-run* test, in which every other copy of a given issue of a publication would contain ad A and every other copy ad B (separately keyed, of course). This, too, is very precise. The main thing is to make sure that the circulation purchased is large enough to provide a statistically significant variation in results between the two ads. But for testing your way to a breakthrough, it can be *slow*.

If you test two ads, wait for the results; then test two more, and so on. A year or so may pass before you discover the "hot button." On the other hand, if you test the control against one ad in publication A and another in publication B (we often do), it is useful, but it does introduce *another variable*, the difference in the two publications. And a truly scientific test has only one variable.

All our experience and common sense tell us that six or eight tests are far more likely to produce a hit than only two. To solve this problem, direct marketing advertisers are turning increasingly to multiple ad testing. We call it "telescopic" testing, because it permits the advertiser to telescope a year's testing experience into a single insertion. Telescopic testing simply applies the direct mail principle of multiple testing to publication advertising. But it requires publications or formats with the *mechanical capability* of running such tests. Perhaps the first magazine to offer this capability was *TV Guide*. Because television programs are different in each region, *TV Guide* publishes *84 different regional editions*. Theoretically, you could do *84 different split-runs*, one in each regional edition, in a single week. (But you wouldn't, because the circulation for each test would be too small.) By testing ad A vs. ad B in the first region, ad A vs. ad C in the next region, and so on, it is possible to test as many as ten or 15 different ads or ad variations simultaneously. By assigning to ad A results the numerical value of 100, we can give the other ad results proportionate numerical values and rank them accordingly.

Of course, an easier way to do multiple testing is by intermixed *cardstock inserts* in the centerfold. The only problem is that these positions are reserved years in advance by repeat advertisers. They are also very costly.

So advertisers began testing new appeals and offers by doing A-B regional splits of *black-and-white pages* and even *half-pages* in the local program section of *TV Guide.* The following examples illustrate what can be done:

- A book series achieved a 252 percent improvement.
- A correspondence course inquiry ad was improved 209 percent.
- A name-getting giveaway program brought its advertising cost per coupon down to 19 cents!

(The technique of applying telescopic testing is discussed in chapter 15). Today there are three basic methods of running multiple tests:

1. *Simultaneous split-runs in regional editions* of a magazine that offers such a service, with one ad used as a control in all the splits.
2. *Free-standing stuffers* or loose newspaper preprints, intermixed at the printing plant before being supplied to the publication.
3. *Full-page card inserts in magazines,* intermixed at the printing plant.

It's a rather expensive game to play, but major direct marketers today are playing for multi-million-dollar stakes. And all it takes is one breakthrough to pay for all the necessary research in a very short time.

A dramatic example of the application of telescopic testing is a series of eight ads created for *Skeptic* magazine, which were tested simultaneously in regional editions of *Time* magazine, all used in the same issue. Carefully study the ads shown in Exhibits 12.4 through 12.11 and see if you can give ratings for ads A through H.

Exhibit 12.4. Ad A—Distrust.

distrust
some of the stuff you hear on the news?
...disillusioned with public officials?
• When the Warren Commission told you that Oswald did it alone —were you a little skeptical?
• When the President announced that the recession was over —were you a little skeptical?
• When William Colby promised that the CIA would never do it again —were you a little skeptical?
Skeptic is the magazine that prints all sides, takes no sides, and lets you make up your own mind. Send for our current issue FREE!
If your answers to the above questions were YES, then congratulations! You're intellectually aware. You're not about to be brainwashed. And you're precisely the sort of independent thinker for whom we edit Skeptic:
—the new magazine that marshals the evidence—then lets you, the judge, decide. Suddenly, you're no longer wondering about all the conflicting reports. With Skeptic, you've now got the essentials.
—the new magazine that gives you the background you need to make important decisions. From now on, you're no longer playing hunches. With Skeptic, you're better equipped to weigh your options.
Skeptic was born out of the belief that we, as citizens, have a right to the truth, not to lies and propaganda. Our magazine is non-political and non-partisan. It is wholly and totally independent, obligated to no one but you.
With each issue, we examine in depth a different subject of major importance to you. We invite in the experts—both pro and con. We instruct them not to pull punches. We then report their opinions and findings to you in some of the most remarkable and revealing articles being published anywhere in the country.
Take the Kennedy assassination, for example. Was the Warren Commission right—or is it the greatest cover-up ever? When Skeptic recently turned back the calendar to November 1963, you were presented with evidence for and against. And once you'd heard and evaluated it all, there might have been fewer doubts in your mind about where the truth in the matter lies.
Or take the faltering economy. Is the recession over and done with, or has it still time to run? When Skeptic took out after Public Enemy #1—Inflation—not long ago, we assembled some of the nation's most knowing people to provide you with a handbook for survival—why inflation occurs, what havoc it wreaks, how you can avoid getting hurt.
Or take the FBI and CIA. What are the chances that they've got your name on a list? That your phone has been bugged? When Skeptic examined the problem, you heard from agency critics—including former employees—as well as the FBI and CIA directors themselves. And in the process you found out some ways to cope with Big Brother—how to learn if your rights have been violated, how to obtain your FBI file.
With Skeptic, you get your answers straight from the top. From the mouths of authorities ranging from Henry A. Kissinger, Theodore H. White and Arthur Schlesinger, Jr. to Eric Hoffer, Clare Boothe Luce and Tom Hayden. That's why Skeptic informs you like nobody else. You're better able to judge. To make decisions. You're even more valuable to your colleagues and associates . . . more interesting to your friends.
Skeptic is published every other month—illustrated, lively, exciting. Because of its forthright character, some people consider it controversial, and you may find it hard to come by locally. But when you use the coupon below to reserve your subscription now —
You will receive a complimentary FREE copy of our forthcoming issue just as quickly as it comes off the presses. No cost . . . no obligation . . . no commitment!
If you like the issue and want to continue as a subscriber, your price for a full year is a very modest $7.50 for the 5 remaining bi-monthly issues. Or if you decide that Skeptic is not for you, just let us know by writing "cancel" on the subscription invoice and mail the bill back within two weeks. You've invested nothing, lost nothing, and you're under no further obligation. But the first issue is yours to keep FREE as a gift, with our compliments!
PLUS . . . Skeptic offers a unique FULL REFUND guarantee! If at any time, for any reason, you're not satisfied, you'll receive a refund of your FULL subscription price—regardless of how many issues you may have received!
ACT NOW for your complimentary FREE issue of Skeptic . . . complete and return the coupon below!
skeptic
WHO KILLED JFK?
skeptic
812 Anacapa St.
Santa Barbara, Calif. 93101
YES, send me the current issue of Skeptic FREE —no cost, obligation or commitment. If I decide to continue, my price for a full year's subscription (all five remaining issues) is only $7.50. But if I don't wish to continue, I need simply write "cancel" across the subscription invoice and mail it back within two weeks. No further obligation on my part, and the current issue is mine to keep free.
Name
Address
City State Zip
6015

Exhibit 12.5. Ad B—The Warren Commission.

THE WARREN COMMISSION WAS RIGHT
THE GREATEST COVER-UP OF ALL
DECIDE FOR YOURSELF
which side is closer to the truth—after reading the major arguments, in this history-making
FREE ISSUE
of Skeptic Magazine!
Since Oswald was known to be right-handed, how come his gun had a left-handed scope? Why does an FBI report claim that separate shots hit the President and ex-Governor Connally . . . when the Warren Commission insists it was a single bullet? And how do you account for the 17 different witnesses—all with evidence contrary to the Warren Commission's conclusions—who were found dead or murdered within three years of that sad traumatic day in Dallas?
Disturbing . . . more than that, agonizing . . . questions that linger to puzzle and plague us still, in 1976. Was the Warren Commission right . . . or are we all victims of the most massive and frightening cover-up in the history of our republic?
The editors of Skeptic Magazine recently decided to take a penetrating, wide-ranging overview of the entire subject, in a special issue entitled "WHO KILLED JFK?" They invited the Commission's staunchest advocates—and severest critics—to present their pro and con views in a totally no-holds-barred fashion. The result: in the few months since publication, "WHO KILLED JFK?" has become the best-selling issue in our history, with every likelihood of becoming a prized collector's item as existing copies become harder and harder to obtain.
skeptic
WHO KILLED JFK?
The JFK special issue is typical of Skeptic's refreshingly different, totally unbiased approach to matters of national and international import that concern us all. Skeptic is a feisty, controversial, completely non-political and wholly independent every-other-month publication. Each issue is devoted to subjects of major importance. Past issues, for example, have been devoted to Spying, the Energy Crisis, Crime, and Inflation.
Skeptic is the only magazine that prints all sides, takes no sides, and invites you to make up your own mind. You get hard facts, trenchant opinions, informed points of view from the leading experts in their fields. From Henry A. Kissinger, Theodore H. White and Arthur Schlesinger, Jr. to Eric Hoffer, Clare Boothe Luce and Tom Hayden. There are no sacred cows grazing in its pages, no editorial bias, no attempts to propagandize or influence. What you will find is some of the most honest, incisive writing being published anywhere in the country today!
With Skeptic, you have the evidence, the background, the essential information you need to draw your own conclusions, make your own decision. You're briefed. You're informed. Better able to judge for yourself. You're even more valuable to your colleagues and associates . . . more interesting to your friends.
Send today for your complimentary issue of Skeptic, "WHO KILLED JFK?" . . . keep it FREE . . . no cost . . . no obligation
If this exciting special issue convinces you that you want to continue receiving Skeptic, your price for a full year is a very modest $6.00 for the 5 issues. (This special introductory rate is a 1/3 savings off the regular $9.00 subscription price!) Or if you decide that Skeptic is not for you, just let us know by writing "cancel" on the subscription invoice and mail the bill back within two weeks. You've invested nothing, lost nothing, and you're under no further obligation. But the special issue, "WHO KILLED JFK?" is yours to keep FREE as a gift, with our compliments! PLUS . . . Skeptic offers a FULL REFUND guarantee! If at any time, for any reason, you're not satisfied, you'll receive a full refund on all unmailed issues. So act today—you've got nothing to lose.
Important: To help us record the response to this ad, would you please do us a small favor? In the appropriate space on the card, please write the letter A. Many thanks.
skeptic Subscription Offices Box 2655, Boulder, Colorado 80302
YES, send me my free issue of Skeptic — no cost, obligation or commitment. If I decide to continue, my price for a full year's subscription (6 issues) is only $6.00 . . . instead of the regular $9.00 price. But if I don't wish to continue, I need simply write "cancel" across your invoice and mail it back within two weeks. And the free issue is mine to keep.
Name
Address
City State Zip
6041

Exhibit 12.6. Ad C—If you agree that thinking for . . . .

If you agree that thinking for yourself is more important than a college degree...
How closely does this "profile" describe you? . . .
You're independent-minded . . . not about to let anybody shove their ideas or propaganda down your throat. You have absolutely no patience with half-baked ideas, half-formed opinions or half-fabricated "facts."
In short, you think for yourself. And that's why you value the head on your shoulders a great deal more than the number of degrees—if any —after your name.
Welcome! Because you're the kind of person for whom we edit Skeptic —the magazine that prints all sides, takes no sides, and invites you to make up your own mind.
Each bi-monthly issue of this totally unbiased and wholly independent publication is devoted to a single subject of major importance. Past issues, for example, have been devoted to Spying, the Energy Crisis, Crime and Inflation.
In Skeptic you get hard facts, trenchant opinions, informed points of view from the leading experts in their fields. From Henry Kissinger and Theodore White to Eric Hoffer and Tom Hayden. Plus valuable regular features like the Survival Handbook, Skeptic Backgrounder, Who's Who and a Skeptic Survey that lets you voice your opinion.
Skeptic gives you the evidence, the background, the essential information you need to draw your own conclusions. You're briefed. You're informed. Better able to judge for yourself. You're even more valuable to your colleagues and associates . . . more interesting to your friends.
SEND TODAY FOR OUR CURRENT ISSUE FREE! Keep it as a gift with our compliments, even if you decide not to continue as a subscriber!
Best of all, Skeptic is great reading! Try it and see—FREE! Mail the coupon for the current issue. If you don't agree that Skeptic is refreshingly different, don't pay for it—just tell us to cancel. If you do like it, your price for a full year is a very modest $6.00 for the 5 remaining bi-monthly issues. (This special introductory rate is a 1/3 savings off the regular $9.00 subscription price!) Or if you decide that Skeptic is not for you, just let us know by writing "cancel" on the subscription invoice and mail the bill back within two weeks. PLUS . . . Skeptic offers a FULL REFUND guarantee! If at any time, for any reason, you're not satisfied, you'll receive a full refund on all unmailed issues. So act today —you've got nothing to lose.
IMPORTANT: To help us record the response to this ad, would you please do us a small favor? In the appropriate space on the card, please write the letter B. Many thanks.
shouldn't you be reading Skeptic?
skeptic 9420-D Activity Road San Diego, California 92126
YES, send me my free issue of Skeptic—no cost, obligation or commitment. If I decide to continue, my price for a full year's subscription (all 5 remaining issues) is only $6.00. But if I don't wish to continue, I need simply write "cancel" across the subscription invoice and mail it back within two weeks. No further obligation on my part, and the free issue is mine to keep.
NAME
ADDRESS
CITY STATE ZIP
6036

Exhibit 12.7. Ad D—Finally a magazine . . . .

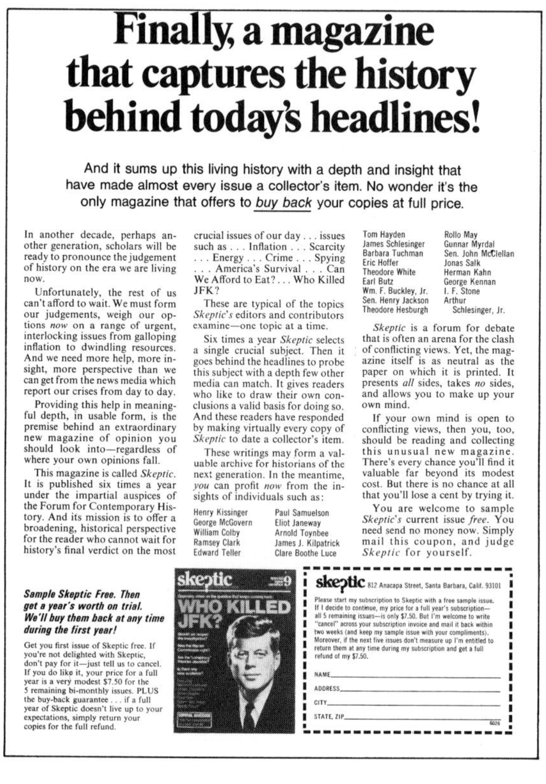
Finally, a magazine that captures the history behind today's headlines!
And it sums up this living history with a depth and insight that have made almost every issue a collector's item. No wonder it's the only magazine that offers to buy back your copies at full price.
In another decade, perhaps another generation, scholars will be ready to pronounce the judgement of history on the era we are living now.
Unfortunately, the rest of us can't afford to wait. We must form our judgements, weigh our options now on a range of urgent, interlocking issues from galloping inflation to dwindling resources. And we need more help, more insight, more perspective than we can get from the news media which report our crises from day to day.
Providing this help in meaningful depth, in usable form, is the premise behind an extraordinary new magazine of opinion you should look into—regardless of where your own opinions fall.
This magazine is called Skeptic. It is published six times a year under the impartial auspices of the Forum for Contemporary History. And its mission is to offer a broadening, historical perspective for the reader who cannot wait for history's final verdict on the most crucial issues of our day . . . issues such as . . . Inflation . . . Scarcity . . . Energy . . . Crime . . . Spying . . . America's Survival . . . Can We Afford to Eat? . . . Who Killed JFK?
These are typical of the topics Skeptic's editors and contributors examine—one topic at a time.
Six times a year Skeptic selects a single crucial subject. Then it goes behind the headlines to probe this subject with a depth few other media can match. It gives readers who like to draw their own conclusions a valid basis for doing so. And these readers have responded by making virtually every copy of Skeptic to date a collector's item.
These writings may form a valuable archive for historians of the next generation. In the meantime, you can profit now from the insights of individuals such as:
Henry Kissinger, George McGovern, William Colby, Ramsey Clark, Edward Teller, Paul Samuelson, Eliot Janeway, Arnold Toynbee, James J. Kilpatrick, Clare Boothe Luce, Tom Hayden, James Schlesinger, Barbara Tuchman, Eric Hoffer, Theodore White, Earl Butz, Wm. F. Buckley, Jr., Sen. Henry Jackson, Theodore Hesburgh, Rollo May, Gunnar Myrdal, Sen. John McClellan, Jonas Salk, Herman Kahn, George Kennan, I. F. Stone, Arthur Schlesinger, Jr.
Skeptic is a forum for debate that is often an arena for the clash of conflicting views. Yet, the magazine itself is as neutral as the paper on which it is printed. It presents all sides, takes no sides, and allows you to make up your own mind.
If your own mind is open to conflicting views, then you, too, should be reading and collecting this unusual new magazine. There's every chance you'll find it valuable far beyond its modest cost. But there is no chance at all that you'll lose a cent by trying it.
You are welcome to sample Skeptic's current issue free. You need send no money now. Simply mail this coupon, and judge Skeptic for yourself.
Sample Skeptic Free. Then get a year's worth on trial. We'll buy them back at any time during the first year!
Get you first issue of Skeptic free. If you're not delighted with Skeptic, don't pay for it—just tell us to cancel. If you do like it, your price for a full year is a very modest $7.50 for the 5 remaining bi-monthly issues. PLUS the buy-back guarantee . . . if a full year of Skeptic doesn't live up to your expectations, simply return your copies for the full refund.
skeptic
WHO KILLED JFK?
skeptic 812 Anacapa Street, Santa Barbara, Calif. 93101
Please start my subscription to Skeptic with a free sample issue. If I decide to continue, my price for a full year's subscription—all 5 remaining issues—is only $7.50. But I'm welcome to write "cancel" across your subscription invoice and mail it back within two weeks (and keep my sample issue with your compliments). Moreover, if the next five issues don't measure up I'm entitled to return them at any time during my subscription and get a full refund of my $7.50.
NAME
ADDRESS
CITY
STATE, ZIP
6026

**Exhibit 12.8. Ad E—Are you fed up with people . . . .**

**Exhibit 12.9. Ad F—9 examples of how Skeptic . . . .**

**Exhibit 12.10. Ad G—5 reasons . . . .**

**Exhibit 12.11. Ad H—Ever feel invisible . . . .**

**Rating the ads**    Have you rated the ads? Okay, let's review the actual results by coupon count. Ranking Ad A—the control ad—as 100, here is the relative pull of each ad.

| Test Ad | A | B | C | D | E | F | G | H |
|---|---|---|---|---|---|---|---|---|
| Rank | 100 | 236 | 144 | 88 | 124 | 143 | 110 | 125 |

If you didn't pick the winning ad—Ad B—which pulled almost three times better than the poorest—Ad D—don't be disheartened. This series of ads was submitted to the readership of *Advertising Age*, asking readers o pick the three best ads in rank order. Less than 1 percent succeeded in this challenge. But a very respectable 31 percent did pick Ad B as the best pulling ad.

Creating print advertising can be both frustrating and rewarding. But because your goal is direct response, you can measure your progress by coupons rather than opinion.

## Self-quiz

1. Good direct response advertising should make its strongest appeal to _____ _____ _____

2. Who are the best prospects? _____ _____ _____ _____

3. Advantages belong to the _____ _____

   Benefits belong to the _____ _____

4. When are benefits more important? _____ _____

5. When are advantages more important? _____ _____

6. Fill in this list of ultimate benefits.

   a. _____
   b. _____
   c. _____
   d. _____
   e. _____
   f. _____
   g. _____
   h. _____
   i. _____
   j. _____
   l. _____
   m. _____
   n. _____

   o. _____
   p. _____
   q. _____

7. Semantics is the hydrogen bomb of _____

8. Most successful headlines have a "hook" to catch the reader and pull him or her in. The most common hooks are such words as:

   a. _____
   b. _____
   c. _____
   d. _____
   e. _____
   f. _____

9. A common error in writing leads is that the writer _____ _____

10. A good writing principle is that body copy should _____ _____

11. What labels may be applied to the section of a classic copy argument?

    a. _____
    b. _____
    c. _____
    d. _____
    e. _____

12. Name four other ways to structure copy.

    a. _____
    b. _____
    c. _____
    d. _____

13. What four-letter word is one of the greatest advertising words? _____

14. Name five unique claims to fame that may prove to be the strongest selling points for a product or service.

    a. _____

    b. _____

    c. _____

    d. _____

    e. _____

15. What is the major advantage of using testimonials in direct response advertising?

    _____

    _____

    _____

    _____

16. Name one of the most important building blocks in the mail order sale.

    _____

    _____

    _____

    _____

    _____

17. Name four ways you can give visual reinforcement to words and ideas.

    a. _____

    b. _____

    c. _____

    d. _____

18. When is a coupon not indicated for a direct response ad?

    _____

    _____

    _____

    _____

19. What is the definition of "telescopic" testing?

    _____

    _____

    _____

    _____

20. What are the three basic methods of running multiple tests?

    a. _____

    b. _____

    c. _____

## Pilot project

You are a copywriter by profession. You have just been employed by a direct response advertising agency. The agency has been appointed by a home study school offering a course in *accounting*. Your copy supervisor has asked you to come up with headlines designed to get inquiries. Develop one headline for each of these ultimate benefits.

Health: _____

_____

Money: _____

_____

Security: _____

_____

Pride: _____

_____

Approval: _____

_____

Enjoyment: _____

_____

Excitement: _____

_____

Power: _____

_____

Fulfillment: _____

_____

Freedom: _____

_____

Identity: _____

_____

Relaxation: _____

Escape: _____

_____

Curiosity: _____

_____

Possesions: _____

_____

Sex: _____

_____

Hunger: _____

_____

# 13

# Techniques of Producing Leads for Salespeople

Twenty years ago the average cost of a sales representative's call was $17.24. By 1969 McGraw-Hill computed the cost at $49.30. The 1978 figure is about $90.00 per call, and climbing! Take note: That's $90 per call, not per sale. Talk to almost any sales executive these days and you'll hear something like, "Our cost per call has gone out of sight. Cold calls have become too damn expensive. I wish we had an efficient lead-generating system." Of course, the sad truth is wishing doesn't make it so.

**Lead generation must be integrated**

Most lead-generating programs are haphazard—too many leads, all at one time. Often there are unqualified leads and leads from unmanned or undermanned territories. Leads are widely scattered within given territories. Lead-call reporting systems are inadequate or nonexistent. Follow-up on sales calls is lacking. These are but some of the ills.

Most lead-generating programs leave much to be desired. For example, a manufacturer with a 200-person sales force dumped 200,000 lead-producing letters over a weekend and produced a flood of 10,000 leads. Less than one-third of the leads were ever called on! Commonplace are call reports that read like this: "I drove 150 miles to follow up this lead. When I asked to see the business executive who mailed the inquiry card, his secretary came out and said, 'Mr. Throckmorton is tied up. Just leave the free umbrella your-company promised and call back the next time you're in town.'" A few leads of this caliber will drive a salesperson off a lead-generating program!

The quantity and quality of leads are related to the products and services featured in the program. For example, an office equipment manufacturer attempted to get leads for his top-of-the-line (big-ticket) equipment. Leads came in a dribble at a time. The marketing manager then said, "Let's see if we can increase leads by featuring our bottom-of-the-line equipment." Leads almost doubled. But the real payoff was that, once the sales personnel were in a true selling position, they were able to move their prospects from bottom-of-the-line to top-of-the-line items.

**Quantity/quality/cost equation**

A company's particular lead problems and experiences will determine the kind of quantity/quality/cost mix to aim for. It is often wise to aim for quantity early in a program, because it is easier to refine and tighten up cost and quality parameters than to loosen them.

The ultimate objective of any lead-generation program is to find the ratio of lead quantity to lead quality that will result in optimum cost efficiency, and provide a flow of leads that will make maximum use of the sales force's time without "flooding" them. Direct marketing offers a great deal of flexibility in adjusting between the two factors of quantity and quality. The quantity of leads can be controlled upward or downward by simply loosening or tightening the qualification parameters built into the response device. This would also affect the quality of leads. Ordinarily, when you reduce the quantity, you increase the quality, and vice versa. Proper testing is necessary to make the delicate adjustment between lead quantity and lead quality that will produce the lowest cost per call.

**A systems approach to improving lead programs**

Lead-generation programs can be as simple as a postcard mailing to a hundred prospects or as complicated as a sophisticated mailing package to a million prospects directed to a demographic and psychographic profile carefully segmented from dozens of merged lists. The systems approach is one of the most in-depth and comprehensive blueprints available to profitable maximization of a sales lead program. Though it may appear complicated, the plan uses a systems implementation approach for optimum control and efficiency to fulfill the primary objectives of any lead or inquiry program. The principles of effective lead generation outlined in this plan, however, can be adapted to any size company simply by extracting the component on which it is built. Here are some of the pitfalls that can all but wreck a lead-generation program:

*Shortsightedness.* As a marketer, not a salesperson, one tends to be preoccupied with the lead-generating phase of the selling process (with which marketers are most involved and familiar) and not always be as attentive as one might be to the larger process as a whole.

*The human factor.* A lead program is affected by a more bewildering number of human influences from within the selling process than most other direct response situations. And the fact that people are "only human" is no help when we're trying to be scientific!

*Complexity of requirements.* Lead-program goals tend to be more complicated than those of most "count your orders" types of selling programs. Precise timing and flow of incoming inquiries become highly critical goals, as does the ethereal balance of lead quantity/cost/quality.

These three problems probably account for as many lead-program failures as unmarketable products. To avoid such pitfalls and to live up to our "scientific/controlled/measurable" self-image, we might do well to look at the total lead-generation-through-sales process in terms of the "systems engineering" discipline. Basically, the systems approach requires that a number of interacting *input* variables be channeled through a *process* which results in measurable *output*. Measurement within and as a result of the process is the *feedback* that adjusts, refines, and fine-tunes the program. New input goes into the process again, ad infinitum.

**Requirements of the systems approach**

The systems approach necessitates an awareness of the *entire* process and the monitoring of everything internal and external that may affect it. Following are essentials to the successful operation of any lead-to-sales system:

**Define what your system is to accomplish**

Look at the total picture. What are the corporate sales volume objectives? What is an acceptable cost per sale? Historically, how many calls or contacts are needed to make a sale? What is the desirable leads-to-sale ratio? How many leads should your sales force be able to handle within prescribed time limits? What is the lead quantity/cost/quality mix needed to maintain or improve conversion ratios? What can you test in your advertising program that promises to improve the whole system?

**Define the interrelation of the elements of the system**

Any one element of the system has some immediate or future effect on the functioning of all elements of the system. You may be the advertising director, but, eventually, the training, compensation, and motivation of the sales force you may never see are going to affect your final output—as will sales force attitudes towards the leads you produce and the promptness with which they can follow them up. Don't lose sight of the total picture! Make every attempt to control the elements of the system.

**Control the interrelationship of the elements of the system**

Many companies, for example, have done an impressive job of educating their dealers and salespeople as to the intent and direction of direct mail testing with mailing packages direct to the dealers. StatTab, direct marketers of computerized bookkeeping services, has a reporting system whereby the home office receives weekly reports on the follow-up activity with every lead routed to field offices: Who is following up the lead? When was the last contact? Has an appointment been set? Such feedback from *within* the system allows them to adjust the operation of the system to avoid lead loss, overleading, and other problems that affect the system output.

Allstate Insurance Company, with some 9,000 agents, uses what could be called a formalized systems approach in their lead-generation programs. The magnitude of that size of sales force demands a total commitment by management down through all relevant departments from marketing to advertising, sales promotion, training, research, accounting, systems, and others. Allstate's lead programs touch every aspect of their lead-generation system.

**Quantify and measure the interrelationship of the elements of the system**

Review leads-to-sales ratios by individual salespersons, offices, and territories. Look at lead-response rates in the light of local competitive activity and local market characteristics. In an ongoing mailing program, examine the size of your active lead pool in relation to the sales force to determine whether mailings need to be stepped up or held back. You may even want to ration leads to individual salespeople based on their follow-up and sales performance. Scrutinize lead-to-sales ratios in analyzing the comparative effec-

# COMPONENTS OF LEAD GENERATOR SYSTEM

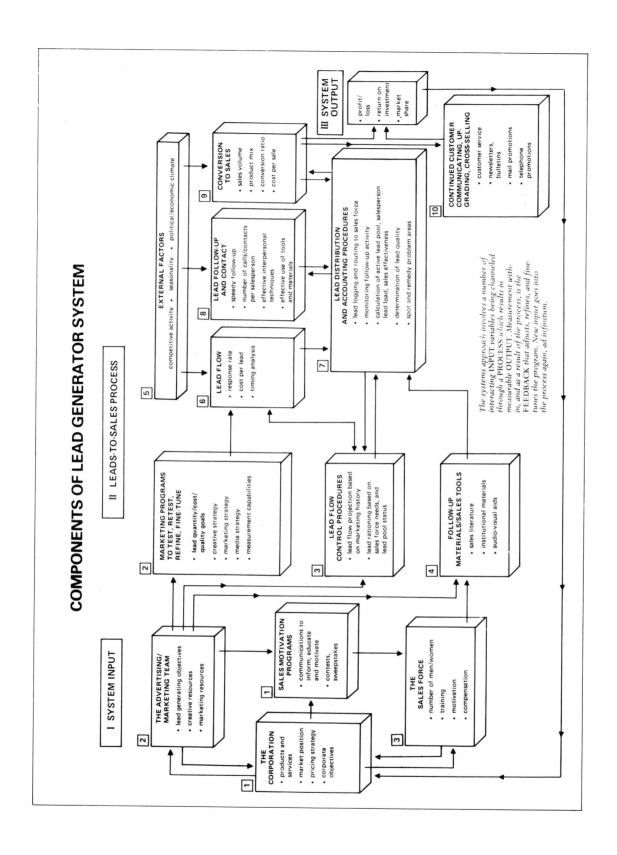

## I SYSTEM INPUT

**2** THE ADVERTISING/ MARKETING TEAM
- lead generating objectives
- creative resources
- marketing resources

**1** THE CORPORATION
- products and services
- market position
- pricing strategy
- corporate objectives

**1** SALES MOTIVATION PROGRAMS
- communications to inform, educate and motivate
- contests, sweepstakes

**3** THE SALES FORCE
- number of men/women
- training
- motivation
- compensation

## II LEADS-TO-SALES PROCESS

**2** MARKETING PROGRAMS TO TEST, RETEST, REFINE, FINE-TUNE
- lead quantity/cost/ quality goals
- creative strategy
- marketing strategy
- media strategy
- measurement capabilities

**3** LEAD FLOW CONTROL PROCEDURES
- lead flow projection based on marketing history
- lead rationing based on sales force needs, and lead pool status

**4** FOLLOW-UP MATERIALS/SALES TOOLS
- sales literature
- institutional materials
- audio-visual aids

**5** EXTERNAL FACTORS
competitive activity • seasonality • political/economic climate

**6** LEAD FLOW
- response rate
- cost per lead
- timing analysis

**8** LEAD FOLLOW-UP AND CONTACT
- speedy follow-up
- number of calls/contacts per salesperson
- effective interpersonal techniques
- effective use of tools and materials

**7** LEAD DISTRIBUTION AND ACCOUNTING PROCEDURES
- lead logging and routing to sales force
- monitoring follow-up activity
- calculation of active lead pool, salesperson lead load, sales effectiveness
- determination of lead quality
- spot and remedy problem areas

**9** CONVERSION TO SALES
- sales volume
- product mix
- conversion ratio
- cost per sale

## III SYSTEM OUTPUT

- profit/ loss
- return on investment
- market share

**10** CONTINUED CUSTOMER COMMUNICATING, UP-GRADING, CROSS-SELLING
- customer service
- newsletters, bulletins
- mail promotions
- telephone promotions

*The systems approach involves a number of interacting INPUT variables being channeled through a PROCESS which results in measurable OUTPUT. Measurement within, and as a result of the process, is the FEEDBACK that adjusts, refines, and fine-tunes the program. New input goes into the process again, ad infinitum.*

tiveness of offers, lists, copy approaches, and media tested in your advertising program.

**Use system feedback to refine and fine-tune the system's operation**

What does the bottom line—profit and loss, return on investment, or market share—dictate in terms of refining marketing and product development strategy, pricing, and distribution strategy? Look back through the entire system and the internal feedback from all elements of the system to determine methods of system refinement that will, in fact, effect the realization of new corporate objectives. Let's look at the elements individually.

**Components of the lead-generator system**

As we proceed through a description of the system, you should study the chart (Exhibit 13.1) showing the interrelationships of the various elements. Let's look at the input variables first.

**System input**

*The corporation: input that drives the system.* For the system to function at maximum efficiency, the corporation's executives must carefully define marketing objectives, constantly monitor system feedback, and be flexible enough to adjust and refine strategies based on feedback.

*The advertising/marketing team: developmental input.* To create a powerful advertising program with profitable results, the marketing team—be it agency, in-house department or both—needs to be aware of the entire selling process, not just the product or service. Advertising people should spend a few days in the field and get first-hand selling experience.

*The sales force: implemental input.* Corporate shaping of the sales force is critical to a smooth-running system. Training, motivational, and compensation objectives should be established with a mind to the important role the sales force plays in the system. Failure to do so can undermine the system.

**Leads-to-sales process**

*Sales motivation programs: better conversion.* The sales force needs to see the direct-response-generated lead as an invaluable resource. This doesn't "automatically" happen. Communication networks must be established between marketing and sales departments. Whether the media are mailing pieces, memos, or presentations, the following ideas must be communicated:

- A direct-response-generated lead can be as valuable as a walk-in or a referral and far more valuable than a cold call.
- Direct response is not a hit-or-miss business. There is a precise method, and often a test scheme, behind the generation of the leads the sales force receives.

For the sake of the system, it's important for a salesperson to know that the few unqualified leads received now and then are a necessary evil of the testing process.

*Marketing programs to test, retest, refine, fine-tune.* All lead-advertising programs have one goal: generating the lead quantity/cost/quality mix that will accomplish the best market coverage, instill the greatest sales force confidence and enthusiasm, and convert to the most profitable sales.

The first test program usually focuses on offers, lists, and media. Don't underrate the importance of premiums or the potential power of media other than mail. From there, future testing can produce refinements in the program and broaden the test area to include creative and graphic approaches and formats. In terms of the system, however, two points are essential at this stage:

- Develop your test objectives in the light of system feedback.
- Whatever you do, build in measurement capabilities and make sure your test structure and sample sizes are such that the measurement is meaningful.

*Lead flow-control procedures: avoid being at the mercy of the flow.* Haphazard mailings lacking sufficient foresight result in inflated costs per sale. Give a salesperson five new leads a week and chances are they'll be treated like gold and given all the requisite attention and follow-through. Hit the same person with 50 in one week, and value judgments will be made as to which are most promising, with some being ignored until next week, some ending up in the circular file. (If your cost per lead is running at $25.00, for example, you can't afford to have too many leads thrown away or "burned off.")

With a few mailings and media tests under your belt, you should be able to predict lead flow within tolerable margins of error. This, of course, depends on thorough analysis of previous lead-flow feedback. With this capability to project future lead flow, you suddenly have the tools necessary to adjust or ration your mailing quantities or media activity based on the size of the sales force in relation to the projected active lead pool.

*Follow-up material and sales tools: reinforce the sales force.* At this point, we have the lead program to arouse interest. Now, it's equally important to have a flexible range of printed and audio-visual materials to help the salesperson tell his story and approach the sale. These should be complementary in creative approach, wherever possible, to the front-end promotion. The reinforced impressions will pay off in retained awareness and acceptance. And don't forget to quantify. The cost of your materials shouldn't be overlooked in computing your costs per sale.

*External factors: system interference.* While we're waiting for the leads to become productive, one element of our system that is not really "input" or "process" will certainly affect "output." We might call it *system interference* from the interaction of our system with other systems.

Eventually, we must account for competitive marketing activity, the political/economic climate, and the effects of seasonality. Although they are difficult to quantify, such factors will have a definite effect on the lead flow and sales and should be considered when evaluating and analyzing the effectiveness of our system. Here come the leads:

*Lead flow: first cost analysis checkpoint.* We now have the raw data that will enable us to compute the response rate and to plot the timing from mail drop to lead flow (these will feed our future lead-control procedures) plus cost-per-lead.

*Lead distribution and accounting procedures: a second chance to impose order on chaos.* The movement of leads through the selling process must be systematic, closely monitored, and fast. Procedures are necessary:

- For logging incoming leads and routing them to the sales force. In campaigns that affect more than one sales office, the most efficient programs are those where all leads come to a central location and are then distributed. Tighter control can then be maintained.
- For checking on follow-up activity. The amount of paperwork you may need for an effective reporting system varies. The important consideration is that your system allows the sales force to give you all the data you need as *effortlessly* as possible. If your reporting forms become too complicated, the red-tape drudgery is going to affect sales force motivation, and this may result in your being fed a lot of misinformation.
- For establishing communication networks whereby sales can feed marketing data regarding lead quality.
- For calculating active lead pools by office and by salesperson and apply these figures to upcoming mailings or media activity.
- For calculating sales effectiveness by office or by salesperson.

*Lead follow-up and contact: molding interest into need.* This is the make-or-break stage of the lead-generating system. Marketing processes and sales processes converge at the point of contact with the prospect. Because the sales process might be mapped out as a self-contained system of its own, it is actually two systems converging for a common goal: the resulting sales volume and profit. External factors, such as other systems beyond ours, also bear heavy influence at this point.

Few sales actions are as important as sheer speed of follow-up. A lead is merely an expression of interest and interest wanes rapidly. Move right in! To protect yourself if you develop an excessive number of leads, you might have ready a portfolio of stock follow-up letters to keep leads "warm" until salespersons can act on them. These letters can sometimes go out from the home office while leads are being transmitted to the local sales offices. Or the letters might be used in situations where speedy contact is made but the prospect asks to schedule the appointment two or three weeks ahead.

Following up a direct response lead requires techniques that are rarely the same as the typical inquiry or referral. The prospect's interest is not usually as strong, and his understanding of the product or service concerned is not usually as thorough. In many cases, a prospect may not really expect a sales call. The salesperson needs to be prepared with a full repertoire of "door openers." Role-playing sessions in sales training programs are helpful in developing the skills necessary to overcome prospect resistance.

Finally, it's impossible to overstate the importance of information exchange between the sales staff and the "lead distribution and accounting" element. It's essential that your ad department or agency people have the feedback they need to fine-tune their lead-producing efforts.

*Conversion to sales: results that refine and improve system operation.* With all elements of the system closely monitored and quantified to the greatest degree possible, the marketer should have sufficient information at hand to determine why the system is or isn't working. Analyze your cost per sale and conversion ratio to determine how your quantity/quality objectives might be refined. Look at resultant sales volume and product mix to determine new promotional angles and points to emphasize that may be worth testing in future promotions. Feed sales analyses by office and salesperson back into lead-accounting and lead-control procedures.

*Continued customer communication, upgrading, and cross-selling: reaping bonus profits.* Don' knock the new customer out of the system at the point of sale. Bonus income and profits will result from promotional programs to upgrade purchases or cross-sell other products and services to the customers you already have. Both the mail and the telephone are effective sources for these added dollars.

Efficient customer service systems are necessary for maintaining the healthy kind of customer relationships you want in your program. Newsletters and bulletins to your customers will also help in making them receptive to your new offers. And don't throw out the leads you haven't sold. A list of unsold inquiries should be set up for future promotions, and the list should be used regularly.

## System output

*Final outcome: input for the continuation and improvement of the system.* Depending on your corporate goals, you should examine the resultant profit, return on investment, or market share in terms of the elements of the lead-generating system. Where do problems occur? Where is greater control needed? Where can effectivness be improved? The answers to these questions are the feedback that drives our perpetual system. With flexible attitudes and flexible operating procedures, the system becomes a controlled, measurable program that drives itself constantly in the direction of operational improvement and greater profit.

## Testing

As you will see in the following case histories, testing is the key to the ultimate development of a successful and cost-efficient lead program. From the testing phase will come the creative and statistical feedback that will help you calibrate the quantity/quality cost equation to meet your specific requirements. You will find, for example, that the degree of qualification will have a direct influence on the quantity and cost of leads as well as a direct effect on your leads-to-sales ratio. Your objectives will be the deciding factor in the determination of the proper mix of an equation that is right for you.

When you test be sure to:

1. *Dramatize your offer.* Xerox uses a "Free Advisory Consultation"—a technique that opens doors for a presentation which helps remove the stigma of just another "sales call." "Guarantees" of product, service, and satisfaction should be dramatized to instill confidence and help eliminate prospect apprehension. "Premiums" (free gifts) are very powerful in stimulating response for a wide variety of offers ranging from insurance to credit-card acquisition programs to office equipment sales. Even an inexpensive premium can dramatically improve results anywhere from 10 percent to 50 percent. In some cases premiums have doubled response.

2. *Use different creative approaches.* There are many ways to position benefits creatively. Test those headlines and copy approaches that touch the "hot button" which triggers a response. If your product costs "less than"—say it loud and clear. But remember there are prospects who are willing to pay more for increased efficiency, convenience, quality, service, and other features.

3. *Try unusual mailing formats.* You can use literally dozens of formats. For example, the standard mailing package vs. a self-mailer; small-to-jumbo-size envelopes or polybag envelopes. How a format works differs from one marketer's offer to the next. For example: on one offer a two-color 11 × 17 brochure did as well as or better than a four-color 17 × 22 brochure. A three-panel 11 × 22 self-mailer performed as well as the control, which was the standard mailing format of an outer envelope, letter, brochure, and reply card. Using publisher's letters, expensive brochures, elaborate involvement devices, and one-side-only letters can significantly increase response. The key is to keep testing.

4. *Use care in list selection.* The right list selection and proper segmentation can significantly and favorably affect your lead program.

5. *Consider the ad preprint technique.* By utilizing trade publication advertising and mailings in combination, you can often increase response 25 percent and more.

6. *Test a single element or a complete package.* These are the two main ways to get meaningful test results. First, you can test a single element or variable in your mailing package. One letter vs. another, for example. If all the other elements of your mailing remain the same, you know any difference in results can be attributed to the letter. On the other hand, you can test two completely different mailing packages against each other. In this case, you won't know exactly which element accounted for the difference in results. But you do know which mailing package does best. And by testing two completely different packages you will increase the chances for a substantial difference in results.

7. *Make sure your tests are statistically valid.* Each portion of the test should be large enough to be meaningful. The quantity can be determined very scientifically by using probability tables (Tables 4.8 and 4.9).

8. *Work on the "beat the champ" principle.* In sports competition, a new champion is never crowned until the old one is counted out. Smart direct marketers operate the same way. Their most successful current mailing package or ad is considered the "champ" or "control." All new approaches are tested against the champ. And marketers continue to use the champ until they find something that beats it in the result column.

9. *Analyze test results carefully.* Look beyond the number of inquiries produced. Your analysis should include the conversions or actual sales that result from each lead-getting effort.

10. *Test for yourself.* It's nice to learn what you can from the testing experience of others. But don't assume your results will turn out the same

way for your market, your product, and your offer. It is better to test for yourself—and find out.

11. *Don't think test results are forever.* Just because something worked best for you five years ago or even two years ago doesn't mean it's best today. Your market changes from year to year, even if your product or service doesn't. Lead-producing efforts should be retested regularly against new lead-producing efforts.

12. *Innovative thinking.* In your attempt to find new breakthroughs, concentrate on testing the big things—products and pricing, offers and premiums, formats and copy.

**Effect of offer on response**

A key factor in the quantity/quality/cost equation is the offer you make to produce leads. It is almost axiomatic that the more appealing the offer, the greater the quantity of leads you can expect. Further, the greater the quantity, the lower the quality is likely to be. Finally, while the cost per lead may be far less where quantity is greatest, cost per sale—the really important criterion—is likely to be higher. Therefore, the marketer seeking leads should systematically test offers that will give him the proper mix among quantity, quality, and cost. You will recall that chapter 2 presents the multiplicity of offer options for direct marketers. The following list is especially applicable to producing leads.

- Free gift for an inquiry
- Choice of free gifts
- Two-step gift offer—for example, an inexpensive gift for an inquiry and a more expensive gift for buying
- Information without obligation
- Free catalog
- Free booklet
- Free fact kit or idea kit
- Free demonstration
- Free survey of needs
- Free cost estimate
- Free visit, often offered by companies selling land
- Free talent test, popular with home-study schools
- Free product sample
- Nominal charge for samples

**Application of lead-producing techniques**

The two following case histories exemplify the value of developing lead programs from the testing stage through analysis, fine-tuning, and implementation.

The first is a case history of a lead-generation program developed by an electronics company. The firm employs a sales force of 600 people through branch offices and distributorships nationwide. The company's primary objective was to design a program that would produce qualified, cost-efficient leads for their sales force and also to test lists, offers, and mailing packages that would be suited to the over-all program.

The first year's mailing program was divided into three cycles:

Cycle 1 to test products, offers, mailing package formats, and lists
Cycle 2 to refine list selection
Cycle 3 to roll out

Almost half of the first year was set aside for the purpose of testing the variables in the direct mail program. These testing cycles provided the hard evidence needed to set the direction for the ongoing lead-generating program. The first cycle was designed to test every element of the program—products, mailing format, premiums, and lists. Let's look at the results of the product test.

**Product test**  *Pocket Secretary vs. VIP.* The company tested the VIP dictating system—their standard product—against the Pocket Secretary, a new mini-dictating machine, as lead generators. Not only did the Pocket Secretary pull 50 percent better in up-front response but conversion figures showed that the average sale from a Pocket Secretary lead was only slightly lower than a sale from a VIP lead. Choosing a product to use as a lead generator is the first important step in your efforts to control the quality and quantity of your sales leads. You might test your most popular item against one with a higher price or a new addition to your line. The results will direct you to the best quality/quantity balance for your sales force.

No less important is the selection of package formats and premiums. Consumer-item direct marketers test heavily in these areas. But in the industrial field such seemingly minor variables are often overlooked. They shouldn't be. Executives of the electronics company we are using in this illustration found that these elements affected more than simply the cost of their direct mail program; those elements also had a direct effect on mailing response. For example:

**Format tests**  *Control format vs. Reply-O format.* Using a standard mailing package consisting of an outer envelope, letter, and separate reply card pulled 10 percent better than the same offer adapted to a Reply-O letter format, which combines letter and reply card.

*Involvement device (stamp/token) vs. non-involvement.* Using an involvement device—in this case, a detachable stamp on the letter to be affixed to the reply card—increased response 20 percent over the same package without the token.

The company also tested long-letter copy against short and found that the long copy pulled better. The firm tested the use of a third-class stamp against a printed indicia on the outer envelope and found that the stamp pulled no better. The company also tested the addition of a telephone option with several mailings and found that it increased response in every case approximately 10 percent. Increases of 10 percent and 20 percent are not as exciting as the results of the product test. But, in an industrial program where every penny counts, knowing what does and does not work for you can dramatically affect your cost per lead.

**Tests on offers**  *Premium vs. free trial.* Every marketer, consumer and industrial, wonders about using a premium. Our electronics company found that the package offering a premium pulled 20 percent better than the same package offering a free trial of the product. Okay, so we use a premium, but what premium? Because the cost of a premium is often 10 times or more the cost of the mailing package, you should select one that is attractive enough to get your qualified prospects to respond but not so attractive that your sales force is burdened with delivering gifts to people who are more interested in the gifts than the product you are selling.

**Tests on premiums**  The company tested four premiums in their first cycle:

- A Spelling Dictionary
- A Dymo Labeler
- A "No-Nonsense" Pen
- A helpful booklet titled "How to Get More Done"

The Spelling Dictionary was used as a control. The Dymo Labeler did 11 percent better; the pen did 37 percent better, and the booklet did 30 percent worse. These results would obviously call for using the pen as the premium. However, the industrial marketer has other factors to consider when applying test results to his lead-generating program.

In the case of our electronics company the sales force was overwhelmingly in favor of the Spelling Dictionary. The product was attractive, light, easy-to-carry. It required no demonstration. And the sales force believed that the book had a higher "quality" appeal to a business prospect than, say, the pen. Taking all this into consideration, the firm stayed with the dictionary, although it was not the best-performing premium.

Testing each of these three elements—product, package format, and premium—provided direction for development of the direct mail package. The biggest breakthrough of the campaign, however, came in list selection.

The firm had been mailing exclusively to compiled lists. Although, over the years, list selection had been refined to the best market segments, still, repeated mailings to the same list caused a continuing fall-off in response. The only way, it seemed, to get the level of response back up to where it should be was to give a bigger and better premium, which cut lead quality and increased cost.

**List tests**  The company decided to test direct response lists. Even firms with a limited market can uncover some direct response lists that will work for them and help expand their potential market. List testing was done in four categories: (1) professional buyers of books and supplies; (2) mail order business inquiries; (3) subscribers to business publications; and (4) travel-and-entertainment cardholders.

Although only the first two categories produced responses at a rate acceptable for this program, over-all results showed a 33 percent increase in response—from 0.47 percent on the compiled lists to 0.70 percent on the direct response lists. Moreover, the sales force noted an increase in the quality of the leads they received from the new lists.

**Results of cycle 1 tests** It became apparent that, by promoting the Pocket Secretary, the Spelling Dictionary, and the stamp involvement device and by using direct response lists, the company could increase response to 1.50 percent. The total effect was a 100 percent increase in response with a substantial improvement in quality of leads.

Using this new package as the control in Cycle 2, the company continued to refine and expand the selection of lists. Because of the testing, the total list universe was increased from 650,000 names previously mailed to a total of two million direct response names. With this as a new base, the firm was in a better position to produce 300,000 leads annually without mailing to any name twice.

How did all this testing affect the cost per lead of the company's program? Here are the results of all three mailings: the cost per lead in Cycle 1, which included most of the testing, was the highest ($34.60/lead). The cost dropped 65 percent to $11.07/lead in the second cycle. And in the roll-out, despite a postal increase, the cost per lead stayed about the same. This campaign shattered some big myths about industrial direct marketing. It proved that the sophisticated testing techniques used for so long by consumer direct marketers to structure their mail programs can be successfully applied to an industrial lead program.

**Case history 2** The second case history is that of the Wallace Business Forms lead-generation program. Wallace Business Forms—one of the world's largest forms printers—is an outstanding example of a firm which has tied its lead-generating program to corporate objectives. The primary objective for the campaign was to increase market share of large users of forms in identifiable markets. The strategy was to use a dual media approach—direct mail and publication advertising—to reach the general computer market plus three vertical markets: banking, schools, and hospitals.

Full-page space ads addressed to the four markets, respectively, were placed in *Computerworld, Bank Systems & Equipment, School Product News,* and *Hospital Financial Management.* The copy positioned Wallace as a data processing problem solver, offering savings in time and money. Minor variations in the copy made each ad market-specific. A response coupon simply offered a free paper savings calculator. Besides attracting response, the ad fulfilled three other purposes: to expose the Wallace name and story, to allow Wallace to mail to the subscriber lists of the several publications, and to provide a "preprint" piece for inclusion in the direct mail package.

The direct mail package consisted of:

1. Outer envelope (Exhibit 13.2), printed on one side, with show-through premium, the paper savings calculator (Exhibit 13.3), plus the promise of a 25 percent savings on business forms cost.

2. The reply card (Exhibit 13.4) with a side flap graphically illustrating the premium, which shows through a die-cut window in the outer envelope.

3. An actual sample of a business form appropriate to the particular market (Exhibit 13.5).

**Exhibit 13.2. Outer envelope of mailing package.**

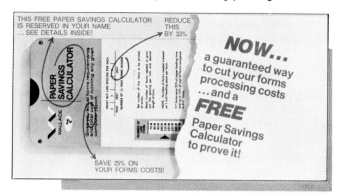

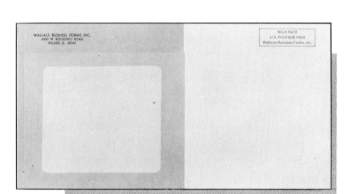

**Exhibit 13.3. Free premium—the paper savings calculator.**

**Exhibit 13.4. Reply form requesting a premium.**

**Exhibit 13.5. Samples of Wallace business forms.**

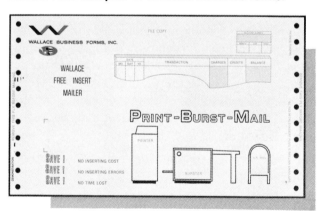

**Exhibit 13.6. First page of personalized four-page letter.**   **Exhibit 13.7. Preprint of space ad.**

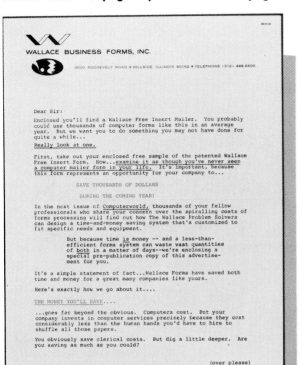

4. A four-page letter personalized to that market (Exhibit 13.6), including an illustration of and benefit copy about the business form included in the mailing.

5. A preprint of the space ad for that market (Exhibit 13.7).

Total combined circulation for the four magazines in which the ad appeared was about 165,000, while 176,000 direct mail packages were sent out.

Almost 80 times as many leads resulted from the direct mail package as from the space ads. This was not surprising, since the ads were intended, as noted, to accomplish important ends other than simply attracting leads. From a standpoint of cost efficiency, the cost per inquiry for direct mail was a bit less than one-tenth that of space.

While space advertising can inform the market, expose the advertiser's name, contact prospects not reachable by direct mail, pave the way for salespeople, and capitalize on the prestige of an influential trade publication, it cannot equal direct mail for furnishing leads in the quantity needed and of the quality desired. Yet the most powerful strategy in lead generation is often the dual media approach, using space to enhance direct mail. This is especially true when advertising in a vertical market publication gives access to the publication's subscriber list.

Several factors are seen as contributing most strongly to the success of the mailings. The inclusion of an appropriate sample form offered dramatic, tangible proof of the quality of Wallace's product and its relevance to the recipient's own business. The copy was highly benefit oriented, with an emphasis on savings in the costs of forms. The premium chosen was valuable in itself because it would help the recipient realize the promised savings and also would qualify the lead by its very specific nature.

WALLACE LEAD PROGRAM

CUMULATIVE DIRECT MAIL RESPONSE

| LIST<br>Total Distribution | COMPUTER<br>WORLD<br>28,417 | CUM.<br>% | SCHOOL PRODUCT<br>NEWS<br>24,776 | CUM.<br>% | HOSPITAL<br>FINANCE<br>4,633 | CUM.<br>% | BANK<br>SYSTEMS<br>10,421 | CUM.<br>% | COMPILED<br>LIST<br>99,809 | CUM.<br>% | COMPILED<br>LIST<br>8,068 | CUM.<br>% | COMBINED<br>175,924 | CUM.<br>% | AVERAGE<br>C.P.I. |
|---|---|---|---|---|---|---|---|---|---|---|---|---|---|---|---|
| 1st Week | 97 | .3 | 28 | .1 | 12 | .2 | | | 1,393 | 1.4 | 22 | .2 | 1,552 | .9 | |
| 2nd Week | 1,325 | | 351 | | 104 | | | | 2,656 | | 128 | | 4,564 | 2.5 | |
| Cumulative | 1,422 | 4.6 | 379 | 1.6 | 116 | 2.3 | | | 4,049 | 4.0 | 150 | 1.7 | 6,116 | 3.4 | |
| 3rd Week | 809 | | 238 | | 81 | | | | 587 | | 92 | | 1,807 | | |
| Cumulative | 2,231 | 7.2 | 617 | 2.6 | 197 | 4.0 | | | 4,626 | 4.6 | 242 | 2.7 | 7,923 | 4.4 | |
| 4th Week | 150 | | 60 | | 13 | | 236 | | | | 19 | | 611 | | |
| Cumulative | 2,384 | 8.4 | 677 | | 210 | 4.5 | 236 | 2.3 | 4,729 | 4.8 | 261 | 3.2 | 8,534 | 4.9 | |
| 5th Week | 89 | | 16 | | 9 | | 200 | | 98 | | 8 | | 420 | | |
| Cumulative | 2,473 | 8.7 | 693 | 2.8 | 219 | 4.7 | 436 | 4.2 | 4,827 | 4.8 | 269 | 3.3 | 8,954 | 5.1 | |
| C.P.I. (GROSS) | $2.29 | | $7.15 | | $4.23 | | $4.78 | | $4.14 | | $5.95 | | | | $4.76 |
| C.P.I. (NET) | After Duplication and Pre-Screening Elimination | | | | | | | | | | | | 6,000 | 3.41 | $7.10 |

**Table 13.1. As a response record, this table cumulatively indicates responses by lists, quantity, percent, and time frame. The gross average cost per inquiry (CPI) as shown is $4.76. However, after duplications were eliminated and inquiries known to be unqualified were pre-screened, the result was a net CPI of $7.10. (Because list owners would not release names, a merge-purge process was not possible.)**

Drawing on the experience of this Wallace program and other successful lead-generation efforts, let us present a checklist to which you might refer before settling on a strategy for your own programs:

1. *Premiums.* Is it valuable or useful enough to improve response? Or is it so general in nature that it will attract too many nonprospects?
2. *Sample.* Is it possible to include a sample of my product in the mailing? If not, am I making it easy for the prospect to obtain a sample or see a demonstration?
3. *Format.* Does it attract immediate attention?
4. *Copy.* Does it stress benefits? Is it addressed specifically to the market it is intended to reach?
5. *Media.* How might a multimedia approach enhance my direct mail effort?

To which we can only add the three words by which all direct marketers live: test, test, and test.

**Use of list data banks**

Once a marketer establishes a universe of lists which produce the best cost-efficient leads, as the electronics company did, then it is practical to establish a list data bank. The benefits are many. A list data bank is a computer file of all lists in a prospect list universe. The computer has the capability to sort the names on these lists according to sales office territories. It is then possible to have a printout for each sales office which specifies the exact number of names on each list that are available for each territory. A list data bank can also identify all names that appear on more than one list. By eliminating the duplicates, the marketer saves the mailing costs that would normally be incurred in mailing to all names on all lists.

The list data bank can generate the following reports:

1. *List availability.* This is a printout by sales office identification number of the names available for that territory. Names are organized into several market groups to separate general lists from special market categories.

2. *Labels generated.* This report—also printed in sales office order—gives an exact count of the number of labels generated for each territory. This report can be used for maintaining list inventory counts as well as lead-distribution control.

3. *Weekly mailing counts.* A breakdown by labels generated for each list source code and each week of mailing. This report helps in the analysis of mailing response.

4. *Unassigned territories.* This report prints out in ZIP code and county sequence the names available in those areas not presently covered by a sales office. The report helps in planning for the addition of offices and salespeople.

**Motivating salespeople and dealers**

Even the most effective lead-generation mailings and ads will mean little if the program is not keyed to the most important person of all, the salesperson. The sales force must be sold on the dollar-and-cents value of the program for them. They must be motivated to follow up and report on the leads. They must be shown how the lead-generation program increases their income. Otherwise, the program will surely die.

A company must successfully communicate the idea that (1) lead generation is not a hit-or-miss business (there's a structured method behind the generation of leads), (2) a direct response-generated lead can be as valuable as a referral and far more valuable than a cold call, and (3) lists that are carefully selected represent the top prospects. A number one key to motivation is getting dealers and salespeople involved at the outset.

**Developing lead flow systems**

When a deluge of sales leads hits the sales force, those personnel simply cannot follow them up properly. The effect can be a lag between receiving the sales lead and the actual sales call. Obviously, this delay has bad effects. The prospect "cools off." He is no longer available to see the salesperson for a number of reasons. For example: his interest has waned, he has called a competitor, or his priorities have shifted. The answer is to space out the leads over time so they can be adequately followed up while they are "hot." Another control mechanism is to make sure that the sales offices receive leads in proportion to the *manpower* or *ability* to follow up. A third control is to devise a means of keeping those leads "warm" until the salesperson does call.

Essential to a successful lead program is a lead-bank system that provides a steady flow of leads in just the right quantity for working promptly while they are "hot." To accomplish this, the marketer must know the percent of response his lead-producing mailing is likely to pull and then mail a sufficient quantity of pieces each week to produce the required number of leads for each territory.

Table 13.2 is a hypothetical table that indicates an optimum lead flow. Assuming a salesperson can average one new call a day, the table shows how many calls each office can make in a working month of 20 days (20 calls per person). This information determines how many mailings are required at a 5 percent return to furnish leads for these calls.

Thus, control can be exercised over mailings so that the two salespersons in Denver, for example, will not be suddenly swamped by scores of sales leads. In their district, 800 mailing pieces would be needed to furnish them with 40 leads, as many as the two salespersons can follow up in one month. ZIP code selectivity helps to target mailings within a district. To keep a constant flow of leads moving to the field at an average of 3,500 a month would require 70,000 mailings per month. A year's campaign (12 months multiplied by 70,000) requires 840,000 mailings.

**Table 13.2. Mailings required for generation of optimum number of leads.**

| District Offices | Number of Salespeople in Each | Total Calls Per Month | Mailings Required at 5% Return |
|---|---|---|---|
| Indiana | 10 | 260 | 5,200 |
| Tennessee | 14 | 220 | 4,400 |
| Virginia | 10 | 220 | 4,400 |
| Michigan | 10 | 220 | 4,400 |
| Illinois | 16 | 280 | 5,600 |
| West Virginia | 13 | 220 | 4,400 |
| New Jersey | 5 | 140 | 2,800 |
| San Francisco | 8 | 180 | 3,600 |
| Maine | 9 | 160 | 3,200 |
| Seattle | 9 | 180 | 3,600 |
| New York City | 10 | 240 | 4,800 |
| Ohio | 10 | 160 | 3,200 |
| Texas | 7 | 140 | 2,800 |
| Utah | 3 | 80 | 1,600 |
| Connecticut | 6 | 100 | 2,000 |
| Pittsburgh | 9 | 200 | 4,000 |
| Philadelphia | 11 | 180 | 3,600 |
| Miami | 3 | 60 | 1,200 |
| Des Moines | 7 | 120 | 2,400 |
| Los Angeles | 2 | 60 | 1,200 |
| Denver | 2 | 40 | 800 |
| Atlanta | 3 | 40 | 800 |
| Totals | 175 | 3,500 | 70,000 |

**Recordkeeping**   Without a system to maintain records and controls, a lead program will flounder and certainly fail. Recorded information should include such factors as: leads received, source of leads, leads distributed, calls made, time between distribution and sales call, and conversions to sales.

Such a system will allow you to analyze the entire program. With this information you can pinpoint weaknesses and establish net cost per lead and cost per sale. Such a system will allow you to get input regarding lead quality and sales efficiency. You can generate a cost-per-sale figure by office, by individual salesperson, and by source of lead.

**Lead follow-up programs**   Most sales executives are entirely happy if they reach the point of providing a steady flow of qualified leads to their sales force. But what about the leads that weren't closed? You're probably producing 10,000 leads a year and you've closed 2,000. So? There are 8,000 prospects out there who expressed an interest but chose not to buy at that time. Should they be forgotten, abandoned? Heck, no! The lead may have cost you from $6.00 to $25.00 or more. A follow-up program can be maintained by mail at a cost of about 20 cents a month per name, chipping away at these qualified prospects until they are ready to buy. The happy result? Optimum conversion to sales!

The customer and inquiry list can become an invaluable source of additional sales. It is easier and less expensive to program information you may never use rather than to re-program information later on. Both lists should be programmed to include such information as:

- Recency of purchase or inquiry
- Frequency of purchase
- Dollar volume of sales
- Annual monetary value
- Date of last purchase or upgrade
- Product line exposed
- Size of company
- SIC classification
- Titles of persons responding

**Mailing to customer and inquiry lists**

Periodic mailings to these lists produce sales as well as maintain valuable customer communication. Mailings that describe new products and other models in the line can be made on a regular basis. Perhaps a newsletter could be mailed periodically featuring case histories, testimonials, and practical tips and ideas along with new product applications. Newsletters are being used successfully today by many companies. Newsletters can serve as a vehicle of communication with customers and prospects and can also be used as a goodwill handout by salespeople.

The possibilities are innumerable. Customers, for example, who have not placed an order for a certain period of time can be asked about the adequacy of their present equipment, material, or program. Fresh leads and fresh sales can be the natural outcome.

Successful lead-generation programs never develop by accident. They require time, money, and tremendous effort. But the payoff derived from a systems approach to lead generation can be very rewarding.

## Self-quiz

1. What is today's average cost of a sales call?

_____

_____

2. Explain the quantity/quality/cost equation.

_____

_____

_____

_____

_____

_____

3. Why is the systems approach to improving lead programs necessary?

_____

_____

_____

_____

4. What is the basic ingredient that makes the systems approach work?

_____

_____

_____

_____

5. Name three pitfalls that can wreck a lead generation program.

a. _____

_____

_____

b. _____

_____

_____

c. _____

_____

_____

d. There are 14 major elements involved in the systems approach.  How many can you name?

_____

_____

_____

_____

_____

_____

_____

_____

_____

_____

_____

_____

_____

_____

6. When testing, what are the five major elements you shouldn't miss?

a. _____

b. _____

c. _____

d. _____

e. _____

Explain two of the above.

a. _____

_____

_____

_____

b. _____

_____

_____

7. List 10 lead-getting propositions

a. _____

b. _____

c. _____

d. _____

e. _____

f. _____

g. _____

h. _____

i. _____

j. _____

8. What was the major breakthrough in the electronics company's case history?

_____

_____

a. Explain in detail_____

_____

_____

_____

_____

_____

b. Which package format did better?_____

_____

_____

c. Did the involvement device

____ increase response

____ decrease response

____ make no difference

Did the addition of a telephone option

____ increase response

____ decrease response

____ make no difference

d. Did the affixing of a third class stamp on the outer envelope

____ increase response

____ decrease response

____ make no difference

e. Did a premium offer do better than a free trial?

____ Yes

____ No

f. In the premium test, the "pen" did 37 percent better than the control. Why, then did the company decide to use the control?

_____

_____

_____

_____

_____

g. Four categories of lists were used for the electronics company. One did 33 percent better. Name the category that did better and explain why.

_____

_____

_____

_____

_____

9. What was the basic media strategy used in the Wallace lead program?

_____

_____

_____

a. What three purposes did the print advertising accomplish?

(1) _____
_____
_____
_____

(2) _____
_____
_____
_____

(3) _____
_____
_____
_____

b. How does the preprint technique work?

_____
_____
_____
_____

c. What are three benefits a preprint mailing can offer?

(1) _____
(2) _____
(3) _____

d. Why do you think the inclusion of a sample (where possible) helps a mailing?

_____
_____
_____
_____
_____

10. What are five advantages of developing a list data bank?

a. _____
_____
_____
_____

b. _____
_____
_____
_____

c. _____
_____
_____
_____

d. _____
_____
_____
_____

e. _____
_____
_____
_____

11. What four important reports can be generated by a list data bank?

a. _____
b. _____
c. _____
d. _____

12. Why is sales motivation an important part of any lead program?

_____
_____
_____
_____

13. What is a leadflow system?

_____

_____

_____

_____

_____

_____

14. What are three benefits of a leadflow system?

   a. _____

   b. _____

   c. _____

15. What are the six essential factors in a lead accounting and reporting system?

   a. _____

   b. _____

   c. _____

   d. _____

   e. _____

   f. _____

16. What is the reason for developing an effective follow-up program to leads who haven't been converted to sales?

_____

_____

_____

_____

_____

17. Name 10 information factors that should be programmed into the customer and inquiry lists?

   a. _____

   b. _____

   c. _____

   d. _____

   e. _____

   f. _____

   g. _____

   h. _____

   i. _____

   j. _____

## Pilot project

You are the marketing manager for a medium-size company selling computer software to the business market. You've been asked to develop a lead program that must generate qualified leads for the sales force.

Input:

1. Product—computer software
2. Average sale—$1,200
3. Market—business and industry (both industrial and retail)
4. Advertising cost per sale—not to exceed $250.
5. Sales organization—six regional offices, 26 district sales offices, 435 salespeople

Implementation:

1. Develop a testing program
2. Select lists and other media
3. Compute a target for the quantity/quality/cost equation
4. Allocate a hypothetical distribution of salespeople to district sales offices
5. Compute the leadflow to each district sales office
6. Create a list data bank
7. Develop a "print" media schedule to include magazines, trade publications, and newspapers
8. Develop lead control and recordkeeping systems
9. Institute a lead follow-up program

# Section IV

# Managing Your Direct Marketing Business

# 14

## Mathematics of Direct Marketing

Creativity in direct marketing brings recognition, awards, and applause. Behind every successful direct marketing operation, however, one or more mathematics majors make the creativity work. They're among the unsung heroes of direct marketing.

**Pricing right**  Take the matter of pricing. You could line up the greatest direct response writers in the country—superstars like Bill Gregory, Hank Burnett, Tom Collins, and Bill Jayme. None could succeed if the price asked for your product left too thin a margin. Neophytes work with *raw* costs: the math boys identify *all* costs. Then they tell you how many orders you need per thousand to break even. If the break-even requirement is unrealistic, you had better increase your margin or drop your proposition.

Let's identify some of the many costs incurred over and above raw product cost. First is the total cost of filling an order: raw product cost plus royalty, if any, plus order processing, shipping expense, free gift, if any, and perhaps a use tax.

Then add administrative overhead, such as rent, light, heat, maintenance, credit checking, and collections. (Each item sold should bear its share of overhead expense.)

What about returned goods, refunds, and cancellations? These may run 10 percent or more, depending upon the item. How about bad debts? Sad to say, not everyone is honest. The "figures man" pumps in a figure for no-pays.

As an example of how hidden costs mount up, let's consider the case of a publisher who decided to sell a book on computer technology for $25.00. The raw cost of the book was $5.00. When all the other costs were pumped in, however, the $5.00 raw cost ballooned to $13.33. The order margin wasn't $20.00. It was $11.67.

Most professional marketers frown on arbitrary pricing, especially for blind items for which there is no comparable product or service. The pros advocate price testing. They would have had the book publisher test at least three selling prices—$19.95, $25.00, and $29.95, for example. Then they would have chosen the selling price that produced the best bottom line.

**Front end, back end**

Direct marketing professionals deal with two sets of figures—front end and back end. They know that front-end figures can lead marketers down the disaster trail. Back-end figures, net profit and loss; these are the figures that really count. Take the case of a gourmet food company. Mangement tested several different ads soliciting catalog requests. The big winner pulled twice as well as the second best ad leaving all the rest far behind. This was the front-end result. But when the back-end figure was computed, conversion to catalog orders from the "winning ad" was only 3.06 percent. Conversion to catalog orders from the third best ad was 20.39 percent, almost seven times as great! Back-end results. That's where it's at.

With the advent of computer tracking of back-end results for all ads by publication, all mailings according to lists became standard procedure. When direct marketing professionals meet privately, they trade horror stories about misleading front-end results. Mailing lists that out-pull all others at the front end may perish in piles of returned goods at the back end with bad debts to match. Ditto for publications that appear to be world beaters in front-end figures and fizzle in back-end figures.

The dictum of the professionals is: *track every lead and every order by source, front end to back end.* To operate in any other way is to live in a fool's paradise.

**Establishing the break-even point**

Authorities agree that the most practical way to determine whether a proposition is viable is to develop a worksheet that will determine your break-even point. In the development of a worksheet it is essential that all items of cost be included. Writing for *Direct Marketing* magazine, Ray Snyder, a highly regarded direct mail consultant, provided a worksheet breaking out all costs for five different propositions (See Exhibit 14.1). This worksheet is worth careful study. Note that the price of items varies from $17.00 to $100. Note also that four of the five promotions are individual mailings, whereas one promotion—Practical English—is an insert which was enclosed with another mailing. Thus, the Practical English promotion cost was only $24.00 per thousand, whereas the cost of the Medical Encyclopedia promotion, for example, was $145 per thousand.

As you follow the Medical Encyclopedia promotion down the column, take special note of items 3 through 8. In this example Ray Snyder was anticipating 10 percent returned goods. Items 4 and 5 take into account the cost of handling the returned goods. Item 6 anticipates there will be a 5 percent bad debt, so this is added to the cost. Items 8a and 8b take into account the cost of setting up an order—plus the cost of processing installment payments: 7 invoices at 25 cents each give us a $1.75 total. Item 9 establishes that the total cost figure of $17.74 has grown from a raw product cost of $10.00.

Item 10 shows that the unit profit after variable costs is $12.26 on the

$30.00 selling price. But this drops to $11.03 (item 12) after the returned goods factor (item 11) has been taken into account. The final figure, that which becomes critical in establishing the break-even point, is a $11.75 margin per order, item 16. Item 17 establishes that the cost of the mailing package, in the mail, for the four-volume Medical Encyclopedia is $145 per thousand. The final computation is to divide the mailing cost per thousand, item 17, by the margin per order, item 16. The simple computation determines that 12.3 order per thousand are required for the total operation to break even.

Further analysis developed for the five items shows a wide variance in the number of orders per thousand required for the break even point. Note that 17.6 orders per thousand are required for the two-volume Practical English set as compared to 12.3 for the four-volume Encyclopedia. This is easily explained by the fact that the Medical Encyclopedia has a selling price of $30.00 and the Practical English set has a selling price of $17.00, with only $10.00 per thousand difference in mailing costs. The insert for the Practical English set, on the other hand, requires only 3.1 orders per thousand to break even. This is explained by the fact that the insert costs only $24.00 per thousand as compared to the solo mailing costing $135 per thousand.

**Exhibit 14.1. Worksheet for determining point of profit in mailings.**

WORKSHEET FOR DETERMINING POINT OF PROFIT IN MAILINGS

| Offer | 4 Volume Medical Encyclopedia | | 2 Volume Practical English | | INSERT Practical English | | 100 Piece Home Workshop | | Polaroid De Luxe Set | |
|---|---|---|---|---|---|---|---|---|---|---|
| 1. Time Price | $30.00 | | $17.00 | | $17.00 | | $59.95 | | $100.00 | |
| 2. a. Cost of Product | 10.00 | | 4.15 | | 4.15 | 30. | 30.00 | | 45.00 | |
| b. Handling | .25 | | .10 | | .10 | | 1.00 | | 1.50 | |
| c. Postage | 1.00 | | .34 | | .34 | | 3.00 | | 2.15 | |
| d. Premium Handling (Incl. Postage) | 1.10 | | 1.05 | | 1.05 | | 2.25 | | 2.00 | |
| e. Use Tax 3% (#1 x "X" %) | .90 | | .51 | | .51 | | 1.80 | | 3.00 | |
| Total Cost: | | $13.25 | | $6.16 | | $6.16 | | $38.05 | | $53.65 |
| 3. Return Percentage | 10% | | 10% | | 10% | | 12% | | 15% | |
| 4. Postage a. and Handling | 1.25 | | .44 | | .44 | | 4.00 | | 3.65 | |
| b. Refurbishing | 1.20 | | .41 | | .41 | | 3.60 | | 6.00 | |
| Cost of Return: | 2.45 | | .85 | | .85 | | 7.60 | | 9.65 | |
| 5. Cost of Return x Return % | | .24 | | .09 | | .09 | | .91 | | 1.45 |
| 6. Bad Debt Percentage | 5% | | 3% | | 3% | | 6% | | 6% | |
| 7. Cost of Bad Debt (#1 x #6) | | 1.50 | | .51 | | .51 | | 3.60 | | 6.00 |
| 8. a. Order Set-Up Charge (X) Avg. - $1.00 | 1.00 | | 1.00 | | 1.00 | | 1.00 | | 1.00 | |
| b. Number of Payments @ Avg. 25¢ each | 7) 1.75 | | 4) 1.00 | | 4) 1.00 | | 8) 2.00 | | 10) 2.50 | |
| Total Process Cost: | | 2.75 | | 2.00 | | 2.00 | | 3.00 | | 3.50 |
| 9. Total Variable Costs | | $17.74 | $8.76 | | $8.76 | | $45.56 | | $64.60 | |
| 10. Unit Profit After Variable Costs (#1 less #9) | $12.26 | | $8.24 | | $8.24 | | $14.39 | | $35.40 | |
| 11. Return Factor (100% less #3) | 90% | | 90% | | 90% | | 88% | | 85% | |
| 12. Net Unit Profit (#10 x #11) | $11.03 | | $7.41 | | $7.41 | | $12.66 | | $30.09 | |
| 13. Fixed Joint & Allocated Charge 2.5% of #12 | .28 | | .19 | | .19 | | .32 | | .75 | |
| 14. Net Profit After J & A 12 less 13 | 10.75 | | 7.21 | | 7.21 | | 12.34 | | 29.34 | |
| 15. Credit for Unit Returned 3 x 2a | 1.00 | | .41 | | .41 | | 3.60 | | 6.75 | |
| 16. Net Profit After Returns Credit 14 plus 15 | 11.75 | | 7.62 | | 7.62 | | 15.94 | | 36.09 | |
| 17. Mailing Cost per M | $145.00 | | $135.00 | | $24.00 | | $145.00 | | $145.00 | |
| 18. Number of orders per M needed to break-even | 12.3 | | 17.6 | | 3.1 | | 9 | | 4 | |

**Exhibit 14.2. Cost work sheet.**

# Cost Work Sheet

COST OF PROMOTION _____

### LINE

1. Selling Price    $ _____
2. Plus Service Charge    _____
3.    Total Selling Price        $ _____
4. Less: Merchandise Cost    _____
5.    Drop Shipping    _____
6.    Delivery    _____
7. Processing, Credit Check & Collection Cost    _____
8. Cost of Returns    _____
9. Bad Debt    _____
10. Money Cost    _____
11. _____    _____
12. _____    _____
13. Total Cost        _____
14. UNIT PROFIT        $ _____ (P)

### CIRCULARIZATION COSTS PER M

15. Circulars    $ _____
16. Inserts    _____
17. Letters    _____
18. Order Forms    _____
19. _____    _____
20. Envelopes    _____
21. _____    _____
22. List Rental    _____
23. Inserting    _____
24. Addressing    _____
25. Mailing    _____
26. Postage    _____
27. Miscellaneous    _____
28. Circularization . . . Cost of Money    _____
29. Total Circularization Cost    $ _____
30. Fixed Overhead per M    _____
31. Total Circularization & Overhead        $ _____ (C)
32. Break-Even Net Sales per M (C ÷ P)        _____

### TOTAL PROFIT AT VARIOUS LEVELS OF NET PULL

| | | | |
|---|---|---|---|
| Projected Net Sales per M (Units) | _____ | _____ | _____ |
| Less: Break-Even Net Sales (Units) (Line 32) | _____ | _____ | _____ |
| Unit Sales per M Earning Full Profit | _____ | _____ | _____ |
| Unit Profit (Line 14) | X _____ | _____ | _____ |
| Net Profit Per M | $ _____ | _____ | _____ |
| M Circulars Mailed | X _____ | _____ | _____ |
| Total Net Profit | $ _____ | _____ | _____ |

Now, let's scrutinize the figures for the use of the 100-piece home workshop. The selling price is $59.95. The raw product cost is $30.00, almost 50 percent of the selling price. By comparison, the Medical Encyclopedia has a raw product cost of only 33⅓ percent. Moving down to item 16 for the 100-piece home workshop, we can see that the order margin is $15.94, not that much greater than that for the Medical Encyclopedia which is selling for half the price of the home workshop. As a consequence, even with the higher selling price, nine orders per thousand are required to break even. The Polaroid Camera with the selling price of $100 at a raw product cost of $45.00 requires the fewest number of orders per thousand to break even (4 orders) among the four solo mailings. Note that selling the camera contributes by far the greatest margin per order, $36.09. The lesson here is that the higher the selling price, assuming adequate margins, the lower the required response per thousand to break even.

Developing a worksheet for every direct marketing project should be a routine procedure. The Alan Drey Company of Chicago, a leading list broker, offers a good example of the type of worksheet that should be used (See Exhibit 14.2). As illustrated, the worksheet not only makes it possible for the marketer to calculate his break-even point, but also enables him to compute total profit possibilities at various levels of net pull.

## The arithmetic of two-step promotions

Up to here, we have assumed that a company uses individual mailings or ads to produce sales. Very often it is more profitable to generate inquiries with various low-cost methods and then convert those inquiries into sales by using special mailings, by telephone, through salesperson calls, or by a combination of these methods.

The case history given in chapter 11 on the Watkins Company of Winona, Minnesota, described the highly profitable application of the two-step method for that company. Space advertising was used to get inquiries, i.e., qualified leads. The catalog was sent only to those who in effect raised their hands and said, "Yes, I would like to receive your catalog." Those qualified inquiries bought (converted) at a 20 percent rate.

When the Hewlett Packard Company first introduced the company's pocket calculator, space ads were used to get qualified inquiries (See Exhibit 14.3). Then the company sent a deluxe mailing package costing more than $350 per thousand to qualified inquirers. A healthy 10 percent converted, producing an almost incredible $40,000 in sales for every 1,000 inquiries.

Robert Kestnbaum, president of R. Kestnbaum and Company, Chicago, points out that particularly for bigger ticket items, the two-step method is often the most profitable. He gives some interesting examples to prove his point.

Inquiries can be generated through any of the media available to the direct marketer. In each case the cost of placing an advertisement, making a mailing, or taking any other action to produce inquiries should be related to the number of inquiries generated to determine cost per inquiry. As an example, if $3,000 was spent to generate each 1,000 inquiries, the cost per inquiry would be $3.00. In addition, there would be a cost of perhaps $30.00 per

**Exhibit 14.3. Space ad for Hewlett-Packard.**

The HP-35 –
A small tribute
to great American
ingenuity. Made in U.S.A.

Don't settle for less.

# Hewlett-Packard presents the world's first pocket calculator that challenges a computer

Slide-rule portability and computer-like power for just $395

Hewlett-Packard's HP-35 is a new time-and-work saver that can free you from countless hours of tedious computation. This cordless wonder is just a bit larger than a pack of king-size cigarettes and weighs a mere 9 ounces. Yet it *challenges a computer* in handling complex problems, including log, trig and exponent functions with a single keystroke. Best of all, it solves these problems on the spot— whether in the lab, on a plane, or at a job site. All this highly sophisticated, highly portable calculating power costs a mere $395.00. So why settle for less? Find out now what the HP-35 can do to make your job a little easier . . . and a lot more productive. Write today for your free Capability Report.

HEWLETT *hp* PACKARD

Mail to:
HEWLETT-PACKARD
Advanced Products, Dept.
10900 Wolfe Road, Cupertino, Calif. 95014

*Please mail me a free copy
of your in-depth Capability Report
on the HP-35 Pocket Calculator*

NAME

TITLE

FIRM NAME

ADDRESS

CITY

STATE                    ZIP

thousand to process inquiries into a usable mailing list. Assuming the average sale was $100, the profit objective was $15.00, and the contribution to circulation was $20.00 after allowance for profit, the inquiry/conversion ratio needed to make a 15 percent profit would now look something like this:

| | |
|---|---|
| Contribution to circularization cost after allowance for profit | $20.00 |
| Total cost of obtaining and processing 1,000 inquiries | $3,030 |
| Cost of follow-up mailing ($175/M) | 175 |
| Total | $3,205 |
| Orders required to break even (16) | 160 |

Under these assumptions, the company must convert 16 percent of the inquiries costing $3.00 each to generate 15 percent pre-tax profits on sales.

Varying the media, kinds of advertisements, appeals, and offers will affect the cost of generating inquiries. Typically, the more highly qualified an inquiry, the more costly it will be to generate, but the higher the conversion rate will be. The thoughtful direct marketer will experiment continuously with various ways of producing inquiries and various means of conversion to fine-tune his program to maximize profits.

Moreover, most companies find that its inquiry list will support repeated conversion mailings. There is, of course a fall off in response to each mailing, but it is profitable to continue making conversion mailings until the incremental cost of the last mailing is greater than the contribution it generates. In our example, the company could continue to make conversion mailings at a cost of about $150 per thousand (M) until the last mailing generated fewer than $750 (7.5 order averaging $100) in sales per thousand pieces mailed.

| | |
|---|---|
| Contribution to circularization cost and profit | $35.00 |
| Profit objective | ($15.00) |
| Contribution to circularization cost | $20.00 |
| Cost per M of conversion mailing | $150.00 |
| Orders required to recover mailing costs | 7.5 |

If a company was looking at a series of conversion mailings, each of which produced 40 percent of the orders produced by the preceding one, the arithmetic for its conversion series would appear as in Table 14.1

Thus the total conversions from this series of four mailings are just under 19.5 percent, and the total sales at $100 each are $19,490. Total contribution would be $6,821. Pre-tax profit would be $3,263 after subtracting $3,558 selling cost, yielding a profit of 16.7 percent on sales.

**Return on investment**
One of the most efficient ways to assess the viability of direct marketing is to measure return on investment. Many major marketers who have set up a separate direct marketing operation as a profit center have found return on investment to be higher than for their sales through traditional channels. A 15 percent return on investment is not unusual.

**Table 14.1. Conversion series.**

| | Circularization Cost | Number Mailed | Number of Orders | Contribution |
|---|---|---|---|---|
| *Contribution per order* . . . . . . . . . . . . . . . . . . . . . . . . . . . | | | | $ 35 |
| Conversion mailing 1, including cost of generating and processing inquiries . . . . . . . . . . . . . . . . . . . . . . | $3,180 | 1,000 | 120 | 4,200 |
| Conversion mailing 2* . . . . . . . . . . . . . . . . . . . . . . . . . | 132 | 880 | 48 | 1,680 |
| Conversion mailing 3 . . . . . . . . . . . . . . . . . . . . . . . . . . | 124 | 832 | 19.2 | 672 |
| Conversion mailing 4 . . . . . . . . . . . . . . . . . . . . . . . . . . | 122 | 813 | 7.7 | 269 |
| Totals . . . . . . . . . . . . . . . . . . . . . . . . . . . . . . . . . . . . . . | $3,558 | 3,525 | 194.9 | $6,821 |

*Mailing cost $150 per thousand.

Dependable Lists, Inc., of New York has established the following formula for ROI for direct marketing:

$$ROI = \frac{(SP \times RE) - TI}{TI} \times 100$$

Where:

$SP$ = selling price (per unit)
$OM$ = order margin (per unit)
$RE$ = replies (per M)
$SC$ = selling cost (per M)
$TI$ = total investment = $([SP - OM] \times RE) + SC$
$ROI$ = percentage return on investment

Dependable Lists provides the following example of the application of ROI for a direct marketer. For example, the selling price per unit is $20.00, the order margin $10.00 per unit, the replies 20 per thousand (or 2 percent), and the selling cost $185 per thousand. Thus the return on investment for this example would be 3.9 percent, not a very attractive return on investment. Having determined this relatively low return on investment, the marketer would pursue alternatives that could increase his ROI. This may become possible by increasing the selling price, lowering the mailing costs, increasing the response per thousand, or a combination. For example, if selling costs were reduced from $185 per thousand to $150 per thousand, with all other factors remaining the same, the ROI would leap from 3.9 percent to 14.3 percent.

The example just cited relates to return on investment on a single promotion. But this is only the beginning. What about the value of repeat business as it relates to return on investment? Repeat business comes at a substantially lower cost than first-time sales. The point can be expressed in a dramatic way with, for example, a continuity book series. The Kleid Company, another leading New York list broker, gives the following example. During the lifetime of a new book club member, the member can typically be expected to spend $35.00 on the publisher's products *in addition to* the member's initial expenditure. Kleid points out that this figure must be factored into the cost per order. It is realistic and valid and it obviously alters the economics significantly. In developing ROI tables for a continuity book publisher, The Kleid Company studied twelve factors:

1. Quantity mailed
2. Total orders received, after credit approval
3. Percentage of response
4. Cost per thousand pieces
5. Raw cost per order
6. Net number of books per starter

7. Net dollar sales per starter
8. Estimated number of returned books
9. Allowance for bad pay
10. Raw profit per starter
11. Percentage of raw profit to sales
12. The relative value of a customer

Not to be overlooked in the determination of ROI is potential income from list rental. I'm referring again to the case history of the Watkins Company, chapter 11. The company's space advertising produced 250,000 inquiries. If Watkins decided to rent those names to other direct marketers at, say, a net profit of $30.00 per thousand, and if the company rented those names ten times over a twelve-month period, $75,000 in additional income would be realized. This figure should be pumped into ROI.

## Improving the figures

Possibilities for substantial increases in profits are always present with a minimal increase in response. Stanley Rapp, president of Rapp & Collins, gives a simple example of how a 10 percent increase can increase profit by 40 percent, and thereby dramatically increase ROI. Taking, for example, a product that sells for $15.00, Rapp sets up the following typical costs and gross profit margins for 1,000 responses (see Table 14.2): product costs, $5,00; indirect costs, $2.00; advertising costs, $6.00; profit, $2.00. He then shows a comparison between 1,000 responses and 1,100 responses, a 10 percent increase.

Knowing that a 10 percent increase in response can increase profits by 40 percent is one thing. Making it happen is often quite another. But an astute direct marketer looks at his figures and asks himself the key question, "What can I do to make these figures come out better?"

The opportunity to increase profits is not limited to increasing response. For example, let's say a direct marketer who mails a catalog to businesses has increased the average order from $32.00 to $44.00, an increase of 37.5 percent. He has achieved his increase in revenue in several ways.

**Table 14.2. Relationship of increased response to profit.**

|  | 1,000 Responses | 1,100 Responses |
|---|---|---|
| Total sales . . . . . . . . | $15,000 | $16,500 |
| Less: |  |  |
| Product cost . . . . . | 5,000 | 5,500 |
| Indirect cost . . . . . | 2,000 | 2,200 |
| Advertising cost . . . | 6,000 | 6,000 |
| Total costs . . . . . . . . | 13,000 | 13,700 |
| Profit . . . . . . . . . . . | $ 2,000 | $ 2,800 |

1. He makes selective price increases, accounting for 10 percent of his total increase.

2. For several multiquantity items (such as business forms), he increased the minimum order requirement, such as "minimum order 100" instead of "minimum order 50" (pull remained consistent).

3. He eliminated several marginal low-ticket items from the catalog.

4. A number of new, related higher-ticket items were offered.

5. A unique checklist was developed for the catalog headed "Do you have enough?" Under the heading were 72 check boxes adjacent to product classifications and page number references.

All these techniques combined accounted for 37.5 percent dollar amount increase per order. Percent of pull was exactly the same as that for the previous catalog.

## Using the good-better-best technique

One of the truly sophisticated techniques, as practiced by the giants in the catalog field, is the good-better-best technique. These marketers almost always feature the "better" item, at the in-between price. The advantage: It's an easy step up for the consumer to opt for the "best," at the highest price; or the consumer may step down to the "good," at the lowest price. The technique at least reaps an order which may not have been produced in any other way.

When sales are computed by catalog analysts, the primary rule they follow is this: the featured "better" item (middle price) must be the biggest seller, or something is obviously wrong. For instance, let's say the "best" item (highest price) is the biggest seller. This means one thing: the market will buy an even higher-priced item. Up goes the average dollar amount.

A takeoff on the good-better-best technique is offering add-on product options at additional cost. This is an excellent technique. Some examples:

• A seller of dictionaries via direct marketing offered the product option of thumb-indexing at $2.00 extra; 25 percent of all orders called for thumb-indexing.

• A seller of Christmas greeting letters offered the add-on option of lithographed envelopes at $20.00 per thousand extra; 21 percent took the option.

• A seller of am/fm radios offered the add-on option of a headset at $5.00 extra; 55 percent took this option.

• A seller of a $29.94 Norelco coffeemaker offered the add-on option of an electric coffee mill at $9.98 extra; a whopping 60 percent took this option. (See Exhibit 14.4.)

Let's look at the arithmetic on the Norelco coffeemaker proposition, with 60 percent taking the add-on option. Here's the way it looked for each 100 orders:

| | |
|---|---|
| 100 orders @ $29.94 | $2,994.00 |
| 60 add-ons @ 9.98 | 598.80 |
| Total revenue from 100 orders | $3,592.80 |

That's a neat 20 percent increase in revenue per order received.

**Exhibit 14.4. Norelco coffeemaker offer included add-on option, increasing revenue per order by 20 percent.**

**Long-term customer value**  Direct marketing professionals consistently find that repeat business is the key to profits. Thousands of customers may try a new publication, a new product, a new service once. But it is the hundreds who give repeat orders who form the basis for a profitable operation. An attrition scale for a typical business service (illustrated in Table 14.3) can be interpreted as evidence of the quick dropoff of repeat orders and the formation of a solid nucleus of repeat customers subsequent to the initial dropoff period.

In reviewing Table 14.3, note that at the end of five months only half of the original 3,000 subscribers remained. Note also how the nucleus of repeat subscribers develops from that point on. For example, 40 percent remained at the end of the ninth month and this group dropped only five percentage points by the end of the twelfth month. These, indeed, are the profitable subscribers. The scale covered an initial twelve-month period. Return on investment need not necessarily be computed for only one year. What about the long term?

**Table 14.3. Typical attrition rate for new magazine subscriptions over one year (based on 3% original response on a 100,000-piece mailing).**

| Month | Number of Subscriptions | Percentage Remaining |
|-------|------------------------|---------------------|
| First | 3,000 | 100 |
| Second | 2,700 | 90 |
| Third | 2,250 | 75 |
| Fourth | 1,800 | 60 |
| Fifth | 1,500 | 50 |
| Sixth | 1,400 | 47 |
| Seventh | 1,300 | 43 |
| Eighth | 1,250 | 42 |
| Ninth | 1,200 | 40 |
| Tenth | 1,150 | 38 |
| Eleventh | 1,100 | 37 |
| Twelfth | 1,050 | 35 |

## Table 14.4. Attrition scale for five-year period.

| Year | Number of Customers | Percentage of Repeat Buyers |
|------|---------------------|------------------------------|
| First . . . . . . . . . . | 1,000 | — |
| Second . . . . . . . . | 342 | 34.2 |
| Third . . . . . . . . . . | 205 | 60.0 |
| Fourth . . . . . . . . | 244 | 71.2 |
| Fifth . . . . . . . . . | 260 | 75.9 |

Table 14.4 tracks 1,000 initial customers through a five-year period. Of the total, only 34.2 percent repeated in the second year. But it is at this point where the nucleus of repeat subscribers forms. Note that through the fifth year 260 repeat customers remained of the 342 who purchased in the second year. This means that a high percentage (76) of the second-year buyers were still repeat buyers in the fifth year.

## Using customer lists to maximize profits

The most precious asset of any direct marketing operation, it is generally agreed, is the customer list. There is another statement, however, which is not always recognized: not all customers are the same. Which leads to this statement: there is no way to maximize profits if you treat all customers the same.

Direct marketers used to throw all their customer names into a pot. They'd keep soliciting names as an undifferentiated group until profits dried up. Then someone said, "Hey, if you want to maximize your profits from your customer lists, you've got to maintain the names in separate groups according to the year of last purchase. This was a breakthrough of sorts. Current-year buyers consistently produced greater profits than customers who had not purchased for one or two years or more. As a result, profits were maximized by grouping customers according to year of last purchase. From there direct marketers learned that frequency of solicitation bore a direct relationship to maximum profits. The pros learned there was a magic number of solicitations they could make in a twelve-month period to former buyers by year of last purchase. And this, too, was a breakthrough. But remember our statement: all customers are different, even if their last purchase was made within the same period. A key factor is making the ability to consume commensurate with customer needs.

Table 14.5 shows a typical example of selling costs as they (a) relate to number of employees in a customer company and (b) as they relate to frequency of solicitation according to number-of-employee categories. The table warrants careful study. Note these basic facts: (1) number of employees

## Table 14.5. Catalog sales analysis by company size and catalog frequency.

| No. of Employees | Selling Cost Per Catalog (In Percent) | | | | | | | |
|------------------|--------|--------|--------|--------|--------|--------|--------|--------|
| | Cat. 1 | Cat. 2 | Cat. 3 | Cat. 4 | Cat. 5 | Cat. 6 | Cat. 7 | Cat. 8 |
| 1 to 99 . . . . . . . . . . | 16.9 | 20.9 | 23.9 | 27.9 | 33.5 | 41.9 | 55.9 | 84.1 |
| 100 to 199 . . . . . . . . | 15.3 | 19.1 | 21.8 | 25.5 | 30.6 | 38.2 | 51.0 | 76.6 |
| 200 to 299 . . . . . . . . | 9.4 | 11.8 | 13.5 | 15.7 | 18.9 | 26.6 | 31.5 | 47.3 |
| 300 to 499 . . . . . . . . | 7.7 | 9.7 | 11.1 | 12.9 | 15.5 | 19.4 | 25.9 | 38.9 |
| 500 to 999 . . . . . . . . | 5.4 | 6.8 | 7.8 | 9.1 | 10.9 | 13.7 | 18.2 | 27.4 |
| 1,000 to 1,499 . . . . . | 5.0 | 6.3 | 7.2 | 8.4 | 10.1 | 12.6 | 16.8 | 25.3 |
| 1,500 to 2,499 . . . . . | 4.6 | 5.8 | 6.6 | 7.7 | 9.2 | 11.6 | 15.4 | 23.2 |
| 2,500 and over . . . . | 2.8 | 3.5 | 4.0 | 4.7 | 5.7 | 7.1 | 9.5 | 14.2 |
| Unclassified . . . . . . | 7.9 | 9.9 | 11.4 | 13.3 | 15.9 | 19.9 | 26.6 | 39.9 |

**Table 14.6. Catalog distribution according to number of employees.**

| Number of Employees | Number of Catalogs |
|---|---|
| 1–99 . . . . . . . . | 4 |
| 100–199 . . . . . | 4 |
| 200–299 . . . . . | 6 |
| 300–499 . . . . . | 7 |
| 500–999 . . . . . | 8 |
| 1,000–1,499 . . | 8 |
| 1,500–2,499 . . | 8 |
| 2,500 and over | 8 |
| Unclassified . . | 7 |

is broken out by nine categories, including unclassified; (2) a series of eight catalogs is mailed to all categories, and (3) the selling cost for each effort is computed for each category.

The effect of profitability as it relates to number of employees is truly startling. On all eight catalog efforts, selling cost as a percent of sales decreases with utter precision as the number of employees increases. (Unclassified relates to those companies for which the number of employees could not be determined. It would be a mix of all categories.)

Having this valuable data, how does one maximize his profits from his customer list? Well let's say that a 28 percent selling cost leaves a satisfactory profit return. On this basis, catalog distribution over a 12-month period would break out as shown in Table 14.6. This sounds like a great way to maximize profits. And it is, so far as it goes. But it's a long way from the ultimate in maximizing profits. Take the first two categories, for example. To reach the targeted profit margin, both categories must be cut off after the fourth catalog has been mailed. But we know that within these two categories there are customers who would respond favorably to a fifth, sixth, seventh, and eighth catalog. If only those customers could be isolated. Unfortunately, under this system, the good fruit is killing off the bad fruit.

## Segmentation by amount of last purchase

A step closer to recognizing that all customers are different is to segment the customer list according to amount of last purchase. Many catalog firms have learned that the dollar amount and frequency of repeat business have a direct relationship to the amount of the last purchase. Therefore, such firms segment their buyers list according to amount of purchase, for example, up to $10.00; from $10.01 to $25.00; and from $25.01 to $50.00.

A further possibility is to separate buyers into cash buyers, credit buyers, and credit card buyers. Another method is to separate buyers into those who order by mail and those who order by telephone.

## The recency-frequency-monetary formula

The ultimate in maximizing profits from a customer list is to be found in the application of the R-F-M formula: R-recency of purchase; F-frequency of purchase; M-monetary amount. These three criteria are the basis for maximizing profits for all the mail order giants. However, any mail order operation of any substance can do likewise. In its simplest form, the method calls for a point system to be established with purchases broken down by quarter of the year. A typical formula might be as follows:

Recency points:
    24 points—current quarter
    12 points—last six months
     6 points—last nine months
     3 points—last twelve months

Frequency points: Number of purchases × 4 points

Monetary points: 10 percent of dollar purchase with a ceiling of 9 points. (The ceiling avoids distortion caused by an unusually large purchase.)

Number of points allotted vary among those using R-F-M formulas, but the principle is the same. Once the system is established and point values are assigned, the opportunities for maximizing profits are almost phenomenal. I've seen sophisticated systems which have scores of categories with profit figures ranging from $50 per thousand catalogs mailed to $1,500 and more. Under the system, each account is isolated from all other accounts. It is assumed that customers buying habits dictate how frequently you can make a solicitation.

Once the R-F-M system is computer programmed, producing a monthly update is a simple matter. Table 14.7 shows what a hypothetical partial printout might look like for a representative group of accounts. The table shows the activity of five accounts for December 1978. Account number 16, 441 bought twice in September and once in December. Recency points were computed in relation to the time interval since each purchase.

**Table 14.7. Analysis of accounts by recency, frequency, monetary—December 1978.**

| Account Number | Month | Recency Points | No. of Purchases | Frequency Points | Dollar Purchases | Monetary Points | Total Points | Cumulative Total Points |
|---|---|---|---|---|---|---|---|---|
| 16,441 | 9 | 12 | 2 | 8 | 32.17 | 3.21 | 23 | 39 |
| 16,441 | 12 | 24 | 1 | 4 | 46.10 | 4.61 | 32 | 71 |
| 16,521 | 1 | 3 | 3 | 12 | 87.09 | 8.71 | 23 | 23 |
| 16,608 | 7 | 12 | 1 | 4 | 21.00 | 2.10 | 18 | 28 |
| 16,708 | 4 | 6 | 1 | 4 | 33.60 | 3.36 | 13 | 18 |
| 16,708 | 8 | 12 | 2 | 8 | 71.00 | 7.10 | 27 | 45 |
| 16,708 | 11 | 24 | 1 | 4 | 206.00 | 9.00 | 37 | 82 |
| 16,921 | | | | | | | | 68 |

Frequency points were computed by multiplying the number of purchases by four. Monetary points were computed by multiplying the dollar amount of purchases and multiplying by 10 percent. Note that under "Cumulative Total Points," this marketer had carried over 16 accumulated points from the previous calendar year, indicating that his customer first bought in calendar year 1977.

In reviewing the list of accounts, note that account number 16,708 spent $206 in November but was given only nine monetary points. This reflects the arbitrary decision of the marketer to give no more than nine monetary points regardless of amount of purchase. Finally, note that account number 16,921 shows no activity for calendar year 1978 but has a total of 68 points for 1977.

The opportunities for manipulating a customer list under the R-F-M system makes all other systems obsolete. Our marketer with eight catalogs could mail all eight catalogs to segments of all employee-number categories and come in under his 28 percent selling-cost requirement every time. Even more significant, however, is the fact that the total selling-cost percentage should drop appreciably because, regardless of the number of employees, only those customers in each category who qualify for the next catalog would receive it.

Installing an R-F-M system requires thought, diligence, perseverance, and investment. But the payoff—maximizing profits—can be beautiful to behold!

## Self-quiz

1. Define "raw cost."

_____

_____

_____

_____

2. Define back-end cost.

_____

_____

_____

_____

3. Typically, the more highly qualified an inquiry is, the_____and_____it will be to generate.

4. Define ROI (return on investment).

_____

_____

_____

_____

5. Name four ways in which a catalog operation might increase profits.

a. _____

b. _____

c. _____

d. _____

6. What is the advantage of the "good-better-best" technique?

_____

_____

_____

_____

7. Define the term "hard-core" customer group.

_____

_____

_____

_____

8. There is no way to maximize profits if you____

_____

9. Name four ways you can segment a customer list.

a. _____

b. _____

c. _____

d. _____

10. Define the R-F-M formula.

_____

_____

## Pilot project

You have been given the assignment to sell a $49.95 calculator by mail. Given the following set of facts, determine your break-even point. (number of orders required per thousand mailing pieces).

1. Merchandise cost—$21.00
2. Order handling expense—$1.00
3. Shipping expense—$1.75
4. Cost of premium (free gift)—$1.25
5. Administrative overhead—10 percent of selling price
6. Returned goods—12 percent
7. Refurbishing cost—10 percent of cost of merchandise
8. Estimated bad debts—10 percent
9. Cost of mailing—$200 per thousand, including a proportionate share of preparation costs.

# 15

## Research and Testing Techniques

"Who needs research?" This is the cry of the old-timers in direct marketing. "We just count replies; that's our research," is their stand. They are living with a myth. The new breed in direct marketing—those who are producing the big breakthroughs—are using research for all it is worth. Research techniques as applied by general advertisers are equally applicable to direct marketers.

**Research tools available**  Bob Kaden of Goldring & Company, a Chicago-based research firm, has worked with a number of direct marketers in applying established research techniques to their direct marketing efforts. A number of research tools are available, and three basic types of research are being applied, as is shown in the following outline, which itself is followed by brief descriptions of the three forms of research.

I. Background research
   A. Focus group interviews (qualitative)
   B. In-depth personal interviews
   C. Awareness, image and attitude studies (quantitative)
   D. Demographic studies (quantitative)
   E. Psychographic research (quantitative)
II. Pretesting research
   A. Benefit analysis (quantitative)
   B. Focus groups
   C. Pretesting strategies/concepts (quantitative)
   D. Pretesting concepts to predict response rate
III. Post-testing
   A. Responder/nonresponder studies (quantitative)
   B. Longitudinal tracking studies (quantitative)
   C. Focus groups (qualitative)

## I. Forms of background research

*A. Focus group interviews (qualitative).* Focus groups are a flexible approach to gathering information leading to the solution of particular research problems.

Because of its less structured nature, the method provides for an extensive study of perceptions, attitudes, and motivations. Its great value lies in the breadth and range of the responses that can be elicited.

In this technique, a small group of respondents are interviewed collectively. When a discussion is started on a particular subject, a snowball effect is achieved. One point or attitude elicits another until a wide range of ideas and attitudes has been exposed and discussed.

Group interviewing is a unique type of research. Properly employed, it is a valuable exploratory tool. Quantified projections should never be made from the results of group interviews. The real value lies only in:

- Identification of relevant behavioral patterns, attitudes, and motivations.
- Establishing priorities among categories and within categories of behavior and attitudes.
- Generally defining problem areas more fully and formulating hypotheses for further investigation.

*B. In-depth personal interviews.* The personal one-on-one (interviewer-to-respondent) interview is a highly effective technique for collecting information among such persons as executives, technical people, the trade, and buyers or persons who are difficult to bring into a focus group. This technique is also appropriate for delving into highly personal topics (e.g., women's personal care products, banking habits, savings plans). The technique is qualitative and a report is prepared that appears similar to a focus group interview report.

*C. Awareness, image, and attitude studies (quantitative).* This is normally a major piece of statistical research. The number of people to be interviewed ranges from as low as 300 respondents to as high as several thousand respondents.

Such studies provide sound, statistically projectable data, such as:

- Number of people aware of the product or service.
- Number of persons trying the product or service and the degree to which they are satisfied with the product.
- Prevailing attitudes toward competitive products and services in terms of the characteristics on which one product or service is distinguished from another.
- How often the product or service is used.
- Attitudes toward such factors as pricing, packaging, and advertising.

*Demographic studies (quantitative).* This is basically a nose-counting technique. This research can help target list selection and general media plan. Its purpose is to determine who uses a product or service in terms of:

- Age
- Income

- Size of family
- Occupation
- Geographic location
- Frequency of product usage

*E. Psychographic research (quantitative).* This highly sophisticated research is a statistically oriented process that categorizes people in terms of life style. The technique segments people into groups by product category. At least 600 subjects are generally required for a proper psychographic study. Non-users of Lanier dictating equipment, for example, might be:

- The sophisticates—persons who read *Psychology Today*, who ski, who like Scotch, who are liberal, who drive two-door cars, and like new challenges.
- The gropers—persons who prefer high quality but are always looking for a bargain, who are not expert in any sport but always are trying, who listen intently to others people's opinions, and who constantly switch from one product to another.
- The unheralded—persons who like recognition, who buy products for their status brand name, who boast about their accomplishments, who like to think they are independent.

## II. Pretesting research

Based on background research studies, creative strategies and objectives are set. Strategies are targeted to the specific kinds of people shown to offer the greatest potential market. Advertising appeals are designed to communicate the desired sales message.

Much confusion arises when one must decide on what pretesting techniques to use. The key to a successful pretesting program is the development of a system. Through a system approach, data are collected in the same manner each time a study is undertaken. Measurements, therefore, are comparable from study to study, and movements toward or away from the objectives are easily observed.

## III. Post-testing

In direct marketing, a unique opportunity exists for determining if and why a campaign is successful and pays off. By contrasting attitudes of those who respond to a promotion to those who do not, one can determine the following:

- If a direct marketing effort produces incremental business.
- If those who receive a direct mail piece develop a better (or worse) image of the sponsoring company.
- Why responders replied and why nonresponders did not. This can help in developing follow-up mailings.
- Tracking the long-term effect of a continuing promotion. (Do sales increase after the second, third, fourth, or fifth drop.)

## Value of research—examples

Here are two examples of the value of research for direct marketers. A major firm selling supplementary learning materials to schoolteachers planned to produce a new catalog. The theme selected by the marketer for their catalog was "Back to Basics." This theme was presented before schoolteachers in a number of focus groups. Without exception, there was violent reaction against the theme "Back to Basics." The marketer got the message and the theme was promptly dropped.

Another major firm—this one in the travel field—wanted to determine the incremental sales value of a direct mail campaign over and above general advertising running in newspapers, magazines, and television. Because the purpose of the direct mail advertising was to induce consumers to buy tickets from travel agencies, no obvious way was immediately apparent to compute incremental sales produced as a result of the direct mail campaign. Post-testing research emerged as the ideal available tool. For the purpose of measuring the impact of direct mail over general advertising, two groups of consumers were selected. The first group received no direct mail promotion. The second did. Prior to the direct mail promotion, both groups were asked about their plans to take a given trip. The intent to travel was similar for both groups. Then, following the direct mail promotion, a questionnaire was sent to both groups. The purpose was to determine the number of respondents who actually did take the trip. The second group—those who received the direct mail promotion—bought $2,000,000 more in tickets than the first group.

## Techniques for producing creative breakthroughs

The value of research for direct marketers cannot be overestimated. Research, however, can measure only what exists. Research and testing may reveal a negative response to stale ideas or a positive response to breakthrough ideas. Generating creative breakthroughs, therefore, should be a subject of great interest and importance to the aspiring direct marketer.

Marketing directors know that creative people are subject to slumps, the "blahs." To keep the creative batting averages high, big-league creative marketing directors constantly motivate their people. And the results are often remarkable.

Brainstorming, first introduced in the 1950s, persists as one of the most effective methods of finding creative solutions to difficult problems. Scores of examples could be cited of breakthroughs that have resulted from brainstorming, but a few will suffice. First, some house rules for brainstorming.

## House rules for brainstorming

*Select a leader.* Let the leader take all responsibility for contact with reality; everyone else in the brainstorming meeting is to "think wild." The duties of the leader are:

- To take notes on all ideas expressed.
- To set a time limit on the meeting, such as 60 minutes.
- To set a quota on ideas to be generated, such as 60 ideas in 60 minutes.
- To admonish any critical thinkers in the group—no negative thinking allowed.
- To say "stop" when an idea has been built up enough.

- To help stimulate new ideas if things lag.

*Rules during brainstorming.*

- Suspend all critical judgment on any ideas expressed.
- Let the leader handle all contact with reality. The rest of the group should "let go" at all times and just react to ideas.
- As each new idea comes, let the leader express the simple meaning.
- Keep building each idea till the leader of the group says, "stop."
- Remember, humor and "play" atmosphere is desirable and important to the process. Don't be afraid to have fun!

*Three-phase process.* Brainstorming is part of a three-phase process. Make all preparations in advance. Do all critical analysis after brainstorming stops.

- Before you start, carefully define problem(s) in writing. Set quotas for ideas. Set a time limit. Review the house rules before the brainstorming session.
- Establish the "formal setting," then *brainstorm.*
- After the session is over, use your normal, everyday judgment to logically develop ideas, selecting the best ideas from all available alternatives.

**Brainstorming example 1**

The problem: Insurance companies are not allowed to give free gifts as an incentive for applying for an insurance policy. How can we offer a free gift and stay within the law? That was the brainstorming problem. Sounds like an impossible problem. Right? Wrong. Brainstorming participants broke through with a positive solution, a blockbuster.

The breakthrough: the brainstorming idea that hit pay dirt was offer the free gift to everyone, whether they apply for the policy or not.

Result: A 38 percent increase in applications.

**Brainstorming example 2**

The problem: How can we avoid paying postage for sending prizes to "no" entrants in an "everybody wins" sweepstakes? (Possible saving in postage to the marketer—if the problem could be solved—was about $250,000.)

The breakthrough: We asked "no" entrants to provide a stamped, self-addressed envelope. We included a prize in the shipping carton for those who said "yes." (The Post Office Department approved the requirement at the time.)

Results: This was the most successful sweepstakes contest the sponsor ever conducted. The sponsor also enjoyed savings of $250,000 in postage.

**Brainstorming example 3**

The problem: We have 36 competitors selling to the schools. They all promise "prompt shipment" of their pompons. How can we dramatize the fact that we ship our pompons in 24 hours and thus capture the bulk of the market?

The breakthrough: We inserted a Jiffy Order Card in the catalog, in addition to the regular order form, featuring **Guaranteed Shipment Within 24 Hours.**

Result: Pompon sales increased a dramatic 40 percent!

**Fantasy games**

Of all the games creative people play, my favorites are fantasy games. These can be defined as games that enable one to reach out for satisfaction of his or her most fervent wishes. Here's a fantasy game anyone can play, in a group or individually. The rules are simple: before you charge into the solution to a direct marketing problem, write three words on the top of a piece of paper—"I wish that. . . ." then complete the sentence with your most fervent wish. Let's take some examples:

*Fantasy 1.* Some time ago, someone probably said, I wish I could find a way to spread my advertising sales cost over several books rather than one. Out of it came the negative option and the Book-of-the-Month Club. A marketing triumph.

*Fantasy 2.* A client recently expressed the wish, I wish we could cut our bad debts in half. A fantasy? Not at all. Brainstorming provided a way to cut the client's bad debts by 80 percent!

*Fantasy 3.* "I wish that we could find a way to contact customers just one week before their supplies are depleted." A unique system to accomplish exactly that came out of this wish.

**Lateral thinking applied**

Recently I sent a memo to all of our writers, asking the question, What do you do when your creative process turns blah? Here is the reply of one of our senior writers: "I use the 'Think Tank.' It's a piece of gadgetry (designed by Edward De Bono, author of many books on the subject of creative thinking) that forces the user to break the habit of logical, vertical thinking and open his mind to creative, uninhibited lateral thought. Here's how I use the Think Tank:

"First, I twist the dials on the sides of the Think Tank to jumble up the words inside. Second, I copy down six random words that appear in the window of the Think Tank. Third, I spend at least five minutes with each word, using word associations and so forth, that relate to the problem I'm trying to solve. Usually one or more of the words will 'trigger' an idea. Here's an example:

"My problem was to come up with some new ideas on how to get more credit card holders for Amoco. I twirled the dial on the Think Tank and the word 'water' popped into the window. In a matter of milliseconds my free, stream-of-consciousness thinking was set in motion and led to a unique idea. Water made me think of boats. Boats need gasoline just as cars do (a good-size cruiser may spend $75 to $100 for a fill-up). There are Amoco gas pumps at marinas on the water. Why not send our regular credit card solicitation package with a special letter and special appeal to a list of boat owners?" (Credit the lateral thinking process with this breakthrough idea.)

**Creative input**

The degree of truly creative output is directly related to two factors: clear and specific definitions of problems to be solved and the right "atmosphere" for developing creative solutions. Frank Daniels, director of Agency/Client Relations of Stone & Adler, gives full time to stimulating creative people. Using a long-established technique for idea stimulation, he provides creative people with eight "stimulators" designed to expand their thinking. The examples that follow were applied to the Lanier company, manufacturers of dictating equipment. Creativity was being stimulated for promoting a minirecorder, Lanier's Pocket Secretary. Each of the eight stimulators is accompanied by a key thought and a series of questions designed to promote creative solutions.

**Can we COMBINE**  Combining two or more elements often results in new thought processes. These questions are designed to encourage brainstorming participants to think in terms of combinations.

*Key thought: combine appropriate parts of well-known things to emphasize the benefits of our product.* "Think of owning a Rolls-Royce the size of a Volkswagen" (Lanier Pocket Secretary).

What can be combined physically or conceptually to emphasize product benefits?

Can the product be combined with another so that both benefit?

Where in the product offer would a combination of thoughts be of most help?

What opposites can be combined to show a difference from competitive products?

What can we combine with our product to make it more fun to own, use, look at?

Can part of one of our benefits be combined with part of another to enhance both?

Can newness be combined with tradition?

Can a product benefit be combined with a specific audience need through visual devices? Copy devices?

What can we combine from the advertising and sales program to the benefit of both? Can salespersons' efforts be combined into advertising?

Can we demonstrate product advantages by using "misfit" combination demonstration?

Can we combine manufacturing information performance tests with advertising to demonstrate advantages?

**TIME ELEMENTS**  Saving time and having extra time are conventional human wants. This series of questions is designed to expand one's thinking toward making time a plus factor in the product offer.

*Key thought: Alter time factor(s) in present offer, present schedules, and present product positioning to motivate action.*

Does seasonal timing have an effect on individual benefits?

Can present seasonal timing be reversed for special effect?

Can limited time offers be effective?
Can early buyers be given special consideration?
Can off-season offers be made?
Are there better days, weeks, or months for our offers?
Can we compress or extend present promotional sequencing?
Can our price be keyed to selected times of the week, month, year?
Can we feature no-time-limit offers?
Can we feature limited time offers?
Can we feature fast delivery or follow-up?

**Can We ADD** An axiom of selling is that the customer often unconsciously compares the added benefits of a competitor's product with those of your product. The products with the most added benefits traditionally sell better. These questions are designed to ferret out added benefits for a particular product.

*Key thought: Look for ways to express benefits by relating functional advantages of unrelated products or things.* "We've taken all the best cassette recorder features and added one from the toaster" (pop-out delivery).

What has been added to our product that's missing from others?

Do we have a deficiency due to excess that can be turned into an advantage?

Is our product usable in many different ways aside from the intended use?

Is our product instantly noticeable? Is it unusual in terms of size, shape, color? What unrelated symbols can we use to emphasize this unique characteristic?

Does our product make something easier? What have we added by taking this something away?

Does our product make order out of chaos or meaningful chaos out of total chaos? What have we added by taking this something away?

What does the purchase of our product add to the buyer's physical situation, mental condition, subconscious condition, present condition, future condition?

Where would the buyer be if he does not purchase? What would be missing from his life?

Does our product give its full benefit to the buyer immediately or does he build up (add) to his well being through continued possession?

**Can We SUBTRACT** Taking away can often be as appealing as adding to. Less weight, less complexity, less fuss, less bother are fundamental appeals. These questions steer brainstorming participants in that direction.

*Key thought: Subtract from the obvious to focus attention on benefits of our product/service.* "We've weighed all the minirecorders and made ours lighter."

What deficiencies does our product have competitively?

What advantage do we have?

What features are the newest? The most unusual?

How can our product use/cost be "minimized" over time?

Can a buyer use less of another product if he buys ours?

Can the evidence of total lack of desire for our product be used to illustrate benefits?

Can the limitations of our benefits be used as an appeal?

What does lack of our product in the buyer's living habits do to him?

Does our product offer a chance to eliminate any common element in all competitive products?

Does our product reduce or eliminate (subtract) anything in the process of performing its work?

Will our product deflate (subtract from) a problem for the buyer?

**Can We Make ASSOCIATIONS**
Favorable associations are often the most effective way to emphasize product benefits. "Like Sterling on silver," a classic example of a favorable association, is an [observation] [saying] [remark] [comment] that accrues to the benefit of the product being compared with other products.

*Key thought: Form a link with unrelated things or situations to emphasize benefits.*

Can we link our product to another already successful product to emphasize benefits?

Can we appeal to popular history, literature, poetry, art to emphasize benefits?

What does the potential buyer associate with our product? How can we use this association to advantage?

When does the potential buyer associate our product with his potential use?

Can associations be drawn with present or future events?

Can associations be made with abstractions that can be expressed visually, musically, with words and so forth?

Can funny, corny, challenging associations be made?

Can associations be made with suppliers of component parts?

Is our product so unique it needs no association?

Can our product be associated with many different situations?

**Can We SIMPLIFY**
What is the simple way to describe and illustrate our major product benefit? As sophisticated as our world is today, the truism persists that people relate best to simple things. These questions urge participants to state benefits with dramatic simplicity.

*Key thought: Dramatize benefits individually or collectively with childishly simple examples, symbols, images.*

Which of our appeals is strongest over our competition? How can we simplify to illustrate?

Is there a way to simplify *all* our benefits for emphasis?

Where is most of the confusion about our product in the buyer's mind? Can we illustrate by simplification?

Is our appeal abstract? Can we substitute simple, real visualizations to emphasize?

Could a familiar quotation, picture, be used to make our appeal more understandable?

Is our product complex? Can we break it up (literally) into more understandable pieces to emphasize benefits?

Can I overlap one benefit with another to make product utility more understandable?

Can I contrast an old way of doing something with the confusing part of our product to create understanding?

Is product appeal rigidly directed at too small a segment of the market? Too broad a segment?

Can we emphasize benefits by having an unskilled person or child make good use of the product in a completely out-of-context situation?

**Can We SUBSTITUTE** The major product benefit for our product is often so similar to major product benefits of competitive products that it is difficult for the consumer to perceive the difference. Substituting another theme, such as Avis did when the company changed its theme to "We Try Harder," can often establish a point of difference. These questions inspire participants to think in terms of substitution.

*Key thought: Substitute the familiar for another familiar theme for emphasis; substitute the unfamiliar for the familiar for emphasis.*

Can a well-known theme for another product be substituted for our theme, or can a well-known benefit for another product be substituted for our benefit?

Can an incongruous situation be used to focus emphasis on our theme or benefits.

Can a series of incongruous situations be found for every benefit we have? Can they be used in one ad? Can they form a continuity series of ads?

What can be substituted for our product appeal that will emphasize the difference between us and our competitors?

Can an obviously dissimilar object be substituted for the image of our product?

Can a physical object be used to give more concrete representation of a product intangible?

Is our product replacing a process rapidly becoming dated? Can we substitute the past for the present, the future for the past or the present?

Can we visualize our product where the competitor's product is normally expected to be?

Can we visualize our product as the only one of its kind in the world, as if there were no other substitutes for our product?

**Can We Make A REVERSAL** The ordinary can become extraordinary as normal situations are reversed. A man doing the wash. A cute miss pumping gas. A trained bear pushing a power mower. These questions are designed to motivate participants to think in terms of reversing normal situations.

*Key thought: Emphasize a benefit by completely reversing the normal situation.*

What are the diametrically opposed situations for each of our product benefits?

For each copy point already established, make a complete reverse statement.

How would a totally uninformed person describe our product?

Can male- and female-oriented roles be reversed?

Can art and copy be totally reversed to emphasize a point?

How many incongruous product situations can be shown graphically? Verbally?

Can we find humor in the complete reversal of anticipated product uses or benefits?

**Test the big things** Whether testable ideas come out of pure research, brainstorming, or self-developed creativity, the same picture applies: *test the big things*. Trivia testing, e.g., testing the tilt of a postage stamp or testing the effect of various colors of paper stock, are passe. Breakthroughs are possible only when you test the big things. Six big areas from which breakthroughs emerge are:

1. The products or services you offer
2. The media you use (lists, print, and broadcast)
3. The propositions you make
4. The copy platforms you use
5. The formats you use
6. The timing you choose

Five of these areas for testing appear on most published lists these days. But testing new products and new product features is rarely recommended. Yet everything starts with the product or service you offer.

Many direct marketers religiously test new ads, new mailing packages, new media, new copy approaches, new formats, and new timing schedules season after season with never a thought to testing new product features. Finally, the most imaginative of creative approaches fails to overcome the waning appeal of the same old product. And still another product bites the dust.

This need not happen. For example, consider the most commonplace of mail order items, the address label. Scores of firms offer them in black ink on standard white stock. Competition is keen: prices all run about the same. From this variety of competitive styles, however, a few emerge with new product features: gold stock, colored ink, seasonal borders, and so forth. Tests are made to determine appeal. The new product features appeal to a bigger audience.

Thinking up new product features and testing for appeal is one way to go. As mentioned, pure research is another and usually more reliable route to follow. Here are some of the questions research can answer about any product or service:

What features in your product or service are favored over those of the competition?

What features offered by the competition are favored over yours?

What new features, not now available, would the consumer like to see in your product or service?

How much more does the consumer believe he would be willing to pay for additional features?

How do your prices compare with the competition's?

More often than not, product research isn't even considered until sales volume falls through the floor. Then, in desperation, someone says, "Maybe we should hire a research outfit to find out what's wrong."

Let's take the case of a successful direct marketer who had enjoyed a consistent 15 percent sales growth for ten consecutive years. Then, bang! Sales dropped 30 percent in the eleventh year. What happened? Competition moved in. Competition with features the originator did not have. So, with the disaster flags up, a research firm was hired. Research showed clearly that the competition had three highly favored major features our marketer didn't have. These features were adapted and improved and two additional features, unearthed through research, were added. Presto! Sales leaped 40 percent the very next season. An important moral appears here: Don't wait for your competition to force you to research your product or service. It might be too late.

## Use projectable mailing sample sizes

Back in the "good old days" when testing was in its infancy, members of the direct mail family lived by faulty test figures. They would mail 1,000 packages of one version of a mailing, and another 1,000 pieces changing one variable, and then they would naively place their faith in the results. Statisticians point out that the differences in results between these minimal mailing quantities are meaningless. For example, if mailing A pulled 1 percent and mailing B pulled 1.2 percent—a difference of 20 percent—no confidence can be placed in the differences. A statistically valid sample, might, in fact, show that mailing A did 40 percent better than mailing B.

A careful study of the tables in chapter 4 will indicate that certain percentages of expected response at certain error limits require fantastic test quantities. Statistical accuracy for certain expected responses at certain error limits could require budgets well beyond the realm of practicality. For instance, statistical accuracy might conceivably require 100,000 mailing pieces on each side of a test. If you were testing six different packages, each against the control package, a total of 1.2 million mailing pieces, would be required and the total test budget would be in the neighborhood of $180,000. Obviously impractical.

Orlan Gaeddert, specialist in circulation research at Time-Life for 16 years, gave some alternatives to this problem in an interview with Rose Harper, president of Lewis Kleid Company. Asked, When are large samples necessary; when are small ones adequate? Gaeddert responds as follows:

The proper sample size is determined by two factors, the normal variation that is anticipated for any random sample and the degree of risk that the user is willing to accept.

You can always make your sampling tolerance as small as you like by increasing the sample size. Do keep in mind, however, that to cut the tolerance in half, you must increase the sample fourfold. This axiom holds for two random samples drawn in exactly the same way.

The risk factor requires subjective judgment. When you know your product and market, you can accept the larger risks of relatively small samples. When trying a new product or a novel promotional concept, it is desirable to minimize risks by running larger tests—perhaps retesting—before making a decision.

The acceptable risk is also conditioned by what you are testing. Low markups require larger samples because there is little room for error. Price tests demand high accuracy and large samples. A large sample is needed initially if you want to track payments or later purchases.

When profit potential is small, which is often true of "one shots," it is not worth using large samples or extensive retesting. Occasionally a new product test or an experiment with a new procedure has very high costs. You may, for example, wish to minimize exposure in the marketplace. In such instances, one must take calculated risks and use minimum-size samples. When testing two packages with roughly similar costs, you can stand rather large sampling tolerances. If the costs are quite different, the solution is complicated.

To the question, How big is the variation for typical samples?, Gaeddert responds:

Chances are that the tolerances for your tests are wider than you think. Assuming that your testing procedures are well controlled and that you are using perfect Nth names samples, a typical test of 10,000 names should pull within 10 percent of the true value about two-thirds of the time. The other one-third of your tests will be off by 10 to 20 percent. In only 38 percent of your tests can you hope to be within 5 percent (plus or minus) of the true value. If you don't have the ideal Nth name sample or have more than the normal number of blemishes in the procedure, your tolerances will be wider than this, perhaps much wider.

The example assumes a 1 percent response from a 10,000 mailing for a total of 100 orders. The easiest way to approximate the expected variation for this situation is: 1 standard deviation = square root of the number of orders. Next, from a normal probability table you find that 68 percent of the errors should fall within one standard deviation (high or low) from the true value. Other formulas apply to other sampling into four or five sub-samples. You will get a vivid demonstration of sample variation.

Where does this leave the old adage about needing 100 orders from a test? Well, if you can live with results that might easily be off by 10 to 15 percent, use a guideline. The point is that you must decide how much risk you can accept for various test situations. Then choose the sample sizes that suit you instead of those that fit somebody else.

If you still insist on using someone else's rules, the following seem to strike the right balance between cost and risk for a variety of direct mail situations:

Packages, promotion concepts . . 10,000 to 25,000 per panel

Price tests . . . . . . . . . . . . . . . . . . . 50,000 to 100,000 per panel
5,000 is a practical unit for a
straight list test. Regression tests
may require 50,000 or more.

To the question, How can direct marketers get more out of list tests? Gaeddert responds:

I find that experience is the great teacher in list testing. Sampling theory can't apply very well when dealing with nonrandom samples, interlist duplication, and the host of other messy problems one encounters. So, by all means tap the hard-won knowledge your list broker has.

List testing is like using a flour sifter with a coarse screen. That is why sequential sampling is a sound and universal practice. If a small sample looks promising, try a bigger bite. Then another chunk if that holds up. Incidentally, sampling variation runs both ways. So if a list has a good track record but looks a little weak in the current test, it too may be worth a retest.

When testing outside mail order lists, a standard sample unit of 5,000 names is practical. In some cases you may go lower, thus buying a limited amount of information about a greater range of lists for the same total test expenditure. I would not, however, test a list with less than 2,500.

A sample of more than 10,000 is seldom justifiable. Believe it or not, the proportion of the list used in testing has hardly any effect on sample variation, unless you test more than one quarter of the total.

On the other hand, when testing the very largest lists—especially compiled lists—you are probably searching for a few segments that work. This may involve a regression test or other advanced statistical techniques. A test of 50,000 would be a good starter, 25,000 an absolute minimum. Sometimes 100,000 or more names are necessary.

**Testing components vs. testing mailing packages**

In the endless search for breakthroughs, the question continually arises: In direct mail, should we test components or mailing packages? There are two schools of thought on this. The prevailing one is that the big breakthroughs come about through the testing of completely different mailing packages as opposed to testing individual components within a mailing package. Something can be learned from each procedure, of course. In my opinion, however, the more logical procedure is to first find the big difference in mailing packages and then follow with tests of individual components in the losing packages, which can often make the winning packages even better.

In package testing, one starts with a complete concept and builds all the components to fit the image of the concept. Consider the differences between these two package concepts:

|  | Package 1 | Package 2 |
|---|---|---|
| Envelope: | 9 × 12 | #10 |
| Letter: | 8-page, stapled | 4-sheet (two sides) computer-written |

|            | **Package 1**              | **Package 2**         |
|------------|----------------------------|-----------------------|
| Circular:  | None                       | 4-page, illustrated   |
| Order form:| 8½ × 11, perforated stub   | 8½ × 3⅔               |

The differences between these two package concepts are considerable. Chances are great that there will be a substantial difference in response. Once the winning package evolves, component tests make excellent sense. Let us say the 9 × 12 package is the winner. A logical subsequent test would be to fold the same inserts into a 6 × 9 envelope. A reply envelope may be considered as an additional test. Computerizing the first page of the eight-page letter could be still another test.

**Questionnaire mailings**

The questionnaire is a research device long used by those engaged in direct marketing. Questionnaires are used for many purposes. This list is indicative of the numerous applications.

- Why merchandise was returned
- Why a customer didn't place a repeat order
- What a customer likes about your merchandise or service
- Whether delivery was prompt and satisfactory
- What other products or services might be desired
- Whether friends might be interested in the same products or service
- The preferable way to buy: cash or commercial credit cards and which credit cards
- The demographics and psychographics of customers
- What publications prospects or customers read
- If a consumable product, the rate at which the product is consumed

It isn't unusual to get responses of 20, 30, 50 percent and more from a questionnaire mailing, particularly to customers. The percentage of response tends to increase considerably when the recipient is told that is is not necessary to sign the questionnaire when returning it. By granting the option of signing or not, the total response is higher. Those who do sign sometimes provide testimonials and are often interested in learning the results of the findings.

To give an example of the research value of a questionnaire mailing, let's take the case of *Advertising Age*. In the fall of 1977 the publication introduced its first home study program titled, "The *Advertising Age* Professional Development Program in Advertising." The program was a huge success.

Following proper direct marketing procedures, *Advertising Age* asked its staff this question: What other home study programs might we develop for our market? The editorial department came up with a number of suggested home study programs. So the next logical question was: Which programs might have the greatest appeal? To answer these questions, *Advertising Age* staff members developed a questionnaire which they mailed to 10 percent of the readership of *Advertising Age*. The questionnaire, as filled in by a typical respondent, is shown in Exhibit 15.1.

The survey clearly indicated a stong interest in sales promotion, advertis-

**Exhibit 15.1.** *Advertising Age* in-house training program questionnaire.

# Advertising Age In-House Training Program Questionnaire.

RETURN TO:

CRAIN BOOKS DIVISION
Advertising Age
740 North Rush Street
Chicago, Illinois 60611

The publishers of Advertising Age are currently formulating plans for a total of nine new in-house training programs, each designed to help people in advertising and marketing improve their professional skills in a particular area.

Your opinions and suggestions can be of immeasurable value in helping us organize our priorities. Can you, therefore, use the checklist below to tell us which of these programs you feel should be developed first. Please rank the nine programs numerically in your order of preference and add any other suggestions you wish for programs not listed here.

1. ☒ Advertising Copywriting.
2. ☒ Graphic Arts Production.
   ☐ Sales Promotion & Merchandising.
   ☐ Publicity & Public Relations.
     ☐ High Performance Business Writing.

☐ Direct Marketing.
☐ Advertising Media.
☐ Consumerism & the Marketplace.
☐ Advertising Research.

☐ Others: *How about mini-courses in presentation techniques? These could be geared for jr. agency staffers*

Comments: *I'd like to see writers trained with an interdisciplinary approach including media, account service and research units. Most writers who train "in house" get no exposure to these important areas.*

☐ OPTIONAL: Check here only if you would like to receive further information on these programs as they are developed.

Information to be sent to: _____

    Name                Title

    Company

    Street Address

    City/State/Zip

MB/pd

ing media, copywriting, and research thus giving *Advertising Age* a clear direction for development of future programs. Also significant was the fact that 76 percent of the respondents (an unusually high figure) signed the questionnaire and 69 percent of the respondents expressed an interest in receiving information about future programs.

*Advertising Age* received a 10.5 percent response to the questionnaire mailing. Votes for suggested programs ranked as follows:

| | Rank | Responses |
|---|---|---|
| Sales Promotion and Merchandising | 1 | 3,235 |
| Advertising Media | 2 | 3,105 |
| Advertising Copywriting | 3 | 3,092 |
| Advertising Research | 4 | 3,079 |
| Direct Marketing | 5 | 2,654 |
| Consumerism & the Marketplace | 6 | 2,582 |
| Publicity and Public Relations | 7 | 2,481 |
| Graphic Arts Production | 8 | 2,311 |
| High Performance Business Writing | 9 | 2,015 |

**How to test print advertising**

For direct marketing practitioners who are multimedia users, testing print advertising is just as important as testing direct mail. And, as with direct mail, it is important that the tests be constructed in such a way as to produce valid results.

Gerald Schreck, media director of Doubleday Advertising Company, New York, gave the following pointers on A/B split tests in the July 12, 1976 issue of *Advertising Age*.

**How to test your print ads with four kinds of splits**

The split helps you determine the relative strengths of different ads. For example, you can run two ads, A and B, in a specific issue or edition of a publication such that two portions of the total run are equally divided and identical in circulation. The only difference is that ad A will run in half of the issue and ad B will run in the other half. For measuring the strength of the ads, a split includes an offer requiring your reader to act by writing or sending in a coupon. Then all you need do is compare the responses with the individual ads. If done properly this method can be accurate to two decimal points. You also have the advantage of real-world testing to find out what people actually do, not just what they say they'll do. And, because all factors are held equal, the difference in results can be attributed directly to your advertising. (See Exhibit 15.2).

*A-B splits.* In an ideal situation, any issue of a split-run publication will carry ad A in every other copy with ad B in the alternate copies.

*Clump splits.* Most often, however, publications cannot produce an exact A-B split. They will promise a clump. That is, every lift of 50 copies, for instance, will be evenly split or even every lift of 25 or 10. The clump can be very accurate when the test is done in large circulations.

*Flip-flops.* For publications that offer no split at all, you can create your own. Take two comparable publications, X and Y. Run ad A in X and ad B in

Y for the first phase. Then for the second phase, reverse the insertions: Ad B in X and Ad A in Y. Total the respective results for A and B and compare.

*The split that isn't.* We recently asked one magazine publisher if he ran splits. The production manager told us, "Oh, yes, we run a perfect split. Our circulation divides exacly—one-half east of the Mississippi and one-half west." Look out. That is not a valid split.

While the A-B split can't tell you why individuals respond to your ad, the technique can tell you what they responded to. And a real bonus is that when you have completed your tests, you'll have a list of solid prospects.

## Twelve ways to key an ad

In an A-B split, how can you compare one run against another run of the same ad? You can "key" coupons or response copy by:

1. *Dating.* On your coupons, try JA379NA for January 3, 1979, in *Newsweek* for ad A and JA 379NB for the same insertion of ad B.
2. *Department numbers.* Use Dept. A for ad A and Dept. B for B in your company's address.
3. *Color of coupon.* One color for A, another for B.
4. *Color of ink.*
5. *Names.* In ad A, ask readers to send correspondence to Mr. Anderson, For B, have them write to Mr. Brown.
6. *Telephone numbers.*
7. *Shape of coupon.*
8. *IBM punches.* You don't even need a computer. Just select a pattern you can read.
9. *The obvious.* Right on the coupon, use "For Readers of *Glamour*" in A and "For *Glamour* Readers" in B.
10. *Address information.* Mr., Mrs., Miss in A, Mr. Ms. for B.
11. *Abbreviations.* In your address, New York for A, N.Y. for B.
12. *Typeface.* In coupon A, all caps for NAME, etc., and in coupon B, upper- and lower-case for Name, etc.

The possibilities are virtually unlimited. All you need is a code that's in keeping with your ad and the publication, one you find is easy to understand and use.

**Exhibit 15.2.
Variations in use of splits.**

| A |
|---|
| B |
| A |
| B |

A-B Split

| A |
|---|
| A |
| A |
| B |
| B |
| B |

Clump Split

| A |
|---|
| B |
| B |
| A |

Flip-flop Split

## Telescopic testing

While it is certainly necessary to construct meaningful A-B split tests, they do have limitations. When the advertiser runs an A-B split test he doesn't know what would have happened if he had been able to run ad C against ads A and B and, additionally, ads D, E, F, and G—all simultaneously, all in the same edition, all under measurable conditions.

Today, testing to find the best ad among a multiplicity of ads all tested under the same conditions is quite feasible. The method is widely known as *telescopic testing.* Telescopic testing is simply the process of telescoping an entire season of test ads into one master test program. (Examples of telescopic testing were given in chapters 11 and 12.) Regional editions of publications and other developments make telescopic testing possible. Indeed, with regional editions you can telescope a year's testing sequences into a single insertion, testing many ads simultaneously. *TV Guide* offers the best opportunity for telescopic testing. *TV Guide* publishes 84 different regional editions. *Woman's Day* offers 26 regional editions. *Time,* with 8 regional editions, makes it possible to test nine different ads or ad variations simultaneously.

Tom Collins, a pioneer in telescopic testing, has established a rule of thumb for estimating the minimum circulation you should buy for your ad tests to make results meaningful. First, start by assuming you need an average of 200 responses per appeal to be statistically valid. Then, multiply your allowable advertising cost per response by 200. Finally, multiply that figure by the number of key numbers in the test. This will give you the total minimum expenditure required to get meaningful results.

To clarify the technique further, let's say you want to test four new ads against a control ad, which we will call ad A. Your tests for the four new ads against the control ad will be structured as follows: A vs. B; A vs. C; A vs. D; A vs. E. Thus we have a total of five ads requiring eight different keys. (Ad A, the control ad, is being tested against a different ad in four separate instances and therefore requires four different keys.)

To read the results in this kind of test, we simply convert ad A to 100 percent, depending on the results achieved. In this way, ad C can be compared with ad E, for instance, even though they are not directly tested against one another. Now, let's say we want to test the four new ads in *TV Guide* against the control ad. Further, using the Collins formula, let's assume we need a circulation of two million to get 200 or more replies for each side of each two-way split. Here's the type of schedule that would be placed in *TV Guide* to accomplish the objective. Note that a careful review of the markets selected for each split (region) shows that all markets are balanced geographically.

| Split 1—Ad A vs. Ad B | | Split 2—Ad A vs. Ad C | |
|---|---|---|---|
| Edition | Circulation | Edition | Circulation |
| SSan Francisco Metro | 750,000 | Northern Wisconsin | 170,000 |
| Pittsburgh | 225,000 | Philadelphia | 230,000 |
| Detroit | 225,000 | Cleveland | 55,000 |
| South Georgia | 67,000 | Kansas City | 230,000 |
| Iowa | 210,000 | Western New England | 175,000 |
| Phoenix | 275,000 | North Carolina | 272,000 |
| Western Illinois | 87,000 | Colorado | 139,000 |
| Northern Indiana | 186,000 | Illinois/Wisconsin | 225,000 |
| | 2,025,000 | Gulf Coast | 125,000 |
| | | Minneapolis/St. Paul | 126,000 |
| | | Central California | 115,000 |
| | | Southeast Texas | 64,000 |
| | | West Virginia | 165,000 |
| | | | 2,091,000 |

## Split 3—Ad A vs. Ad D

| Edition | Circulation |
|---|---|
| Central Ohio | 210,000 |
| Michigan State | 309,000 |
| Western New York State | 65,000 |
| Central Indiana | 230,000 |
| San Diego | 255,000 |
| New Hampshire | 141,000 |
| Portland | 195,000 |
| Eastern Virginia | 160,000 |
| Kansas State | 92,000 |
| Tuscon | 70,000 |
| North Dakota | 65,000 |
| Eastern Washington St. | 145,000 |
| Evansville-Paducah | 104,000 |
| | 2,041,000 |

## Split 4—Ad A. vs. Ad E

| Edition | Circulation |
|---|---|
| Eastern New England | 665,000 |
| Chicago Metro | 475,000 |
| Orlando | 140,000 |
| Oklahoma State | 184,000 |
| St. Louis | 235,000 |
| Eastern Illinois | 100,000 |
| Missouri | 141,000 |
| Eugene | 45,000 |
| Idaho | 57,000 |
| | 2,042,000 |

A recap of this test reads as follows: five simultaneous ad tests, distributed among 43 markets, with a total circulation of 8,199,000, at a total cost of $23,650, or a cost per thousand of $2.88. Historically, winning ads from this type of test can be determined within two to three weeks of issue date.

Telescopic testing is not limited to regional editions of publications. Newspaper inserts serve as an ideal vehicle for such testing. The test pieces are intermixed at the printing plant before being shipped to the newspaper. All test pieces, however, must be exactly the same size. Otherwise, newspapers cannot handle them on their automatic inserting equipment.

Using full-page card inserts in magazines is still another way to test simultaneously a multiplicity of ads. Scores of magazines now accept such inserts. It is important to remember that in telescopic testing we are looking for breakthroughs, not small differences. As Collins puts it, "We are not merely testing ads, we are testing hypotheses. Then when a hypothesis appears to have been proved by the results, it is often possible to construct other, even more successful ads, on the same hypothesis."

Test hypotheses tend to fall into four main categories:

1. What is the best price and offer?
2. Who is the best prospect?
3. What is the most appealing product advantage?
4. What is the most important ultimate benefit? (By "ultimate benefit" we mean the satisfaction of such basic human needs as pride, admiration, safety, wealth, peace of mind, and so on.)

Old American Insurance Company of Kansas City, Missouri, is a prime example of an advertiser who uses hypotheses in determining the type of ads to be developed for telescopic testing. The company developed a free Social Security Fact Kit which they offered to send to anyone requesting information about their Guaranteed Issue Life Insurance. Five ads were developed, as illustrated in Exhibit 15.3.

**Exhibit 15.3. These five ads for Old American Insurance Company were tested in a single issue of *TV Guide*.**

# FREE!

## Social Security Fact Kit

It's yours without cost or obligation if you're 50 to 80

What you don't know about Social Security could cost you thousands of dollars now or in the years ahead! Send today for your free SOCIAL SECURITY FACT KIT—Handbook, Benefit Calculator and Earnings Request Form. It's a public service offer from . . .

**Old American Insurance Company**
4900 Oak Street. Dept. M-251
Kansas City, Missouri 64141

**Ad A**

## Over 50... and need more life insurance

### WE GUARANTEE TO ISSUE YOU A POLICY

if you're between 50 and 80—regardless of your health condition—even if you've been turned down elsewhere!

**Send for free details.**

Along with them you'll receive a FREE 3-piece SOCIAL SECURITY FACT KIT. It explains the benefits you may be entitled to—perhaps *now*—and how to collect them! Write to:

**Old American Insurance Company**
4900 Oak Street, Dept. M-252
Kansas City, Missouri 64141

**Ad B**

## Will you get all the benefits you're entitled to?

*You may not*—unless you know what benefits are available and how to apply for them!

Find out—with the 3-part SOCIAL SECURITY FACT KIT, offered to persons 50 to 80 as a *free* public service! Write:

**Old American Insurance Company**
4900 Oak Street, Dept. M-253
Kansas City, Missouri 64141

**Ad C**

# FREE Social Security facts now available by mail.

**Kansas City, Mo.**—You may be entitled to Social Security benefits you don't even know about! How can you find out?

Read the newest edition of "Your Social Security Handbook." The handbook, a benefit calculator and an earnings request form make up the free Social Security Fact Kit, offered to persons 50 to 80 as a public service.

There's absolutely no obligation on your part. For your free kit, write to:

**Old American Insurance Company**
4900 Oak Street, Dept. M-254
Kansas City, Missouri 64141

**Ad D**

# People 50-80

## FREE KIT helps you get all the Social Security benefits you're entitled to!

Thousands of dollars may be yours right now—or in the years ahead. Don't miss out! Send today for your free SOCIAL SECURITY FACT KIT—Handbook, Benefit Calculator and Earnings Request Form. It's a public service offer to persons 50 to 80 years old. Write to:

**Old American Insurance Company**
4900 Oak Street, Dept. M-255
Kansas City, Missouri 64141

**Ad E**

These five quarter-page ads were tested in a single issue of *TV Guide*. Combined circulation from the selected regions was 2,969,303. Total cost for the five-way test was $2,931, including split-run charges of $1,000. The control was ad A which was split-tested in each region against all other ads. Rating control ad A as 100, here are comparative results: Ad A—100, Ad B—6.5, Ad C—40.4, Ad D—62.4, Ad E—38.9.

Note the tremendous difference in relative response. The story does not end there. The telescopic test merely indicated which ad pulled the greatest number of inquiries. To determine the true efficiency of each of the test ads, Old American Insurance Company tracked the process to the final result, actual sales of life insurance. Ad A—the big winner front-end—performed poorly at the back end. In actuality, the best lead ad, from a final cost point, fell between the best lead response and the poorest lead response. Telescopic testing found the best ad from a front-end response standpoint: careful tracking by keys revealed the best ad from a sales efficiency standpoint.

Research and testing are the backbones of a highly successful direct marketing operation. Good luck in all your efforts!

**Self-quiz**

1. Name the three basic types of research that can be applied to direct marketing.

   a. _____

   b. _____

   c. _____

2. What are the three phases of the brainstorming process?

   a. _____

   _____

   _____

   b. _____

   _____

   _____

   c. _____

   _____

   _____

3. What is lateral thinking?

   _____

   _____

   _____

   _____

4. What are the six big factors to test?

   a. _____

   b. _____

   c. _____

   d. _____

   e. _____

   f. _____

5. Low markups require
   ☐ small test samples    ☐ large test samples

6. Short of using probability tables ☐ 5,000    ☐ 10,000 is a practical unit for a straight list test.

7. Which is more desirable?
   ☐ Testing components of mailing packages?
   ☐ Testing complete mailing packages?

8. Name five applications for questionnaires.

   a. _____

   b. _____

   c. _____

   d. _____

   e. _____

9. Name six ways to key a print ad.

   a. _____

   b. _____

   c. _____

   d. _____

   e. _____

   f. _____

10. Define telescopic testing.

    _____

    _____

    _____

    _____

11. Name the four categories into which test hypotheses seem to fall.

    a. _____

    b. _____

    c. _____

    d. _____

## Pilot project

You have a list of 100,000 customers who have bought from your consumer merchandise catalog. But, as is often the case, you know little about your customers except that they have bought from you. The time has come to draw a profile. Construct a questionnaire designed to determine both the demographics and psychographics (lifestyle) of your customers.

# Appendix

**Operating guidelines for ethical business practice**

The future of direct marketing will depend greatly on how direct marketers deal with consumers. To promote a fair, long-term relationship between consumers and marketers, the Direct Mail/Marketing Association maintains a watchdog committee to formulate fair standards of practice for direct marketing. These standards of ethical practice appear below.

1. Advertisers/marketers, whether selling products or services or raising funds for nonprofit organizations, should make their offers clear and honest. They should not misrepresent a product, service, publication or program and should not use misleading, partially true or exaggerated statements. All descriptions and promises should be in accordance with actual conditions, situations and circumstances existing at the time a mailing is made. Advertisers/marketers, whether selling products or services or raising funds for nonprofit organizations, should operate in accordance with the Better Business Bureau's basic principles contained in the BBB Code of Advertising and be cognizant of and adhere to the Postal Laws and Regulations, and all other laws governing advertising and transaction of business by mail.

2. Advertisers/marketers should not make offers which purport to require a person to return a notice that he or she does not wish to receive further merchandise in order to avoid liability for the purchase price, unless all the conditions are first made clear in an initial offer that is accepted by the purchaser by means of a bona fide written order. Attention is suggested to more detailed specifications regarding negative option plans which have been formulated by the Federal Trade Commission.

3. Mailings should not contain vulgar, immoral, profane or offensive matter nor should advertisers/marketers use the mails to promote the sale of pornographic material or other matter not acceptable for mailing on moral grounds. Advertisers/marketers, whether selling products or services or raising funds for nonprofit organizations, should not use the mails to promote the sale of products or services by means of a lottery.

4. Advertisers/marketers, whether selling products or services or raising funds for nonprofit organizations, should not disparage any person or group on ground of sex, race, color, creed, age or nationality.

5. The terms and conditions of guarantee should be clearly and specifically set forth in immediate conjunction with the guarantee offer. Guarantees should be limited to the reasonable performance capabilities and qualities of the product or service advertised.

6. Advertisers/marketers should not make exaggerated price comparisons, claims on discounts or savings; nor employ fictitious prices.

7. A product or service which is offered without cost or obligation to the recipient may be unqualifiedly described as "free." "Free" may also be used conditionally where the offer requires the recipient to purchase some other product or service, provided all terms and conditions are accurately and conspicuously disclosed in immediate conjunction with the use of the term "free" and the product or service required to be purchased is not increased in price or decreased in quality or quantity.

8. Photographs and artwork representing or implying representation of a product or service or fund raising program for nonprofit organizations should be faithful reproductions of the product, service or aid offered by the fund raising program. All should be current and truly representative. All descriptions and promises should be in accordance with actual conditions, situations, and circumstances existing at the time of the promotion. Photographs and artwork representing or implying situations related to a product, service or program should be in accord with the facts. If models are used, clear disclosure of that fact should be made in immediate conjunction with the portrayal.

9. If laboratory test data are used in advertising, they should be competent as to source and methodology. Advertisers/marketers should not use excerpts or laboratory test material in support of claims which distort or fail to disclose the true test results.

10. Advertisers/marketers, whether selling products or services or raising funds for nonprofit organizations, should not use unsupported or inaccurate statistical data or testimonials; or testimonials originally given for products or services other than those offered by such advertisers/marketers; or testimonials making statements or conclusions known to be incorrect. If testimonials are used, they should contain no misstatement of facts or misleading implications and should reflect the current opinion of the author.

11. Advertisers/marketers who sell instruction, catalogs, or merchandise-for-resale or sell or rent mailing lists should not use misleading or deceptive statements with respect to the earnings possibilities, lack of risk, or ease of operation.

12. Advertisers/marketers, whether selling products or services or raising funds for nonprofit organizations, should not use promotional solicitations in the form of bills or invoices (pro forma invoices) deceptively.

13. Advertisers/marketers, whether selling products or services or raising funds for nonprofit organizations, should not mail unordered merchandise for which payment is demanded.

14. Advertisers/marketers, whether selling products or services or raising funds for nonprofit organizations, should not use any list in violation of the lawful rights of the list owner; and should promptly bring to the attention of the lawful owner of any list any information they may have regarding any possible violation of his proprietary rights therein.

15. Advertisers/marketers, whether selling products or services or raising funds for nonprofit organizations, who permit the outside use of their mailing lists should at all times be aware it is not in the best interests of the public or of themselves to allow their lists to be used by organizations that do not observe the DMMA Guidelines for Ethical Business Practices.

16. Advertisers/marketers, whether selling products or services or raising funds for nonprofit organizations, who rent, exchange or purchase mailing lists should make every effort to ascertain the origin, current ownership and market profile of such mailing lists in the interests of directing their promotions only to those segments of the public most likely to be interested in their causes or to have a use for their products or services.

17. When products or services are offered on a satisfaction guaranteed or money back basis, any refunds requested should be made promptly. In an unqualified offer of refund or replacement, the customer's preference shall prevail.

18. Advertisers/marketers should be prepared to make prompt delivery of orders solicited in their copy. Unforeseen contingencies should be reported to the customer promptly when delivery is unavoidably delayed. A reply device should be included, enabling the customer, if he or she wishes, to cancel the order and obtain a refund of any purchase price already paid.

19. Advertisers/marketers, whether selling products or services or raising funds for nonprofit organizations, should not use misleading or deceptive methods for collecting money owed by delinquent accounts.

20. Advertisers/marketers should distribute products only in a manner that will provide reasonable safeguards against possibilities of injury to children and/or adults.

21. Advertisers/marketers who are raising funds for nonprofit organizations should make no percentage or commission arrangements whereby any person or firm assisting or participating in a fund raising activity is paid a fee proportionate to the funds raised, nor should they solicit for non-existent or non-functioning organizations.

22. All advertisers/marketers including those firms who use, create, produce or supply materials and/or lists for direct mail advertising should make conscientious efforts to remove names from their mailing lists when so requested either directly or in accordance with the DMMA Mail Preference Service.

# Glossary

**ACG.** See Address coding guide.

**Action devices.** Items and techniques used in a mailing to initiate the desired responses.

**Active buyer.** A buyer (see Buyer) whose latest purchase was made within the last 12 months.

**Active member.** Any member (see Member) who is fulfilling the original commitment or who has fulfilled that commitment and has made one or more purchases in the last 12 months.

**Actives.** Customers on a list who have made purchases within a prescribed time period, usually not more than one year. Also subscribers whose subscriptions have not expired.

**Active subscriber.** One who has committed himself for regular delivery of magazines, books, or other goods or services for a period of time still in effect.

**Add-on service.** Service of the Direct Mail/Marketing Association which gives consumers an opportunity to request that their names be added to mailing lists.

**Address coding guide (ACG).** Contains the actual or potential beginning and ending house numbers, block group or enumeration district numbers, ZIP codes, and other geographic codes for all city delivery service streets served by 3,154 post offices located within 6,601 ZIP code areas.

**Address correction requested.** An endorsement which, when printed in the upper left-hand corner of the address portion of the mailing piece (below the return address), authorizes the U.S. Postal Service, for a fee, to provide the new address (where known) of a person no longer at the address on the mailing piece.

**AIDA.** The most popular formula for the preparation of direct mail copy. The letters stand for Get Attention, Arouse Interest, Stimulate Desire, Ask for Action.

**Assigned mailing dates.** The dates on which the list user has the obligation to mail a specific list. No other date is acceptable without specific approval of the list owner.

**Audit.** A printed report of the counts in a particular list or file.

**Back end.** The activities necessary to complete a mail order transaction once an order has been received, or the measurement of a buyer's performance after he has ordered the first item in a series offering.

**Bangtail.** A promotional envelope with a second flap which is perforated and designed for use as an order blank.

**Bill enclosure.** A promotional piece or notice enclosed with a bill, an invoice, or a statement which is not directed toward the collection of all or part of the bill, invoice, or statement.

**Bingo card.** A reply card inserted in a publication and used by readers to request literature and samples from companies whose products and services are either advertised or mentioned in editorial columns.

**Bounce back.** An offer enclosed with mailings sent to a customer in fulfillment of an order.

**Broadcast media.** A direct response source which includes radio, television, and cable television.

**Broadside.** A single sheet of paper, printed on one or both sides, folded for mailing or direct distribution, and opening into a single, large advertisement.

**Brochure.** Strictly, a high-quality pamphlet with specially planned layout, typography, and illustrations. The term is also used loosely for any promotional pamphlet or booklet.

**Bucktag.** A separate slip attached to a printed piece containing instructions to route the material to specific individuals.

**Bulk mail.** A category of third class mail covering a large quantity of identical pieces but addressed to different names which are specially processed for mailing before delivery to the post office.

**Business list.** Any compilation or list of persons or companies based on a business-associated interest, inquiry, membership, subscription, or purchase.

**Buyer.** A person who orders merchandise, books, records, information, or services. Unless another modifying word or two is used, it is assumed that a buyer has paid for all merchandise to date.

**Cash buyer.** A buyer who encloses payment with order.

**Cash rider.** Also called "cash up" or "cash option" in which an order form offers installment terms, but a postscript offers the option of sending full cash payment with order, usually at a saving over the credit price as an incentive.

**C/A.** Change of address.

**Catalog.** A book or booklet showing merchandise with descriptive details and prices.

**Catalog buyer.** A person who has bought products or services from a catalog.

**Catalog request (paid or unpaid).** A request for a catalog by a prospective buyer. The catalog may be free, or there may be a nominal charge for postage and handling, or there may be a more substantial charge which is often refunded or credited on the first order.

**Census tract.** A geographical area established by local committees and approved by the U.S. Census Bureau which contains a population segment with relatively uniform economic and social characteristics with clearly identifiable boundaries about 1,200 households.

**Cheshire labels.** Specially prepared paper (rolls, fanfold, or accordion fold) used to reproduce names and addresses to be mechanically affixed, one at a time, to a mailing piece.

**Circulars.** A general term for printed advertising in any form, including printed matter sent out by direct mail.

**Cleaning.** The process of correcting or removing a name and address from a mailing list because it is no longer correct or because the listing is to be shifted from one category to another.

**Cluster selection.** A selection procedure based on taking a group of names in series, skipping a group, taking another group, and so on. For example, a cluster selection on an Nth name basis might be the first 10 out of every 100 or the first 125 out of 175. A cluster selection using limited ZIP codes might be the first 200 names in each of the specified ZIP codes.

**Coding.** (1) Identifying devices used on reply devices to identify the mailing list or other source from which the address was obtained. (2) A structure of letters and numbers used to classify characteristics of an address on a list.

**Collate.** (1) To assemble individual elements of a mailing in sequence for inserting into a mailing envelope. (2) A program that combines two or more ordered files to produce a single ordered file. Also the act of combining such files. Synonymous with merge as in merge-purge.

**Compiled lists.** Names and addresses derived from such sources as directories, newspapers, public records, retail sales slips, and trade-show registrations to identify groups of people who have something in common.

**Compiler.** An organization that develops lists of names and addresses from directories, newspapers, public records, registrations and other sources, identifying groups of people, companies, or institutions with something in common.

**Complete cancel.** Refers to a person who has completed a specific commitment to buy products or services before canceling.

**Comprehensive.** Complete and detailed layout for a printed piece. Also: "comp," "compre."

**Computer compatibility.** The ability to use data or programs of one computer system on one or more other computer systems.

**Computer letter.** A computer-printed letter providing personalized fill-in information from a source file in predesignated positions in the letter. It may also be a full printed letter with personalized insertions.

**Computer personalization.** Printing of letters or other promotional pieces by a computer using names, addresses, special phrases, or other information based on data appearing in one or more computer records. The objective is to make use of the information in the computer record to tailor the promotional message to a specific individual.

**Computer service bureau.** An internal or external facility providing general or specific data processing services.

**Consumer list.** A list of names (usually with home address) compiled or resulting from a common inquiry or buying activity indicating a general or specific buying interest.

**Continuity program.** Products or services bought as a series of small purchases rather than all at one time. Generally based on a common theme and shipped at·regular or specific time intervals.

**Contributor list.** Names and addresses of persons who have donated to a specific fund-raising effort.

**Controlled circulation.** Distribution at no charge of a publication to individuals or companies on the basis of their title or occupation. Typically, recipients are asked from time to time to verify the information that qualifies them to receive the publication.

**Controlled duplication.** A method by which names and addresses from two or more lists are matched (usually by computer) to eliminate or limit extra mailings to the same name and address.

**Conversion.** The process of changing from one method of data processing to another or from one data processing system to another. Synonymous with Reformatting.

**Conversion.** Securing specific action such as a purchase or contribution from a name on a mailing list or as a result of an inquiry.

**Co-op mailing.** A mailing in which two or more offers are included in the same envelope or other carrier with each participating mailer sharing mailing costs according to a predetermined formula.

**Cost per inquiry (CPI).** A simple arithmetical formula—total cost of mailing or advertisement divided by the number of inquiries received.

**Cost per order (CPO).** Similar to Cost per inquiry except based on actual orders rather than inquiries.

**Cost per thousand (CPM).** Refers to total cost per thousand pieces of direct mail "in the mail."

**CPI.** See Cost per inquiry.

**CPO.** See Cost per order.

**CPM.** See Cost per thousand.

**Coupon.** A portion of a promotion piece of advertisement intended to be filled in by an inquirer or customer and returned to the advertiser to complete the action intended.

**Coupon clipper.** A person who has given evidence of responding to free or nominal-cost offers out of curiosity with little or no serious interest or buying intent.

**Deadbeat.** A person who has ordered a product or service and, without just cause, has failed to pay for it.

**Decoy.** A unique name especially inserted in a mailing list for verification of list usage.

**Delinquent.** A person who has fallen behind in his payments or has stopped scheduled payment for a product or service.

**Delivery date.** The date on which a specific list order is to be received from the list owner by the list user or a designated representative of the list user.

**Demographics.** Socio-economic characteristics pertaining to a geographic unit, such as county, city, sectional center, ZIP code, group of households, education, ethnicity, and income level.

**Direct mail advertising.** Any promotional effort using the U.S. Postal Service or other direct delivery service for distribution of the advertising message

**Direct response advertising.** Advertising through any medium designed to generate a response by any means (such as mail, telephone, or telegraph) that is measurable.

**DMMA mail order action line (MOAL).** A service provided by DMMA to assist consumers who have encountered problems while shopping by mail they cannot resolve themselves.

**Donor list.** (See Contributor list).

**Dummy.** A preliminary mockup of a printed piece showing placement and nature of the material to be printed. Also a fictitious name with a mailable address inserted into a mailing list to check on usage of that list.

**Dupe (duplication).** Appearance of identical or near-identical entities more than one time.

**Duplication elimination.** A controlled mailing system which provides that no matter how many times a name and address is on a list, and no matter how many lists contain that name and address, it will be accepted for mailing only one time by that mailer. Also referred to as "dupe elimination."

**Envelope stuffer.** Any advertising or promotional material enclosed in an envelope with business letters, statements, or invoices.

**Exchange.** An arrangement whereby two mailers exchange equal quantities of mailing list names.

**Expire.** Refers to former customer who is no longer an active buyer.

**Expiration.** A subscription which is not renewed.

**Expiration date.** The date on which a subscription expires.

**Fill-in.** A name, address, or other words added to a preprinted letter.

**First-time buyer.** A person who buys a product or service from a specific company for the first time.

**Former buyer.** A person who has bought one or more times from a company but has made no purchase in the last twelve months.

**Free-standing insert.** A promotional piece loosely inserted or nested in a newspaper or magazine.

**Frequency.** The number of times a person has ordered within a specific period of time, or in toto. (See also Recency and Monetary).

**Friend-of-a-friend (friend recommendation).** The result of one person sending in the name of someone considered to be interested in a specific advertiser's product or service. A third-party inquiry.

**Front end.** The activities necessary or the measurement of direct marketing activities leading to an order or a contribution.

**Fund-raising list.** Any compilation or list of persons or companies based on a known contribution to one or more fund-raising appeals.

**Geographics.** Any method of subdividing a list based on geographic or political subdivisions (ZIP codes, sectional centers, cities, counties, state, or regions).

**Gift buyer.** A person who buys a product or service for another.

**Gimmick.** An attention-getting device, sometimes three-dimensional, attached to a direct mail printed piece.

**Guarantee.** A pledge of satisfaction made by the seller to the buyer and specifying the terms under which the seller will make good his pledge.

**Hot-line list.** The most recent names available on a specific list, but no older than three months. In any event, use of the terms "hot-line" should be further modified by such terms as "weekly," or "monthly."

**House list.** Any list of names owned by a company as a result of compilation, inquiry or buyer action, or acquisition that is used to promote that company's products or services.

**House-list duplicate.** Duplication of name and address records between the list user's own lists and any list being mailed by him on a one-time use arrangement.

**Inquiry.** A request for literature or other information about a product or service. Unless otherwise stated, it is assumed no payment has been made for the literature or other information. A Catalog request is generally considered a specific type of inquiry.

**Installment buyer.** A person who orders goods or services and pays for them in two or more periodic payments after delivery of the products or services.

**Inter-list duplicate.** Duplication of name and address records between two or more lists, other than house lists, being mailed by a list user.

**Intra-list duplicate.** Duplication of name and address records within a given list.

**K.** Used in reference to computer storage capacity, generally accepted as 1,000. Analogous to M in the direct marketing industry.

**Key code (key).** A group of letters or numbers, colors, or other markings used to measure the specific effectiveness of media, lists, advertisements, and offers (or any parts thereof).

**Keyline.** Can be any one of many partial or complete descriptions of past buying history coded to include name and address information and current status.

**KBN (kill bad name).** What is done with undeliverable addresses, i.e., nixies. You KBN a nixie.

**Label.** A piece of paper containing the name and address of the recipient applied to a mailing for address purposes.

**Layout.** An artist's sketch showing the relative positioning of illustrations, headlines, and copy. Positioning subject matter on a press sheet for most efficient production.

**Letterhead.** The printing on a letter which identifies the sender.

**Lettershop.** A business organization that handles the mechanical details of mailings such as addressing, imprinting, and collating. Most lettershops offer printing facilities, and many offer some degree of creative direct mail services.

**List (mailing list).** Names and addresses of individuals or companies having in common a specific interest, characteristic, or activity.

**List broker.** A specialist who makes all necessary arrangements for one company to make use of the lists of another company. A broker's services may include most or all of the following: research, selection, recommendation, and subsequent evaluation.

**List buyer.** Technically, this term should apply only to one who actually buys mailing lists. In practice, however, it is usually used to identify one who orders mailing lists for one-time use. A List user or Mailer.

**List cleaning.** The process of correcting or removing a name or address from a mailing list because it is no longer correct. Term is also used in the identification and elimination of house list duplication.

**List compiler.** A person who develops lists of names and addresses from directories, newspapers, public records, sales slips, trade-show registrations, and other sources for identifying groups of people or companies with something in common.

**List exchange.** A barter arrangement between two companies for the use of mailing lists. The arrangement may be list for list, list for space, or list for comparable value—other than money.

**List maintenance.** Any manual, mechanical, or electronic system for keeping name and address records (with or without other data) so that they are up-to-date at any (or specific) points in time.

**List manager.** A person who, as an employee of a list owner or as an outside agent, is responsible for the use, by others, of a specific mailing list. The list manager generally serves the list owner in several (or all) of the following: List maintenance (or advice thereon), list promotion and marketing, list clearance and record keeping, and collecting for use of the list by others.

**List owner.** A person who, by promotional activity or compilation, has developed a list of names having something in common. Or one who has purchased (as opposed to rented,

reproduced, or used on a one-time basis) such a list from the developer.

**List rental.** An arrangement in which a list owner furnishes names on his list to a mailer, together with the privilege of using the list on a one-time basis only (unless otherwise specified in advance). For this privilege, the list owner is paid a royalty by the mailer. "List rental" is the term most often used, although "list reproduction" and "list usage" more accurately describe the transaction, since "Rental" is not used in the sense of its ordinary meaning of leasing property.

**List royalty.** Payment to list owners for the privilege of using their lists on a one-time basis.

**List sample.** A group of names selected from a list for the purpose of evaluating the responsiveness of that list.

**List segmentation.** See List selection.

**List selection.** Characteristics used to define smaller groups within a list (essentially, lists within a list). Although very small select groups may be very desirable and may substantially improve response, increased costs often render them impractical.

**List sequence.** The order in which names and addresses appear in a list. While most lists today are in ZIP code sequence, some are alphabetical by name within the ZIP code; others are in carrier sequence (postal delivery); and still others may use some other (or no) order within ZIP code. Some lists are still arranged alphabetically by name, or chronologically, or with many variations or combinations.

**List sort.** The process of putting a list in a specific sequence from another sequence or from no sequence.

**List test.** A part of a list selected for the purpose of trying to determine the effectiveness of the entire list. A List sample.

**List user.** A person who uses names and addresses on someone else's list as prospects for the user's product or service. Similar to Mailer.

**Load up.** The process of offering a buyer the opportunity of buying an entire series at one time after the customer has purchased the first item in that series.

**Mail dates.** Dates on which a user has the obligation by, prior agreement with the list owner, to mail a specific list. No other date is acceptable without express approval of the list owner.

**Mailer.** (1) A direct mail advertiser. (2) A printed direct mail advertising piece. (3) A folding carton, wrapper, or tube used to protect materials in the mails.

**Mailgram.** A combination telegram-letter with the telegram transmitted to a postal facility close to the addressee and then delivered as first class mail.

**Mailing machine.** A machine that attaches labels to mailing pieces and otherwise prepares such pieces for deposit in the postal system.

**Mail order action line.** A service of the Direct Mail/Marketing Association which assists consumers in resolving problems with mail order purchases.

**Mail order buyer.** A person who orders and pays for a product or service through the mail. Those who use the telephone or telegraph to order from direct response advertising may be included in this category although, technically, they are not Mail order buyers.

**Mail preference service (MPS).** A service of the Direct Mail/Marketing Association wherein consumers can request to have their names removed from or added to mailing lists.

**Match.** A direct mail term used to refer to the typing of addresses, salutations, or inserts onto letters with other copy imprinted by a printing process.

**Match code.** A code determined either by the creator or the user of a file to be used for matching records contained in another file.

**MOAL.** See Mail order action line.

**Monetary value.** Total expenditures by a customer during a specific period of time, generally 12 months.

**MPS.** See Mail preference service.

**Multiple buyer.** A person who has bought two or more times. Not one who has bought two or more items. Also multibuyer or repeat buyer.

**Multiple regression.** Statistical technique used to measure the relationship between responses to a mailing with census demographics and list characteristics of one or more selected mailing lists. Used to determine the best types of people and areas to mail. This technique can also be used to analyze customers, subscribers, and so forth.

**Name.** Single entry on a mailing list.

**Name acquisition.** The technique of soliciting response to obtain names and addresses for a mailing list.

**Name-removal service.** That portion of the Mail preference service offered by Direct Mail/Marketing Association wherein a consumer is sent a form which, when filled in and returned, constitutes a request to have the person's name removed from all mailing lists used by participating members of the association and other direct mail users.

**Negative option.** A buying plan in which a customer or club member agrees to accept and pay for products or services announced in advance at regular intervals unless the person notifies the company within a reasonable time after each announcement not to ship. (See Federal Trade Commission Trade Regulation Rule).

**Nesting.** Placing one enclosure within another before inserting into a mailing envelope.

**Net name arrangement.** An agreement between a list owner and a list user at the time of ordering or before in which the list owner agrees to accept adjusted payment for less than the total names shipped. Such arrangements can be for a percentage of names shipped or names actually mailed, whichever is greater, or for only those names actually mailed, without percentage limitation. They can provide for a running charge or not.

**Nixie.** A mailing piece returned to a mailer (under proper authorization) by the U.S. Postal Service because of an incorrect or undeliverable name and address.

**No-pay.** A person who has not paid (wholly or in part) for goods or services ordered. "Uncollectible," "Deadbeat," and "Delinquent," are often used to describe the same person.

**Novelty format.** An attention-getting direct mail format.

**Nth name selection.** A fractional unit that is repeated in sampling a mailing list. For example, in an "every tenth" sample, you would select the 1st, 11th, 21st, 31st, etc., records; or the 2nd, 12th, 22nd, 32nd, etc., records, and so forth.

**Offer.** The terms under which a specific product or service is promoted.

**One-time buyer.** A buyer who has not ordered a second time from a given company.

**One-time use of a list.** An intrinsic part of the normal list usage, list reproduction, or list exchange agreement in which it is understood that the mailer will not use the names on the list more than one time without specific prior approval of the list owner.

**Open account.** A customer record that, at a specific point in time, reflects an unpaid balance for goods and services ordered, without delinquency.

**Order blank envelopes.** An order form printed on one side of a sheet with a mailing address on the reverse. The recipient simply fills in the order, folds the form and seals it like an envelope.

**Order card.** A reply card used to initiate an order by mail.

**Order form.** A printed form on which a customer can provide information to initiate an order by mail. Designed to be mailed in an envelope.

**Package.** A term used to describe, in toto, all of the assembled enclosures (parts or elements) of a mailing effort.

**Package insert.** Any promotional piece included in a product shipment. It may be for different products (or refills and replacements) from the same company or for products and services of other companies.

**Package test.** A test of elements, in part or in their entirety, of one mailing piece against another.

**Paid cancel.** Refers to a person who completes a basic buying commitment or more before canceling a commitment. See Completed cancel.

**Paid circulation.** Distribution of a publication to persons or organizations which have paid for a subscription.

**Paid during service.** Term used to describe a method of paying for magazine subscriptions in installments, usually weekly or monthly, and usually collected in person by the original salesperson or a representative of that company.

**Peel-off labels.** A self-adhesive label attached to a backing sheet which is attached to a mailing piece. The label is intended for removal from the mailing piece and for attachment to an order blank or card.

**Penetration.** The relationship of the number of individuals or families on a particular list, e.g., in toto, by state, ZIP code, or SIC, compared to the total number possible.

**Personalizing.** Individualizing of direct mail pieces by adding the name or other personal information about the recipient.

**Phone list.** A mailing list compiled from names listed in telephone directories.

**Piggy-back.** An offer that hitches a free ride with another offer.

**Poly bag.** Transparent polyethylene bag used instead of envelopes for mailing.

**Pop-up.** A printed piece containing a paper construction pasted inside a fold and which, when the fold is opened, "pops up" to form a three-dimensional illustration.

**Positive option.** A method of distribution of products and services incorporating the same advance notice technique as "Negative option" but requiring a specific order on the part of the member or subscriber each time. Generally, it is more costly and less predictable than "Negative option."

**Postal service prohibitory order.** A communication from the U.S. Postal Service to a company indicating that a specific person or family considers the company's advertising mail to be pandering. The order requires the company to remove all names listed on the order from its own mailing list and from any other lists used to promote that company's products or services. Violation of such order is subject to fine and imprisonment. The names listed on the order are to be distinguished from names removed, voluntarily, by the list owner at an individual's request.

**Postcard.** A single-sheet self-mailer on card stock.

**Postcard mailer.** A booklet containing business reply cards which are individually perforated for selective return to order products or obtain information.

**Premium.** An item offered to a buyer, usually free or at a nominal price, as an inducement to purchase or obtain for trial a product or service offered via mail order.

**Premium buyer.** A person who buys a product or service to get another product or service, usually free or at a special price, or who responds to an offer of a special product (premium) on the package or label, or sometimes in the advertising, of another product.

**Preprint.** An advertising insert printed in advance and supplied to a newspaper or magazine for insertion.

**Private mail.** Mail handled by special arrangement outside the U.S Postal Service.

**Prospect.** A name on a mailing list regarded as a potential buyer for a given product or service but who has not previously made such a purchase.

**Prospecting.** Mailing to get leads for further sales contact rather than to make direct sales.

**Protection.** The amount of time before and after the assigned mailing date during which the list owner will not allow the same names to be mailed by anyone other than the mailer cleared for that specific date.

**Psychographics.** Characteristics or qualities used to denote the life style or attitude of customers and prospective customers.

**Publisher's letter.** A second letter enclosed in a mailing package to stress a specific selling point.

**Purge.** The process of eliminating duplicates or unwanted names and addresses from one or more lists.

**Pyramiding.** A method of testing mailing lists in which one starts with a small quantity and, based on positive indications, follows with larger and larger quantities of the balance of the list until finally one mails the entire list.

**Questionnaire.** A printed form to a specified audience to solicit answers to specific questions.

**Recency.** The latest purchase or other activity recorded for an individual or company on a specific customer list. See also Frequency and Monetary.

**Recency-Frequency-Monetary-Value Ratio.** A formula used to evaluate the sales potential of names on a mailing list.

**Renewal.** A subscription that has been renewed prior to or at expiration or within six months thereafter.

**Repeat buyer.** See Multi-buyer.

**Rental.** See List rental.

**Reply card.** A sender-addressed card included in a mailing on which the recipient may indicate his response to the offer.

**Reply-o-letter.** One of a number of patented direct mail formats for facilitating replies from prospects. It features a die-cut opening on the face of letter and a pocket on the reverse. An addressed reply card is inserted in the pocket, and the name and address which appear thereon show through the die-cut opening of the letter.

**Reproduction right.** Authorization by a list owner for a specific mailer to use that list on a one-time basis.

**Response rate.** Percentage of returns from a mailing.

**Return envelope.** Addressed reply envelope—either stamped or unstamped, as distinguished from business reply envelopes which carry a postage payment guarantee—included with a mailing.

**Return postage guaranteed.** A legend that should be imprinted on the address face of envelopes or other mailing pieces if the mailer wishes the U.S. Postal Service to return undeliverable third class bulk mail. A charge equivalent to the single-piece third class rate will be made for each piece returned. See List cleaning.

**Return requested.** An indication that a mailer will compensate the U.S. Postal Service for return of an undeliverable mailing piece.

**Returns.** Responses to a direct mail program.

**RFMR.** See Recency-Frequency-Monetary-Value Ratio.

**Roll out.** To mail the remaining portion of a mailing list after successfully testing a portion of that list.

**ROP.** See run of paper or run of press.

**Rough.** A dummy or layout in sketchy form with a minimum of detail.

**Royalties.** Sum paid per unit mailed or sold for the use of a device such as a list, imprimatur, or patent.

**Running charge.** The price charged by a list owner for names run or passed but not used by a specific mailer. When such a charge is made, it is usually made to cover extra processing costs. However, some list owners set the price without regard to actual cost.

**Run of paper or run of press.** A term applied to color printing on regular paper and presses as distinct from separately printed sections made on special color presses. Also sometimes used to describe an advertisement positioned by publisher's choice in other-than-a-preferred position for which a special charge is made.

**Salting.** Deliberate placing of decoy or dummy names in a list to trace list usage and delivery. See also Decoy and Dummy name.

**Sample buyer.** A person who sends for a sample product, usually at a special price or for a small handling charge, but sometimes free.

**Sample package (mailing piece).** An example of the package to be mailed by the list user to a particular list. Such a mailing piece is submitted to the list owner for approval prior to commitment for one-time use of that list. Although a sample package may because of time pressure differ slightly from the actual package used, the list user agreement usually requires the user to disclose any material differences when submitting the sample package.

**Scented inks.** Printing inks to which a fragrance has been added.

**Sectional center (SCF or SCF center).** A U.S. Postal Service distribution unit comprising different post offices whose ZIP codes start with the same first three digits.

**Selection criteria.** Definition of characteristics that identify segments or subgroups within a list.

**Self-cover.** A cover of the same paper as the inside text pages.

**Self-mailer.** A direct mail piece mailed without an envelope.

**Sequence.** An arrangement of items according to a specified set of rules or instructions. Refers generally to ZIP code or customer number sequence.

**SIC.** See Standard Industrial Classification.

**Software.** A set of programs, procedures, and associated documentation concerned with the operation of a data processing system.

**Solo mailing.** A mailing that promotes a single product or a limited group of related products. It usually consists of a letter, brochure, and reply device enclosed in an envelope.

**Source code.** A unique alphabetical or numeric identification for distinguishing one list or media source from another. See also Key code.

**Source count.** The number of names and addresses in any given list for the media or list sources from which the names and addresses were derived.

**Split test.** A technique in which two or more samples from the same list—each considered to be representative of the entire list—are used for package tests or to test the homogeneity of the list.

**Standard Industrial Classification (SIC).** Classification of businesses, as defined by the U.S. Department of Commerce.

**State count.** The number of names and addresses in a given list for each state.

**Statement stuffer.** A small printed piece designed to be inserted in an envelope carrying a customer's statement of account.

**Step up.** The use of special premiums to get a mail order buyer to increase his quantity of purchase.

**Stock art.** Art sold for use by a number of advertisers.

**Stock cut.** Printing engravings kept in stock by the printer or publisher for occasional use, in contrast to exclusive use.

**Stock formats.** Direct mail formats with illustrations or headings preprinted and to which an advertiser adds his own copy

**Stopper.** Advertising jargon for a striking headline or illustration intended to attract immediate attention.

**Stuffer.** Advertising enclosure placed in other media, e.g., newspapers, merchandise packages, and mailings for other products.

**Subscriber.** A person who has paid to receive a periodical.

**Swatching.** Attaching samples of material to a printed piece.

**Syndicated mailing.** A mailing prepared for distribution by firms other than the manufacturer or syndicator.

**Syndicator.** A person who makes available prepared direct mail promotions for specific products or services for mailing by a list owner to his own list. Most syndicators also offer product fulfillment services.

**Tabloid.** A preprinted advertising insert of four or more pages, usually about half the size of a regular newspaper page, designed for inserting into a newspaper.

**Teaser.** An advertisement or promotion planned to excite curiosity about a later advertisement or promotion.

**Test panel.** A term used to identify each of the parts or samples in a split test.

**Test tape.** A selection of representative records within a mailing list designed to enable a list user or service bureau to prepare for reformatting or converting the list to a form more efficient for the user.

**Throwaway.** An advertisement or promotional piece intended for widespread free distribution. It is generally printed on inexpensive paper and most often distributed by hand, either to passersby or house-to-house.

**Tie-in.** A cooperative mailing effort involving two or more advertisers.

**Til forbid.** An order for continuing service which is to continue until specifically cancelled by the buyer.

**Title.** A designation before (prefix) or after (suffix) a name to more accurately identify an individual. Prefixes: Mr., Mrs., Dr., Sister. Suffixes: M.D., Jr., President, Sales Manager.

**Tip-on.** An item glued to a printed piece.

**Token.** An involvement device usually consisting of a perforated portion of an order card which is designed for removal from its original position and then placed in another designated area on the order card to signify desire to purchase the product or service offered.

**Town marker.** A symbol used to identify the end of a geographical unit of a mailing list. It was originated for "towns" but is now used for ZIP codes, sectional centers, and so forth.

**Traffic builder.** A direct mail piece intended primarily to attract recipients to the mailer's place of business.

**Trial buyer.** A person who buys a short-term supply of a product or who buys the product with the understanding that it may be examined, used, or tested for a specified time before he must decide whether to pay for it or return it.

**Trial subscriber.** A person who orders a publication or service on a conditional basis. The condition may relate to delaying payment, the right to cancel, a shorter than normal term or a special introductory price.

**Uncollectable.** Refers to a person who hasn't paid for goods and services at the end of a normal series of collection efforts.

**Unit of sale.** A description of the average dollar amount spent by customers on a mailing list.

**Universe.** The total number of persons who might be included on a mailing list. All of those who fit a single set of specifications.

**Update.** Adding recent transactions and current information to the master (main) list to reflect the current status of each record on the list.

**Up front.** Securing payment for a product offered by mail order before the product is sent.

**Verification.** The process of determining the validity of an order by sending a questionnaire to the customer.

**Wide Area Telephone Service (WATS).** A service providing a special line allowing calls within a certain zone, on a direct dialing basis, for a flat monthly charge.

**Window envelope.** An envelope with a die-cut portion on the front to permit the viewing of the name and address printed on an enclosure. The "die-cut window" may or may not be covered with a transparent material.

**Wing mailer.** Label-affixing device that uses strips of paper on which addresses have been printed.

**ZIP code.** A group of five digits used by the U.S. Postal Service to designate specific post offices, stations, branches, buildings, or large companies.

**ZIP code count.** The number of names and addresses in a list, arranged within each ZIP code.

**ZIP code sequence.** Arrangement of names and addresses in a list according to the numeric progression of the ZIP code in each record. This form of list formatting is mandatory for mailing at bulk third class mail rates based on the sorting requirements of the U.S. Postal Service regulations.

*Source: Direct Mail/Marketing Association.*

# Index